P9-DMI-848

RED HOT PEPPERS

ALSO BY JEAN ANDREWS

A FIELD GUIDE: SHELLS OF THE FLORIDA COAST, 1993

THE TEXAS BLUEBONNET, 1993

AN AMERICAN WILDFLOWER FLORILEGIUM, 1992

TEXAS MONTHLY FIELD GUIDE: SHELLS OF THE TEXAS COAST, 1992

PEPPERS: THE DOMESTICATED CAPSICUMS, 1984

TEXAS SHELLS: A FIELD GUIDE, 1981

SHELLS AND SHORES OF TEXAS, 1977

SEA SHELLS OF THE TEXAS COAST, 1971

RED HOT PEPPERS

WRITTEN AND ILLUSTRATED BY
JEAN ANDREWS

MACMILLAN PUBLISHING COMPANY   NEW YORK   MAXWELL MACMILLAN CANADA   TORONTO

MAXWELL MACMILLAN INTERNATIONAL   NEW YORK   OXFORD   SINGAPORE   SYDNEY

Copyright © 1993 by Jean Andrews
Illustrations copyright © 1993 by Jean Andrews

Credits for permission to publish certain recipes in this book appear on page 225.

All rights reserved. No part of this book may be reproduced or transmitted in any form or by any means, electronic or mechanical, including photocopying, recording, or by any information storage and retrieval system, without permission in writing from the Publisher.

Macmillan Publishing Company
866 Third Avenue
New York, NY 10022

Maxwell Macmillan Canada, Inc.
1200 Eglinton Avenue East
Suite 200
Don Mills, Ontario M3C 3N1

Macmillan Publishing Company is part of the Maxwell Communication Group of Companies.

Library of Congress Cataloging-in-Publication Data

Andrews, Jean.
    Red hot peppers / written and illustrated by Jean Andrews.
       p.   cm.
    Includes bibliographical references (p.   ) and index.
    ISBN 0-02-502251-2
    1. Cookery (Hot peppers)   2. Hot peppers.   I. Title.
    TX803.P46A53   1993   93-25604   CIP
    641.6'384—dc20

Macmillan books are available at special discounts for bulk purchases for sales promotions, premiums, fund-raising, or educational use. For details, contact:

    Special Sales Director
    Macmillan Publishing Company
    866 Third Avenue
    New York, NY 10022

10 9 8 7 6 5 4 3 2

Printed in the United States of America

TO ISABELLA OF CASTILE, FEMINIST QUEEN OF SPAIN, WHOSE INTUITION AND SUPPORT

OF THE COLUMBUS QUEST MADE THE DISCOVERY OF PEPPERS POSSIBLE;

A REMARKABLE WOMAN WHO SPENT MORE TIME ON THE

BATTLEFIELD THAN IN THE KITCHEN.

CONTENTS

FOREWORD

y first affair with peppers, *Peppers: The Domesticated Capsicums,* changed my life, as most affairs do. In the beginning it had been a rather private arrangement, just peppers and me. After that book was published, the world intruded on our togetherness. I was invited hither and yon to tell the pepper story, and in so doing I learned that people out there thought I had written a food book. This came as quite a shock to me, but if food people wanted to hear about peppers, I was ready and willing to tell them a story. As I met the movers and shakers in the food world, I kept hearing, "We love your book, but would you tell us more about cooking with them?"

I had already been delving deeper into the directions taken by the *Capsicum* peppers after Christopher Columbus discovered them, and it appeared to me that as peppers moved through the trade routes they had a great effect on the cuisines in the lands along the way. Once *Capsicum* reached the Old World, they fell into the hands of spice merchants. I began to wonder, why did the spice trade go one way and not another five hundred years ago? who carried it? why did some people respond to the introduction of peppers and others didn't? why do some cui-

sines have certain characteristics and not others? and on and on. These questions took me not only to libraries, where I found much about the spice trade and a little about the early movements of capsicums, but also to many countries along the pepper trail, including much of Africa and Monsoon Asia (India, Nepal, Bhutan, Sri Lanka, Thailand, and Indonesia) plus the Szechuan and Hunan provinces in China and the Silk Route.

Our swift little pod had done a significant part of its travel within the first fifty years after Columbus brought it back to Spain, which makes for a very long-ago story in times very, very different than those we now live in. The more I looked into this saga, the more convinced I became that the presumptive pepper trail by which Columbus took the American plant to Spain and whence it progressed to Europe was not the only pathway followed into Europe and the Middle East. So I set out to learn what I could about our peripatetic pod.

At the onset I learned that the historical background for studying *Capsicum* cookery is complex. In most peppery food areas throughout the world, political and economic systems that consisted of either a small local privileged upper class or conquering Europeans attempted to dominate the daily lives and actions of the native masses. This form of class system deeply affected the cuisine, creating a division in the quantities and varieties of food consumed by different sections in the same populace, and forming by force, in the case of slavery, the food patterns of large populations. Within most of these cultural groups, religion added its food taboos. These factors combined to produce cuisines unlike our typical Americanized-European cookery.

I also discovered that, in spite of the necessity for every human of every race on earth to eat regularly, little has been written concerning the foodways of various culture groups in relation to their total cultural history. There are excellent food books like *Food in Chinese Culture*, edited by K. C. Chang, but in thumbing through book after book on the history and culture of a particular group, one finds chapters on such topics as racial composition, political organization, economics, family, philosophy, religion, science, art, literature, recreation and amusement, and secret societies, but little or nothing on foodways. Are they just taken for granted or is it because the day-in, day-out preparation and serving of family meals has always been "woman's work" and therefore less important? The manner in which food is selected, prepared, and served is always the result of the culture in which it takes place, as indeed are the accessories and rituals that accompany the rudimentary activity of eating.

Now, I can say, with a sigh of relief, that I see a growing interest in the study of foodways as a means for understanding culture. Although food is eaten as a response to hunger, it is more than filling one's stomach to satisfy nutritional requirements; it is also a premeditated selection and consumption process providing emotional fulfillment. The way in which food is altered reveals the function of food in society and the values that society supports. I have tried to give my readers some background on the cuisines that have embraced capsicums, but it is preposterous to attempt to describe the foodways or food culture of many groups in one chapter. Each paragraph begs for elaboration, qualification, and more work is required to round out the story.

Special thanks go to the scholars who read and approved the text of this book. Professors Alfred Crosby, author of *Ecological Imperialism* and *The Columbian Exchange*; Terry Jordan, ethnogeographer and author of *The American Backwoods Frontier* plus too many other books to list; Robert King, linguist and expert on things Indian; L. Tuffly Ellis, historian and former director of the Texas State Historical Association; Elizabeth Fernea, author and Middle East specialist; botanists and *Capsicum* authorities W. Hardy Eshbaugh and Charles Heiser, Jr., and authors of *Seeds to Civilization* and *Of Plants and Man*; Billie L. Turner and Guy L. Nesom, taxonomists; Tom Mabry, plant chemist; medievalist Ernest N. Kaulbach and linguist Frances Karthunen who helped with translations. Special thanks go to Carol Kilgore and Kathi Helmi for early editing, and Guido Davita for translating. On the few occasions when the vast libraries at the University of Texas at Austin did not contain the material I needed, the interlibrary loan staff at the Texas State Library acquired it for me. Without their diligence in digging out obscure references I could have not put this book together. To all the originators of the recipes included here, most of whom I have come to know personally, my heartfelt appreciation. Enjoy!

PART I

THE
PEPPER

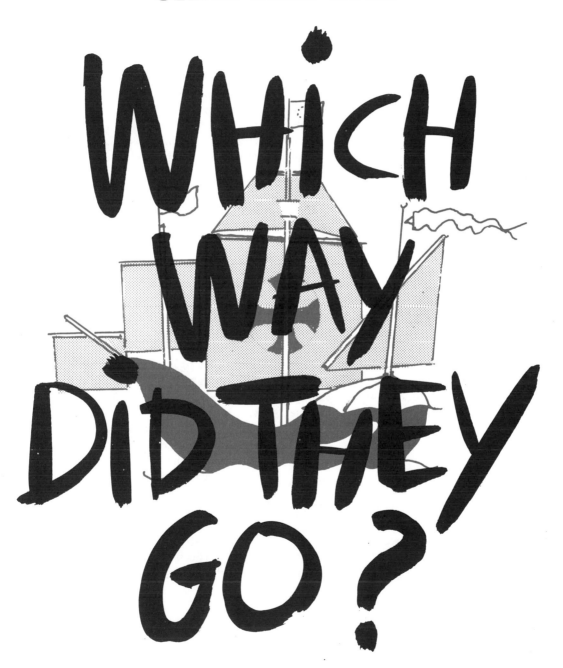

CHAPTER ONE

WHICH WAY DID THEY GO?

hat is it, spice, herb, condiment, vegetable, garnish, medicine, decoration, icon, or landscape feature? It's all of the above. It's SUPERPOD! *Capsicum* pepper has become, after salt, the most frequently used seasoning agent and condiment in the world and an important green vegetable throughout the temperate zones. Capsicum cookery is found not only in Mexico, the American Southwest, the Caribbean, and most points south, but also in the Far East, Africa, the Balkans, and the Mediterranean. Capsicums certainly must have what it takes to have earned such veneration as a culinary ingredient in so many varied cuisines.

In my book *Peppers: The Domesticated Capsicums* I explored the domesticated capsicums of the western hemisphere[1] but I did not discuss the cuisines that favor capsicums. Since the publication of that book, I have traveled all through the peppery places of the Far East. I have poked through markets, visited kitchens, and searched out home gardens and commercial fields, where I carefully examined capsicums and collected *Capsicum* seed, which I brought home and cultivated. From all of this I have concluded that only two of the four or five *Capsicum* species that were domesticated from their wild state in the western hemisphere have come to play a significant role in the cuisines of the eastern hemisphere. How

did these American capsicums get there in the first place? What happened to cause the movement of domesticated capsicums out of the New World, their place of origin? Where and why were certain ones adopted and not others? I will try to answer those questions and more, as well as to show how the Portuguese were more responsible for the distribution of capsicums and other New World foods to the eastern hemisphere than were the Spanish who discovered them in the western hemisphere. The five characters in this play are the cousins *Capsicum—annuum, frutescens, chinense, baccatum,* and *pubescens.* In the world's theaters, the lead role is played by C. *annuum,* while C. *chinense* is second. The first three have overlapping parts, in fact, the characters of those three are so hard to distinguish that the role played by C. *frutescens* will probably be eliminated. Although their parts are more limited, the last two are easily recognized, rugged individualists.

We all know what happened in 1492, but did you know Columbus also discovered capsicums? Prior to his first voyage to the West Indies, tropical capsicums were unknown in the New World north of present-day Mexico and the Caribbean and nowhere in the Old World. (In correspondence botanist W. Hardy Eshbaugh told me recent evidence suggests that *Capsicum annuum* var. *glabrisculum/aviculare* may have extended into a corridor north of the Rio Grande, Southern Arizona, Coastal Louisiana, and Florida.) The first pictures and descriptions of capsicums published were in a German herbal written by the physician Leonhart Fuchs[2] in 1542. For that reason we must assume that the major post-Columbian distribution of *Capsicum* took place between 1492 and 1542, although Fuch's herbal may have been in preparation as early as 1532. In the herbal Fuchs discussed several capsicums and

---

1. At the time of the Discovery, four or five of the more than twenty different wild capsicums had been domesticated through selection by the skillful agriculturists who inhabited the New World, and no others have had their genetic makeup altered to produce another domesticated species since that time. *Capsicum annuum* var. *annuum* (cayenne, bell pepper), the most common of the group, was domesticated in Mexico; C. *frutescens* ("Tabasco"), then only semidomesticated and now unsupportable, could have come from anywhere in the American tropics; C. *chinense* (habanero, Scotch bonnet) originated in Amazonia; C. *baccatum* var. *pendulum* (ají amarillo) arose in the highlands of Peru or Bolivia; and C. *pubescens* (rocoto) is an Andean domesticate. See Chapter 3 for specifics.

---

2. Fuch's botanical masterpiece appeared in 1542 as *De historia stirpiuim* in Latin. The following year (1543) an edition in the vernacular German was called *New Kreüterbuch.*

presented the first illustrations of the fruiting plant. All appear to be *C. annuum* var. *annuum,* the annual pepper. The question is, how did they get there? And why are they the Mesoamerican species and not those which scholars have shown to be indigenous to South America and the West Indies at the time of the Discovery (*C. chinense* and *C. frutescens*)? Even if a wild *C. annuum* was the only one of its kind found in the West Indian islands visited by Columbus during his first three voyages or by others who followed him to the West Indies or went to Brazil, there would not have been sufficient time for a wild plant to have been domesticated and developed into the several types of fruits shown by Fuchs in 1542, only fifty years after the discovery of *Capsicum* peppers by the Spaniards. Those fifty years between 1492 and 1542 are our critical time frame.

Writing about African peppers, Eshbaugh, without giving reasons, mentions the possibility of *Capsicum annuum*[3] growing in the West Indies at the time of the discovery, when earlier studies indicate that at that time it grew only in Mesoamerica,[4] the place where it was domesticated.[5] If that was the case, the Spaniards could not have introduced the Mexican chilli to the West Indies directly from Mexico, as Mexico was not discovered by the Spaniards until 1517, and the conquistador Hernando Cortés did not invade Mexico until 1519. Notwithstanding that the Mexican *C. annuum* var. *annuum* may have been available to Spanish explorers before the discovery and invasion of Mexico, the Nahuatl word *chilli* was not, and *chilli* is the name by which capsicums became known in India and the Far East.[6] This narrow Mexico-Fuchs time frame, now but seventeen years, helped convince me that the Spaniards had acquired the Mexican domesticates somewhere within the Spanish Main before Cortés captured Moctezuma, but where and how did they get there? The search was on!

The distribution map (page 6) giving rise to these questions resulted from research by some of the leading *Capsicum* scholars, including Charles B. Heiser, Jr., Paul G. Smith, Barbara Pickersgill, W. Hardy Eshbaugh, and M. J. McLeod.[7] Taking

---

3. Geographer William C. Sturtevant, in a paper written in 1961, also states that *Capsicum annuum* and/or *C. frutescens* were being grown by the Tainos (Arawaks) at the time of contact. He based his statement on the records of the Columbian chroniclers and a paper written by Heiser and Smith in 1953. That paper was written when only those two species were accepted and before they isolated *C. chinense.* I think Sturtevant's diagnosis might have been different if he had seen the later paper, which discussed the dominant *Capsicum* species in the West Indies—*C. chinense.* Not that *C. annuum* could not have been there, and I think it was, but evidence other than that he cited will be needed, as much more has been learned about the genus since 1953.

4. Mesoamerica (middle America) extends from mid-Mexico through the northwestern tip of Nicaragua.

5. Peter Martyr (1493) reported that maize, which along with *C. annuum* var. *annuum* was first domesticated in Mexico, was brought to Iberia when Columbus returned from his first voyage in 1493. Carl O. Sauer, writing in 1966, tells us the maize-beans-squash complex, which originated in Mesoamerica, was growing in island *conucos* (mounded gardens).

In addition, by the time of the Discovery, the Mexican domesticated turkey, immediately favored and noted by Europeans because it was superior to their domestic fowl, had "passed, along with other Mesoamerican traits and intruders, into Coiba country and was taken from there to Darién (Panama) and on to Santo Domingo (West Indies), between which places there was frequent communication [among the Spanish]," Sauer continues. People carrying the turkey and some corn to feed it could have carried peppers. I think the Spanish picked annual peppers up somewhere in the Spanish Main (West Indies Islands + southern littoral of Caribbean + intermediate sea) before Cortés's conquest of Mexico in 1521, and the Portuguese got them from the Spaniards at some undocumented place.

6. Nahuatl, the language of the Aztec overlords of Tenochtitlán was the official trade language within large stretches of pre-Columbian Mesoamerica, and it is still spoken by a million and a half people in Mexico. The Nahuatl word *chilli,* meaning the *Capsicum* plant, is not found in Emilio Tejera's dictionary of indigenous words of Santo Domingo where the Spanish first headquartered. All of the early writers—Chanca, Martyr, C. Columbus, F. Columbus, de las Casas—used the South American/Caribbean name *ají* when speaking of peppers. It was not until Cortés opened Mexico in 1521 that the word *chilli* became known. Dr. Francisco Hernández, the king's historian and physician, who lived in Mexico from 1570 to 1577, was the first to use *chilli* in print.

7. The pre-Columbian distribution of *Capsicum* was deter-

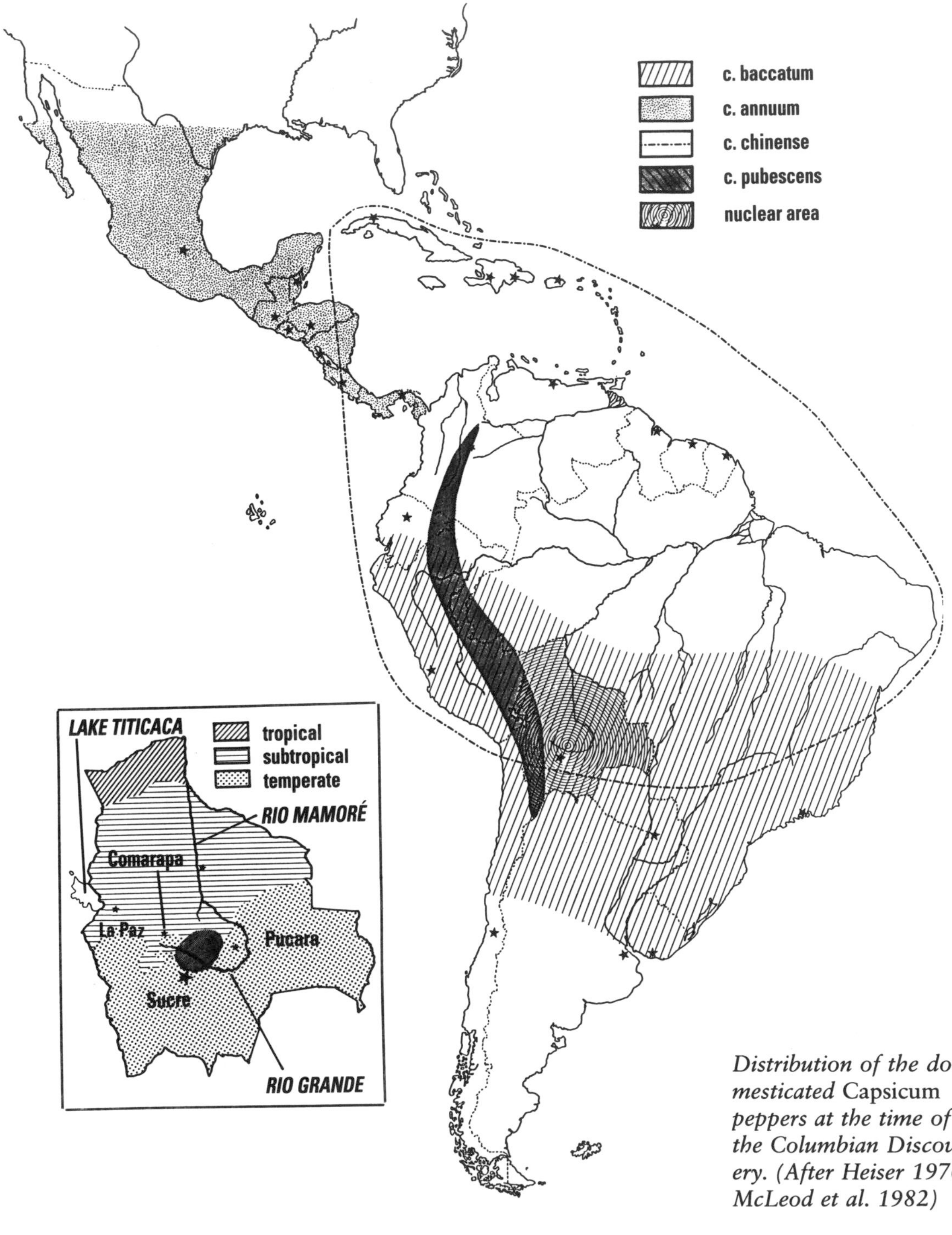
c. baccatum
c. annuum
c. chinense
c. pubescens
nuclear area
LAKE TITICACA
tropical
subtropical
temperate
RIO MAMORÉ
Comarapa
La Paz
Pucara
Sucre
RIO GRANDE

Distribution of the domesticated Capsicum *peppers at the time of the Columbian Discovery. (After Heiser 1976; McLeod et al. 1982)*

such a map at face value, we should be able to place a specific explorer in a specific region, thereby allowing us to speculate on which *Capsicum* species he would probably have encountered. That assumes, however, that no pre-Columbian trade and/or migration had begun to spread the Mesoamerican *C. annuum* to the West Indies as migration had carried the *C. chinense* from South America to those islands. Given the slow transportation and communication systems at the end of the fifteenth and beginning of the sixteenth centuries, in order for New World *C. annuum* to have been as widely distributed in the Old World as it became within such a short period after the discovery, Columbus had to have found domesticated *C. annuum* var. *annuum* within the Spanish Main, either on the mainland where the map depicts, or from the islands before 1519 to 1521. I think he found it in both places. I have envisioned several possible scenarios that might account for *C. annuum* having been found by Columbus on his first voyage.

Archaeological reports published in 1967 prove that *Capsicum annuum* was being cultivated by man as early as 5000 B.C.,[8] if not earlier, in the Tehuacan Valley of southeastern Puebla and northeastern Oaxaca in Mexico. Later studies summarized by geographer David Watts demonstrate migrations by nonagricultural groups of Paleo-Indians (incorrectly called Ciboney by Las Casas) from the coast of Mesmoamerica to the West Indies by way of the Mid-Caribbean Island chain occurred after 5000 B.C. and before 2500 B.C. In fact, within that period, when the sea level was lower than it has been since then, during certain seasonal conditions of winds and current, the movement of rafts equipped with mat sails

---

mined by research using methods such as archaeological evidence, comparative genetics, chromosomal studies, along with Vavilov's method of analyzing the geographic distribution of morphological (shape) variance.

8. This proves capsicums to be the earliest spice used by humans.

from Cap Gracias a Dios, Nicaragua, to Jamaica and Española may have been quite easy, even for novice sailors who were big game hunters from the mainland following sea mammals—manatee and seals. They could have brought the indigenous Mesoamerican red peppers with them.

During this same period of lower sea levels, birds could have performed their function of *Capsicum* seed dispersal as they had when they moved peppers from their place of origin in South America north to Mesoamerica before prehistoric man had made his way to that region. The greater exposure of the submerged mountain range between Mesoamerica and Jamaica resulting from the lower sea level would make distances shorter; therefore, the flight of land birds along the island chain would have been easier than anytime after 2000 B.C.

In the meanwhile, the Paleo-Indians who settled in Española would have had plenty of time—three thousand undisturbed years—to have consciously or unconsciously selected bigger and bigger peppers from those that came from Mesoamerica with their ancestors, even though they were not farmers.

Later migrant agriculturalists—Arawaks from South America, who traveled north along the Antilles to Española—overran those more primitive peoples following their own journeys between A.D. 250 to A.D. 1000. These farmers, who brought with them the Amazonian *C. chinense,* could have undertaken the cultivation and domestication of wild Mesoamerican pepper transported by the Paleo-Indians so long before—they had time enough before Columbus arrived.

However, the most feasible scenario has the already domesticated *Capsicum annuum* following the established pre-Columbian trade routes running from Mesoamerica up and down the Central American corridor, across northern South America, and north through the Antilles.

Let's speculate on where and how Columbus acquired those cayenne types (*Capsicum annuum* var. *annuum*) that set the Old World on fire. In a

Christopher Columbus, after an engraving by P. Mercuri

letter to the king and queen and their treasurer after his first voyage (1492 to 1493) Columbus did not mention peppers by name but spoke of the natives eating meat with very hot spices. Among the entries in the log[9] of that first voyage is one for November 4, 1492, from Cuba in which we are told that Columbus brought samples of black pepper and cinnamon to show the natives what he was looking for. Several weeks later, on November 21, we learn that Martín Alonzo Pinzón, the defiant captain of the caravel *Pinta*, left the group and sailed from Cuba in search of gold. Then, on Christmas day the two remaining ships reached the coast of Española, where the ill-fated *Santa Maria* ran aground and was lost. Lack of space on the *Niña* for the shipwrecked crew necessitated leaving thirty volunteers on the island. A fortress was built from the

timbers of the wrecked ship and was named *Navidad* (Christmas). Near that site, on New Year's Day 1493, Columbus recorded a momentous culinary circumstance in his journal: "The pepper which the local Indians used as spice is more abundant and more valuable than either black or malegueta pepper[10] [grains of paradise—a fiery African native of the ginger family]" (see the map on pages 10–11). He left a recommendation that those who were to remain on Española collect as much of it as possible. Two weeks later, near Samaná Bay at the other end of the island, Columbus continued to record what they were seeing. Besides cotton and other things, there was much *ají*, the native pepper. He found it to be much stronger than black pepper, and the people wouldn't eat without it. He estimated that one could load fifty caravels a year with it in Española. Mark your calendars! January first is *Capsicum* discovery day.

The account of the first voyage by the royal historian Pietro Martire d'Anghiera (Peter Martyr) is of great importance—not only does he write of maize[11] found growing in the islands in

---

9. There are several translations of the log of Columbus with minor variations. Those I have looked at have been translated by V. W. Brooks, J. M. Cohen, C. Jane, R. H. Funson, and S. E. Morison.

---

10. Varieties of tiny chillies, both *Capsicum annuum* var. *annuum* and *C. frutescens,* are commonly called maleguetas after the African spice *Aframomum melegueta,* which is not related to either black or red pepper. According to Fuchs, malegueta pepper is named for Melle or Méléga in the northern Niger area of Guinea, Africa. This member of the ginger family is a small, aromatic, sorghum-sized seed confusingly called Guinea pepper or grains of paradise, terms also applied to chillies and cardamom. It was known in Lyons and Venice during the thirteenth century as a less expensive substitute for black pepper. Following Portuguese establishment at Elima on the Bight of Benin on the west African coast, Elima became the center for a flourishing business in ivory, slaves, gold dust, and malegueta pepper. During the sixteenth century that littoral was first known as Malegueta Coast, then as the Grain Coast. After the Discovery, several chillies of the cayenne type also came to be called "ginnie" pepper.

11. The unique North American symbiotic maize-beans-squash complex recognized by geographer Carl O. Sauer in 1966, and referred to as the Three Sisters by Native Americans, is a concept critical to any study of capsicum diffusion. I suggest that chillies were an adjunct to that triad and were not only grown and eaten with them, but also traveled with them throughout the tropical and subtropical world and from

Although Columbus had discovered peppers January 1, 1493, on Espanola during his first voyage, he gives a better description of them on his second voyage. "In those islands there are also bushes like rose bushes which make a fruit as long as cinnamon full of small grains as biting as pepper; those Caribs and the Indians eat that fruit as we eat apples."

1492 but describes the pungent spice used by the natives. In that description is found this relevant remark: "When it [pepper] is used there is no need of Caucasian pepper. The sweet pepper is

there into more temperate areas. In that case they would be called the Three Sisters and Little Brother—no one would ever take a pepper to be female.

called *boniato,* and the hot pepper is called *canibal,* for they are sharp and strong as cannibals." "Sweet pepper" is a key piece to our puzzle. There may be some other sweet varieties of *Capsicum chinense* than the rocotillo in Peru, but those species growing in the West Indies are renowned for their pungency. It is improbable, therefore, that the reference is to a pepper of that

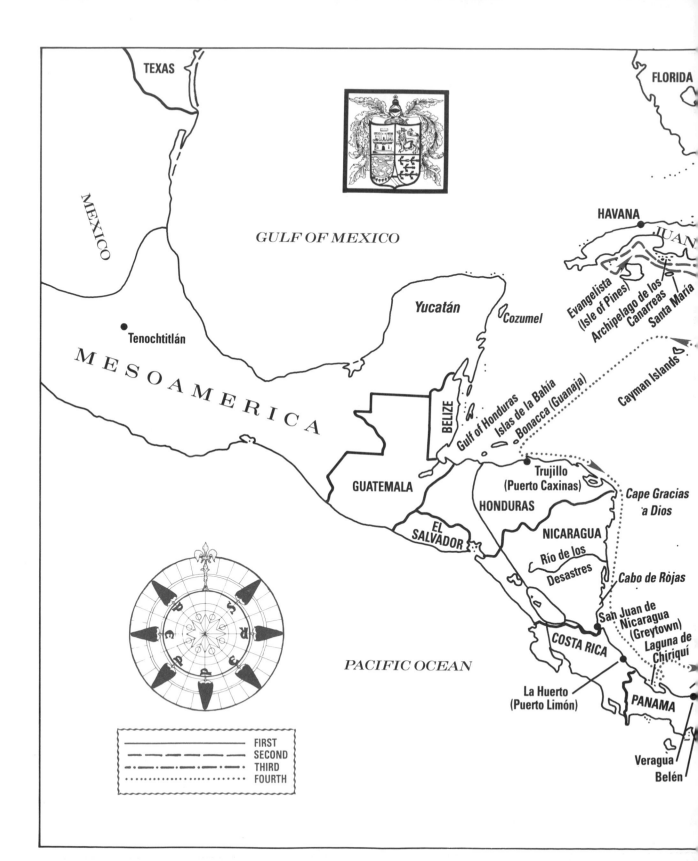

TEXAS

FLORIDA

MEXICO

GULF OF MEXICO

HAVANA

Yucatán

Cozumel

Evangelista
(Isle of Pines)

Archipelago de los
Canarreas

Santa María

Tenochtitlán

M E S O A M E R I C A

Gulf of Honduras

Islas de la Bahía

Bonacca (Guanaja)

Cayman Islands

BELIZE

GUATEMALA

Trujillo
(Puerto Caxinas)

Cape Gracias
'a Dios

HONDURAS

EL
SALVADOR

NICARAGUA

Río de los

Desastres

Cabo de Ròjas

San Juan de
Nicaragua
(Greytown)

COSTA RICA

Laguna de
Chiriquí

PACIFIC OCEAN

La Huerto
(Puerto Limón)

PANAMA

Veragua

Belén

FIRST
SECOND
THIRD
FOURTH

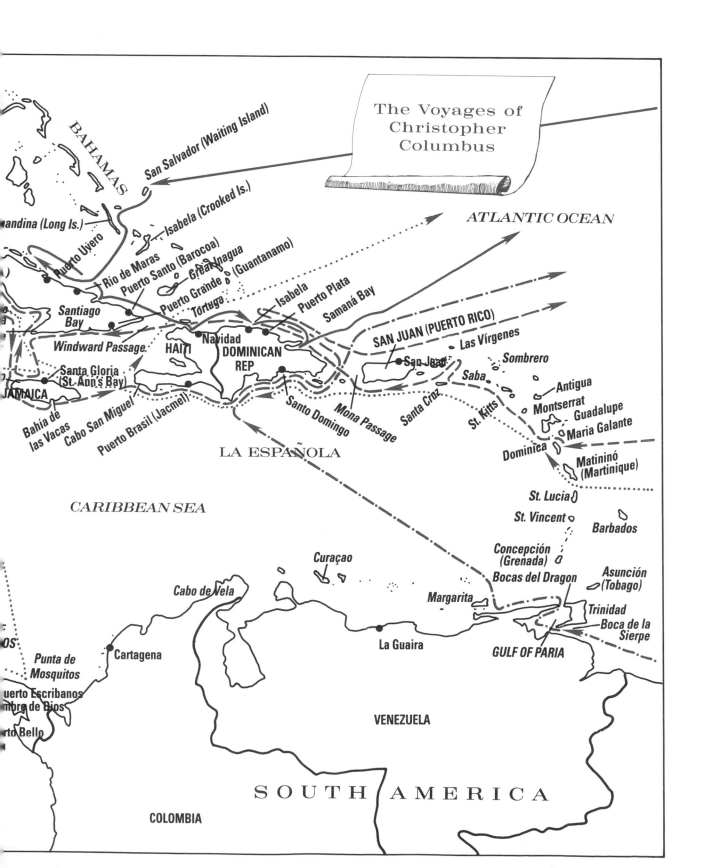

The Voyages of
Christopher
Columbus

BAHAMAS

San Salvador (Waiting Island)

ATLANTIC OCEAN

Isabela (Crooked Is.)

andina (Long Is.)

Puerto Uyero

Río de Maras

Puerto Santo (Barocoa)

Great Inagua

Puerto Grande (Guantanamo)

Isabela

Puerto Plata

Samaná Bay

Santiago
Bay

Tórtuga

SAN JUAN (PUERTO RICO)

Las Vírgenes

Navidad

San Juan

Sombrero

Windward Passage

HAITI

DOMINICAN
REP

Saba

Antigua

Santa Gloria
(St. Ann's Bay)

Santa Cruz

Montserrat

JAMAICA

St. Kitts

Guadalupe

Bahía de
las Vacas

Cabo San Miguel

Santo Domingo

Mona Passage

Maria Galante

Puerto Brasil (Jacmel)

Dominica

Matininó
(Martinique)

LA ESPAÑOLA

St. Lucia

CARIBBEAN SEA

St. Vincent

Barbados

Concepción
(Grenada)

Curaçao

Asunción
(Tobago)

Bocas del Dragon

Cabo de Vela

Margarita

Trinidad

Boca de la
Sierpe

La Guaira

GULF OF PARIA

OS

Punta de
Mosquitos

Cartagena

uerto Escribanos

mbre de Dios

to Bello

VENEZUELA

SOUTH AMERICA

COLOMBIA

species, but refers instead to a Mesoamerican *C. annuum* var. *annuum* that already had sweet varieties at that time.

On the second journey (1493 to 1496), Diego Chanca, physician to the voyage, wrote that the aborigines ate a vegetable called *agí* to give a sharp taste to fish and bird dishes. Columbus also logged peppers on his second voyage. In a letter to the sovereigns written during that trip, Columbus listed peppers as one of the things he brought to them; however, the third voyage (1498 to 1500) was so plagued with problems for Columbus that he or his chroniclers did not mention foods. Fortunately for my tale, Columbus took his illegitimate fourteen-year-old son, Ferdinand, with him on his fourth voyage (1502 to 1504).[12]

The first continental landing made by the adventurers was on the coast of Honduras, where they encountered people of the high Mesoamerica culture who were very unlike those of the Caribbean islands. Soon the Europeans overtook and captured a huge native trading canoe carved from a single log.[13] Ferdinand described this vessel, eight feet wide and as long as a galley, filled with exotic merchandise covered with a canopy of palm leaves, and carrying a crew of twenty-five. Amid the cargo was maize, roots, and "victuals like they eat in Española," along with woven cotton fabrics, all from Mesoamerica. In fact, there was such a wide selection of native goods aboard that his father Christopher exclaimed, "Thanks to God, that he has given us a sample of all the things of that land without danger or fatigue to our people." Recalling Dr. Chanca's letter in which he reported the Indians eating *ají* (capsicum) on everything they ate, I like to believe that capsicums were in that canoe along with the other native foodstuffs.[14] For certain, the fiery pods wouldn't have been left behind!

In a letter titled CHRISTOPHER COLUMBUS, VICEROY AND ADMIRAL OF THE INDIES, TO THE MOST CHRISTIAN AND MIGHTY KING AND QUEEN OF SPAIN, OUR SOVEREIGNS, NOTIFYING THEM OF THE EVENTS OF HIS VOYAGE AND THE CITIES, PROVINCES, RIVERS AND OTHER MARVELS, ALSO THE SITUATION OF THE MANY GOLDFIELDS AND OTHER OBJECTS OF GREAT RICHES AND VALUE, we learn that on his final voyage in the fall of

---

12. Columbus's second son, Ferdinand was born in 1488 at Córdoba as a result of a liaison during the six years Christopher waited, unemployed, in the shadow of King Ferdinand and Queen Isabella's battle tents as they pursued the final destruction and surrender of the Moors at Granada.

Ferdinand Columbus and Bartolomé de Las Casas, a record-keeping Dominican friar who traveled in the Indies, had access to Columbus's papers, and both recorded full narratives of his life and voyages.

13. According to Samuel Eliot Morison, at the time of the European arrival in America, oceangoing canoes such as these were used by the Arawak and Carib Indians for interisland trade. Ferdinand's description of the canoe and its contents leaves no doubt that it was Honduran. The Amerindian mariners hugged the coast just as the contemporary Mediterranean mariners did. Although some did venture into the open sea, it was only to reach offshore islands from Mesoamerica or interisland within the West Indies.

---

14. During the spring semester of 1991, botanist Dr. Charles B. Heiser, Jr., professor emeritus at the Indiana University, held the Jean Andrews Visiting Professorship in Tropical and Economic Botany at The University of Texas at Austin. I was privileged to have conversations with him on this question at that time. The following pertinent correspondence was an outgrowth of those conversations.

In August of 1991, while reexamining Fuchs's herbal at my request, Heiser found something of particular interest to the diffusion of New World plants. He reports: "Fuchs describes four American plants—maize, beans, squash, and peppers (maybe more, but I haven't had time for checking). The cucurbit is *Cucurbita pepo*. This, like *Capsicum annuum*, at that time was found in Mesoamerica and not in the West Indies. (The species in the West Indies was most probably *Cucurbita moschata*.) Therefore, I think it likely that Columbus got the squash seed the same time as he did *C. annuum*." These statements are based on place of origin—*C. pepo* in Mesoamerica; *C. moschata* from South America had traveled with the Arawaks to the West Indies—without mentioning the possibility of a pre-Columbian movement from Mesoamerica to the West Indies. Nevertheless, it backs up my theory that the Mesoamerican plants were available within the Spanish Main before the discovery and conquest of Mexico. That herbal illustrates both Sauer's (1966) corn complex and peppers, thereby adding weight to Stoianovich's (1966) thesis that "there is little chance that corn came from the New World to Europe by itself," and to my theory that peppers traveled as part of that complex.

1502, soon after the Honduran landing, the explorers reached the coast of Nicaragua, where they spent some time repairing and refitting their ships. During that sojourn Columbus questioned the natives about gold and other things. Afterward he wrote to their majesties, "According to reports they are all acquainted with red pepper." It was his practice to collect a sample of all things new and different he saw to take back to show to the king and queen. There is no doubt in my mind he collected some of those "red peppers" for his sovereigns, and based on the pre-Columbian distribution maps, they would have been *Capsicum annuum* var. *annuum*.

A little later in 1502, when the Spaniards arrived in Panama, they found corn, beans, and perhaps peppers, where they had been carried from Mexico gradually, down through Central America. From there the pre-Columbian trade route went east across *Tierra Firme,* and thence north into the Antillean islands (see the map on pages 10–11). With the post-Columbian help of the Spanish, these foods quickly traveled from the isthmus to all of the West Indies. The listing of maize, also indigenous to Mesoamerica, among the foods brought to Spain in 1493, indicates that an exchange between its Mesoamerican homeland and the West Indian islands had already begun. Although it is highly possible that Mesoamerican capsicums like those described by Martyr had already reached some parts of the West Indies at the time of Columbus's first voyage, we can be assured they spread rapidly after the contact on the mainland in 1502.[15]

Fray Bartolomé de Las Casas, the Apostle of the Indies, spent many of his ninety-two years in the New World, first arriving in 1502. He recorded his careful observations in his *Apologética Historia,* believed to have been drafted in Española between 1526 and 1529.[16] Two of the three capsicums he describes as being cultivated in the West Indies fit the illustrations found in Fuchs's herbal. One *ají* was long, red, and finger shaped; a second was globular like a cherry and more pungent. A third was a wild capsicum that bore very small fruits. The first fits the description of Fuchs's Mesoamerican cayenne type.

Now, a look at the Portuguese enterprise. During the seventeenth century, botanical writers, including Charles L'Éscluse, reported that some of the capsicums in India were called Pernambuco pepper and Brazilian pepper. Evidence such as this supports the Portuguese introduction of the first *Capsicum* peppers into India, but gives no clue as to what species, though Pernambuco was a Portuguese colony on the eastern point of Brazil; therefore it would seem those peppers were *Capsicum chinense* (see the map on pages 14–15). By early in the sixteenth century the Portuguese had also introduced what they called Spanish pepper to Pamrukan, Java. The origin of that common name poses another question. Why Spanish and not Brazilian or Pernambuco? Where

---

15. Although it sounds unlikely at first, we are told by South African anthropologist M. D. W. Jefferies that in 1502 (the same year that the Spanish made their first American mainland contact), the Portuguese introduced corn to their Cape Verde Islands from an earlier introduction to their colonies in Guinea. That corn would have had to have been from a West Indian source via Iberia, the Canaries, or the Azores because at that time the only New World mainland contact the Portuguese had made was in Brazil (1500), and there was no corn there yet.

16. Writing in 1864, O'Gorman reveals that Las Casas's observations cannot be definitely dated, the best we can do is to say he made them between the time of his first arrival in Española in 1502 and his last visit to that island in 1532. In Seville some twenty-five years after making the first draft, Las Casas separated the *Historia* and the *Apologética* and enriched them with numerous interpolations. Since Las Casas remarked that the peppers he saw were "like those already known in all Spain," it would be very significant to know when he was referring to them growing in Spain—at the time of his first sighting, at the time of his first draft, or when he made his final revision. His first visit to Española coincided with Columbus's discovery of the mainland in 1502. During his second stay in the West Indies (1508 to 1515), Las Casas farmed a grant of land on the river Arimáo in Española between 1513 and 1514. I tend to think he made his agricultural observations during that sojourn, which was well before the discovery of Mexico, thereby strengthening my Mesoamerican trade thesis.

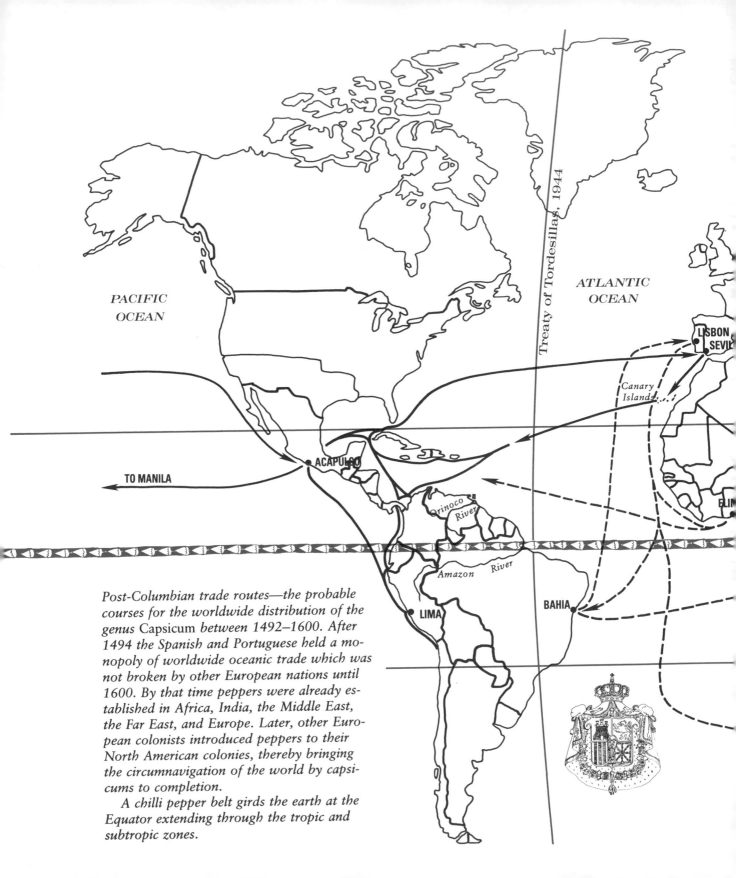

PACIFIC
OCEAN

ATLANTIC
OCEAN

Treaty of Tordesillas, 1944

LISBON
SEVIL

Canary
Islands

TO MANILA

ACAPULCO

ELIM

Orinoco River

Amazon River

LIMA

BAHIA

Post-Columbian trade routes—the probable
courses for the worldwide distribution of the
genus Capsicum between 1492–1600. After
1494 the Spanish and Portuguese held a monopoly of worldwide oceanic trade which was
not broken by other European nations until
1600. By that time peppers were already established in Africa, India, the Middle East,
the Far East, and Europe. Later, other European colonists introduced peppers to their
North American colonies, thereby bringing
the circumnavigation of the world by capsicums to completion.

A chilli pepper belt girds the earth at the
Equator extending through the tropic and
subtropic zones.

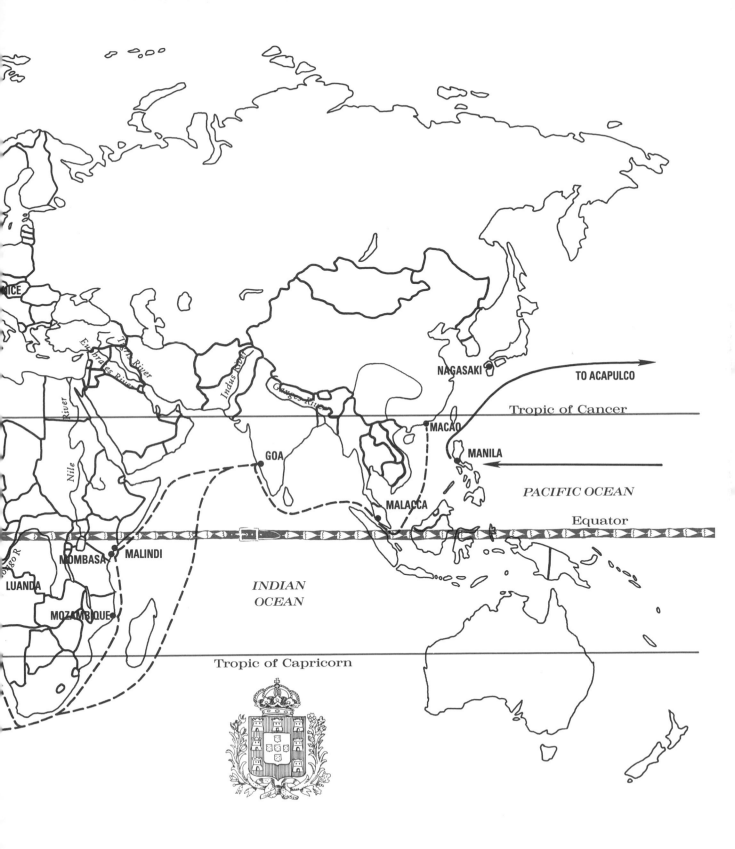

VENICE

Euphrates River

Tigris River

Indus River

Ganges River

Nile River

Congo R.

NAGASAKI

TO ACAPULCO

Tropic of Cancer

MACAO

MANILA

GOA

PACIFIC OCEAN

MALACCA

Equator

MOMBASA

MALINDI

LUANDA

INDIAN
OCEAN

MOZAMBIQUE

Tropic of Capricorn

had the Portuguese acquired "Spanish pepper"? The Spanish did not become active in the Pacific until 1565 and neither they nor other European ships were permitted to trade in Indian and Indonesian ports during the period of Portuguese supremacy (1497 to 1600) in the Far East.

To answer that very significant query will require looking at some obscure facts and circumstances regarding the goings-on of the Spanish and Portuguese during the fifty years before and after the Discovery. More than half a century before Columbus discovered America, the Portuguese, under the auspices of Prince Henry the Navigator, had begun their exploration and colonization of the west coast of Africa. At that time the rulers of both Portugal and Spain knew that the valuable spices came from the Far East, but both countries were dependent on Venice as their source, and Venice was the eastern Mediterranean middleman for the hated Muslims at the caravan terminus of Aleppo (now Halab, Syria) and in Alexandria, Egypt. As soon as the Iberian powers independently won their freedom from the forces of Islam, they each set out to find a way to the fabled Indies that would bypass those two centers. Spices in general, and the pungent black seed of a botanically unrelated Indian vine, black pepper (*Piper nigrum*), in particular, were not the only motivation for the Portuguese venture, but they were a predominant factor.[17]

Before the feats of Columbus, an Arab-speaking Portuguese, Pero de Covilha, reached India by way of the Mediterranean and the Red Sea. Although his was a shorter route to India, Islamic barriers made it unfeasible. Therefore, the Portuguese continued cautiously coasting[18] south along western Africa, and rounding the Cape of Good Hope the Portuguese captain Bartolomeu Dias sighted the Indian Ocean in 1487–88. With that, the rivalry between the two great Iberian powers came to a head. As Portugal was about to reach the Malabar coast of western India, Spain chose to play her trump card, Christopher Columbus. Consequently, after the Discovery the Portuguese hastened their exploration of the west African coast in an effort to reach the spice lands in order to catch up with Spanish achievements. Soon thereafter, a Portuguese ship under the irascible, brutal Vasco da Gama, with the guidance of the finest Arabian navigator in Malindi, Ahmad-Ibn-Madjid, arrived in India in 1497. Now the Iberian feud became testy.

Shortly after the discovery of America, the Borgian pope Alexander VI decided to put an end to the squabbling between those two Catholic powers. In 1493 and 1494 with the Treaty of Tordesillas,[19] he drew an imaginary longitudinal

17. As stated by Charles Boxer in 1969, the four principal causes of Portuguese exploration in chronological order were: (1) crusading zeal, (2) desire for Guinea gold, (3) quest for Prester John, a powerful if implausible schismatical Christian priest-king, (4) search for spices. The spices, however, only become a significant objective after the death of Prince Henry in 1460. By that time West African slave trade was going strong.

18. Fernand Braudel relates that coasting or hugging the shoreline was prevalent in the Mediterranean and much of India during the fifteenth and sixteenth centuries. Mediterranean sailors were fainthearted when it came to taking their boats across the seas, even though yearly voyages to London and Antwerp were not uncommon. Sailing close to shore provided protection against the elements, and having the coastline in sight aided navigation. The small capacity of the boats made necessary almost daily stops to renew water, wood, and supplies. These stops gave ample opportunity for bartering and exchange, and for accidentally spreading seed in food scraps. Merchants would voyage with their wares, and every seaman, from captain to cabin boy, had a packet of merchandise on board. The long trips were a sequence of selling, buying, and exchanging the cargo. The only things resembling our "destination-conscious" modern shipping were the large specialized salt and grain ships. The others were more like floating markets. The practice of seamen carrying merchandise for sale persisted throughout the days of the sailing merchant ships.

19. The most important of the papal bulls was the *Inter coetera*, which granted to Spain and Portugal everything they could discover on their side of the imaginary line. In 1529 the Treaty of Zaragossa attempted to settle the problem that resulted when that first line went through the then-unknown Far East. Spain and Portugal made an agreeable exchange that allowed Spain to retain the Philippines, which fell within

line, 370 leagues west of the Cape Verde Islands,[20] which continued around the globe, even though no one knew what route it would take in the Far East. Then he proclaimed that Spain could explore and trade in the area to the west, while granting Portugal the eastern half, effectively barring to Spain the route around southern Africa.

The Portuguese did not leap into power in the Far East immediately. Pedro Álvares Cabral followed da Gama in 1500; his fleet of thirteen ships contained two vessels laden with trade goods, which could have included the New World capsicums. In 1502, while Columbus was exploring the coast of Mesoamerica, da Gama returned to India. After a new trading post was set up at Cochin, a better harbor, he went back to his rewards in Portugal. But it was not until the Portuguese seized Muslim-dominated Goa in 1510 that their Far Eastern efforts under Governor Afonso de Albuquerque showed any results. By the time of Albuquerque's death in 1515 the Portuguese were shipping spices from the Far East to Lisbon and thence to Antwerp, making Lisbon the greatest commercial city in Europe.

Although Cabral had discovered Brazil on his voyage to India in 1500, no exploration was attempted. For the first thirty years after his landfall the Portuguese, fully occupied in the Far East, made no use of Brazil except as a source of brazilwood for dye. Salvador was founded in 1502, but no other colonies were established until after 1530 with the introduction of sugar plantations.

Meanwhile, to the north of Brazil the Spanish were dominating the scene. Spanish mercantilism dictated that her colonies should exist for the sole benefit of the mother country. Although there ensued rapid envelopment of the areas considered to be economically alluring—those with gold deposits, ample labor supply, easy access, and abundant land for agriculture and grazing—total occupation of these territories never took place. Española, in the heavily populated West Indies, became their first center and served as a base for the conquest and settlement of the other islands, while Cuba became the base for exploration and conquest of the mainland. But the center of Spanish interest persisted only until 1530, when the gold and labor force became depleted. After that, Spanish immigration to the West Indies came to a standstill, and African slaves began to be imported through the Portuguese to replace the Amerindians, who verged on extinction by 1540.[21] The imported European domesticated pigs, cattle, and horses did so well on the islands that the archipelago became the suppliers of those animals to the conquistadors. Their traditional grains and olives did not prosper, however, as the Spaniard had little understanding of the nature of the Antillean environment, which was tropical and had a seasonal cycle of rainfall reversed from that of Iberia. As a result, the settlers urgently needed foodstuffs from the mother country during the early years. This need was compounded by a persistent emphasis on European crops and a rejection of the native food from the *conucos* (mounded gardens).

The famed Spanish convoy system, which ex-

Portuguese territory by the lines of those treaties. Those treaties unwittingly determined the Old World destination of many New World plants.

20. The Cape Verde Islands off the coast of present day Senegal, West Africa, were important Portuguese bases during the fifteenth century. Because the Portuguese introduced New World plants to these islands and Guinea very early, they are significant locations in the movement of these plants around the world.

---

21. Writing in 1987, David Watts describes the West Indies as being inhabited by eight to ten thousand Europeans in 1509. Between the time ninety men in the initial Columbus band set foot on the islands until then, three million native Americans died—three hundred Arawaks and Caribs for each Spaniard. In the highlands of Mexico the Spanish encountered a climate and landscape more comparable to their Estremadura and Andalusia than the tropical West Indies. In contrast to the more primitive inhabitants of the islands, Philip Means disclosed that those the Spaniards met in Mexico were a disciplined people practicing an advanced type of intensive agriculture within a society somewhat similar to their own feudal system.

isted as the only legal link between the Caribbean and the rest of the world, was not implemented until 1561, long after capsicums had become established in the Old World. Although two fleets supposedly departed from Spain each year for the Caribbean, several years could pass without New World ports hosting a single Spanish ship. Even less shipping took place during our "critical period," despite the need to supply approximately ten thousand residents of the newly established Spanish colony. This paucity of Spanish shipping allowed the daring Portuguese to enter the region surreptitiously with their African slaves and other trade goods. This illicit trade was aided by Spain's own subjects in the Americas, not from disloyalty, but rather from dire necessity.

In the first half of the sixteenth century only a thin trickle of exchange existed between Seville and the New World. Portuguese trade between Lisbon and the New World was greater. At the same time, back on the Iberian peninsula, relations, including commerce, between the two Iberian powers were surely cordial if not friendly, since the royal houses were now linked by marriage. Evidently there was communication between Lisbon, Seville, and Barcelona that could have contributed to the rapid spread of *Capsicum*.

The grain trade in Iberia was another contributing factor. At the time of the conquest and throughout the early movement (1492 to 1550) of New World economic plants—maize, tomatoes, tobacco, squash—bread grain in Portugal was deficient, and the little country depended on a well-established trade with neighboring Spain and North Africa for its cereal supply. Surely the traders would have been aware of the new maize and its attendant plants—squash, beans, and capsicums.

By the 1550s the Portuguese merchants had penetrated all of Spanish America and in particular its capital cities and important ports: Mexico City, Santo Domingo, and Cartagena. A considerable Portuguese trading network that spread throughout the New World in a matter of twenty years was centered on Lisbon, and extended to both the African and the American sides of the Atlantic, with connections in East Africa and the Far East. Even though there was a direct trade route between Portuguese Africa (Elmina in present Ghana and Luanda in Angola) and Portuguese Brazil (Bahia in Pernambuco) after 1535, throughout the sixteenth and seventeenth centuries nothing went from Brazil to India without going to Lisbon first.

Very few Spanish ships actually made the West Indian trip, even though the demand for European goods was so great in the Indies that Spanish merchants could not meet it. That neglected Indies trade, therefore, was a standing temptation to slavers, smugglers, and illicit traders, mostly Portuguese, in the first half of the sixteenth century. From the early years of the century African slaves had been employed in the sugar production of Española, and later throughout the Spanish Main and in coastal Mexico.[22] Portuguese slavers supplied other slave traders licensed by the Spanish government, and often ran cargoes across on their own account. That slave trade presented opportunities to acquire Mesoamerican foods, including capsicums.

Slaving was not the only opportunity. The Mesoamerican plants could have been available on the Iberian peninsula, or at refitting stops in the Spanish Canary Islands and the Portuguese Azores, which were frequented by both Spanish and Portuguese ships sailing with the prevailing winds to New World ports where they were resupplied with local foods. Even Columbus went to Lisbon via the Azores before he returned to Seville at the end of his first voyage.

---

22. By 1550 the Spanish population in the West Indies had dwindled until it did not exceed fifteen hundred. Española had a thousand Spaniards and twelve to thirteen thousand Africans. In fact, Africans were the bulk of the people on the islands. The first Negro slaves were brought to the West Indies in 1502 directly from Spain, where enslavement of Jews, Moors, and Negroes was an established institution.

The climate on those Portuguese Atlantic islands—Madeira, the Azores, Cape Verde, and São Tomé—proved to be agreeable to the cultivation of Mexican produce. Scholars have studied and written copiously about maize, as you can see in the bibliography, so I started looking at its early movements because little has been written about capsicums. Without going into all the details, I have concluded that the Portuguese started growing corn and capsicums (*Capsicum annuum* var. *annuum*) in their islands in the Azores, and Madeira as well as Guinea on the Senegal coast of western Africa, and Angola as soon as they acquired the seed from a yet undetermined Spanish source late in the fifteenth century.[23] From there the crops arrived in Cape Verde, São Tomé, and Principe by 1502. The date of 1502 is very interesting, because that is the same busy year that Columbus began his fourth voyage, which took him to the mainland of Mesoamerica for the first time, and da Gama made his second voyage to India. If maize was introduced to the Cape Verdes in 1502, the seed could not have come from the first Columbian landfall on the North American continent (1502 to 1504), but would have had to have come from an earlier West Indian source (the Spanish), through a suspected movement to those islands over existing native trade routes prior to the first voyage of Columbus.

After the introduction of those New World plants to Portuguese eastern Atlantic holdings, it was no longer necessary to return to the New World for them. The Portuguese added the new agricultural products to their regular cargoes while carrying on their long-established and highly profitable European trade in sugar, slaves, gold, ivory, and "ginnie pepper" (grains of paradise). It is probable that *Capsicum* seed was transported from this area to India via Mozambique as soon as soon as it was obtainable. If there had been an early introduction of the Caribbean/South American chillies, a preference for the Mesoamerican capsicums would have caused them to be replaced.

The Portuguese monopoly assured by the Treaty of Tordesillas resulted in their becoming the primary carriers of New World plants to the Old World. Not only could the Portuguese receive credit for the introduction of American flora and fauna to Africa, India, and the Far East, but also directly and indirectly to parts of Europe. As a result of those Portuguese introductions to India and/or East Africa, long-established Arabic-speaking traders were able to transport the American exotics from the Malabar coast and/or East Africa to the Middle East, whence they traveled to eastern Europe via Constantinople and Venice. In addition, Portuguese convoys returning from India could have transported those introduced American foods, along with indigenous Asian spices, in cargoes from their new colonies east of the Pope's line back to Antwerp via Lisbon, as we shall see.[24]

In the five hundred years since the Discovery, the Caribbean/South American capsicums such as Scotch bonnet and habanero (*C. chinense*), never have become popular in Spain, Mexico, and the United States, or in Africa, where the Portuguese had direct trade routes to Brazil. In fact, they are only now gaining acceptance in those places.

---

23. Personal correspondence with Professors Murdo MacLeod, historian at the University of Florida, and Samuel M. Wilson, anthropologist at the University of Texas at Austin, has assured me that the Portuguese were not present or active in any way in the Caribbean before the introduction of slaves from Africa around 1509. This would reaffirm my suggestion that the New World seed that went to West Africa within the first ten years following the Discovery was not acquired directly from the West Indies by the Portuguese.

---

24. The Flemish botanist Matthia de Lobel (1538 to 1616) observed that capsicums had been brought from Goa and Calicut at a very early date. From that, George Watt, writing at the turn of the century, declared, "There can be no doubt that the Portuguese very possibly began exporting them in competition with black pepper."

Capsicum chinense is a native of the tropics and therefore harder to grow in temperate and subtropical climates. Its ripe fruit does not keep well, does not dry readily for year-round storage and use—whole or ground, does not travel satisfactorily, or have the versatility of its multifaceted temperate cousin, *C. annuum* var. *annuum*. For the most part, the first New World plants introduced to the Old World were from the hot, humid, tropical Caribbean islands. It was not until plants were available from the Mexican highlands after 1519 to 1521, and Peru after 1528 to 1531, that pepper varieties more suited to the climates of Europe were accessible.

Using the distribution of coffee[25] as an analogy, I feel it would have taken seeds from only a few blistering pods to introduce the spice that burned its way through the kitchens of the Far East. Having found coffee growing wild in Ethiopia before A.D. 1000, the Arabs assured their monopoly by heating the coffee beans to prevent germination and by guarding their plantations. It took but seven viable beans stolen by a seventeenth-century pilgrim to Mecca from Mysore, India, to introduce coffee cultivation to India. If Meccan pilgrims collected coffee seed, perhaps they gathered chilli seed, too.

Considering that capsicums of the type that went to India have approximately twenty-five to sixty seeds in one pod, and that in the tropics they begin producing fruit within two and a half to three months and continue throughout the year, it takes little imagination to project a few seeds into enough capsicums to change the cuisines of much of the world's population. Old World peasants, whether in the Balkans, Venice, India, or Indonesia, never grew black pepper, cinnamon, cloves, nutmeg, or cardamom in their gardens—their cultural requirements made it impossible—but once the *Capsicum* seed became available, they had a spice that they could grow for their own use.

As ecological historian Alfred W. Crosby, Jr., who coined the phrase "the Columbian Exchange," says, "The most important changes brought on by the Columbian voyages were biological in nature." If the effect of New World capsicums on Old World cuisines is any gauge, their transfer must have been one of the most significant achievements of the Admiral of the Ocean Sea. Inconceivable as it may seem today, at that time the Old World was without turkeys, corn, potatoes, squashes, common beans, peanuts, sweet potatoes, lima beans, cacao (chocolate), vanilla, avocados, tomatoes, pineapples, manioc (also called yuca, cassava, and tapioca), and *Capsicum* peppers, but not for long. Within the lifetime of the conquistadors, most of these foods were established throughout the world except for the Pacific Islands, New Zealand, and Australia. By 1542, only fifty years after their discovery by Columbus, three varieties of capsicums were recognized on the Malabar coast of India.

It is still difficult to perceive the rapidity of the spread of New World foods, especially corn, beans, squash, sweet potatoes, and capsicums, throughout the world.[26] Meanwhile in the Americas, Old World plants and animals were also quickly assimilated. In combination with the great variety of native American foods their addition triggered a dynamic nutritional change. Food historian John C. Super asserts that during

---

25. Coffee first came to the notice of Europeans traveling in the Levant in the sixteenth century. In 1615 Venetian traders shipped coffee beans to Europe. The Dutch had introduced tea five years previous to that, and the Spaniards had initiated cocoa (made with water) drinking eighty years before that. These beverages accompanying dessert were quite revolutionary at the end of the seventeenth century.

26. I think that disbelief in the rapidity with which New World food plants spread has bred a school of thought that insists there is evidence that maize, for example, was grown in Guinea, Turkey, and Granada, Spain, before Columbus; however, none of the evidence is botanical. Until biological evidence is found to support the claims, we should not doubt that the Old World and the New World each had unique flora and fauna up to the point of the Columbian exchange.

the sixteenth century it is unlikely that any other area in the world had such multiplicity of staples and abundance of animal protein as Spanish America, making possible the rapid expansion of the Spaniards in the Americas during the first half of the sixteenth century.

Africa

You will recall a growing Portuguese presence on the west coast of Africa in 1415 as their search for gold, slaves, and spices led them further south along that long, uncharted coast toward the southern tip. Amid civilizations strikingly different from their own, they set about to exploit the continent in order to trade in slaves and ivory. The slave trade with the Americas coupled with the introduction of New World foods inaugurated a yet uncompleted cultural and economic revolution within Africa.

SUB-SAHARAN AFRICA

West Africans could have obtained the American peppers by several means. In writing about African agriculture, Marvin Miracle tells us that the Portuguese established friendly relations with the ruler of the Kingdom of Congo after their arrival in 1482, and within twenty years (1502) the Kingdom of Congo was sufficiently influenced by the Portuguese for the Pope to recognize it as a Christian state. In 1521 the son of the king of Congo, who as a boy had been sent to Portugal for education, was made the first bishop of Congo. Thus any superior crops that the Portuguese knew about at this time could easily have been introduced either by the Portuguese or by Africans sent to Portugal during this period.

The Africans, already accustomed to using the burning seed of *Aframomum melegueta* (called grains of paradise) in their food, readily accepted the fiery American capsicums, which soon supplanted that spice both at home and abroad. After the early establishment of capsicums in Guinea the Portuguese probably carried African grown chillies along with the Far Eastern spices to Lisbon and their mercantile colony in Antwerp, where much of their spice cargo was marketed. In 1597 John Gerard, the English herbalist, reported that "ginnie" peppers were in England. That he was not referring to *A. melegueta* is evident, as he clearly describes capsicums, adding that they went from "Ginnie, India, and those parts, into Spaine and Italy: from whence wee have received seede for our English gardens." Today the most used capsicums in Africa are *Capsicum annuum* var. *annuum* of the cayenne type, while *C. chinense* and the small *C. frutescens* are less common.

MEDITERRANEAN
NORTH AFRICA

In 1492 Arabic-speaking Muslims of Mediterranean stock occupied a broad band of territory from the Black Sea to Morocco, thereby isolating Christendom from direct communication with the peoples of Asia. North Africa, a cultural world far apart from the sub-Saharan region, was crossed by the highly cultivated Saracen Moors as they overran Spain. After their seven-hundred-year occupation of Spain, they were finally defeated by the armies of King Ferdinand and Queen Isabella. Following their defeat, the Moors could have introduced the New World plants during their century-long flight into the Muslim world of North Africa and from there into the rest of that domain around the Mediterranean.

As evidence of the early arrival of American plants in northern Africa we find maize being cultivated in Ethiopia by 1547, and it is entirely possible the Portuguese introduced it in Ethiopian Massawa as early as 1520. In the southern Balkans maize was known as Egyptian or Arabic grain. Traian Stoianovich, a Balkan economist,

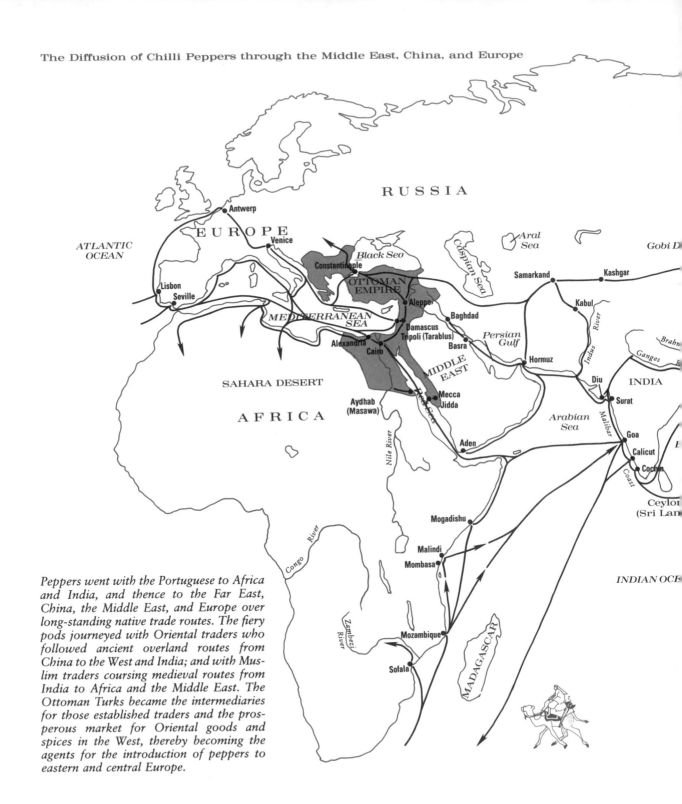

Peppers went with the Portuguese to Africa and India, and thence to the Far East, China, the Middle East, and Europe over long-standing native trade routes. The fiery pods journeyed with Oriental traders who followed ancient overland routes from China to the West and India; and with Muslim traders coursing medieval routes from India to Africa and the Middle East. The Ottoman Turks became the intermediaries for those established traders and the prosperous market for Oriental goods and spices in the West, thereby becoming the agents for the introduction of peppers to eastern and central Europe.

expressed the opinion that maize did not travel alone—where it went so went beans, squash, and I would add capsicums. The Moors' long-standing trans-Sahara gold, slave, and melegueta pepper trade provided further opportunity for contact with West Africa, and the American plants introduced to that coast.

Monsoon Asia

The southern and eastern part of the distant Far East is referred to as Monsoon Asia, even though seasonal monsoon wind conditions do not apply to the entire area. It covers less than a seventh of the earth's land surface, yet embraces half its population and almost a third of the cultivated land in the world. Some of the world's oldest civilizations are to be found within its boundaries, and everywhere millennia-old customs, food habits, dress, and farming methods still prevail among the peasants. This is the land that held the vaunted "riches of the Orient" that drove the western rulers and merchants of the fifteenth century to send their frail ships into the unknown. Those ships brought the new-found food plants to the Far East, where they were readily established and incorporated into the cuisines of the area.

INDIA

After first landing in Calicut, India, the Portuguese quickly determined that Cochin, to the south, was a better harbor for their purposes. A bit later they captured Goa, long an important Muslim trading entrepôt, and installed their Far East headquarters in that more favorable location. As the capital of Portuguese India, it was in Portuguese hands from 1509 to 1961, and even today is visibly different from Mother India.

Asian shipping was permitted to continue as before, provided a license was purchased and customs on the cargo were paid to the Portuguese.[27] New World economic plants—tobacco, pineapple, peanuts, henequen (source of sisal for rope), and capsicums, to name a few—soon became a vital part of that cargo.

Coasting between Goa, Diu, Surat, or Hormuz to the Persian Gulf, or in convoys across the Arabian Sea to the Red Sea, American capsicums quickly joined the other spices following those two ancient medieval trade routes—the Aleppo and the Alexandria routes—long used by the Turks, Arabic-speaking mariners, and other Muslims to carry the lucrative trade from Monsoon Asia to the Levant; the travelers followed the Silk Roads with their toiling caravans from the Ganges delta over the Burma Road, or from the commercial center of Kabul on the caravan road from Turkey and Persia at the head of the Indus River to China; and they also sailed the sea lanes to Malacca and Indonesia used by coasting Chinese, Gujarati, and Arabic traders—these were some of the routes over which the New World foods traveled (see the map on pages 22–23). These new foods melded into the principally vegetarian cuisines of China, India, Indonesia, and other areas of the Far East.

Unlike Spain, Portugal did not yearn to establish an empire on land; her goal was a seaborne empire. They made no attempt at extensive inland conquests; yet, such an empire as they coveted required garrisons, factories, and support facilities at strategic spots along the various coasts. Within their Goan headquarters, India's

---

27. Most of the Portuguese ships used in that area were built with European plans in Gujarat or Goa using the superior Indian teakwood. The small wooden-plank Gujarat and Goan boats, designed for coasting with the monsoon winds, employed no nails but were sewn together with coconut fiber cord (coir). While in Goa and Cochin on the Malabar coast of India, I was able to examine and photograph boats of the same construction that are still used by fishermen along both the Arabian Sea and the Bay of Bengal.

Portuguese invaders had among them not only conquerors and traders but also missionaries, who set forth to make good Roman Catholics out of the local "heathens." Those faithful Jesuits carried seeds for their mission gardens wherever it was their fate to be sent, and we can rest assured they didn't forget them when they went to India, for one of their routines was to introduce the cultivation of maize as a means of gaining the trust of the indigenous peoples. The missionaries were also involved in trade as a means of supporting their work.

The new spice was welcomed by Indian cooks who, at home with burning black pepper and biting ginger, were accustomed to pungent, spicy foods. The easily cultivated and naturalizing varieties of *Capsicum annuum* var. *annuum* and *C. frutescens* were, for them, a lot more heat with a lot less grinding and expense; they also grew readily and fruited abundantly in a sympathetic environment. Into the curries they went.

CEYLON, MALAYSIA, INDONESIA, THAILAND

The Buddhist island of Ceylon (Sri Lanka), populated today with Sinhalese, was of strategic importance on the oceanic trade routes of Monsoon Asia. It has, in turn, been Portuguese, Dutch, and British before gaining its independence; however, the latter two occupying forces did not put out the fire that the Portuguese had ignited. Food in Sri Lanka is very pungent.

Islam, introduced by Arab traders at an early date, reached the eastern monsoon area long before American capsicums. Although it seems at least twenty years tardy, 1540 is the only date I've found for the arrival of New World capsicums in the East Indies (Indonesia) by way of the Arab and Gujarati traders who had been active in Southeast Asia for a thousand years and/or the overpowering Portuguese. Muslim ships, sailing between Malaccan waters and the Persian Gulf or Red Sea, regularly frequented Atzeh, at the tip of Sumatra. Since 1511, Malacca had served as a forward base for Portuguese trading and missionary expansion into China, Japan, Thailand, and eastern Melanesia, and by 1550 the Portuguese had a permanent base at Macao on the South China coast. Their *Nao da Macao,* the trading galleon romanticized in the novel *Shōgun,* ran from Goa via Malacca to Macao and thence to Nagasaki, Japan, until the mid-seventeenth century. From any of these Portuguese ports of call, local seagoing craft—Malaccan, Javanese, Siamese, Cambodian, and Chinese, as well as Indian and Arabic—could easily have carried American peppers throughout the East Indies and the Spice Islands (Moluccas), even to the Philippines and China. The chillies might also have been found at the Arab and Persian trading colonies that had been established during the seventh and eighth centuries in Canton and Hangchow, on China's southeast coast.

It has been suggested that dried or fresh chillies were taken as a condiment or food by sailors and inhabitants of the monsoon area, who inadvertently spread the seed when they stopped for meals (see footnote 18). Native navigators who found the New World plants in Portuguese and later Spanish ports of Melanesia, Indonesia, the Philippines, and Guam carried them from island to island. Not to be outdone, the birds hopped in. Even today flocks of pigeons descend from the mountains to feed on ripe red capsicums, thus carrying seed to remote places. Though some Pacific islands were inaccessible to early sailors, few are so remote that chilli seeds could not have been deposited there by birds. In any case, capsicums soon spread in cultivation throughout that tropical area and then escaped from gardens to become naturalized in the wild, where they have been so successful and their adoption by the denizens of the zone so complete that only recently do present inhabitants of the region even consider the suggestion that chillies are not indigenous to that area. Today, these people are born with capsaicin in their veins.

SOUTHWESTERN CHINA

The Chinese are considered by anthropologist Berthold Laufer to be the foremost masters of plant economy in the world, with all useful plants of the universe being cultivated there. During the Ming dynasty of the sixteenth century, Chinese were contemplative, intelligent, and broadminded people with an active foreign policy, who seldom rejected whatever good things foreigners offered. Considering communications and travel time in the sixteenth century, it took but a brief time for the American economic plants newly introduced to India to have been added to the baggage carried so laboriously from the Gangetic delta at the Bay of Bengal through Burma to Chendu in Szechuan over what is now known as the Burma Road. They also could have traveled from the Indian Ocean up the Indus River to Afghan Kabul, to meet the historic course followed by Marco Polo, winding its toilsome way from Turkey through Persia and Afghanistan to China. Yet another perilous route from the Indian Ocean began at Portuguese Diu and Surat on the Gulf of Cambay, from which it followed rivers that were tributaries to the Ganges, which wound its course to the mountainous bed of the Brahmaputra River, then up and across the Himalayas to Szechuan (see the map on pages 22–23).

It was over these torturous trails that emissaries, emperors, Arabic and Indian traders, religious pilgrims, and ordinary men came and went for centuries. Ancient Ming dynastic records show the origin of New World food plants in China to be the territory northwest of Tibet bordering Szechuan known as Si-fan. Here again, within the lifetime of the conquistadors (about 1492 to about 1550), American food plants took root in Chinese soil. Alfred W. Crosby, Jr., declares that "No other large group of the human race in the Old World was quicker to adopt American food plants than the Chinese." Capsicums and tomatoes not only helped revolutionize the taste of cooking in the southwestern area, but they also supplied rich, new sources of vitamins

C and A and specific minerals, improving the diet. After their introduction, seasonal dietary deficiencies were no longer a major problem, as vital nutrients were available during most of the year.

The Southeast, with its ports in Fukien, including Canton and Amoy, had intimate trade relations with the Portuguese for at least thirty-five years before the founding of the Portuguese trading colony at Macao in 1550, and later with the Spanish colonies in the Philippines. Coastal Chinese did not fail to notice and incorporate the valuable new plants the *Fo-land-chi* (Portuguese) had brought to Asia, but there were no roads from the seaports to carry those new foodstuffs six hundred miles to Szechuan during the Ming dynasty. As a consequence, peppers entered China two ways—to the east by sea, and to the southwest by overland routes.

Japan and Korea

JAPAN

The Portuguese sailed to feudal Japan around 1549 and opened those islands to New World foodstuffs. The Japanese themselves could have encountered chillies on their trading forays into Southeast Asia, where they had had colonies in the Philippines, Thailand, and Indonesia from the beginning of the seventeenth century. Modeling ships after Spanish vessels in the Philippines, they sailed across the Pacific to New Spain before Spain slammed that gateway shut in 1611, causing Japanese envoys to return from missions to Mexico aboard Spain's Acapulco-Mania galleon.

KOREA

From its isolated location on a peninsula west of Japan you would hardly think of Korea as a hot spot, but according to the per capita consumption of chillies, it is the hottest spot on the *Capsicum* trail. Korea took no part in the spice trade either before or during the era of that exotic commerce.

The first contact Koreans had with Europeans was in Peking, where Portuguese Jesuit missionaries were hard at their job of converting the "heathen" to the Roman Catholic form of Christianity. Books were the first European import into Korea by way of Peking, but later the missionaries themselves went. New World plants would have had to come the same way.

The Middle East

The Middle East, a term not always satisfactory to some geographers, encompasses an area little comprehended and largely unknown by those of us in the United States until recent tragic events brought it to our consciousness. It is a territory extending from Iran to Libya and from the Sudan to Turkey, having a characteristic Mediterranean climatic regime of summer drought and winter rain (except in the extreme north and south) that sets it apart from its neighbors. Until the twentieth century, this seemingly measureless area has been largely isolated from the main currents of economic and political activity, but the discovery of oil changed all that—rapidly.

Arabic, the dominant tongue, is the language of the Koran and as such is one of the great unifying forces of the Muslim/Islamic world. Long before the advent of the Portuguese, Arabic-speaking traders and seamen were the great explorers of the Indian Ocean to the Cape of Good Hope and on to the China Seas, as their far-flung bases on the southern China coast witness. Following the fall of the Roman Empire, the Arabs developed a vast empire with a rich scientific, literary, and artistic culture. They expanded knowledge while the lights of civilization and learning burned low in Europe during the Dark Ages. After A.D. 622, a Muslim flood raged through North Africa all the way to Spain, where it persisted for seven hundred years. It was the Muslim obstruction of the old routes to the Far East that drove the peoples of Europe to seek new directions to reach the Oriental luxuries they craved, and in so doing encountered a new world. The traders of the Middle East played a leading role in the distribution of capsicums and other New World plants.

TURKEY AND THE ARABIAN CARAVAN ROUTES

Strategically situated as a bridge between Europe and Asia, ancient Turkey (Anatolia) and the courses of the Tigris and Euphrates rivers have served as channels for the stream of humanity flowing between the East and West for ages. Barley, wheat, onions, peas, lentils, and dates are some of the important food crops first domesticated in that region, confirming a preoccupation with agriculture since prehistoric times.

The area was overrun by central Asiatic Turks riding down from Asia, who were in turn invaders, slaves, mercenaries, and adventurers, but who eventually ruled the land. Following the thirteenth-century Mongol invasion, the Turkish dynasty of the house of Ottoman, ruling through a military and religious autocracy, rose to become the major power in the fifteenth-century Western world. It was they who built a unified political system on the foundation of the Arabic language and the Islamic religion.

A Turkish document, written between 1498 to 1513, mentions a New World plant, the common bean, for the first time, and by 1539 New World maize was already playing a pivotal role in that area. It could have been that these first Columbian foodstuffs, including capsicums, came to Turkey from Spain via the Ottoman contacts with exiled Spanish Moors or expelled Spanish Jews who conceivably distributed them through-

out North Africa all the way to Egypt. The majority of those Jews settled in Turkey. But, due to the nature of trade and the extent of warfare in that critical period, I suspect those were not the most likely carriers. The clandestine firearm trade between Spain and the Turks is another plausible answer.[28] The procurement of weapons caused nations that were uncompromising rivals before the world to be "blood-brothers in the privacy of the counting-house," according to anthropologist John Witthoft.

Yet another possibility is that capsicums arrived in Turkey from India or Egypt[29] with Ottoman agents traveling medieval seaborne trade routes, via the Persian Gulf and/or the Red Sea, then to Venice and/or Istanbul. The northern route went from the Indian Ocean by way of Muscat, Ormuz (now Hormuz), and the Persian Gulf to Basra (al Basrah, Iraq) to Baghdad, then followed the Euphrates River to Aleppo, on to Antioch (Antakya, Turkey), and from there across

---

28. Most early inventions having to do with the technology of guns were Muslim/Moorish discoveries. Their early firearms used flint stone to spark the gun powder. At the time of the European conquest of America, gunflints from Albania were preferred. Gunflints are tangible evidence of international commerce and technical excellence. Archaeologists working in Mesoamerica and South America have found that the Spaniards used Albanian gunflints in their miquelet locks to slaughter and conquer the Amerindians. It made no difference where the flints came from, just so they were the best, consequently, rival armies often used flints from the same source. Huge numbers of guns of the Spanish and Turkish types were produced during that period. All of the early gunflints of Spain actually came from Albania, and were but one small item in a prosperous commerce reported by Witthoft in 1966. The mariners on the trading ships that stopped for supplies at frequent intervals could have noticed new foods and carried them with them.

29. Peppers, like maize, could have been introduced to Abyssinia (Ethiopia) and Egypt from the Portuguese in India or by coasting Muslim traders from any of the Portuguese garrisons established to refit the India fleet along the Swahili coast of East Africa—Mozambique, Mombassa, Malindi, Sofala. The supplies for these garrisons came from India or possibly the Portuguese Atlantic islands, not from Lisbon. In 1949 A. C. A. Wright wrote that the Portuguese had an embassy at Massawa, the main port of Ethiopia, from 1520. The Turks centered their activities at Harar, Ethiopia.

or around Turkey to Istanbul or from Aleppo to the Syrian (not Libyan) port of Tripoli (later Alexandretta, now Iskenderun) and then by sea to Constantinople (Istanbul) or Venice. The southern route began at Aden, passing through the Red Sea to Suez and Cairo, from there by a riverless overland course to Jerusalem, Damascus, Aleppo, and on to Istanbul and/or Venice; or overland to Alexandria and thence by land or sea (see the map on pages 22–23). By whichever route, Aleppo was a key point. In 1600 Venice operated sixteen trading houses and a consular office in Aleppo with quays at Tripoli to service the Adriatic shipping. European traders rarely went beyond the cities at the edge of the desert. The realm of caravans[30] was dominated by Muslim traders.

Since Hormuz, at the strategic entrance to the Persian Gulf, was a Portuguese colony and center for trade in Arabian horses, Oriental goods, Indian cottons, and spices from 1515 to 1662, there is the possibility that European and Turkish traders drawn to that center carried capsicums and other New World plants, even the American turkey, to Anatolia. Though any of these traveling merchants could have brought them to Europe, the exchange probably resulted from Ottoman armies following ancient trade routes of those merchants, through the Persian Gulf, across Asia Minor to the Black Sea and on into the Balkans and Greece. I think the fact that Turks, like others were to do later, quickly recognized the value of American maize as food for livestock,[31] and required peasants in the occupied lands to grow

it and other new food plants as provisions for both animals and men of their armed forces, explains the rapid movement of the American corn complex (see footnote 11).

Another entryway was the ancient Malabar spice route through the Red Sea to Alexandria, Egypt, and on to Greece, Venice, and Germany. The Portuguese blockades were not completely effective in halting the trade in that narrow body of water. It was difficult to outmaneuver such ancient mariners as the skilled Muslim seafarers, who easily sailed their agile little boats across the Indian Ocean with alternate monsoons, guided by their substantial knowledge and the use of the astrolabe, or Jacob's staff. Their significant navigational skills led Islam to dominate a large part of the Old World until the fifteenth century. The area around the Red Sea was part of the Turkish Empire during our period of 1492 to 1542, throughout which there was a marked revival in the Red Sea spice trade.

Europe

As you should be aware by now, I feel certain that chillies came to Europe several ways. After I present a few more puzzling facts of the case, you can decide for yourself or use the information to ferret out a better solution.

Keep in mind that in early sixteenth-century Europe the peasant majority received its food supply from communally cultivated cereal crops. These were supplemented by "garden" crops. New crops could be tried out in gardens around the house. Only after a crop proved successful in

30. Depending on which Indian seaport they sailed from, the vast convoys of ships reached the Red Sea in May or November every year. Fernand Braudel describes the scene. At Jedda they were met by congregations of caravans that could contain as many as 20,000 people and 300,000 animals at one time. Jedda was also the port that served the pilgrims journeying to nearby Mecca.

31. Stoianovich recounts that in Hungary corn/maize is known as maritime millet or grain in reference to its arrival there by way of the Black Sea or the Adriatic. He asserts that there is little chance that corn came alone from the New

World to Eastern Europe; but rather it arrived as part of Sauer's whole beans-maize-squash complex. In the New World, peppers were closely associated with that complex.

the garden was it allowed space in the communal fields. Virtually no records of garden crops were kept, so this important part of agriculture is a dark spot in the early history of agriculture. It is probable that the New World plants such as maize, chillies, sunflowers, squashes, beans, and tobacco were first grown in the European peasant's home garden. Capsicums were, and still are for most of the world, a garden crop.

THE BALKANS

The Turkish military conquest led by Suleiman the Magnificent of the wealthy but divided Balkan peninsula was the prelude to the introduction of paprika chillies. During our "critical period" in *Capsicum* history the Ottomans took Belgrade (1521), Rhodes (1522), and Hungary (1526), and stood before Vienna (1529) before turning back. A vast area that included not only the Balkans but North Africa, Egypt, and Syria, as well as Asia Minor, was under the domination of the Ottoman Empire until the Mediterranean Sea battle of Lepanto (1571) sealed its fate. As previously mentioned, Turkish military policy required the peasants of occupied lands to cultivate garrison gardens, which produced the food needed for the multitude of men and herds of animals in the army, and it was no different here.[32] Some authors believe maize was being grown in the Balkans by 1520 to 1530. This may well be so, for maize had become entrenched in the folklore of the region by the beginning of the eighteenth century. We are told by the French historian Fernand Braudel that the establishment of a system to provision the army was followed by another equally important, but less rigid requirement. which was "the construction of roads and fortified posts, the organization of camel trains, the setting in motion of all the supply and transport convoys," and finally the transmission of Turkish civilization to the conquered. Over these supply routes came the treasures of Asia, as well as New World foods.

By the middle of our "critical" period (1492 to 1542), the Portuguese dominated the sea lanes of the Indian Ocean and Hormuz, which functioned as the center for the seaborne goods destined for Persia and the rest of the Middle East. At the same time, the Venetians considered the hazardous sea voyage from the Adriatic to Egypt to be the main impediment to their trading endeavors in the Turkish-dominated Mediterranean. Thus, it would seem the Persian Gulf route or overland from the Red Sea to Aleppo would be the more likely capsicum trails to the Balkans.

GERMANY AND CENTRAL EUROPE

Contrary to what appears to be the obvious route—America to Spain to Europe—I suggest that capsicums arrived by two separate routes. The first could have gone to western Europe by one of the traditional ways—the western, with the Portuguese by sea directly from Lisbon or from Lisbon via Africa and the Atlantic islands or from Seville to Antwerp and Genoa; but the second went to eastern Europe via Venice or Istanbul by means of the Muslim Turks[33] (see the map on pages 22–23).

Iberians and western Europeans may have

---

32. The Turkish standing army, as described by Schevill, was usually made up of twelve to fourteen thousand Janissaries (unmarried infantry); ten to twelve thousand cavalry, each with four horsemen; plus irregulars. Two hundred thousand took part in the invasion of Hungary. It would take a lot to feed all those mouths on a daily basis.

33. According to geographer N. J. G. Pounds, spices came from southeastern Asia either by the overland or the oceanic route to respectively Venice or Lisbon. Venetian spices were distributed mainly by the Alpine routes to central and western Europe, and only occasionally by galley to western ports. The Portuguese spices were distributed by sea, most going to Antwerp for redistribution in northern Europe. The sixteenth century avenue regularly taken by cane sugar along with spices from India or Arabia, according to Braudel, passed through Venice to Germany on the way to markets in Flanders (Antwerp). Such statements reinforce my proposed eastern Mediterranean entry route.

been familiar with American peppers, but they did not appreciate their spice value until long after the pod's mid-sixteenth-century introduction to the Balkans. It took the Napoleonic blockade of European ports in the first decade of the nineteenth century to put them on the table, when they were reintroduced from Hungary and the Balkans as a substitute for more favored imported spices being denied entrance.

In 1535 Gonzalo Oviedo wrote that capsicums had been carried to Italy and Spain, and in 1542 Leonhart Fuchs was the first herbalist to report that capsicums were cultivated in Germany, where they were grown in pots. According to English herbalist William Turner, they were in England before 1538; author Zoltan Halasz finds them in the Balkans before 1569; and botanist Carolus L'Écluse found them in Moravia by 1585. Evidently believing that the foreign *Capsicum* plants had come to Europe from India, Fuchs called a long cayenne type *Indianischer pfeffer* (Indian pepper), a bulbous-shaped one *Breyter Indianischer pfeffer* (broad Indian pepper), and a more or less conical pod *Calechutischer pfeffer* (Calicut pepper). He also made one reference to *Piper Hispanum* (Spanish pepper), which was not illustrated. Could the *Hispanum* have come with the Albanian gunflint trade and the others with Indian spices? These names imply that he considered them to be native to that port where the Portuguese first entered India. Even today, in Calicut, the Tamil-speaking populace call the dry, red cayenne-type chillies *kappal molakai,*[34] which translates as "the pepper from the ship" or "the ship's pepper." In a letter written in 1569 they were referred to as *Türkisch rot pfeffer* (Turkish red pepper). Fernand Braudel affirms that Fuchs's Germany received spices and pepper

from Venice. The Venetians got them from the Middle Eastern spice centers, which, in turn, got them from India.

SPAIN AND PORTUGAL

Fifteenth- and sixteenth-century Spanish and Portuguese peoples had different attitudes toward agriculture, which may have contributed to the Portuguese having had a greater influence on the worldwide distribution of American food plants than the Spanish, even though the Spanish received them first. According to ethnobotanist Edgar Anderson, "The Portuguese had a highly specialized horticulture, an enthusiasm for unusual vegetables in fine variety, and a special flair for agricultural botany; while the Spanish exhibited aristocratic disdain for the dirty details of vegetable growing." *Quien sabe?*

The early French botanist Carolus L'Écluse, on a visit to Spain in 1564, saw the "American *Capsicum* where women had pepper plants hanging in the entrance to their gardens throughout the entire year. The fruit has various shapes and is used both fresh and dry as condiments." In Portugal he also found many types being cultivated at the monastery of Ulysitton on the banks of the Tagus River. Some of those were "endowed with a yellow color," and were so hot that "the sharpness would burn the jaws for several days."

ITALY AND THE MEDITERRANEAN

Although in 1535,[35] thirty-seven years after the discovery of America, the chronicler Gonzalo de Oviedo recorded that they were "carried to Spain and Italy," capsicums were not used there as food to any extent until much later. At first most were grown in pots as rarities. Later the larger sweet capsicums probably went to the Italian peninsula

---

34. This was related to me by T. P. Ramamoorthy, Ph.D, a Tamil botanist with The University of Texas at Austin, whose family is of Cochin, India. Calicut, Cochin, and Goa (in that order) were the ports first reached and dominated by the Portuguese in the late fifteenth and early sixteenth centuries.

35. In 4(3):31 of *The Journal of Gastronomy,* the date which I attributed to Oviedo's report of the introduction of chillies to Italy should be 1535, the date of his *La Historia de las Indias,* and not 1526, the date of his *Sumario de la Natural Historia de las Indias.* Those nine years could make a considerable difference.

along with the tomato, which was recorded by the Italian herbalist Pietro Matthiholi in 1544. Capsicums were shown in a painting by an anonymous follower of the Italian painter Michelangelo Amerighi Caravaggio in 1607.[36]

During the reign of Charles V (1519 to 1558), the people of Spain did not eat capsicums as did their more adventurous kinsmen in America, so it is unlikely that they carried those first capsicums with them in their journeys throughout the Spanish kingdom of the Hapsburgs, which encompassed not only Spain and the Netherlands but also the southern half of the Italian peninsula, including Naples. Although the Mediterranean peoples could have cultivated capsicums sometime after the introduction of the more acceptable Mexican varieties, they did not adopt them or the tomato as a part of their cuisine for two hundred years.

Geographically and, at the time of the Discovery, politically, the Mediterranean was effectively divided into two parts by Sicily and the Italian peninsula. The eastern half was dominated by Islamic peoples and the western half by Christians. Venice was dependent upon the Turks for her spices and wheat, while Florence and Genoa relied on the Iberians for imported goods. Communication between the two halves was slow, as Venice had few commercial connections to Lisbon, and trade between the eastern and western basins of the Mediterranean was at a virtual standstill. In the western Mediterranean, Genoa traded with Bruges in Belgium. Hapsburg Italy and the Netherlands, with Antwerp as its market center, were the two poles of Western European commerce.

For centuries the Mediterranean, bustling with maritime commerce along its littoral, had been the highway to the Levant,[37] with long-established trade and affiliations. The ships of the western Christians used the Strait of Messina to enter the eastern part, while the eastern Islamic ships passed through the Sicilian channel to go west. There were also continuous mule trains transporting goods across the Italian peninsula from one coast of the peninsula to the other. In spite of this exchange, the two halves of the sea maintained their sovereignty and their own spheres of influence organized into closed circuits. Between the middle of the fifteenth and sixteenth centuries Spanish imperialism gained control of the western sea. By contrast, the eastern Mediterranean was the Ottoman sea. These two parts of the Mediterranean, commanded by warring rulers, were physically, economically, and culturally different from each other. Interchange between the eastern and western halves of the Mediterranean slowly resumed with the decline of the Ottoman Empire, but capsicums had been in Europe more than a quarter century by then.

The daughter of Ferdinand and Isabella, Joanna, married the short-lived Hapsburg Philip I. Joanna's son was the Hapsburg Charles of Ghent, King of Spain (1516 to 1556), who became Charles V, Emperor (1519 to 1558) of Austria and Spain. He had little time for Spain. After 1535 the riches of the New World, pouring in through Seville, became a major consideration of the Austrian Hapsburgs. (Now you understand why Montezuma's feathered headdress and other Aztec treasures are in the museums of Vienna and not in Madrid.) Although the contacts between Spain and Germany were strong during the long reign of Charles, they did not produce any recorded plant introductions from Spain to Germany. In 1580 Spain and Portugal were

---

36. Days spent poring over books containing hundreds of Italian still-life paintings covering three centuries revealed little, if any, interest or acquaintance with New World fruits and vegetables. The Caravaggio-like painting had a squash, one tomato, and two pepperoncini-type peppers—one red and one yellow. A couple more had tomatoes. Obviously, the plants were not widely known in Italy.

---

37. The Levant is the non-European coast of the eastern Mediterranean extending from Greece to Egypt.

united under Phillip II, the son of Charles V.

Although the Turks got a grip on the heel of the Italian boot during this same period, I do not think that they introduced capsicums to the Italian Peninsula or acquired capsicums from Italy at that time or place. I believe sweet capsicums and tomatoes[38] came to western Italy from Spain[39] for several reasons: first, the historic record of western Mediterranean trade linking Seville and Barcelona with the southern half of Italy (formerly Naples) and Sicily (the part of Italy where the use of sweet capsicums and tomatoes is predominant today); second, the pungent capsicums the Turks carried to the Balkans were not that sweet capsicum type that came to be favored by both Italian and Spanish cooks; and finally, the use of capsicums and spices in the Balkans is more Indian in nature, while that of the western Mediterranean is unique to that region.

ENGLAND

Although during the Victorian period spicy Indian food was in vogue, England does not have a peppery cuisine; however, our mother country was a vital stop on this round-the-world journey of the pod. It has not been possible thus far to determine through documented evidence how it was that capsicums arrived in England by 1538. We know that British[40] trade with either the West or the East Indies was not established at that time, so capsicums must have been exported to England from Europe. The English could have acquired the seed from Spain or in the nearby

port of Antwerp, the crossroads of Europe, where considerable Portuguese and Spanish mercantile enterprises flourished at that time. Spain and the Netherlands, which included Antwerp, were united in the Hapsburg Empire. We have seen that sugar and spices came from India, through Germany and Antwerp on their way to Great Britain, so why not peppers? In 1548 the names the English herbalist William Turner gave for capsicums were "in englishe Indishe peper, and the duche indisshouer pfefer." John Gerard, a later herbalist, wrote in 1597 that the peppers being grown in pots in England were "ginnie peppers," indicating they had come from west Africa.

Capsicums straight from Spain were also a prospect. The first of Henry VIII's six wives was Catherine of Aragon, Spain. Although Catherine did not marry Henry until 1509, she had come to England in 1501 to marry his short-lived brother, bringing with her a retinue of one hundred and fifty, which included cooks, bakers, and carvers. This Spanish connection continued for more than thirty years, until her death.[41] John Frampton, an English merchant, in his translation of the Spaniard Nicholas Monardes's herbal, refers to the close relationship that existed between England and Spain when he remarks, "the afore saied Medicines . . . are now by Marchauntes and others brought out of the West Indias into Spaine, and from Spain hether into Englande, by suche as dooeth daiely traffike thether." The Portuguese could have brought them to England, as there is a report of five Portuguese ships tied up at Falmouth, England, in 1504, heavily loaded with black pepper and spices from Calicut. It was from English gardens that our world-traveling *Capsicum* returned to the Western Hemisphere.

---

38. Edgar Anderson (1958) reports that the Italians learned about the use of tomatoes from the Turks. Their original name for tomato is *pomo di moro*, the "apple of the Moors," later corrupted to *pomo d'oro*, *pomo d'amour* (or love apple).

39. At the end of the sixteenth century the English herbalist John Gerard assumed peppers came to Spain and Italy from Guinea and India.

40. English privateers first ventured into the Spanish Main after 1560, but trade was not their objective. Their early activities were carried on without establishing bases.

---

41. I like to think that Catalina de Aragon, the fifth and last child of Ferdinand and Isabella, the sponsors of the Discovery of Peppers by Cristóbal Colón, was responsible for the introduction of the *Capsicum* to England and then to Anglo-America. A wish-filled scenario—yet a possibility!

North America

Except in the two Spanish colonies of Santa Fe, New Mexico, and St. Augustine, Florida, the introduction of domesticated capsicums into Anglo-America north of Mexico, which at that time included Texas and the southwestern states, took place after the early years of distribution—1492 to 1600. Nevertheless, I think we would be remiss not to look at our own territory, Today we can enjoy a wide variety of capsicums in a plethora of peppery dishes offered by our indigenous Tex-Mex, southwestern, Creole/Cajun, and nouvelle cuisines, about which reams have been written. A number of our contributing chefs are among those who have pioneered and/or written about the peppery foods of the United States.

Both the British and the Dutch had ample sources for capsicums by the time they began to colonize North America in 1604. Red peppers, along with other food plants, arrived in Bermuda on the good ship *Elizabeth* in 1613. On December 2, 1621, Captain Nathaniel Butler, governor of the Bermudas, sent the governor of Virginia large cedar chests, "wherein were fitted all such kindes and sortes of the country plants and fruicts, as Virginia at that time and until then had not, as figgs, pomegranates, oranges, lemons, plantanes, sugar canes, potatoe, and cassada rootes [cassava], papes [papaya], red-pepper, the pritle peare [prickly pear], and the like." In spite of this early record, capsicums did not take hold in the colonies until later, when the plantation system and African slavery were introduced. Chillies were still curiosities in 1785 when George Washington grew two kinds of them in his Mount Vernon, Virginia, botanical garden. The plantations in the southern colonies had a climate more suitable for the cultivation of capsicums, and the African slaves, both from the West Indies and directly from Africa, had developed a diet that demanded chillies. Chillies probably came with the slaves from the West Indies.

A small still-life painting by the American artist Raphael Peale records green bell peppers in Philadelphia in 1814. And so capsicums traveled from the New World to the Old World and back again to the Western Hemisphere. My account is incomplete and like all chronological reports may mistake appearance for reality. It cannot be claimed that all the questions concerning the circulation of chillies are settled, but they have been highlighted. It is hoped someone will accept the challenge to resolve the perilous passage of the peerless pod. In the meantime, let's see how that peregrination affected the cuisines of the lands it touched.

CHAPTER TWO

THE HOT SPOTS

he real hot spots in the world of peppery food are Mexico, Guatemala, much of the Caribbean, most of Africa, parts of South America, India, Bhutan, Malaysia, Thailand, Indonesia, southwestern China, the Balkans, the United States—Louisiana, Texas, and the Southwest—plus Korea. In these places capsicums are consumed on a meal-to-meal basis—in fact, one fourth of the adult population of the world uses pungent chillies in its food daily. There are other areas—in North America and parts of Europe—where sweet or mildly pungent capsicums are commonly used as part of the daily fare, but more as a vegetable or an occasional condiment. The popularity of peppery foods is growing so much throughout the world that suppliers find it difficult to keep up with the demand.

We have followed the probable trail of the captivating *Capsicum* and can see that it forms pathways girdling the equator and spreading north and south through the tropics and subtropics in a wide pantropical belt (see the map on pages 14–15). To understand why intensive use of the tropical peppers is typical in those warm climes requires a look at the food patterns of the inhabitants of capsicum's natural habitat. I won't go into a detailed account of the cuisine of each hot spot; that has already been done in other food books for the most part, but I will look at some generalized patterns of cuisines and meals, resulting, I hope, in a better understanding of why *Capsicum* cookery is the way it is.

Culinary behavior, the deliberate processing of a foodstuff for the purpose of changing it in some calculated manner, has occurred in all cultures throughout human history, yet everyone does it differently. This personal method or style of culinary behavior is what we call cuisine. Partaking of a cuisine different from your own is, in essence, a culinary handshake introducing you to another culture.

A cuisine is one of the most characteristic and least complicated expressions of a culture. A cuisine consists of a limited number of foods; there is an established and repetitive way of flavoring the basic components; it prefers certain methods of preparation; and it is eaten by prescribed rules. A cuisine reveals the beliefs of a society, both positive and negative. Some, such as food taboos, result in the group not utilizing all the food that nature has placed at their disposal. A cuisine is essentially very conservative and resistant to change. Notwithstanding that conservatism, new foods are regularly added, and are prepared with the habitual seasonings, using time-honored cooking techniques. For example, Indian curries had been around for thousands of years before America was discovered, but chillies were readily incorporated, becoming the dominant seasoning in a rather intricate flavor principle. (A flavor principle, as described by Elizabeth Rozin, is a distinct combination of seasoning ingredients used consistently by an ethnic group.)

In my travels through the lands where peppery cookery dominates, I have noted a pattern in every locale, be it Africa, Mexico, India, China, Sri Lanka, Indonesia, South America, Thailand, or Bhutan. What I began to realize as I savored the local dishes was that there is always a basic starch—it could be rice, maize, yams, manioc, wheat, barley, potatoes, or whatever starch food was native to the area—that is eaten with a sauce (stew, gravy, ragout, curry) containing legumes, vegetables, and occasionally a little meat. The meals were vegetarian for the most part, either by choice or by necessity, and the sauce differed from place to place according to the spices, herbs, and amount of chilli used to season it. Plants of the genus *Capsicum* are indigenous to the American tropics and were introduced to the subtropics in the Western Hemisphere in pre-Columbian times. As a result of cultivation as early as 6500 to 5000 B.C. or seven thousand years ago, they were apparently the earliest spice used by humankind— the use of black pepper, ginger, and turmeric in

India did not begin for another three to four thousand years. When capsicums were introduced by Europeans at the beginning of the sixteenth century to similar environmental conditions in the tropics and subtropics of the Old World, the American pepper quickly became pantropic.

The natives of those hot regions were accustomed to eating spicy foods to spark up their bland starch and legume diet. But their own spices were costly to produce and to use. The new spice was welcomed because it produced fruit within a short time and it yielded practically year round. In addition, it shipped and stored easily and was therefore inexpensive and readily available, even to the poorest. A little went a long way.

Much has been said about the cooling effect that results from eating capsicums as being the reason they are consumed with such gusto in hot lands. Yes, they make you sweat when you eat them in the tropics, but they also make you sweat when you eat them in an air-conditioned room, and you don't see tropical inhabitants munching on peppers as they sweat in the cane fields and rice paddies in order to cool off. Rather, pepper eaters eat them in their food because they like the taste and because they are convenient.

The common denominator in pepper cookery, a starch base, which I had observed in my travels, is the "core" of the principal meal as defined by anthropologist Sidney Mintz, and is accompanied by a periphery, or "fringe," composed of foods of every sort, which provide flavor and sauce for the core. The fringe makes it possible for people to eat with zest large quantities of the monotonous core food by providing some supplementary contrasting flavor. This meal model holds for most of the Third World countries day in and day out. The huge mound of rice or other starch routinely piled on a plate and heartily consumed with little time lost continues to amaze me.

Legumes (pulses)—beans, peas, lentils, chick peas, peanuts—are almost invariably cooked to make a sauce (page 36) to spoon over the starch when served. To the sauce may be added a little meat or fish, pickled vegetable, spicy condiment, or other taste enhancers—chillies being a prime example.

Capsicums were a welcome addition to such monotonous and often dry diets because the pungent ingredient, capsaicin, in chillies increases the production of body fluids (page 62). First, the appetite is aroused, then an increased flow of saliva facilitates chewing and swallowing the starchy food, and digestion of those starches is aided by stimulation of the flow of gastric juices.

Through the ages creative cooks in Turkey, India, Szechuan, Indonesia, Bhutan, Hungary, Thailand, the Caribbean, and Africa have skillfully embroidered new designs on their cuisines with their vivid *Capsicum* threads. Today our own inventive chefs are creating spectacular new culinary combinations to delight our senses and titillate our taste buds. The recipes of many of the pioneers of *Capsicum* cookery are presented in this book.

Latin America

Now that scientists have determined that peppers originated in South America, one might think that all of those countries would have equally peppery foods; however, that is not the case. According to Alfred W. Crosby, Jr., "More than three of every four inhabitants of the southern temperate zone are entirely of European ancestry." He classifies Argentina, Uruguay, southern Brazil, and Costa Rica, plus the United States and Canada as Neo-Europes. It is principally these countries that do not have traditional fiery cuisines. The Latin American countries where the populations are largely mixtures of European-Amerindian-African stock are the places where pungent peppers are used more frequently in cookery.

The basic starch staples of pre-Columbian America—maize, bitter and sweet manioc, potatoes—are still being grown and used, but in many areas, food staples from the Old World have been accepted as well. When the Europeans came to America, they brought with them plant and animal foodstuffs never imagined by the Native Americans. Cows, horses, sheep and large, barking war dogs (American dogs were small, fat, and barkless animals raised for food) were but several of the wonders that arrived with Columbus on his second voyage, as well as wheat, chickpeas, barley, and sugarcane. Then came onions, garlic, citrus, apples, peaches, cucurbit melons, grapes, rice, chickens, pigs, and on and on. Although the Amerindians were forced to grow and prepare Old World food for their conquerors, in the beginning they rarely added those foods to their traditional meals, which at the time of the Conquest were mainly vegetarian, with the addition of occasional game, domesticated dogs, insects, and seafood.

Of those post-Columbian plant introductions to the Americas, the one that probably had the most far reaching and longest lasting effect, not only on cookery but also on demographic and sociological events, was sugarcane. In Europe at the time of the discovery of America, sugar had come into general use, but it was still the luxury it had been since the Crusaders returned with it from the Holy Land. In their efforts to bypass Venice and any dealings with the hated Turks, the Portuguese introduced it to their own colonies on the eastern Atlantic islands and Brazil. The Spaniards took it to the West Indies, where Native Americans were forced to labor in its cultivation. The tragedy of that effort is only too well known (see footnote 21 on page 17). The introduction of sugarcane culture with the attendant African slave trade had a significant influence on the movement of New World plants, including *Capsicum*. Let's look at how Latin Americans use those foods today.

When the Spaniards arrived in Mexico, they soon realized the Aztecs were accomplished gastronomes who had a wide range of ingredients at their command and ate with a high level of refinement. After the Spanish occupation, the European and Aztec cuisines melded to produce a unique Mexican cuisine.

Elizabeth Lambert Ortiz, an authority on Latin American cooking, remarks that Mexican cooking, resting firmly on its Amerindian origins and interwoven with Spanish cookery, is the most exotic. Beans, corn, squash, tomatoes, avocados (from the Nahuatl word for testicle), and chillies are vital in Mexican cuisine, which is characterized by sauces featuring the rich flavors of *Capsicum annuum* var. *annuum*. The flavor principles of Mexican food are tomato, chilli, and cumin while those of Central America are lime, coriander, garlic, and chilli. Although Spanish influences can be recognized in Caribbean cookery, it is mainly a mix of Amerindian and African, as a by-product of the plantation system with its European overlords. To this early mixture has been added the tastes of more recent migrants—East Indian, Asian, South European. The many migrations, voluntary or forced, to the Caribbean area have created one of the most ethnically heterogeneous areas in the modern world. Each group has brought its influence to bear on the rice-and-legume-based cuisine. Peppers, principally the habanero type (page 75) and Scotch bonnet (page 85), both *C. chinense,* are used more as condiments than as seasonings. Venezuela has no identifiable cuisine but has been influenced by other Latin American countries. In Colombia the cuisine is less traditional, with peppers appearing primarily in the daily table sauces. Rice, seafood, poultry, and coconut milk are used extensively, and *arepas* (biscuit-sized cornbread) are more common than tortillas. In Ecuadorian cooking, potatoes and vegetables are important, and there is always a peppery table sauce.

Peruvians like their food *picante,* and they have the indecently hot rocoto, *Capsicum pubescens* (page 56), along with the barely milder *C. baccatum* var. *pendulum* (page 56) and *C. chinense* (page 55), plus the introduced Mexican *C. annuum* var. *annuum* to provide variety. The Amerindians of Peru had domesticated the potato, quinoa, lima beans, squash, and several peppers, which they combined with the meat of wild game or the several domesticated animals and birds—llamas, alpacas, muscovy duck, and guinea pig. This broad native base, with Spanish and other more recent influences, has produced a delightfully different cuisine.

The long coastline of Chile provides a great variety of seafood that is prepared in interesting ways and served with delicious Chilean wines, but, as a whole, the cuisine is not peppery. In Argentina, renowned for its beef and wine, Spanish cooking has been modified by the large influx of Italians and Germans. Uruguay, Paraguay, southern Bolivia, and southern Brazil are characterized by the *caboclo* culture, a mixture of Amerindian, Afro-South American, and Portuguese. Brazilian cuisine is one of the most varied of Latin America, and its manioc–yam–sweet potato base has been greatly influenced by the early introduction and assimilation of great numbers of Africans, who readily adopted the local peppers. That predominant Afro-Bahian cuisine began to change when Europeanization followed independence in 1822. Bread came in with the nineteenth century, and French recipe books took their toll on traditional Brazilian cookery. Today the three styles of cooking—Bahian, Cariocan, and Paulista—are a mixture of Portuguese, African, and Amerindian, with the Cariocan of Rio de Janeiro leaning heavily on pepper sauces made from varieties of *Capsicum chinense* and the malegueta pepper (another name for bird peppers, which are very small varieties of *Capsicum* and not *Afromomum melegueta*).

Sub-Saharan Africa

On their arrival in coastal Africa the Portuguese found a culture strikingly unlike their own, but one that offered a rich prize in raw materials and slaves. Initially, the Portuguese control of the coasts of Africa had little effect on the food habits of its people. Not until after the discovery of Brazil in 1500 and the introduction of sugar plantations there in 1535, which impelled the importation of huge numbers of African slaves to its shores, did a significant exchange of plants between South America and Africa occur. Approximately a third of the principal commodities produced today in African tribal economies were not known to its peoples before the arrival of the Portuguese. The West Africans were not only accustomed to food made pungent with grains of paradise (*Afromomum melegueta*) (see footnote 10 on page 8), but their tropical climate was a ready-made environment for most of the New World plants. The entire east coast of Africa also readily accepted the New World plants, using them in a cuisine heavily influenced by the foodways of India.

Africa is so immense that it is not fair to generalize, but for the most part the main dishes of many African countries combine grains with legumes into a one-dish vegetarian meal. Porridge made of a cooked starch that may be manioc, sorghum, millet, rice, yams, or maize, according to region, is served with a great variety of stews (sometimes called relishes) seasoned with tomatoes, onions, chillies, or other available vegetables. Most of the peppers and other vegetables used in these stews come from gardens cultivated near the huts. Legumes are the primary source of protein, while meat, beef in particular, is an exception in the traditional diet.

Today food in Africa covers a wide range of tastes, but chillies are the common denominator. Whether you are using the hot pepper seasoning berberé in Ethiopia, the piri-piri sauce and stews of Ghana, Nigeria, Senegal, and the Ivory Coast, or curry in Kenya and South Africa, you will be eating the American pepper and, most likely, at a concentration that is not easy for beginners to tolerate. Pili-pili, a sauce made of chillies, onion, garlic, lemon juice, tomatoes, and horseradish, is used throughout Africa. Pili-pili, beri-beri, and piri-piri are sound-alikes that could be different spellings of a local name for the same sauce type.

For some reason, the capsaicin content of peppers grown in most of Africa is higher than that of peppers grown in most other places. Pharmaceutical companies that use capsaicin in their products have known this for a long time; consequently, most of the chillies they use have been imported from Africa; however, India and China have taken the lead recently. Nevertheless, one bite and you'll agree that African chillies are hotter than similar American ones.

Monsoon Asia

The majority of the people in the world live in Monsoon Asia. That mass of Oriental humanity is still rural and agriculturist in nature. Their foodways went unchanged for thousands of years until the strange plants from the New World arrived five hundred years ago. American peanuts, sweet potatoes, corn, squashes, tomatoes, and chillies were hungrily adopted into their traditional eating patterns.

INDIA

The dramatic culinary change that spread throughout the Far East began in India. Who could have dreamed that a few innocuous red pods from the cargo of a lumbering Portuguese carrack, unloaded at Calicut, Cochin, or Goa,[1] would literally fire the imaginations of the cooks of the Far East? At the very same time that the seaborne Portuguese were introducing entirely new foods from the New World to the coastal regions of the subcontinent, a Moghul[2] invasion was sweeping across the northern passes from Afghanistan. The invaders brought new foods and cooking techniques from the Old World to a mixed race of people who, with time, would assimilate and modify both into their own unique and varied cuisine. The Portuguese enriched themselves, while the Moghuls enriched the culture of India.

When one thinks of Indian food, curry comes to mind. Today, it is impossible to imagine a curry without *Capsicum* peppers. Curries are dishes with a varying amount of gravy-type liquid to which is added legumes, meat, fish, and/or vegetables along with a quantity of bruised spices and chillies. The term "curry" has become a generic one for sauce. A little "curry" gives a lot of flavor to a large mess of rice or *chapatis* (soft, flat, griddle-fried bread). Various sour, bitter, sweet,

---

1. It was a very exciting experience for me to stand at the sites of the ancient Portuguese quays below the majestic cathedrals in Old Goa (now Panaji) and picture just such a scene. The cities on the Malabar coast, where there are large numbers of Catholic Christians with Portuguese names, are quite distinct from other Indian towns. Not only is the architecture different, but the Catholics wear simple Western-style clothing instead of the typical woman's sari or man's sarong.

2. The Moghuls (Mughul in Persian) were Central Asian Turks who invaded India from Afghanistan and ruled from 1527 to 1707. Do not confuse them with the Mongols of Chinese Mongolia, although at an early date there was a mixture of Turkish and Mongolian blood long since diluted to little more than a memory.

or astringent dishes are served with it. The side dishes are presented either directly on a platter (*thali*) or a large leaf around the central pile of rice or bread, or in small containers served on the *thali* and little piles on the leaf. The diner helps himself to the various items, mixing these with rice or folding them up in pieces of flatbread. This is often accompanied by a cooling yogurt *raita* (page 201). Sweet dishes are eaten separately at the end. Indian recipes are very flexible, presenting only the basic ingredients and methods to be used. The rest is up to the cook.

In most Indian cooking whole spices are bruised and put into hot oil to release the flavors into the oil (mustard oil, sesame oil, coconut oil, ghee—clarified butter—but never olive oil).[3] Although other ingredients are added to this spice mixture, the whole spices are not meant to be eaten but are to be set aside unobtrusively by the diner. Even when the spices are ground into a powder (*masala*; page 106), they are frequently heated in oil first. Onions,[4] garlic, and ginger pastes along with several basic gravies/sauces are prepared and kept on hand for use with various combinations of spices in the cooking of curries. For the most part, cooking is done in a *kadhai,* a deep frying pan. The Indian flavor principles are garlic, cumin, ginger, turmeric, coriander, and cardamom, along with chilli and black pepper.

Because the Gujarati of western India were a seafaring and shipbuilding people who conducted an ancient and flourishing trade with the Indonesian archipelago, their very hot, spicy cookery

was not only incorporated into Indonesian foodways, but was influenced by them. As a consequence of early trade contacts with Indonesia, the dishes of eastern and southern India, as well as those of Gujarat, are probably closer in taste to Indonesian and Malaysian dishes than to the Central Asian Moghul meat dishes. Similarly, the tandoori roast meat of the northwest has closer links with Central Asia through Afghanistan than with the rest of India. Those coastal areas encountered chillies first, which may account for their greater popularity in those areas. In 1900 Goa was the principal *Capsicum*-growing region in India, and the fiery pods were known as Goa peppers (*Gowai mirchi*) in Bombay. From India the peppery cuisine progressed through Burma to Thailand.

BHUTAN AND NEPAL

Bhutan and Nepal, two small Oriental countries tucked in the Himalayas adjoining India's northern borders, probably should not be considered together because, as a result of their long isolation, their cultures are quite different. Both have only recently opened their borders to tourists. The factors that have influenced their basically vegetarian cuisines, however, are similar enough to be discussed jointly. Chinese and Indian influences and religious food taboos are about equal in the kitchen, and so is the quantity of peppers—plenty. Nepalese Hinduism has absorbed Buddhism and imposed its food taboos on its followers. As a result, no beef is eaten in Nepal, and only male sheep, goats, and water buffalo are slaughtered in the prescribed ways for food. A succulent Nepalese water buffalo fillet was one of the best pieces of meat I have ever eaten anywhere.

Bhutanese waiters become greatly distressed and are quick to point out that they consider your order to have too much starch or that you chose two preparations too near alike. This idea

---

3. Putting spices in hot oil to release the flavor is a practice of critical importance to the story of the movement of peppers because the same method is used in the Balkans, though not in Italy and the western Mediterranean.

4. During my second two-month "food trip" to India I discovered why my curries had never tasted quite right. I had been using our white or yellow onions in their preparations, while only the much sweeter purple onion is available to cooks in India. For authenticity, use purple onions or shallots in all Indian recipes calling for onions.

of balance between the starch, *fan,* and the vegetable and meat, *ts'ai,* is a typical Chinese food attitude (page 44). In late October the rooftops of the already colorful Bhutanese homes are ablaze with scarlet peppers spread on to dry, and long red clusters punctuate the gaily painted eaves.

THAILAND

If asked the main characteristic of Thai food, you would not be wrong in saying "hot." Although many influences can be detected in modern Thai cooking, it is the Indian that prevails. There is good reason for this, because Indian culture and the Buddhist religion were dominant in ancient Siam. In the twelfth and thirteenth centuries migrations of Thai peoples followed the rivers leading to Siam from the Central Asian regions of Hunan and Szechuan. The influences of Hinduism, Buddhism, and Confucianism formed the character of Southeast Asian civilization. Although there were Portuguese, English, and Dutch trading posts, no European power ever colonized Buddhist Siam.

Although predominately vegetarian, Thai cuisine is highly refined, and presentation is important. You will be served many curries and curry-type dishes, but you will never encounter the use of yogurt or beef in traditional Thai cooking. A large quantity of many spices and chillies of the cayenne type are used. Instead of following the Indian practice of heating them whole in oil, a Thai cook grinds the spices, herbs, and chillies into a paste and then stirs that paste into hot coconut oil to which the other ingredients are added.

Until quite recently, only very hot chillies, like those cultivated in India, were grown and used in Thailand. In fact, there is no Thai word for "sweet pepper." In the last few years a sweet pepper has been introduced for consumption by foreigners, and several chillies, including the yellow

'Santa Fe Grande' ('Caribe'), have found their way into gardens, but the general populace does not use them. It would be hard to convince most Thais that capsicums were not native to their country.

INDONESIA

Indonesia is made up of thirteen thousand islands, some quite large, populated with one fifth of the world's inhabitants. The fabled Spice Islands are among these islands. Throughout history spices have drawn traders and adventurers to these tropical islands, and as a consequence the food is less distinctive than in some of the other countries in that part of the world. The strongest culinary influence is Chinese, which is to be expected when you remember that Chinese traders had sailed here for spices by the first century A.D., centuries before the first European set foot in the area. Large-scale immigration from India is generally ruled out, even though Hinduism and Buddhism became established as early as the third century A.D., and the food bears the effects of that contact. The ancient and steady flow of Arab traders injected large doses of Islam into the veins of Indonesians, and the formative influences of Islam, Hinduism, Buddhism, and Confucianism defined the distinctive character of Southeast Asia and spilled over into Indonesia. The offspring of those traders and native women, schooled in the religion of the father, acquired its food taboos, which they spread among their mother's people. Again, the Portuguese, bent on commerce and not colonization, came and left peppers, peanuts, and pineapples along with other American food plants that were absorbed into the native cuisine.

Many foods are cooked with coconut and/or wrapped in banana leaves. *Satay,* skewered meat which is barbecued, is served with the popular peanut sauce. All the islanders use chillies, utilizing them more as a condiment than as a seasoning, and no meal can be eaten without a *sambal* (page 103). These searing table sauces are mixtures of tomatoes, garlic, onion, chillies, lime juice, and often a touch of fish or shrimp paste, which are ground together daily in small amounts. However, those in a hurry can buy sambals in bottles like our catsup, but there the resemblance ends. Soy sauce, garlic, molasses, and New World peanuts are the defining Indonesian flavor principles.

MALAYSIA

The cookery of Muslim Malaysia is very similar to that of Indonesia, but the Malaysians were even more influenced by the Chinese, who constitute a majority of the racial stock. A special Chinese-based cuisine is the "nonya" cooking of Malaysia and Singapore (*nonya* is Malay for a well-to-do Chinese lady). Sri Lanka and India have both had more input in Malaysian cookery than in Indonesian. Their transplanted curries and biryanis (rice with meat or vegetables) are very evident in Malaysia. The food is often coconut based and also made very hot with peppers.

PHILIPPINE ISLANDS

Many young Americans do not remember that the seven thousand Philippine Islands were governed by the United States following the Spanish-American war of 1898, when Cuba and the Philippines were ceded to the United States, until they were granted independence in 1945. They might be surprised that English is the language that the Filipinos in the various islands resort to in order to overcome local language barriers. Westernization from that forty-seven-year tenure was extensive but not complete. Spanish is the other language that a Visayan Filipino might use when trying to speak with a Tagalog Filipino,

because Spain owned the islands from the day that exceptional mariner, Ferdinand Magellan, planted Spain's flag and cross in 1519 until the day the Americans took over, 379 years later. Calling those years the period of Spanish domination is in reality quite misleading. In actuality it was a period of Mexican influence, because the so-called Spaniards were natives of New Spain in the Americas and the Philippines were governed by the Spanish Viceroy of Mexico. Not until Mexico won its independence from Spain in 1821 was the governing of the Philippines directed from Spain by "real" Spaniards.

At the coming of the Spaniards the Philippine Islands, from the standpoint of geography and ethnicity, were really a part of the East Indies. The inhabitants were mostly Muslim Malays only a little removed from the primitive stages of culture. To the Spaniards and also the Portuguese, so recently out from under the Moorish yoke, anyone who was dark and Muslim was a Moor, so they called the local Muslim folk Moros. The Moros are dominant in the southern islands. Even though Indonesian traits are evident, the culture of the Philippines evidences a greater Chinese influence than from any other society, and nowhere greater than in the Cantonese-style cuisine that makes great use of soy sauce, rice wine, gingerroot, garlic, and/or meat broth, and/or fermented black beans. After almost four hundred years of Mexican influence one would expect significant vestiges to be evident in the local cookery because peppers, along with other New World plants, entered the islands after 1565, when the Acapulco-to-Manila galleon (see map, pages 14–15) became an agent for distribution of goods between the Orient and New Spain for more than 250 years. As a whole, Filipino food is not peppery, and the rich, dark red sauces of Mexico made with ancho pastes are nowhere to be found. With soy sauce replacing anchos, *adobo,* the national dish, has little resemblance to its Spanish or Mexican ancestor. Today, either small bowls of vinegar-based chilli-pepper sauces or bottled hot sauces are served as table sauces to be added at the diner's discretion. Peppers appear as vegetables in Chinese-style dishes. Although menus in the Philippines may be peppered with Spanish words, the food is not. The Filipinos accepted the new foods only by adapting them to their traditional cookery.

However, several dishes were carried over from the Mexicans, such as filled pastry or *empanadas,* tamalelike *sumans* of squash or rice wrapped in banana or palm leaves, beans, corn on the cob, and several others. The hot chocolate drink drunk there is exactly like that of Mexico, even down to the molinillo, the flanged, wooden beater twirled between the palms of the hands to make it. It was fascinating for me to recognize Amerindian words for foods being used in the native dialects because this affirms that the plant was not present before the Spanish brought the plant and its name.

ENGLISH	SPANISH	VISCAYA	ORIGIN
avocado	*aguacate*	*abokado*	Nahuatl (*ãhuactl*)
chocolate	*cacao*	*cacao*	Nahuatl (*cacahuatl*)
corn	*maiz*	*mais*	Arawak
papaya	*papaya*	*kapaya*	Arawak
peanut	*mani*	*mani*	Arawak
chili/pepper	*chile*	*sili*	Nahuatl (*chilli*)
pineapple	*piña*	*pinya*	Latin (*pinus*)
potato	*papa*	*papa*	Quechua
squash	*calabasa*	*calabasa*	Arabic via Spain
sweet potato	*camote*	*camote*	Nahuatl (*camohtli*)
tobacco	*tabaco*	*tabaco*	Arawak
tomato	*tomate*	*kamati*	Nahuatl (*tomatl*)

Southwestern China

Food in China is a cultural obsession. Few other cultures are as food oriented as the Chinese. The Chinese fare, using preparation methods based on the duality of things (Tao), is very different from Western food. It is a cuisine that emphasizes variety of preparation, a blending of small pieces, short cooking times (fuel is precious), and the use of whatever foods are available except for dairy products. And, as a consequence of centuries of population pressure on the food supply, it is chiefly vegetarian. The basis of the Chinese way of preparing food from raw ingredients to morsels ready for the mouth is the division between *fan,* which consists of grains and other starch foods, and *ts'ai,* vegetable and meat dishes. A balanced meal must have appropriate amounts of both *fan* and *ts'ai.*

China, so long isolated from the world, is divided into four regions on the basis of geographical features that separated the ancient peoples, allowing them to develop differently in each area. Each of these geographical units evolved a distinct, highly refined cuisine, which began to intermix regionally during the Han dynasty.[5] For the purpose of our pepper discussion, only the Southwest, including Yunnan, Kweichow, Szechuan, Hunan, Xinjiang, and Hupeh, will be of concern to us.

Southwest China, like the southwestern United States, favors hot and spicy foods prepared with

5. Restaurants originated in China during the T'ang dynasty (A.D. 618–907). In the Sung dynasty, which followed, sex was added to the menu of those sociable meeting places. Even though that delicacy is no longer offered, the Chinese probably eat out more than any other culture.

vitality and zest. The hot and humid climate of the Chinese Southwest is a companion to a cuisine that features a pungent, peppery taste combined with delicate flavors. Although there are more similarities than differences in Chinese culinary practices, why is that area so different from the other regions?

For whatever reason, it was only in the landlocked areas of the Southwest, communicating with India and the Middle East through the plodding silk caravans, that chillies markedly influenced the cookery. Once there, it was readily available at little cost. Szechuan-Hunan cuisine is characterized by a passionate use of chillies, pepperlike fagara (page 105), garlic, and fermented soybean products, vinegar, sugar, and peanut and rapeseed oil (canola, page 104) are common. Wise and complex use is made of nuts and poultry, and pungent flavors of all sorts are harmoniously blended and quickly cooked. The flavor principles of southwestern China are soy sauce, brandied wine, and gingerroot, plus sugar for "sweet" dishes, vinegar for "sour," chillies for "hot." If American Chinese restaurants are any measure, we know that in restaurants featuring Szechuan or Hunan menus we can expect the food to be Hot. I found only two or three pepper cultivars of the cayenne type (*Capsicum annuum* var. *annuum*) in the markets of those two Chinese territories, but what they lacked in variety they made up for in quantity.[6]

---

6. Since 1949 there have been many changes in Chinese life; naturally they would affect food habits. I'm certain regional differences have become less obvious as a result of the commune system combined with increased food importation, better transportation, and improved communications, as well as advances in storage, irrigation, and agricultural technology. There has been little systematic inquiry to determine the extent of change in culinary practices. What the Western tourist eats is not the daily fare of the people but is redolent of pre-1949 cookery. For an excellent "case study" in which scholars of food-in-culture have presented a descriptive history of food habits in China, read *Food in Chinese Culture*, edited by K. C. Chang.

East Asia

JAPAN

Nowhere was Chinese influence more direct than in Japan. With the introduction of Buddhism about A.D. 645, Japanese society was modeled on T'ang China. This influence carried over into cookery and became the basis of Japanese cuisine, which relies on seafood and rice, with soy sauce, saki, sugar, and sometimes gingerroot as flavor principles. The Portuguese were the first Europeans to come to Japan, later came the Spanish and the Dutch. First among them were their merchants, then their missionaries. Although the Portuguese Jesuits did not cooperate in missionary activities with the Spanish Franciscans, Augustinians, and Dominicans from the Philippines, they all had good luck with conversions for a while, so much so that around 1637, except for contact with the Dutch and Chinese, the Japanese closed their doors to all foreigners, and did not reopen them until the second half of the nineteenth century. It was those Iberian missionaries who introduced peppers to Japan.

Japan produces peppers for export, but they are not used in their own classic cookery. Japanese food emphasizes raw and colorful dishes requiring only a minimum of cooking and served with cereal foods and the ever-present pickled vegetables. Although the Japanese have a long historical involvement with the chilli, it was the American occupation forces and their catsup and pepper sauce that really got the Nipponese into nipping peppers. Douglas MacArthur's introduction of American ideas of nutrition to Japan after World War II changed not only the eating habits but also the physiques of postwar generations, as witnessed by a comparison of the heights of young native-born Japanese today with those of their grandparents. Post–World War II affluence and westernization have taken their toll on Buddhist beef avoidance in the home of Kobe beefsteaks.

KOREA

It came as a great surprise when I learned that Korea has the highest per capita consumption of chillies per day. Northern China has had the greatest influence on the rice-based vegetarian-by-necessity cookery of Korea. Next to cereal foods, vegetables provide the bulk of the diet. Here the rice is eaten plain, without sauce or condiments, but at the same time as the soup and crispy-tender stir-fried vegetable dishes, or with a soupy one-dish meal. Fresh red or green chillies are cooked in the vegetable, seaweed, and fish dishes rather than as part of separate condiments. When meat is eaten it is skewered and cooked on small grills. Along with chillies, the flavor principles are soy sauce, brown sugar, sesame seeds, and garlic. Spices and herbs are not customarily used. A long, narrow, red cayenne type is the most commonly used *Capsicum*. *Kim ch'i*, pickled Chinese cabbage, combined in a thousand ways with such things as ginger, chillies, turnips, cucumbers, and/or shrimp or fish, is served with every meal. This ubiquitous fermented condiment is usually made every September at harvest time. Although Korea was dominated by the Japanese for many years, their food is more highly seasoned, and more elaborate cooking methods are used than in Japan.

The Middle East

TURKEY

Originally from the North and West of China, the varied people now known as Turks were a nomadic group who shared a common culture with the Mongolians. Their language is an offshoot of the Ural-Altaic cluster distantly related to Mongolian, Finnish, and Hungarian. They wandered into Central Asia, becoming one with the Iranian nomads through annihilation and absorption. Famed as warriors, the Seljuk Turks became the mercenaries of the Near Eastern and Mongolian armies that initiated the fall of the Byzantine Empire, allowing the emergence of the Ottomans. Intermarriage was so common between the Mongol ruling class and the Turkish troops that after a time the rulers became Turks in language and culture. The Turks of Anatolia, now Turkey, and the vast Ottoman Empire were mainly farmers. Although today industrialization is spreading, the remaining Turkish nation is still largely a rural country of small villages.

The peasants' diet has changed little throughout the ages. The main meal is a bulgur (wheat) or rice pilaf served with vegetable stews, yogurt, and lots of wonderful crusty bread. Lamb is the most important meat; however, meat is not regularly eaten in the villages. The evening meal of the urban upper classes usually has two or three vegetable dishes, a pilaf, and increasingly some meat (mainly lamb) or fish. Islamic taboos include alcohol, blood, and the flesh of horses, pigs, asses, and carrion eaters. Tediously wrapped or stuffed vegetables are favorites. Preparing a Turkish meal takes patience and a lot of hard work. Most urban workers eat restaurant food at noon; consequently, the restaurant meals in Turkey are very much like home food. Both groups have a taste for very sweet sweets but don't ordinarily eat them with meals. There has been a considerable Persian influence, resulting in a cosmopolitan cuisine.

Peppers of the cayenne type are abundant. Unlike the cayennes we are familiar with, the Turkish cayennes are very flavorful but only mildly pungent. Fresh green ones (*yesil biber*) are chopped into salads and stews or are roasted whole and served with meat, on kebabs, or with stews. Pickled green peppers are a familiar condiment. Allowed to ripen and then air dried, the very flavorful red ones (*kiemiz biber*) are carefully seeded and veined then crushed into small flakes, which are served in little bowls to be sprinkled liberally on prepared foods. When ground into a fine powder, like our paprika, it is used more often during cooking to add flavor and color. When in season, a very flavorful, pale green bell type is stuffed with seasoned rice and steamed. Turkish food is not pungent but is very delicately flavored with herbs such as parsley, thyme, dill, dried mint, and fennel. The shallot-like onions are more subtle than ours, and garlic is not allowed to overpower the herbs.

Turkish grain-based cookery is one of the seminal cuisines of the world, and Ottoman conquests carried that cuisine's influence into Persia, Greece, the Balkans, Asia Minor, and North Africa, while the Moghuls delivered it to India, where it persists to this day. It predominates in the eastern Mediterranean. Wheat bread, yogurt, kabobs (cooked on skewers), the sunken tandir/tandoor oven, pilaf, Arabic coffee (page 20), olive oil, and Oriental spices are but a few of the foods and food practices that the Ottoman invaders carried with them to their new territories. The Asiatic Turks began to arrive in the Middle East during the eleventh century. As they conquered the Saracen lands of the Arabian region, Islam conquered them. The new converts spread their doctrine with zeal and fury. Through the ages the Turks have so intermixed with the people they conquered that the physical mongoloid traits have practically disappeared, but their yogurt hasn't.[7]

---

7. One way that intermixing occurred was through the Ottoman system of army recruitment. The entire standing army was continually replenished either by capture or a levy on the children of the Christian population. Every four years they selected a number of the most promising fourteen- to eighteen-year-old boys, whom they educated as Turks and Muslims. They became the sultan's slave family, and the best went on to be entrusted with the affairs of government. Other than the sultan, there was hardly a born Muslim wielding a sword or scepter.

THE ARAB WORLD

The culinary traditions of the Middle Eastern countries are highly intermixed. Although there are a few recognizable "national dishes," the cuisines of Turkey, Syria, Lebanon, Iran, Egypt, Iraq, Saudi Arabia, Tunisia, Algeria, Morocco, Israel, and Greece are a closely related complex that has been passed down from mother to daughter. The Muslim invasions within the region introduced Arabic dishes throughout. Peasant food was brought by the soldiers and court cuisine by their generals. The best of the two sources became the melting pot for a new culinary tradition, and trade between the Arabic and then the Ottoman empires made the ingredients available.

The literature dealing with the spice trade in the fifteenth and early sixteenth centuries is filled with references to the exploits of "Arabs and Muslims" and their influence on the arts, trade, and technology of that world. It is well to remember that about the time of the birth of Christ, Arabs were involved in complex trading patterns to the east with India, to the north with Europe, and throughout the Roman Empire. When Islam began (A.D. 632 is usually the date given), the Arabs quickly became an international force, conquering most of the present-day Middle East and much of Spain, Sicily, and east to India. The high culture of the Arab Muslim Empire was approximately A.D. 632 to 1000.

With the rise of cities, a complex cuisine developed. *The Baghdad Cookery Book of 1226* contains 160 recipes, some very intricate. The nomadic Bedouin in the Arabian peninsula continued to eat as they had always eaten—primarily dates, bread, and camel and goat meat and milk; settled agricultural peoples had available to them a wider variety of foods and spices. The new food plant, rice, entered from India via Syria, Iraq, and Iran and was cultivated throughout the Arabic world all the way to Spain. In the cities a new cuisine developed, using products from the traders as well as what was grown locally. A big change came with the introduction of plants from the New World—especially tomatoes.

Although Arabs were active in the spice trade at an early date, spices were not used in their food until later because they could get too much by trading them. Sugar, another Indian native, went first to Iran and then spread throughout the Mediterranean. Increased transport and travel brought foodstuffs from one part of the empire to another. With the Crusades came some European ("Franc") influences. Iran's had been the most distinguished culture in the Middle Eastern area and at one point things Iranian, such as a taste for sweet and sour, were in. Presentation was, and still is, paramount, resulting in the use of turmeric, bixa (achiote, page 104), and saffron to add color to the very complex dishes. Meat, rice, and sugar were for the rich, lentils, beans, and honey for the poor. Pork and wine were, and are, taboo to all. The fall of Baghdad to the Mongols in 1258 marked a decline in the interest in the culinary arts. As religious puritanism grew, preoccupation with gastronomy shrank.

Today lamb is still the favored meat; preferred vegetables are eggplant, cauliflower, okra, cucumbers, spinach, onions, and garlic; favorite fruits are pomegranates, apricots, dates, oranges, grapes, apples, and melons. Lemon juice is used profusely. Fresh mint, dill, and parsley are the chief herbs, and cinnamon is the most frequently used spice. Foodways have changed little in the centuries that have elapsed since the Mongols on their shaggy ponies galloped down from the steppes of Mongolia. Chicken is still eaten with nuts, rice with legumes, and meat with fruit. For the most part, tomatoes have usurped the place of fruits in meat dishes. Herbs, spices, flower waters, and color are loved by all. Rice and yogurt play important roles. Ingredients are finely ground or pounded, rolled into little forms, simmered in broth, drowned in syrup, or cooked

with yogurt as they were long ago. Desserts may be pastries filled with ground nuts and sticky honey, or thickened milk puddings. It is a delightful, but laborious and time-consuming cuisine in which capsicums play little part.

There is a greater variety of peppers available for cooking in Mediterranean North Africa because the countries in that area not only have the pungent types that made their way north with the Arabic trans-Sahara slave trade from the west coast, but they also had the advantage of the busy Mediterranean commerce and Arabian traders. The excellent Moroccan paprika (page 102) is made from the types of peppers used for Spanish paprika, probably a relatively recent introduction. The food style is Mediterranean, with heavy Middle Eastern accents of dried fruits, almonds, olives, spices, and stuffed or wrapped vegetables. Couscous, the traditional Berber grain dish of the Maghreb area—Morocco, Algeria, Tunisia—served with the pungent *harissa* sauce (pages 101, 150), is but one example of a culinary tradition formed by invaders.

Invaders of another type are bringing about a chilli change in these areas if the growing sales of pepper products from Louisiana and Texas are indicators. When the oil boom in the Middle East began, oil field workers from the vast fields in Louisiana and Texas went by the thousands to man the rigs until the locals could be trained to do the new work. With them went their indispensable hot pepper sauces, which have caught the fancy of the Arabs.

Europe

Today we do not think of Europe as a place where peppers are incorporated into the cuisine; however, some countries have done so, particularly the Balkans. As an outcome of the long Dutch tenure in Indonesia, resulting from their capture of the Portuguese Indonesian spice empire at the beginning of the seventeenth century, a taste for spicy Indonesian foods was taken home. Today Indonesian restaurants serving *rijstaffel* (rice table) are not uncommon in Holland, but in general food there is anything but *picante*. However, modern Dutch horticultural skills are producing those dazzlingly colorful bell peppers that enhance our tables and challenge our growers.

THE BALKANS AND HUNGARY

The arrival of our bright red pod did indeed cause a revolution in the eating habits of the Balkans, but the change was not overnight. The peppers that landed in the Balkans, where they are known as *paprika*, are of the cayenne type similar to the New Mexican chile, having a mild to hot pungency, and are used more as a seasoning.

Among crops introduced directly to the Balkans by the Turks during the period of occupation (fifteenth to nineteenth centuries), or by North Balkan Christian market gardeners working abroad or in other parts of the Turkish empire, or diffused due to population migrations within the empire are cultivars of *Capsicum annuum* var. *annuum*. The Greeks called this new spice *peperi* or *piperi* after the Latin *piper*, meaning "black pepper," which may have derived from *pipali* (*peepul*), a Sanskrit word meaning "sacred fig tree." The Bulgarian people modified it to *piperke, peperke, paparka*. When the so-called Turkish pepper reached Hungary, the name was slightly altered to become *paprika*. It was in Hungary, during the sixteenth and seventeenth centuries, that paprika slowly but surely changed the cookery as the plant itself was changed. The original fiery peppers were bred to reduce the capsaicin content and to increase the flavor and coloring power of the tapering, elongated cone-shaped pods.

Zoltan Halasz, in his book on Hungarian paprika, tells us that this paprika is added to typical Hungarian stews and goulash (*gulyas*) and is prepared in two basic ways: (1) The paprika is added to a roux made of heated lard and flour to which various spices are added, and is used to thicken the dish; and (2) onions are cooked in hot lard, paprika is added to the hot mixture, and then the meat and other ingredients are incorporated. Dishes prepared by the second method are called paprikas. It is important to dissolve the paprika in hot, but not burning, fat. One cannot fail to notice that this method of preparation is more akin to the Indian and Persian method of sautéing spices in hot oil before adding the other ingredients than it is to the Mediterranean use of peppers as a vegetable or table sauce, which supports the scenario of origin via India. Balkan cookery has two strong influences, Turko-Middle Eastern and Austro-European. The techniques of East and West are combined and passed from mother to daughter. Yogurt, herbs, and chillies are characteristic of Balkan kitchens.

SPAIN AND PORTUGAL

Many Americans equate Spain and Portugal with Mexico when they think of food, and expect it to be full of chillies, but in fact their dishes are not spicy. The stay-at-home Spaniards and Portuguese never did develop the taste for chillies that their more adventurous kin who emigrated to the Americas did.

In spite of shared territory and origins, the two Iberian cultures are not alike. Although both of their cuisines are simply cooked, the Portuguese use market produce more inventively and with more herbs and spices than the Spaniards. One of the things that sets Portuguese meat cookery apart from the Spanish is the paste, like the Mexican *adobo* (page 104), made of sweet red peppers the Portuguese use as a dry marinade to season meats and poultry. Both chillies and sweet peppers are used in cooking, and a sauce made of piri-piri (page 151) peppers is kept in a bottle on the table to use over almost everything the Portuguese eat. These caustic little peppers are said to have first come to Portugal from Angola, Africa.

Reflecting long years of foreign domination, many Spanish cooks use a lot of Phoenician-introduced saffron, garlic, and parsley, along with Moorish cumin and Roman olive oil. Protein comes more from seafood than red meat in their cookery. Spanish cuisine is very regional. The first peppers that arrived from New Spain were looked upon more as curiosities and ornamentals than as something to be eaten. The tomato met the same fate. The Moorish *gazpacho* (soaked bread), brought to Andalusian kitchens from Morocco, began as a soup of olive oil, garlic, almonds, and vinegar thinned with water. Much later some of the new American foods, such as tomatoes and sweet peppers, along with local onions and cucumbers or whatever might be in the garden, were incorporated into the traditional mixture.

When the Moors returned to Morocco after their defeat in 1492, they brought the new American tomatoes and peppers home with them. The famous Spanish paellas, based on short-grained rice introduced by the Moors, use only a little chopped sweet pepper.

When West Indian peppers first arrived in Spain, their need for a hot, humid habitat made them difficult to grow. It was not until the more readily cultivated *Capsicum annuum* var. *annuum* arrived from highland Mexico that any culinary interest in peppers developed. In Spain I found fields where some of the biggest, brightest red bell peppers I have ever seen were growing. Others produced smaller tomatolike peppers for paprika. I saw no chillies growing, although they are cultivated to a lesser degree. *Chilindrón* dishes blending red bell peppers, tomatoes, on-

ion, garlic, and succulent ham with other meats, except beef, are typical of northeastern Spain. *Sofrito* (page 108), with a *Capsicum* base, is a traditional Spanish seasoning mixture. The use of chillies in table sauces such as romesco (page 152) and piri-piri (page 151) is reasonably commonplace. The tomato has had greater effect on Spanish and other Mediterranean cuisines than have peppers. In the past the Iberians have not favored a peppery cuisine, but usage of chillies is growing.

THE MEDITERRANEAN

After the decline of the Ottoman Empire, interchange between the eastern and western halves of the Mediterranean cautiously resumed. One would expect such interchange to have some effect on the cuisines of the Mediterranean region, and it did. Although there are differences from country to country, there is a similarity that makes Mediterranean cuisine distinctly different from that in other parts of Europe.

Since ancient times, Mediterranean cuisines have been based on fish, bread, goat meat, and olive oil; later, citrus and tomatoes were added. The corn dish called polenta[8] and spaghetti, considered so typically Italian, are foreign introductions. The sweet, highly flavored, strong-colored, tomato-shaped pepper that is grown today and used to make a high-quality paprika in both Spain and Morocco is not like those long podded types favored in the paprika regions of Yugoslavia. Therefore, it was probably not introduced to Morocco by the Ottomans but later by the Spaniards. Pungent peppers are grown to a limited degree in the Mediterranean area, especially the

8. As further evidence of contact between Venice and the Ottomans, polenta originated in Macedonia, where it was originally made from coarse wheat. New World corn and the recipe probably journeyed to northern Italy together. Spaghetti was an outcome of Marco Polo's journeys.

North African countries, but they are the exception rather than the rule, and are used primarily as table sauces such as rouille, harissa, and romesco rather than as a seasoning. Mediterranean cookery favors the type of sweet pepper we call ethnic peppers and uses them as vegetables more than as seasonings and condiments as Balkan cooks do.

North America

The foodways of North or Anglo America are not as peppery as other American countries we have discussed because its history is completely different. When the first Anglo colonists arrived in temperate North America, they encountered Native American agriculturists growing the "three sisters"—corn, beans, and squash—but not the tropical "little brother" chilli, and wild game and fish in abundance. From the Amerindians the colonists learned to grow the new crops using local methods, finding them easy to cultivate, simple to prepare, and easy to store—just the thing to take when the new Americans gathered their families and moved farther west. The familiar European staple, wheat, was demanding to grow and took too long to mature, while a crop of maize could be ready in six weeks without plow or horses. To this they added hogs and chickens, which could fend for themselves in the wilderness, as supplements for the abundant wild game, fish, and native foods from the land.

A major influence on North American cuisine was the diversity of cultures. Not only were many of the foods of the Native Americans adopted, but their methods of preparation, such as the making of hominy, succotash, and maple syrup. Successive groups from other European societies brought their foodways to enrich those found in the new continent, each making its own contribution. Among other things, the British gave us apple pie; the French influenced the making of soups, chowders, and fricassees; the Spanish brought sugarcane, oranges, and wine-making, as well as the technique of barbecuing, which they learned from the native Caribbeans; the Dutch added cole slaw; the Scotch brought oatmeal; the Irish returned the potato to the New World; Germans contributed sausages; Italians gave us pasta, and on and on. To all of these has been added the touch of the African slave, who brought us okra and watermelons. Later events resulting from our twentieth-century wars, along with increased travel and immigration, brought added Oriental and Middle Eastern influences. A willingness to experiment and borrow from these other cultures is yet another characteristic of North American cookery.

Cultural diversity was significant, but the most important North American tradition of plenty was based on a primeval abundance, which became the basis of the emerging cuisine. That abundance made a virtue of large helpings simply served. Lack of domestic help eliminated foods that required careful preparation. The dishes were simple, the food nutritious, and served separate from one another without sauces or garnishes to mask the flavors. Pork was the principal meat in the South and West until this century because the self-reliant pig was an ideal meat source for colonists. Maize in its myriad forms, from corn on the cob to porridge to cornbread, was the plant staple. The new enthusiasm for democracy made a virtue of simple and often tasteless food.

The spicy seafood, rice, and cayenne dishes that evolved after the French-Canadian followed the great Mississippi River into the crawfish- and oyster-filled bayous of southern Louisiana; the flavorful blending of French, Spanish and Afro-American influences with a love for peppers that emerged into Creole cooking; the memories of pungent, tortilla-based cookery that Mexicans brought with them north of the Rio Grande and combined in their Texas kitchens with the new ingredients to create Tex-Mex cooking, still full of chillies, and only faintly resembling anything in Mexico, but good!—those are the exceptions. To them is added the new southwestern cookery in which daring young chefs have borrowed from the Mexican, the Amerindian, the cowboy, and newcomers from the rest of the United States to produce a flavorful and color-filled piquant mélange unique to the area—such are the taste teasing pepper pockets where pepperphilia predominates.

The Tie That Binds

In all the places we have discussed, the chillies that prevail over all the others are the Mexican native, *Capsicum annuum* var. *annuum* and all its varieties. There are many cultivars of the first species, especially in Mexico and the southwestern United States, however, the cayenne type of that species dominates the Eastern Hemisphere. A generalized comparison of the usage in the West—Mexico, the U.S. Southwest, and Guatemala—with the East—Africa and Monsoon Asia

(I can't speak for the Balkans)—might go like this: In both worlds, East and West, a meal lacks a certain spirit without chillies. Peppers are an integral ingredient of the sauces that go over the starch. Pulverized peppers go into the meat, and small ones are eaten as a side dish or in condiments. The West fills large sweet or hot pods with cheese or meat and fries them in fat or bakes them. The East fires up its curries and stews with chopped, ground, or whole small pods. Both regions like pungent sauces to slosh over cooked dishes. In both the East and the West peppers are combined with other spices and herbs in side dishes or sauces more than served alone. The meals of the East and the West may not be alike in the makeup of the dishes, but the biting taste of each suggests the other. The tie that binds is the pungent chilli.

If you have to serve a dinner that was acceptable to all and balanced nutritionally to the entire populations of the places we have discussed—Latin America, Monsoon Asia, southwestern China, Japan, Korea, and Africa—what would you serve? That universal menu could be chicken, rice, squash, and chilli sauce, with tea for a beverage and a banana for dessert. Of course, each locale would use their characteristic flavorings to make the dish palatable from their point of view.

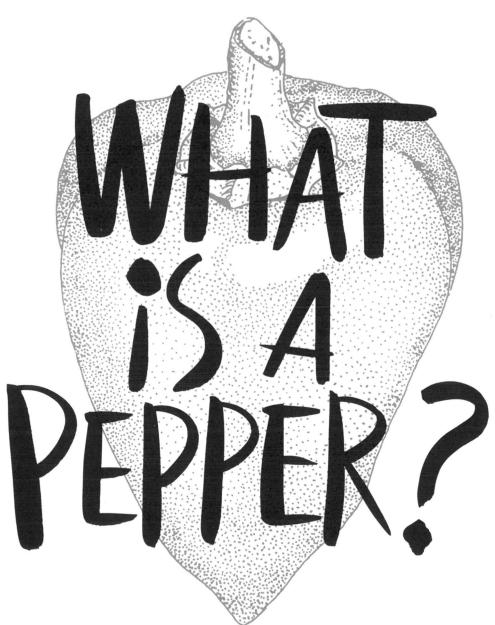

CHAPTER THREE

WHAT IS A PEPPER?

How do you account for the popularity of the pepper pod[1]—neither pepper nor a pod? The genus *Capsicum* is a rather mixed-up group of plants. Not just the name is cause for argument; even the defining characteristics of the genus are still being debated. However, there are some things on which all agree. To begin with, *Capsicum* is no relation to its namesake, black pepper, which is the seed of a woody vine, *Piper nigrum*, a native of India. Nor is it any kin to *Pimenta diocia*, allspice, the fruit of a native American tree of the myrtle family.

The confusion in names arose as a result of the confident Columbus, who was so certain he had landed in some part of the East Indian Archipelago when his search for black pepper and other spices prompted him to sail west from Spain five hundred years ago that he called the pungent spice the natives used on everything they ate *pimiento*, after the *pimienta* (black pepper) for which he was searching. Later the Spanish explorers added to the chaos by calling aromatic allspice, the second indigenous spice they found, *pimenta*, or Jamaican pepper. *Capsicum* "peppers" are also not related to what is known as the Guinea or ginnie pepper, *Aframomum melegueta* (see footnote 10 on page 8), a pungent African spice from Guinea known as grains of paradise, which, along with its kin, cardamom, are members of the ginger family. Ginnie pepper was brought to the Americas with African slaves, who loved it; but they learned to like the American capsicums even more. Today, only the name is used.

If it is not the *pimienta*, then just what is the capsicum? The genus *Capsicum* is in the family Solanaceae, as is the deadly nightshade, potato, tobacco, petunia, and others. Thousands of years ago some tropical Amerindians cultivated, improved, and developed the ancestral *Capsicum* into a wide variety of fruits that grow from sea level to an altitude of ten thousand feet, but are killed by frost. The genus *Capsicum* consists of perennial herbaceous to woody shrubs native to the American tropics. In areas subject to freezes, it is grown as an annual. Scholars are not in agreement as to its place of origin—either somewhere in southwestern Brazil or in Central Bolivia. Long before humans migrated across the Bering Strait to America, and before that migration reached Mesoamerica, it had been carried by birds, one of its natural means of dispersal,[2] to other parts of South America. Centuries later, when the Europeans arrived, birds and/or pre-Columbian Amerindians had not only carried the indigenous spice to Mesoamerica and the Caribbean, they had domesticated[3] the four or five species which are cultivated today. Each of the domesticated species had been developed independently in different geographical regions from small-fruited wild species. No new species have been domesticated since Columbus first stumbled on to the red and green capsicums of the New World.

All species of the wild *Capsicum* have certain common characters: small pungent, red fruits that may be round, elongate, or conical; fruits at-

---

1. Both the *Capsicum* and the bean pod are fruits, but the chilli is not a pod despite that traditional designation. A pod is dry, dehiscent fruit that splits open along two sutures to release the seed.

2. Recent observations by W. Hardy Eshbaugh reveal that rainwater acts as a dispersal agent for certain wild species in Peru by knocking the fruit off the plant and washing it downhill to streams that carry it to new locations.

3. Domestication is an evolutionary process operating under the influence of human activity. In plants there is genetic modification from their wild state through selection, or by using modern biotechnology. According to Heiser (1973) domestication is completed when man controls the breeding of the organism. A domesticated type is usually incapable of survival without the care of humans, although some domesticates—horses, pigs, and a few domesticated plants—can revert to a wild-type existence. "Domesticated" and "cultivated" are often used synonymously, but in fact they have quite different significance.

tached to the plant in an erect position; fruits readily removed from the calyx; and seeds dispersed by birds. Wild *Capsicum* flowers have a stigma-bearing style that extends beyond the anthers to facilitate pollination by insects. Domesticated cultivars have short styles, which promote self-pollination. Once people began to grow the *Capsicum* plants they, unconsciously or perhaps even consciously, selected seed from those fruits more difficult to remove from the calyx because they would remain attached until harvest, making it harder for birds to pluck. It was also observed that if the capsicums hung down and were hidden among the leaves, the hungry birds had trouble extracting them. As a result, pendent fruit became more desirable, and today most domesticated capsicums have pendent fruit instead of erect. Size increased as larger and larger fruits were selected, and the weight of those larger and heavier fruits also helped the capsicums become pendent.

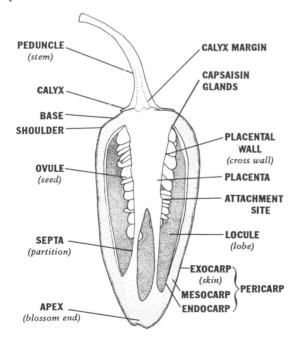

PEDUNCLE
(stem)

CALYX

BASE

SHOULDER

OVULE
(seed)

SEPTA
(partition)

APEX
(blossom end)

CALYX MARGIN

CAPSAISIN
GLANDS

PLACENTAL
WALL
(cross wall)

PLACENTA

ATTACHMENT
SITE

LOCULE
(lobe)

EXOCARP
(skin)
MESOCARP ⟩ PERICARP
ENDOCARP

CROSS-SECTION OF A PEPPER

In the case of many domesticated plants, the color, flavor, size, and shape were changed through selection by humans. All mild and sweet capsicums are the result of domestication. All wild capsicums are pungent (mouthwarming). This pungency, unique in the vegetable kingdom, results from the presence of a group of closely related compounds.

According to botanist W. Hardy Eshbaugh, writing in 1993, there are more than twenty-five species of *Capsicum*, four of which have been domesticated. Many of the wild capsicums are harvested and one, *Capsicum annuum* var. *glabriusculum (chiltepín)*, is cultivated[4] to a limited degree, and is the only wild capsicum widely used in the United States. There are four or five domesticated species: *C. annuum* var. *annuum*, *C. frutescens*, *C. chinense*,[5] *C. baccatum* var. *pendulum*, and *C. pubescens*. Studies to be reported in a forthcoming monograph on the genus *Capsicum* may call for the merging of the first three closely related species, or, at least, the second and third.

I feel a capsule of *Capsicum* taxonomy will not be hard to swallow, and will be good for you.[6] Judging from the scholars' map (page 6) that shows the distribution of each of these species at the time of the Discovery, Columbus should have first encountered domesticated *Capsicum chinense*, although the wild *C. annuum* and *C. frutescens* might have been around. These

---

4. Cultivated: to cultivate means to conduct activities involving the care of a plant; it is concerned with human activities. A plant can be cultivated before it is domesticated. Once humans began to select for particular qualities in a plant species, they had begun the workings of domestication.

5. The diffusion of capsicums to Africa and Asia took place in such a short time that many years later Europeans thought they originated in the Orient. Evidence of that is the name "chinense" given to a species by Nicholas Jacquin in 1776 when he stated that he had named it for its home.

6. Those interested in more information than is given in this chapter may want to go to *Peppers: The Domesticated Capsicums,* or some of the material listed in its bibliography.

are the ones that were predicted to be found at the initial points of European contact before 1502—the Caribbean islands and the coast of South America from Brazil to Central America. However, in previous pages I have theorized that the domesticated *C. annuum* var. *annuum* had already been introduced to the West Indies (page 7). Twenty-seven years later, when the relentless Hernando Cortés invaded Mexico, he encountered *C. annuum* var. *annuum*. Later conquistadors would meet *C. baccatum* var. *pendulum* and *C. pubescens* in the Andean regions of South America.

Capsicum annuum var. *annuum*, *C. frutescens*, and *C. chinense* are the only ones that became established in the Old World, where the dubious *C. frutescens* grows spontaneously or semiwild. All three are known to grow in Africa, but only *C. annuum* var. *annuum* and *C. frutescens* are significant in India and the Far East. It is thought that, near the beginning of the twentieth century, *C. pubescens* was introduced from its Andean homeland to the highlands of Central America and Mexico, although it could have moved into Mesoamerica with the conquistadors much earlier. It requires a cool, freeze-free climate with a long growing season, and the fleshy fruit deteriorates rapidly; as a consequence its use is more limited than the others. For some reason, the widespread Andean *C. baccatum* var. *pendulum* has never caught on outside South America. I had good luck growing several of these flavorful *ajís* in my Texas garden, but perhaps its sprawling habit makes it undesirable commercially.

Virtually all of the capsicums that are found in markets around the world are *Capsicum annuum* var. *annuum*. If you plant seed saved from a garden where several cultivars of that variety are grown, you can expect considerable variation in the offspring. Consequently, there are untold numbers of varieties of this species. Interspecific sterility barriers prevent it crossing at all with *C. pubescens*, and only under special conditions will it cross with *C. baccatum* var. *pendulum*. It will cross with the other two, *C. frutescens* and *C. chinense*, and some of the resulting hybrids have produced viable seed. Some scholars have thought that *C. annuum*, *C. frutescens*, and *C. chinense* have a common ancestor, and that the latter two are closely related. In fact, recent evidence has caused the pioneering *Capsicum* scholar, Charles B. Heiser, Jr., and others to conclude that from both practical and biological standpoints there is no justification for recognizing *C. frutescens* and *C. chinense* as separate species. If they are combined, the code of nomenclatural priority requires the earliest name be used—in this case it would be frutescens instead of chinense, which will probably bring about another period of confusion in *Capsicum* names. However, whatever the name they'll taste the same.

The only way you can differentiate between the various *Capsicum* species is by the corolla and its calyx (the flower). Let's start with the easy ones. The flowers of *Capsicum baccatum* var. *pendulum* and *C. pubescens* are so different from the flowers of the other three species that if you saw those plants in bloom you would have no doubts. *C. baccatum* var. *pendulum* has a white flower with yellowish spots and white anthers that turn brownish yellow with age. *C. pubescens* has a beautiful purple flower with a tiny white border, and to make recognition even easier, its seeds are black. The flowers of the other three have white to greenish-white petals and purple anthers. The flowers of *C. chinense* and *C. frutescens* are slightly greenish, while those of *C. annuum* var. *annuum* are milky white. Occasionally the annual pepper will have two flowers per node, but never more than two, so don't confuse it with *C. chinense*, which *always* has two or more. Unless you are growing the plants yourself, you will probably not be confronted with this problem.

For the most part, it is impossible to positively identify a species by the fruit alone. But don't

THE DOMESTICATED CAPSICUMS

C. chinense   *C. baccatum pendulum*   *C. frutescens*   *C. annuum annuum*   *C. pubescens*

worry, only three cultivars that are not *Capsicum annuum* var. *annuum* are grown commercially in the United States at this time, *C. frutescens* 'Tabasco' and *C. chinense,* the dátil and habanero. Your problem in the kitchen or market will be in distinguishing one *C. annuum* var. *annuum* cultivar[7] from another.

If you purchase seed or plants for your garden, record the cultivar name. The common names frequently vary from place to place and will often be different for the same variety, depending on whether it is fresh or dried. The cultivar name should be the same everywhere because it has been registered.

When Columbus first came upon capsicums, the Arawaks of the West Indies called it *axí,* which the Spanish transliterated to *ají (ajé, agí).* That language is extinct now, and so are the Arawaks (see footnote 21 in chapter 1). As I've said earlier, it is highly probable that capsicums traveled from South America to the West Indies in prehistoric times with the name *ají* already attached. Today in the Dominican Republic (formerly Española) and a few other places in the Caribbean along with much of South America, the pungent varieties are still called *ají.* However, *uchu* and *huayca* are other ancient words used for capsicums by some Amerindian groups in the Andean area. The Spanish called it *pimiento* or *pimientón* (depending on the size) after *pimienta,* or black pepper. These names traveled with the plant to Spain, but not throughout Europe, where it is called *peperone* in Italy, *piment* in France, and *paprika* by the Slavs in the Balkans.

---

7. A cultivar is a population variant or hybrid that has originated and persisted under cultivation. The word is formed from "cultivated variety" and is abbreviated as "cv." There are hundreds of bell pepper cultivars, for example, each with a name in conformity with the International Code of Nomenclature of Cultivated Plants, and that name must be markedly different in the way it is written from the scientific name, which is regulated by the International Code of Botanical Nomenclature. Examples of cultivar names: *Capsicum annuum* var. *annuum* cv. 'Caloro'; *Capsicum frutescens* cv. 'Tabasco'.

At the time the Spanish arrived in Mexico, the Nahuatl-speaking natives called their fiery fruit *chilli.* The Nahuatl stem *chil* refers to the chilli plant and also means "red." To the generic word *chilli,* the term that described the particular chilli cultivar was added (e.g., *tonalchilli* means "chilli of the sun or summer," *chiltecpin* means "flea chilli"). The term *chilli* first appeared in print in 1651. In Mexico today, the Spanish word *chile,* which was derived from *chilli,* refers to both pungent and sweet types and is used in combination with a descriptive adjective, such as *chile colorado* (red chilli) or a word that indicates the place of origin, such as *chile poblano* (chilli from Pueblo). The same variety can have different names in different geographic regions, in various stages of maturity, or in the dried state. Consequently, the names of capsicums in Mexico can be very confusing.

The Portuguese language uses *pimenta* for capsicums and qualifies the various types—*pimenta-da-caiena,* cayenne pepper; *pimenta-da-malegueta,* red pepper; *pimenta-do-reino,* black pepper; *pimenta-da-jamaica,* allspice; while *pimentāo* is pimento, red pepper, or just pepper. *Ají* and *chile* are not found in a Portuguese dictionary, nor did they carry the words *chilli* or *Capsicum* with them in their travels.

The Dutch first, then the English, were probably responsible for spreading the current capsicum names to the Eastern part of the world, because in Australia, India, Indonesia, and Thailand in general, "chilli" (chillies) or sometimes "chilly," is used by English speakers for the pungent types, while the mild ones are called capsicums. Until very recently only mild varieties were to be had in Australia, while Indonesians and Thais don't use sweet capsicums at all, so they have no word for them. Each Far Eastern language has its own word for chillies—*prik* in Thai, *mirch* in Hindi, to name but two.

The United States is where the greatest confusion exists. Here we find both the anglicized spelling, "chili" (chilies) and the Spanish *chile (chiles)* used by some for the pungent fruits of the *Capsicum* plant, while "chili" is also used as a short form of "chili con carne," a variously concocted mixture of meat and chillies. *The Oxford English Dictionary* gives "chilli" as the primary usage, calling "chile" and "chili" variants. *Webster's New International Dictionary* prefers "chili," followed by the Spanish *chile* and the Nahuatl *chilli*. In the American Southwest, "chile" refers to the long green or red chilli that is/was known as the Anaheim or long green or red chile but is now preferably called New Mexican chile by the folks there. New Mexicans even went so far as to enter that name in the *Congressional Record* of November 3, 1983 (misidentified as *Capsicum frutescens* instead of *C. annuum* var. *annuum*). In an English-speaking country it seems somewhat inconsistent to choose the Spanish *chile* over the anglicized "chili" or "chilli"—the original Nahuatl name used by a majority of the English speaking world today. It would be so much less confusing if they were called what they are—capsicums—but getting Americans to call peppers capsicums would be like getting us to use the metric system; "chilli" instead of "chili" or "chile" is more realistic. To make matters even more confusing, "pimento," an anglicized version of *pimiento,* has been adopted by the Georgia Pimento Growers Association for their mild product, but the word is not always used.

Not because one name is right and another is wrong, but for the sake of consistency and clarity, in this book "capsicum" or "peppers" will be used when speaking of the fruit of the *Capsicum* in general, both sweet and pungent; "chilli" for the pungent types; "chili" for the spicy meat dish; and "pimento" for the sweet, thick-fleshed, frequently heart-shaped red capsicum. If *chile* (in italics) is used, it will refer to a native Mexican cultivar or, unitalicized, to the long green or red New Mexican chile type. Whenever possible the name of the specific fruit type/group or cultivar name will be used. It is hoped that the reader will follow suit, thereby helping to stabilize the trou-blesome situation. Like Gertrude Stein's rose, a jalapeño is a jalapeño is a jalapeño.

The important thing to remember is that each variety has its own character, and if another variety is substituted, the flavor of the dish will change. Therefore it is essential that not only the specific capsicum but also its specific form (fresh, dried, canned, pickled, etc.) be used and not just hot pepper or green pepper. Reading the cultivar descriptions starting on page 65 will make this easier.

Nutritional Physiological Considerations

Capsicums are not only good, they are good for you. Nutritionally, capsicums are a dietary plus. They contain more vitamin A than any other food plant and are also an excellent source of vitamin C and the B vitamins. By gram weight, jalapeños contain at least twenty times more vitamin A and more than twice the vitamin C than fresh oranges (see chart). Capsicums also contain significant amounts of magnesium, iron, thiamine, riboflavin, and niacin. Even though chillies are not eaten in large quantities, small amounts are important where traditional diets provide only marginal vitamins. In *Peppers* I give a detailed account of the nutritional value of capsicums along with the story of their use by the Hungarian scientist Albert Szent-Györgyi in his discovery of vitamin C.

Vitamin C is a very unstable nutrient. It is readily destroyed through exposure to oxygen in the air, by drying, and by heating, and it is soluble in water. In other words, cooking is very damaging to it. Keep cut or peeled capsicums well covered to prevent contact with oxygen, and don't allow them to stand in water for more than one hour. Nevertheless, considerable vitamin C is retained in cooked and canned green capsicums. Green capsicums are higher in vitamin C than red capsicums because vitamin C diminishes with maturity. Vitamin A is just the opposite, increasing as the capsicum matures and dries. Also, vitamin A is not lost when exposed to oxygen, and is quite stable during the cooking and preservation process.

1 GRAM UNCOOKED	VIT. A (ICU.S)	VIT. C (MG.S)
Bell pepper	50	1.20
Fresh orange	2.24	.538
Carrot	30.5	.35
Potato	.375	.016
Tomato	8.49	.22

Weight-conscious readers may be happy to learn that capsicums and a few other pungent spices will cause their metabolic rate to increase after eating them. This diet-induced thermic effect requires six grams of chilli to burn off an average of forty-five calories in three hours.

Pepper seeds, like all seeds, have some protein and fat (oil). They also have a little manganese and copper, but otherwise add little nutritionally. In North America the seeds are traditionally removed, but in other countries this is seldom customary—especially in small chillies. Removing seeds from fresh green or red chillies reduces the pungency to some extent because the seeds absorb capsaicin from the placental wall to which they are attached. In dry chillies or any peppers that have large, mature seeds (like ancho and New Mexican chile types) they have become woody in texture, and some find that quality undesirable; however, others grind them to give a nutty flavor to sauces (like cascabel). Higher grades of paprika and pepper flakes have had the seed and veins (cross walls) removed before grinding. Whether you leave the seeds in or remove them is strictly a matter of personal preference, having little effect on the nutritional value.

In recent years much has been written concerning the nutritional and medical attributes of capsicums as reported in scientific studies. Dur-ing this same period the public has become more health conscious, which has led to increased nutritional awareness. "Low-calorie," "low-cholesterol," "complex carbohydrates," "high-fiber," "low-sodium," "unsaturated oils," and "low-fat" have become part of our daily vocabulary, and food growers and processors are responding to public demand by providing for these nutritional requirements. Health authorities are in agreement that a change in our traditional American food style is vital to good health. Capsicums conform to these food restrictions, and at the same time their distinctive flavor peps up an otherwise bland, creamless, butterless, eggless, saltless meal. Capsicums are a real health food!

Capsaicin, the Pungent Principle

People don't eat capsicums for the vitamins and fiber, they eat them because they are pungent. Take away the vitamins and the fiber and people would still eat chillies, but take away the capsaicin and they don't want them. A unique group of mouth-warming amide-type alkaloids (capsaicinoids) containing a small vanilloid structural component is responsible for the burning sensation associated with capsicums, acting directly on the pain receptors in the mouth and throat. This vanilloid element is present in other pungent plants used as spices, such as ginger and black pepper. For some time capsaicin was believed to be the only active pungent principle of *Capsicum*, but more recently studies have added other compounds[8] to the pungent group of which capsaicin

---

8. Vanillyl amide compounds or capsaicinoids in *Capsicum* are predominantly capsaicin (C, 69 percent), dihydrocapsaicin (DHC, 22 percent), nordihydrocapsaicin (NDHC, 7 percent); homocapsaicin (HC, 1 percent), homodihydrocap-

is the most important part. Three of these capsaicinoid components cause the sensation of "rapid bite" at the back of the palate and throat, and two others cause a long, low-intensity bite on the tongue and midpalate. Differences in the proportions of these compounds may account for the characteristic "burns" of the different capsicum cultivars. In both sweet and pungent capsicums, the major part of the organs secreting these pungent alkaloids are localized in the placenta to which the seeds are attached. A lesser amount occurs in the dissepiment (veins or cross walls), which is the white part extending from the placenta dividing the interior cavity into sections or lobes (see the figure on page 55). The seeds contain only a low concentration of capsaicin. Historian Bartolomé de Las Casas made an astute observation about the pungency in capsicums four and a half centuries ago:

> This is what one should know. The part that burns are the seeds and the veins [*rayas*] that form inside the compartments where the seeds appear. All that is between these and does not come in contact with the veins is not pungent, it is sweet and smooth.

The response to some additives in food used at optimal levels is the sensation in the mouth of a warm, mouth-watering quality. A sensory analyst and *Capsicum* authority from India, V. S. Govindarajan, insists that this response should be defined by the term "pungency," rather than the other less desirable connotations generally used—hot, stinging, irritating, sharp, caustic, acrid, biting, burning. He also suggests that pungency be given the status of a gustatory characteristic of food as are sweet, sour, bitter, saline, astringent, or alkaline.

The capsaicin content is influenced by the

---

saicin HDHC, 1 percent). Several more analogues of these in trace amounts bring the number to ten. C and DHC are the primary heat contributors, but the delayed action of HDHC is the most irritating and difficult to quell.

growing conditions of the plant and the age of the fruit, and could possibly be variety specific. Dry, stressful conditions will increase the amount of capsaicin. Beginning about the eleventh day, the capsaicin content increases, becoming detectable when the fruit is about four weeks old and reaching its peak just before maturity, then dropping somewhat in the ripening stage. Sun-drying generally reduces the capsaicin content, the highest retention being obtained when the fruits are air-dried, with minimum exposure to sunlight. Many people swear to me that sweet capsicums in their garden had crossed with "hot" ones, resulting in their sweet ones producing pungent fruit the same year. With the evidence hot in their hands it is hard to make them believe that a cross will not evidence itself in the same growth cycle. What actually happened to their nonpungent bell or banana pepper is not a phenomenon particular to *Capsicum* in the plant world. Even though the cultivar planted had been bred until it was non-pungent, non-poisonous, etc., it still held some of the original gene that produces capsaicin or a particular poison, but that gene had been silenced. Then, for some undetermined reason, the silenced gene in a sweet chilli reappears or reexpresses itself under certain circumstances—possibly climatic—causing those latent characteristics to build up as the fruit matures toward the end of a stressful season.

Ethnobotanist Gary Nabhan explains that the distasteful and sometimes poisonous alkaloids found in plants serve to keep their seed out of the wrong animals and get them into the right ones in order to guarantee seed dispersal as the animal moves from the feeding place. Once dispersed by the animal, the seed must be able to germinate. If a wild chilli seed is to germinate, it must pass through the creature's digestive tract undamaged. Birds have a digestive tract that softens the seed without significant damage. Most wild chilli seeds require this trip through a bird's digestive system to germinate. The capsaicin discourages other animals from eating chillies, while the red color attracts the birds to the ripe fruit—many small animals cannot see red. Birds, the only other animal besides man thought to eat chillies on purpose, lack appropriate pain receptors and are therefore untouched by the chillies they consume with such relish.

Capsaicin is hard to detect by chemical tests. It has virtually no odor or flavor, but a drop of a solution containing one part in 100,000 causes a persistent burning on the tongue. The original method for determining the heat in capsicums is the Scoville Organoleptic Test, which is a taste test, developed in 1912, that relies on the physiological action of the compound. It is a highly subjective method and has been largely replaced by the use of high-pressure liquid chromatography (HPLC), a highly reproducible technique for quantifying capsaicinoids in capsicum products; however, the results are still given in Scoville Units. HPLC only measures the relevant amount of capsaicinoid compound of one particular pod, from a particular location, particular season, and particular plant. The same cultivar may test differently when grown under different circumstances. The results of such procedures can only be considered to be a general guide. In your kitchen, you should taste a tiny portion to estimate the pungency and adjust your usage accordingly. Don't be afraid, just do it. Instead of rating the pungency of the various cultivars described in Chapter 4 in Scoville Units, a simple scale of one to ten has been used because I was not able to find two published Scoville Unit rankings in agreement.

Capsaicin is eight times more pungent than the piperine in black pepper, but unlike black pepper, which inhibits all tastes, capsaicin only obstructs the perception of sour and bitter; it does not impair our discernment of other gustatory characteristics of food. Capsaicin activates the defensive and digestive systems by acting as an irritant to the oral and gastrointestinal membranes. That irritation increases the flow of saliva and gastric acids. Eating capsaicin also causes the neck, face, and front of the chest to sweat in a reflexive response to the burning in the mouth. Very little capsaicin is absorbed as it passes through the digestive tract, an uncomfortable consequence of which is jalaproctitis (burning defecation). This is probably the basis for the Hungarian saying "Paprika burns twice." There is little evidence that constant consumption of chillies has an effect—either positive or negative—on the average person. If stomach ulcers are present or developing, however, the stimulation of gastric acid secretions caused by eating chillies is a potential hazard.

Eating capsicums not only increases the flow of saliva and gastric secretions but also stimulates the appetite. These functions work together to aid the digestion of food. The increased saliva helps ease the passage of food through the mouth to the stomach, where it is mixed with the activated gastric juice. These functions play an important role in the lives of people whose daily diet is principally starch-based.

Emotional upsets, nicotine, or caffeine greatly increase the amount of acid in the stomach, and ulcers are often the result. It is only common sense to recognize that eating stimulating chillies while emotionally tilted, smoking, sipping coffee, or having a few margaritas will really fill your stomach with acid. The good news is, your body has a complex physical-chemical barrier to protect the stomach lining from the acid. The bad news is that alcohol and aspirin will readily penetrate that barrier. One aspirin causes the loss of only a small amount of blood, but in conjunction with alcohol it can bring on excessive bleeding.

There is a preventive measure you can take if you dearly love to mix chillies with margaritas or some other alcoholic imbibement. Fat takes hours longer than carbohydrates or proteins to digest, so stimulants such as alcohol take longer to affect someone who has eaten a fatty snack such as cheese before drinking. Cheese serves to coat the stomach. If you have a finicky stomach, eat some cheese or drink some cream before indulging in food highly spiced with chillies and washed down with wine, beer, or margaritas.

There are several ways to put out the fire. Capsaicin is not soluble in water. No amount of water will wash it away, but cool water will give temporary relief by changing the surface temperature. In 1984 I discovered that the addition of a small amount of chlorine or ammonia to water ionized the capsaicin compound, changing it into a salt that is soluble in water. This works miracles on your hands, but of course you can't drink chlorine or ammonia. Like many organic compounds, capsaicin is soluble in alcohol. Again this works on the skin, but caution must be noted when you drink it because we have already seen that alcohol penetrates the barriers nature has provided to protect your stomach lining—as well as being intoxicating. For your burning mouth, try using vodka as a mouthwash and gargle, then spit it out—great for the designated driver.

Recently it was determined that your burning mouth can be relieved by lipoproteins such as casein, which remove capsaicin in a manner similar to the action of a detergent, breaking the bond the capsaicin has formed with the pain receptors in your mouth. Milk and yogurt are the most readily available sources of casein. It is the casein, not the fat, in milk that does the job, therefore butter and cheese will not have the same effect. *Raita,* the traditional cool yogurt and chopped vegetable accompaniment to fiery curries, has served this function for generations in India.

Capsaicin or the burning sensation produced by it may prove to be a nonhabit-forming alternative to the addictive drugs used to control pain. The fact that the vanilloids occur in most pungent plants has led neurobiologists to conclude that the mammalian nervous system has specific neuroreceptors for those compounds. Not only birds, but other creatures, such as snails or frogs, do not have similar neuroreceptors. Studies of capsaicin and its relationship to substance P, a neuropeptide that sends the message of pain to our brains, has led investigators to conclude that capsaicin has the capacity to deplete nerves of their supply of substance P, thereby preventing the transmission of those hurt-filled signals. Already this ability of capsaicin is being used to treat the pain associated with shingles, rheumatoid arthritis, and phantom-limb pain. Obviously, Native Americans had a sound basis for treating toothaches and the pain of childbirth by eating chillies, one that the rest of the world has been slow to recognize.

Aroma, Flavor, and Color

I am often asked if certain capsicums, especially ornamentals, are edible. Yes, all capsicums are edible, but, like the Orwellian pigs, some are more edible than others. Flavor makes the difference. The flavor compound of capsicums is located in the outer wall (pericarp); very little is found in the placenta and cross wall and essentially none in the seeds (see the figure on page 55). Color and flavor go hand in hand because the flavoring principle appears to be associated with the carotenoid pigment: Strong color and strong flavor are linked. For example, the red bells are far superior in flavor to the less expensive greens. Unfortunately, most people don't consider anything but the heat or price when they select a cultivar. *Capsicum pubescens* (the rocoto) and the various varieties of *C. chinense* are more aromatic and have a decidedly different flavor than those of *C. annuum* var. *annuum,* but for most Anglo-Saxons those two species are too pungent to enjoy. Being able to recognize the differences in flavors of the various cultivars is most important in cooking. Using a different variety can completely change the character of a dish. You cannot substitute an ancho for a chipotle or a bell pepper for a banana pepper without a noticeable difference.

Color in a painting is the most compelling element, and it is an important adjunct in foods as well. Few foods are more stimulating to our visual sense than an array of brilliant red, yellow, green, orange, purple, and brown capsicums.[9] Even if you don't eat capsicums, their use as garnishes can enhance the total appearance of your dish or table. The carotenoid pigments responsible for the color in capsicums make them commercially important as natural dyes in food and drug products throughout the world. Red capsanthin, the most important pigment, is not found in immature green capsicums. All capsicums will change color as they mature from green to other hues. Green capsicums are simply gathered before they are fully ripe. Brown-colored capsicums result from the retention of the green chlorophyl, which mixes with the red pigment to make brown in the mature fruit. Unripe capsicums have better keeping quality and are less difficult to transport than ripe ones; consequently, they are more available and less expensive in the market. Unfortunately for the consumer, the distinctive *Capsicum* flavor develops only as the fruit ripens, reaching its peak at maturity.

Taste and smell are separate perceptions. If you are not conscious of the distinctive aroma of a capsicum, you should be—it adds to the pleasure of eating it. Americans are learning to appreciate aroma in capsicums as Asians and Africans have long done. Several aroma compounds produce the fragrance. The taste buds on the tongue can discern certain flavors at dilutions up to one part in two million, but odors can be detected at a dilution of one part in one billion.

---

9. While other guests were sitting lethargically at the table following a long, sumptuous dinner party, I emptied a sackful of peppers I had brought to my hosts into the middle of the table. Even as the bright pods, representing nearly all species were falling into a vibrant pile, the sated guests jumped up, began touching the peppers, talking animatedly all at one time, and dashing for cameras—completely revitalized. I am continually amazed at the way chillies excite people as no other food does.

The more delicate flavors of foods are recognized as aromas in the nasal cavity adjacent to the mouth. Sensory cells with this function are much more discerning than the tongue. Compare the aroma of a jalapeño with that of a habanero— you'll recognize the specific odor of each immediately. The enchantment of peppers is like that of a lovely woman whose charm of shape and subtle perfume entice you to her and whose inner fire creates a mystique and desire.

Why Chilli Lovers Love Chillies

What is it about a fruit that makes one quarter of the adults on the earth eat it every day in spite of the fact that nature designed it to burn in order to protect it—they can't all be capsimanics suffering from chilliphilia, can they? There is something singularly human surrounding the acquired taste for chilli. Psychologist Paul Rozin has probably looked into that question more completely than anyone else, writing numerous fascinating papers detailing the results of his studies. I can do no better than to summarize his findings.

Rozin looked first for adaptive/evolutionary explanations, since such explanations are commonly offered. One by one he has shot them down for lack of demonstrable evidence. Nor has he found any antibacterial effect; capsicums do not help preserve food, and capsicums weren't used to disguise spoiling food in their original New World setting. The fact that the chilli is used in greatest quantity in mild climates such as Korea and highland Mexico negates the claim for a sweating/cooling effect. There are, however, other, more probable theories. The extremely high vitamin A and C content gives them a nutritional advantage that early man may or may not have recognized. By activating the flow of saliva, capsicums aid in chewing often dry, starchy foods and increase their flavor. Capsicums have a wide range of aromas, flavors, colors, and pungencies that provide variation to monotonous diets. The burning in the mouth gives a feeling of fullness (a meat quality) to repetitious, bland meals. In Europe the initial adoption of the chilli was medicinally and socially motivated. Of these modifying values, flavor enhancement and salivation are those most likely to have been realized and utilized.

The heat produced by capsaicin is a principal reason for liking capsicums. The initially negative feeling becomes positive. Regular consumption of chilli has only a slight desensitizing effect, good news for the chilli lover who craves the burn.

Liking to eat chillies is definitely an acquired taste. Young children do not care for them. In the first stage, or initial exposure to chillies, few like them. The second stage is liking them—and not everyone does. In the beginning, preference comes about from the enhancement of the flavors of other foods. This progresses into a liking for the burn. Professor Rozin concludes, "Chilli is currently consumed for one reason: it tastes good."

What is a capsicum? An old dictionary of "Aztequismos" defined *chile* as *el miembro viril* (virile member). However, since this book concerns food and why we like to eat capsicums as a food, I'll not go into the medical or physiological aspects that concern such reactions as opponent-endorphin responses and benign masochism. If you want to know more, I suggest reading the work of Paul Rozin and Andrew Weil or looking at my *Peppers*. Happy mouth-surfing!

LOOK AT ME! CULTIVAR DESCRIPTIONS

The peppers you are about to see are shown off the plant and without foliage, much as you will find them in the marketplace. They have been drawn in the same scale relative to each other, so you will not see tiny fruit drawn large in order to fill the space on the page.

BANANA PEPPER AND 'HUNGARIAN WAX'
Capsicum annuum var. *annuum* Linné

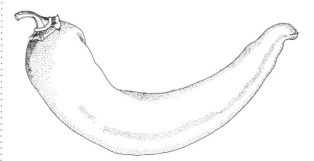

COLOR: Pale yellow-green to yellow, maturing to bright red

SHAPE: Elongated cylinder, tapering to a point; wax type

SIZE: 5½ to 6 inches long by 1½ inches wide

PUNGENCY: Sweet, 0; hot, 5

SUBSTITUTES: 'Cubanelle' for sweet; 'Caloro' or 'Santa Fe Grande' for hot

OTHER NAMES: 'Sweet Banana', 'Hungarian Yellow Wax'

USES:
  FRESH: In salads, vegetable dishes, and stews; as garnish; stuffed like celery; fried
  PICKLED: As garnish; in salads or sandwiches; as a condiment

SOURCES:
  FRESH: Home garden, farmers' markets
  DRIED: Not used dried
  PROCESSED: Pickled banana peppers available in food stores
  SEEDS: Most seed suppliers.
  AVAILABLE CULTIVARS: 'Early Sweet Banana', 'Giant Yellow Banana', 'Hungarian Yellow Wax', 'Long Sweet Yellow'

This beautiful, flavorful pepper is a crisp addition to an hors d'oeuvre tray, but its availability depends on location. It is a favorite of the home gardener. The sweet form is known as the banana pepper and the hot is called Hungarian wax. Both are long, tapered, yellow fruits that cannot be distinguished until you take a bite. They are commonly used in their immature yellow state. The ripe red banana pepper is good in salads and vegetable dishes, but the fully ripe Hungarian is almost too hot to eat. This cultivar was introduced from Hungary in 1932.

BELL PEPPER
Capsicum annuum var. *annuum* Linné

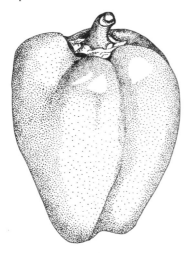

COLOR: Green to red, orange, yellow, brown, purple

SHAPE: Blocky. A few cultivars, such as the tomato-shaped 'Sunnybrook' or the long, narrow 'Ruby King', do not conform. Bell type

SIZE: 4 to 6 inches long by 3½ to 4 inches wide

PUNGENCY: Sweet, 0, except for 'Mexi-bell', 3 to 5

SUBSTITUTES: Banana, 'Cubanelle', pimento peppers

OTHER NAMES: Capsicums, mango, morrón, pimentón, or any one of the hundreds of hybrid cultivar names

USES: Stuffed (parboiled 2 to 3 minutes first); fried; in casseroles, vegetable dishes, salads, relishes, soups, sauces; as a garnish, crudité

SOURCES:

FRESH: Food stores, farmers' markets, home garden

DRIED: Bell peppers are not dried whole; dehydrated flakes can be found in the spice section of food stores

PROCESSED: Ripe red ones are canned as a pale substitute for pimento

SEEDS: There is a multitude of cultivars; any seed company will have one or more.

AVAILABLE CULTIVARS: 'Ace Hybrid', 'Argo', 'Big Bertha', 'Klondike Bell', 'Ma Belle', 'Oriole', 'Staddon's Select', 'Yolo Wonder'

Who can't recognize a bell pepper? Sweet peppers of the type known as bell peppers are the most used *Capsicum* in the United States. Sweet peppers were developed through the process of selection by the Amerindians before Columbus discovered America, and were known as bell peppers as early as 1681. A pepper of the tomato type was probably the precursor of the ubiquitous bell. A small still life painted in 1814 by Raphael Peale depicted green bell peppers, thereby recording their early presence in the markets of Philadelphia. Since that date American growers have developed several hundred different bell cultivars with a conglomeration of names such as 'Bull Nose', 'Big Bertha', 'Keystone', 'Dutch Treat', and 'Bell Boy'. 'Calwonder' ('California Wonder'), which was introduced in 1928, is the most popular.

The bell, a thick-fleshed, sweet pepper used primarily as a vegetable, is consumed most frequently in the unripe green stage, even though they may ripen to red, orange, yellow, brown, and deep purple. In the midwestern United States the bell types are frequently called mangoes, even though they are in no way related to that tropical fruit. The food historian William Woys Weaver explains that seventeenth-century merchants in England imported stuffed pickled mangoes from India. English cooks, with no source for that tropical fruit, substituted such things as cucumbers and unripe peaches in their efforts to reproduce the delicacy. When the recipe arrived in the American colonies, baby muskmelons and bell peppers replaced the exotic mangoes, and the name was transferred to the peppers (see pages 202–203 for the recipe). Most older cookbooks call for bell pepper when a recipe requires sweet green pepper.

The fruit can grow erect or pendent, and there may be two to four locules, or lobes. The four-lobed fruits sell better. When selecting bell peppers, choose those that are well shaped, firm, and thick fleshed. Pale, blemished, wrinkled, limp specimens are not desirable. The fully ripe red or colored fruit is much more flavorful and digestible than the common unripe green ones. Holland is producing beautiful, colorful, large bell peppers for the American market that are quite delicious but expensive, and the colorful, tasty bells have become favorites of American chefs. Some American growers are beginning to compete for the market the Dutch have created, and bells are also grown in Mexico for export to the United States; however, they are not commonly eaten in Latin America.

The bell does not need to be peeled before using; however, in recipes for stuffed peppers it is advisable to parboil them. This can be done in the microwave by putting them in a plastic bag or covered dish with a tablespoon of water for a minute or two, depending on the number of peppers. Roasted and peeled bells impart a new flavor dimension to salads and casseroles. Store the fresh peppers in the vegetable drawer of the refrigerator (see page 95).

CASCABEL
Capsicum annuum var. *annuum* Linné

COLOR:
  FRESH: Dark green to reddish brown
  DRIED: Dark reddish brown with translucent, glossy skin
SHAPE: Oblate; cherry type
SIZE: 1 inch long by 1 to 1½ inches wide
PUNGENCY: Hot, 4
SUBSTITUTES: Catarina, cayenne, guajillo, japonés

OTHER NAMES: Bolita, bola, trompo, coban, trompillo
USES: Ground/powdered in sauces, tamales, sausages, casseroles; as a seasoning; toasted or untoasted
SOURCES:
  FRESH: Not used
  DRIED: Imported, found in Mexican food stores, border town markets
  PROCESSED: Probably not imported
  SEEDS: Mexico or specialty seed suppliers.
  CULTIVAR: 'Real Mirasol'

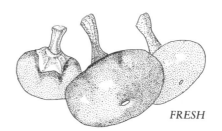

FRESH

DRIED

The Mexican cascabel is a cherry pepper look-alike when it is fresh, but there the resemblance ends. When the ripe fruit dries to a dark reddish-brown color, the skin becomes translucent and the seeds rattle around inside, hence its name *cascabel,* or "jingle bell." The thick-fleshed cherry pepper does not dry satisfactorily. At times the smaller elongate catarina and the larger guajillo, which also dry with a translucent skin and seeds that rattle, are often incorrectly labeled cascabel. This round red pepper may grow erect or pendent. It is cultivated in the Mexican states of Durango, San Luis Potosí, and Coahuila. When ground—seeds and all—the nutty flavor of the roasted cascabel makes a wonderful sauce. Smaller varieties such as bolita (little ball) and bola are made into pickles.

Do not confuse the round cascabel with the smaller, conical 'Cascabella' (see page 92).

CAYENNE
Capsicum annuum var. *annuum* Linné

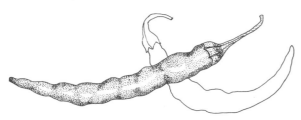

COLOR: Dark green to red

SHAPE: Elongate cylinder, wrinkled, curved; cayenne type

SIZE: 5 to 6 inches long by ½ to ¾ inches wide

PUNGENCY: Hot to very hot, 7 to 8

SUBSTITUTES: Jalapeño, serrano, Thai

OTHER NAMES: A pepper of the cayenne type was one of the first capsicums introduced to the Far East. It has become the most common type of *Capsicum* grown in the world, with different names in every country.

USES: In Creole and Cajun dishes; in Indian, Indonesian, Thai, Pakistani, Hunan, and Szechuan cooking; in meat and vegetable dishes, salad dressings; as a table spice

SOURCES:

FRESH: Farmers' markets, home gardens, and some food stores throughout the country

DRIED: In any ethnic or supermarket spice section, powdered or whole

PROCESSED: Powdered in the spice section of almost any food store; used in some pepper sauces and Cajun and Creole seasonings

SEEDS: Most seed suppliers carry one or more varieties.

AVAILABLE CULTIVARS: 'Cayenne Langer', 'Cay-enne Large Red Thick', 'Cayenne Pickling', 'Golden Cayenne', 'Hades Hot', 'Hot Portugal', 'Japanese Fuschin', 'Jaune Long', 'Long Red', 'Long Slim', 'Mammoth Cayenne', 'Ring of Fire'

The cayenne chilli could be called the Cajun or Creole pepper because it is such an integral part of those cuisines. It has been said this pre-Columbian cultivar probably originated in French Guiana on the northeastern coast of South America and was named for the Cayenne River, but this is very doubtful. The Portuguese obtained it soon after the Discovery, when neither they nor the Spaniards were near the Cayenne River. It was probably growing in Española because it fits the descriptions of the early chroniclers and the picture in Fuchs's herbal. It possibly arrived in Louisiana, soon after Spain took over, via Spanish trade routes from Mexico serving the important port of New Orleans. Spain gained control of New Orleans from France in 1762, after one hundred years of French occupation. The Spanish held sway from 1762 to 1802, and the French and Spanish cuisines melded into a "native born," or Creole, cuisine. In 1800 the migration of French Acadians added a new touch to the local culinary scene, but the cayenne remained a staple. No Creole or Cajun specialty is complete without its special bite.

After the discovery of America, the cayenne was distributed to India and the Orient. This long, curved, sharp-pointed fruit with its wrinkled skin and biting pungency is the fruit type for a group of peppers often called finger or chilli peppers. It ranges in size from 3 to 12 inches in length, with a narrow shoulder. In the United States it is cultivated commercially in Louisiana and is grown in home gardens throughout the country. Although the long, slender, curved fruit is typical, a blocky and shorter type has been developed in recent years. In Mexico peppers of the cayenne type are mirasol/guajillo and de árbol. Although the Far Eastern cultivars have been grown for centuries, they have neither common nor cultivar names (see page 68 for cayenne pepper).

In commercial circles the dried cayenne is known as ginnie pepper.[10] What is sold as powdered cayenne pepper may or may not contain cayenne peppers. It is usually made from one or more very pungent, small red varieties grown in India, Japan, Africa, Louisiana, South Carolina, and Mexico. This is the red chilli powder called for in Indian, Pakistani, and Indonesian recipes. Cayenne pepper has become synonymous with dried chilli powder or packaged "red pepper."

CHERRY
Capsicum annuum var. *annuum* Linné

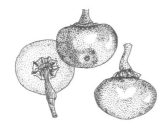

COLOR: Medium green to red

SHAPE: Oblate; cherry type

SIZE: ¾ to 1 inches long by 1¼ to 1½ inches wide

PUNGENCY: Sweet or hot, 0 to 4

SUBSTITUTES: Any pickled pepper

OTHER NAMES: Hot cherry, Hungarian cherry, sweet cherry

USES: In pickles, relishes, jams, salads, condiments; as a garnish

SOURCES:

FRESH: Home gardens, farmers' markets

DRIED: Not used dried

---

10. An African spice, *Afromomum melegueta* or grains of paradise, is the original "ginnie pepper"; however, after the Portuguese introduction of the American cayenne-type pepper to Africa, it was also called Ginnie pepper.

PROCESSED: Pickle section in food markets

SEEDS: Most seed suppliers have at least one cultivar.

AVAILABLE CULTIVARS: 'Bird's Eye', 'Cerise', 'Cherry Jubilee', 'Cherry Sweet', 'Christmas Cherry', 'Red Giant', 'Super Sweet', 'Tom Thumb'

This rotund pepper has been around since before Columbus discovered America. It was portrayed by early herbalists such as Fuchs (1543) and L'Escluse (1611). Its shape is similar to that of a cherry, hence its name. This name is applied to a group or type of pepper that has fruits that are globose or oblate. They can be sweet or hot, large or small, erect or pendent, and are grown as often as ornamentals as they are for fruit. The cherry pepper does not dry satisfactorily and is used almost entirely as a pickled condiment. There are many cherry-type cultivars.

In Mexico the hot cascabel has the outward appearance of a cherry pepper; however, it has very thin flesh, which dries readily and becomes translucent. The cascabel is only used when dried.

CHILTEPÍN (CHILTECPÍN)
Capsicum annuum var. *glabriusculum* (Dunal, 1852)
Heiser & Pickersgill, 1975

COLOR:

FRESH: Green to red, some nearly black; glossy

DRIED: Brownish red

SHAPE: Ovoid

SIZE: ¼ inch long by ¾ inch in diameter

PUNGENCY: Very hot, 8 to 9

SUBSTITUTES: Really nothing, but try cayenne pepper,

Thai peppers, 'Tabasco' peppers (not the sauce)
OTHER NAMES: Amash, amomo, bird, bravo, chilillo,
chilipiquin, chilpaya, chilpequin, chiltipiquín, del
monte, huarahuao, max, piquén, to name a few
USES: Fresh or dried, they are mashed together with
anything on your plate; in table sauces; for seasoning meats, vegetables, soups, and stews
SOURCES:
FRESH: In the lower part of the Southwest, grows
wild in backyards, fence rows, anywhere birds
stop; in the rest of the country, found in some
markets.
DRIED: Ethnic food markets, Native Seeds.
SEARCH (see Source section, page 224), home
gardens
PROCESSED: Some pickled in the Southwest; er-
ratic availability in markets
SEEDS: Native Seeds.SEARCH (see Source section,
page 224); specialty seed houses, friends in the
Southwest; ask your friendly neighborhood
birds to help you

A little dish of these tiny fireballs always stays on
my kitchen counter. I use one in almost everything, from salad dressings to cream sauces, to
kill the blandness. There are many names for this
wild little chilli. Two of the most common ones
are chiltepín for the ovoid type, and chilpequin
for the longer, more acute form. The variously
spelled common name is a corruption of the original Nahuatl (a language spoken by the Aztec
people living in Mexico when Cortés arrived and
still spoken by at least 1½ million people in Mexico) name, *chiltecpín* (pronounced *chill-tech-
peen*) used by pre-Columbian Amerindians.
South Texans call them all chilpequin or chilipe-
quin; however, in Mexico *chiltepín* (pronounced
chill-tey-peen) is used for the more common
ovoid shaped chilli. Previously I have referred to
this semiwild pepper as *Capsicum annuum* var.
aviculare (Dierbach, 1829), D'Arcy and Eshbaugh, 1973, *Phytologia,* 25(6):350. However,
C. annuum var. *glabriusculum* has priority over
var. *aviculare*; therefore, it wins even though I

preferred the commonly used *aviculare,* which
refers to birds.

Many think they have discovered a new pepper when they find a slightly different chiltepín,
but there are so many intergrades in size and
shape and color—some are even black—throughout its range from the American Southwest to
Colombia that there is no use getting excited. To
add to the confusion within this extensive range,
the tiny forms of *C. frutescens* are also commonly
termed bird peppers. The numerous vernacular
names for the chiltepín are applied to both species, depending on geography.

Farmers in the state of Sonora, Mexico are
now cultivating and marketing this semiwild little chilli. As a result, a second domestication is
taking place as evidenced by larger, nondecidu-
ous fruits.

Unlike most chillies, the chiltepín prefers partially shaded to shady locations. It also does well
in pots. I've had the same plant in a big clay
container for over five years. Older plants become quite woody. The difficulty in harvesting
this little fruit, combined with the fact that most
are only found in the wild, makes it *very* expensive, ten dollars or more per pound. But a little
goes a long way, and you have to be quick—the
birds are waiting!

One of the favored ways to use chiltepíns is to
fill a small sauce bottle about three-fourths full
with the whole fruits, then to fill the bottle with
vinegar. Let it sit awhile, then douse vegetables,
soups, or what have you with it. I often use
kitchen sherry or tequila instead of vinegar for a
mellow sauce; refill as needed. When cooking
with them, crush the peppers in a mortar or a
custard cup and add a little water; use this pepper water to season with instead of throwing
whole peppers into your stew. It is less of a surprise for the guest who might get a whole pepper
in a mouthful of stew. Use it to season roasts,
turkey, and capon before cooking them by making holes in the meat with a larding tool or ice
pick and poking chiltepíns deep inside.

For deeper insight into the bird chilli, read Gary Nabhan's chapter "For the Birds: The Red-Hot Mother of Chiles" in his delightful, award-winning book *Gathering the Desert.*

'CUBANELLE'
Capsicum annuum var. *annuum* Linné

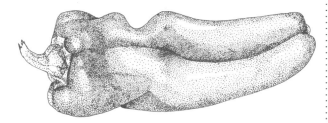

COLOR: Pale yellow-green, to orange, to red; at times all those colors at once; glossy

SHAPE: Elongated cylinder, undulating, sunken apex; Cuban or ethnic type

SIZE: 6 inches long by 2¼ inches wide

PUNGENCY: Sweet, 0

SUBSTITUTES: Red, yellow, or orange bell (green, if hard pressed); banana; 'Szegedi' or any sweet ethnic type

OTHER NAMES: Italian pepper

USES: Always used fresh; fried, in salads, as a vegetable, stuffed, in any recipe calling for a bell pepper

SOURCES:

FRESH: Home gardens, farmer's markets, some ethnic food stores on the East Coast

DRIED: Cannot be air-dried; perhaps can be dehydrated as you would bells

PROCESSED: Not processed

SEEDS: Commercially available, but you may need to search the catalogs.

AVAILABLE CULTIVARS: 'Biscayne', 'Cubanelle', 'Cubanelle PS'

The name 'Cubanelle' is derived from "Cuba"; however, it is thought to be of Italian origin, having been introduced to America in 1958. With the addition of the Italian diminutive ending *-nelle,* the meaning is presumably "little Cuban." Possibly, the Italians first acquired it from Cuba or vice versa. This large-fruited, very colorful cultivar of the wax type is characterized by a thick, sweet flesh that is much more flavorful but not quite so thick as those of the bell type. The 'Cubanelle', and other peppers of the ethnic type such as 'Shepherd', 'Laparie', 'Sweet Hungarian', 'Romanian', 'Szegedi', and 'Gypsy', have long been popular where there are large populations of people of Italian or Slavic descent; recently they have gained considerably in general popularity. It is delicious when used for the same dishes as the less flavorful green bell pepper and will become more readily available with public demand.

Italian cooks cut this pepper into ½- to 1-inch strips, which they sauté in olive oil. More olive oil and garlic are added to the cooled pepper strips. Covered bowls of this are always kept in the refrigerators of Italian homes for snacks on French-type bread or for sandwiches at suppertime (see the recipe on page 136).

DATIL
Capsicum chinense Jacquin

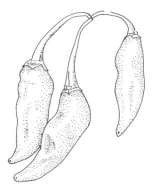

COLOR: Yellow-green to golden yellow

SHAPE: Elongated with a slight neck, pointed apex, shallowly wrinkled; long wax type

SIZE: 2 inches long by ¾ inches wide in the center

PUNGENCY: Very hot to very, very hot, 10

SUBSTITUTES: Habanero, Scotch bonnet

OTHER NAMES: Mindoran

USES: In sauces, relishes; as a seasoning

SOURCES:

FRESH: Home gardens, farmer's markets, food stores in and around St. Augustine, Florida

DRIED: Heat-dried fruits available packaged in St. Augustine, Florida, area

PROCESSED: Numerous sauces and relishes bottled in St. Augustine, Florida, area

SEEDS: From growers in St. Augustine, Florida, area

This little-known pepper has the same potential as the 'Tabasco' and probably originated in much the same fashion. Like the 'Tabasco', which came to Louisiana in the 1840s from Mexico, and through isolation and selection, it became a cultivar so different from its original Mexican parent that no *Capsicum frutescens* variety like it occurs in Mexico today, and there is no *C. chinense* variety like the datil in the West Indies at the present time. It is thought the first dátil was brought to the United States from the West Indies even earlier than the 'Tabasco', but it has remained in and around the area to which it was originally introduced. There it still awaits widespread recognition.

In 1763, after two hundred years of occupation and trade, Spain lost her Florida territory to England. Four or five years later, Dr. Andrew Turnbull brought fourteen hundred indentured laborers, mostly male but a few with families, to his plantation in New Smyrna, Florida, from Greece, Italy, Corsica, and English (formerly Spanish) Minorca. Five hundred died during the first five months, and at the end of nine years only six hundred of the original group were living.

Tradition has the datil pepper being brought to St. Augustine, Florida, around 1776 when the surviving Minorcans fled to that city to escape the abuses at Turnbull's plantation. It is my educated guess that the Minorcans did not bring the datil with them to America because *Capsicum chinense* did not grow in the Mediterranean at that time (or now, for that matter); instead, the pepper appeared in Florida as a result of the convenient and long-standing trade in slaves and other goods between St. Augustine and the West Indies—Havana in particular—during the Colonial period (1565–1821) or shortly thereafter. Though they probably didn't bring them to this country, I do not hesitate to credit the Minorcans with giving the new pepper its name. In the Minorcan language, a Catalan Spanish derivative, *datil* means "date." Mediterranean peoples knew the date because it had been introduced to that region by the Phoenicians long ago. It is unlikely the Spaniards resident in colonial Florida would have been familiar with dates, nor would the African slaves brought from the West Indies, most of whom were of Mande-speaking tribes from the Guinea region, to whom the word *datil* was alien. The original Minorcans would have had to have named it because their American-born children had not seen dates on trees. Unless further research provides some additional documentation, its precise origin will remain clouded by the haze of time. However the original Minorcan immigrants pronounced *datil* when they named it, today Floridians call it "dat-el," rhyming with "that."

About forty to fifty commercial growers cultivate small plots of datils, making it the first *Capsicum chinense* to be grown for profit in the United States (though recently commercial farmers have begun growing habaneros). This commercial production has been going on for at least seventy years.

The wrinkled, golden little fruits look somewhat like fresh dates while they are still on the palm tree, hence their name. Like its cousin, the habanero, the datil is quite aromatic and very, very *picante*. A little goes a long way.

The datil is used by food processors in the

green state because the fully ripe fruit will not keep more than two or three days; consequently almost everyone uses it that way. However, it is much more fragrant and flavorful when golden. For that reason I'd recommend growing some of your own. Try it, you'll like it.

DE ÁRBOL
Cadpsicum annuum var. *annuum* Linné

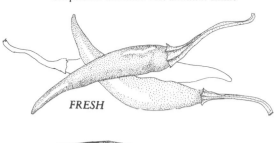

FRESH

DRIED

COLOR:
  FRESH: Green to red
  DRIED: Bright red
SHAPE: Elongate conical, narrow shoulders, pointed apex; cayenne type
SIZE: 3 inches long by ¾ inch wide
PUNGENCY: Hot, 7
SUBSTITUTES: Cayenne, chiltepín, japonés, dried Thai
OTHER NAMES: Alfilerillo, bravo, cola de rata, cuauhchilli, ginnie pepper, pico de pájaro
USES: In table sauces
SOURCES:
  FRESH: Seldom used fresh; found in home gardens in the United States
  DRIED: Found packaged in the spice section of many supermarkets and ethnic food stores
  PROCESSED: Not processed
  SEEDS: Catalogs of specialty seed companies; from packaged dried fruits

This very narrow, curved chilli keeps its bright red color when dried. It is used with the seeds, as

all chillies are in Thailand. Although it is not very flavorful, it is very, very *picante,* making it desirable for sauces or as a capsaicin pickup with less pungent but more savory varieties.

'FLORAL GEM'
Capsicum annuum var. *annuum* Linné

COLOR: Yellow to orange to bright red; glossy; calyx yellow
SHAPE: Elongated cylinder, indented blossom end; wax type
SIZE: 1½ inches long by 1 inch wide at shoulder
PUNGENCY: Hot, 6 to 7
SUBSTITUTES: 'Cascabella'
OTHER NAMES: None
USES: Pickled; fresh in table sauces
SOURCES:
  FRESH: Home garden, farmer's markets; uncommon
  DRIED: Not used dried
  PROCESSED: Pickled in food stores; supply irregular
  SEEDS: Hard to locate, try catalogs of specialty seed houses.
  AVAILABLE CULTIVARS: 'Floral Gem Jumbo', 'Floral Grande'

Even though it is bright red when mature, 'Floral Gem' is known as one of the yellow wax types because it is processed only in the yellow stage. Home gardeners, of course, can use it in any of its color phases. The cultivar was first released in 1921. Later, it was one of the chillies used to develop the 'Caloro', which came out in 1966.

The plant's spreading, almost vinelike habit is responsible for its name. It is the only commercially grown yellow annual chilli with an indented end and is processed by B. F. Trappey and Sons of New Iberia, Louisiana, for their brand Torrido Chili Peppers. Unfortunately, these are not always on the shelf. Trappey—now owned by the McIlhenney Company—provides the growers with seed, but it is difficult to get them gathered because pickers no longer care to pick the small peppers. If you are lucky enough to find a jar, use them in salads or chopped and cooked with meats, sauces, or beans.

'FRESNO'
Capsicum annuum var. *annuum* Linné

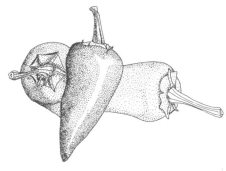

COLOR: Yellowish green (never yellow) to red; glossy
SHAPE: Conical, pointed apex; wax type
SIZE: 3 inches long by 1½ inches wide at shoulder
PUNGENCY: Hot, 5 to 7
SUBSTITUTES: Jalapeño, 'Santa Fe Grande', serrano
OTHER NAMES: Hot chili
USES: Used green, as a seasoning, in sauces; pickled, same uses as for the jalapeño
SOURCES:
  FRESH: Home gardens, farmer's markets, some food stores in the Southwest
  DRIED: Never dried, flesh too thick
  PROCESSED: Pickled; but not found regularly in food markets
  SEEDS: Catalogs of a few specialty seed houses
AVAILABLE CULTIVARS: 'Fresno', 'Fresno Grande'

This very glossy, medium-size wax type that stands erect amid dark green foliage was released in 1952 by Clarence Brown, who named it 'Fresno' in honor of Fresno, California. It is used only fresh because the thickness of the flesh precludes drying. Its resistance to tobacco mosaic, a disease fatal to peppers, caused it to be used to develop 'Caloro' in 1966. A seed company in turn used 'Caloro' to develop 'Fresno Grande'. 'Fresno' turns a bright red when ripe, but is used in the green stage. Off the bush the mature red fruits look very much like the ripe 'Santa Fe Grande'; however, 'Fresno' is green or red, never orange or yellow, and 'Sante Fe Grande' is never green. In the Southwest, where it is grown, it is often called hot chili. 'Fresno' should not be overlooked as an ornamental in beds or pots.

Brown also developed the smaller conical 'Cascabella' (see page 92).

GUAJILLO, DRIED; MIRASOL, FRESH
Capsicum annuum var. *annuum* Linné

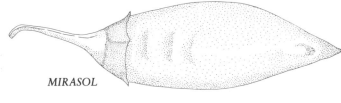

MIRASOL

GUAJILLO

COLOR:
  FRESH: Green to red to brownish red
  DRIED: Translucent reddish brown
SHAPE: Elongate conical, pointed apex; cayenne type

SIZE: 3 to 5 inches long by ½ to 1¼ inches wide, very variable

PUNGENCY: Hot, 4 to 5

SUBSTITUTES:

FRESH: Serrano, jalapeño, Thai

DRIED: Cascabel, New Mexican chile

OTHER NAMES:

FRESH: Miracielo

DRIED: Cascabel, puya, pullia, puya, travieso, trompa, perhaps costeño and chilhuacle

USES:

FRESH: In table sauces; used like the serrano

DRIED: In sauces and seasonings; for color

SOURCES:

FRESH: Home gardens; not yet available in markets in the United States

DRIED: Primarily in the Southwest or in ethnic food stores

PROCESSED: Not processed

SEEDS: Catalogs of specialty seed companies.

AVAILABLE CULTIVARS: 'La Blanca 74', 'Loreto 74', 'Real Mirasol'

The mirasol/guajillo is one of the most variable chillies. Not only can the thin-skinned fruit vary from small to large, smooth to wrinkled, erect to pendent, the plant is also quite inconstant in its growth patterns. Next to the ancho, the guajillo is the most used dried chilli in Mexico, and there is good reason. The flavor is very distinctive and only small amounts of the dried fruits are required to both flavor and color the dishes prepared with them. The coloring quality is excellent.

Mirasol means "it is looking at the sun," yet most of the fruits are pendent, except in the earliest stages (a very variable characteristic). Since this cultivar is pre-Columbian in origin, it may well be that the attachment position has changed from erect to pendent through selection for larger, heavier fruit over the years while the name stayed the same. Gourds (*guaje*) are used for rattles; therefore the dried form of this chilli, with seeds that rattle when shaken, are called *guajillo*,

or "little gourd." One of the most used capsicums in Peru is known there by the name mirasol. However, it is not the same as the Mexican cultivar described here but rather is a larger fruit whose species identity is not known to me—probably not *Capsicum annuum* var. *annuum*. Amal Naj, a journalist friend from India, told me he knew a chilli in India called the same thing. It's an obvious name for a fruit that points toward the sun.

The guajillo is often incorrectly called *cascabel* (jingle bells); however, the true cascabel is a globular-shaped chilli with a completely different flavor and coloring quality. Guajillos are used in stews and soups, as a condiment with chicken dishes, and in *chilaquiles,* a traditional Mexican dish using stale tortillas. They are wonderful for chili con carne or any dish that you want to make a rich, red color. There are two other very localized chillies in Mexico that may be only regional variations of the mirasol/guajillo—the costeño and chilhuacqui. Both are used dried in the same manner as the guajillo. I grow my own guajillos, and let them dry on the bush.

HABANERO
Capsicum chinense Jacquin

COLOR: Green to yellow-orange, or orange, or orange-red

SHAPE: Round to oblong, undulating, pointed apex; habanero type

SIZE: 1 to 2½ inches long by 1 to 2 inches wide

PUNGENCY: Very, very hot, 10+

SUBSTITUTES: Nothing can match its flavor and aroma, but try 5 jalapeños for each habanero

OTHER NAMES: Congo, bonda man Jacques, bonnie, ginnie, Guinea pepper, pimenta do chiero, siete caldos, Scotch bonnet, and pimenta do cheiro (in Brazil)

USES: In table sauces, cooked sauces; as a seasoning

SOURCES:

FRESH: In some markets on the East Coast catering to Caribbean people, home gardens; increasingly in supermarkets and specialty food stores

DRIED: Does not dry well on the bush. The dried ones being sold have only heat; the flavor that distinguishes the fresh habanero is all gone

PROCESSED: Bottled sauces, canned; in specialty shops and some supermarkets

SEEDS: Catalogs of some specialty seed companies; not easily found

Wow! Handle the habanero, meaning "from Havana or *La Habana*," with care! Some folks equate the Yucatecan habanero and West Indian Scotch bonnet, as I did in the past, but they are not the same cultivar, though they are the same species. The habanero is consistently lantern shaped, while the other golden pepper has no neck and is regularly inverted at the apex when mature, giving it the form of a Scotsman's tam-o'-shanter, or "bonnet," hence its name. The pointed apex of a glossy, smooth, mature habanero is never inverted into a basal fold to produce the appearance of the Scotsman's headpiece. There are some varieties of *Capsicum chinense* and *C. baccatum* var. *pendulum* that have the inverted shape of a Scotch bonnet when they are pale yellow-green and immature, but they don't stay that way. These balloon out when mature into a somewhat crinkly, lobed, blocky fruit the size and color of a golden habanero. Although called Scotch bonnet and habanero, they are too irregular and crinkly to be either; nevertheless, people unfamiliar with *C. chinense* call them by those names because they recognize a similarity. There is also an ornamental *C. annum* var. *annum*, sometimes called the squash pepper, that maintains a somewhat similar shape through all stages.

To add to the confusion, there is yet another *Capsicum chinense*, the West Indian hot, a habanero type. This blocky pepper is always red and not quite as aromatic and flavorful as its glowing orange cousin in Yucatán, yet it is often referred to as a red habanero. In fact, in a West Indian farmer's field of mixed peppers there can be found several habanero look-alikes.

Except for *Capsicum pubescens* in a few highland areas in Mexico and Central America, the lantern-shaped habanero holds the undisputed claim of being one of the hottest chillies in North America. It was developed and grows in Yucatán, Mexico, but there are other habanero types throughout the Caribbean, most of which are incorrectly called habanero. After *Peppers* was published, I learned about another *C. chinense*, the datil, which has been said to have grown for more than 100 years in the St. Augustine, Florida, area and is cultivated commercially to a limited extent there (see page 71). It is probably an equal to the habanero in pungency. Some brave soul will have to make a comparative test of the datil, habanero, Scotch bonnet, West Indian hot, and *C. pubescens*. The habanero is highly aromatic, with an unmistakable flavor. Do wear gloves when working with these. I especially like to cook black bean soup with a habanero, and it is an agreeable companion to lamb in stews and curries. A fresh table sauce made with chopped habaneros, lime juice, and salt is a staple throughout the Caribbean.

Habaneros can be grown in home gardens; however, the germination period is quite long. It requires a warm, moist environment to produce a compact plant filled with clusters of glowing orange lanterns. A sight to behold, the habanero is well worth the wait, both aesthetically and gastronomically.

JALAPEÑO
Capsicum annuum var. *annuum* Linné

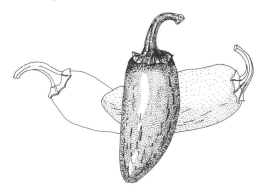

COLOR: Bright to deep blackish green; matures red

SHAPE: Cylindrical, blunt apex; jalapeño type

SIZE: 3 inches long by 1½ inches wide

PUNGENCY: Hot to very hot, according to season, soil conditions, and state of maturity, 1 to 5 +

SUBSTITUTES: 'Caloro', 'Caribe', 'Fresno', 'Santa Fe Grande', serrano

OTHER NAMES: Acorchado, bola, bolita, candelaria, cuaresmeño, gorda, huachinango, jarocho, mora, morita

USES: In condiments, sauces, soups, stews, meat and vegetable dishes, appetizers, desserts; as a garnish

SOURCES:

FRESH: Most supermarkets (it's becoming more readily available throughout the United States; although some commercial growers in the Southwest raise jalapeños, most are imported from Mexico), home gardens

DRIED: Will not air-dry, must be smoked. Smoked peppers are called chipotles, and when chipotles are canned with vinegar they are *adobado* (page 104).

PROCESSED: Canned sliced or whole, pickled (*en escabeche*), prepared with other canned or frozen foods; in cheeses, sauces, candies, etc.

SEEDS: Most seed suppliers will have at least one cultivar.

AVAILABLE CULTIVARS: 'Early Jalapeno', 'Espinal-teco', 'Jalapa', 'Jalapeno M', 'Jaloro' (yellow), 'Jarocho', 'Jumbo Jal', 'Mitla', 'Papaloapan', 'Peludo', 'Pinalteco', 'Rayado', 'San Andres', '76104', 'TAM Mild Jalapeno-1'

It is probably safe to say that the jalapeño is the best known chilli of all in North America, and its popularity and celebrity continue to grow. A jalapeño even soared to outer space on an early manned space flight, becoming our first "astro-pod." This fiery fruit originated in Mexico and was named for the city of Jalapa in the state of Veracruz. In Mexico only the pickled form of this cultivar is called jalapeño; the fresh green fruits are called *cuaresmeño* (Lenten chilli) and *candelaria* (candlemas chilli). A shorter, fat variety is known as *chile gordo* (fat chilli). The flesh of the jalapeño is too thick to air-dry satisfactorily; therefore, the ripe red ones are dried (*ahumado*) by smoking in an oven similar to a Chinese smoke oven. This smoked jalapeño is called *chipotle,* as is any pepper when it has been dried by smoking. "Chipotle" is the common spelling for *chilpotle,* which is from the Nahuatl word *pochilli,* or "smoked chile." The chipotle is sold dried or pickled (*adobado*) in cans. Chipotles are much hotter than green jalapeños because the amount of capsaicin in all peppers increases with maturity.

The skin of the jalapeño is usually marked with corky striations. The food industry has found that consumers want jalapeños to have these lines and will pick striated ones over the unlined fruits even though they have no effect on the flavor. There are more than a dozen named jalapeño cultivars, including one out of which researchers at Texas A & M University have bred most of the heat. The idea behind that new cultivar was to provide a processor with a neutral jalapeño so a specific, controlled amount of capsaicin could be added, thereby regulating the degree of pungency in order to be able to label the product accurately—mild, medium, hot. The only problem is that no grower will plant a tame jalapeño. Obviously, the public likes to play jalapeño roulette.

Store fresh jalapeños in the refrigerator in heavy plastic zip-lock bags or tightly closed jars from which all air has been expelled. They freeze well. Before freezing, blanch for 2 minutes; this helps preserve the capsaicin; then spread them in a flat pan and freeze. When frozen, bag them loosely, seal well, and use as needed. Dried chipotles can be stored in tightly closed plastic bags in a cool, dry place.

Jalapeños can be pickled and canned Mexican style (*en escabeche*) with vinegar, oil, and spices or in the American style without spices. If you have to substitute a pickled jalapeño when a recipe calls for a canned or fresh one, you must rinse out the vinegar lest you change the flavor of the dish.

NEW MEXICAN CHILE (ANAHEIM)
Capsicum annuum var. *annuum* Linné

COLOR:
  FRESH: Bright green to red
  DRIED: Brownish red
SHAPE: Elongate, flattened, tapering to a blunt point; New Mexican/Anaheim type
SIZE: 7 to 10 inches long by 1¾ to 2 inches wide
PUNGENCY: Mild to hot, depending on cultivar, 1 to 4

SUBSTITUTES: Poblano for fresh, ancho or guajillo for dried
OTHER NAMES: Anaheim, California long green chile, chilacate, chile college, chile colorado, chile de ristra, chile verde, 'Chimayo', 'Hatch' long green/red chile, 'New Mexico No. 9', pasado, and many other cultivars. Frequently, packaged dried fruits are incorrectly labeled guajillo
USES: Stuffed (*relleno*); in soups, stews, sauces, casseroles; fried; as a garnish; in soufflés, etc., as well as for decoration
SOURCES:
  FRESH: Most food stores in the Southwest, but becoming more available throughout the country
  DRIED: Same as for fresh.
  PROCESSED: In the spice section of food markets; sold as pizza pepper, red pepper flakes, powdered (sometimes as paprika and also in commercial chili powder), as well as pure; also sold as canned green chiles, whole or chopped
  SEEDS: Most seed suppliers will have one or more cultivars, such as 'Anaheim', 'Anaheim M', 'Anaheim TMR 23', 'Big Jim', 'California', 'Chimayo', 'Colorado', 'Coronado', 'Eclipse', 'Española Improved', 'New Mexico No. 9', 'NuMex', 'Red Chile', 'R-Naky', 'Sandia' (hot), 'Sunrise', 'Sunset', 'TAM Mild Chile', 'TMR 23', etc.

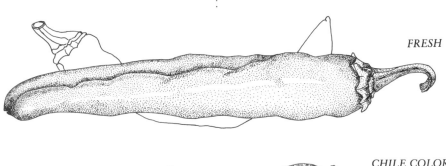

FRESH

*CHILE COLORADO
(DRIED)*

This is the beautiful long green or red pepper that originated in New Mexico. The ancestor of this much-used cultivar was probably brought to New Mexico from Mexico in 1597, when Captain General Don Juan de Oñate colonized that territory for Spain.[11] In 1896, almost three hundred years later, a California rancher named Emilio Ortega, who had been raising cattle in New Mexico, took some of the local pepper seeds with him when he returned to Oxnard, California. He then started a pepper cannery in Anaheim, California. The first New Mexican chile cultivar developed from these seeds was named 'Anaheim', and is of the cayenne type. Some consider the New Mexican chile type (same as Anaheim) a type apart from the cayenne.

Meanwhile, back in New Mexico, Dr. Fabian Garcia was working with fourteen strains of a similar pepper. Of the fourteen strains being studied, number nine proved to be the favorite. In 1917 Garcia released the 'Improved No. 9', which became the most widely grown long green/red pepper for many years to come. Today there are many cultivars. After the fall harvest the bright red strings of the mature fruits are hung to dry. These *ristras* have virtually become the symbol of the region, where they are not only consumed in enormous quantities but are also celebrated in art, song, and pageantry.

Several years ago, the scientists of the National Pepper Conference recommended that the official name be designated as the long green/red chile, instead of calling the pepper by one of the many cultivar names or the Anaheim type. This did not satisfy the New Mexican growers, producers, and pepper fanciers, who wanted it to be known as the New Mexican chile. The New Mexicans did not stop until they got that designation into the *Congressional Record* in Washington, D.C. So it must be official, and hereafter various cultivars will be called the New Mexican chile type.

Unless very young and tender fruits are available, the fresh fruits must be roasted and peeled before using. In the fall, throughout the Southwest, you will see roadside chile roasters being patronized by the New Mexican chile lovers as they prepare to stock their freezers with the new fall crop. You can't believe the amount those folks consume. Select firm, bright-colored, unwrinkled fresh fruits and clean, pliable dried ones. Producers have begun recently to dry the green fruits by smoking them, a process that gives them a distinctive flavor.

The fresh green chiles are dehydrated after being roasted or smoked to make a product with a flavor completely different from other chile flavors. Called *pasados* or *chile pasados,* they are rehydrated (page 99) and used in stews and sauces.

The most popular dish prepared with the New Mexican chile is *chiles rellenos* in which the chiles are filled with cheese, dipped in a batter, and fried. Although this is the most commonly used pepper in the Southwest, it has not played a significant part on the Mexican food menu in Mexico or Texas; however, interest in it is growing.

Store fresh New Mexican chiles in the refrigerator for immediate use, and freeze or dry them for future use, but DO NOT attempt to put up this nonacid vegetable at home except in vinegar- and salt-based relishes and sauces—to do otherwise would be risking botulism (see pages 196–198 for a description of methods).

---

11. New Mexicans do not like to credit Oñate with introducing peppers to New Mexico because he was a Spanish Creole. Perhaps they are not aware that his wife was Mestizo, the granddaughter of the conquistador Cortés and the great-granddaughter of the Indian chieftain Montezuma, a remarkable lineage.

PASILLA, DRIED; CHILACA, FRESH
Capsicum annuum var. *annuum* Linné

COLOR:

FRESH: Dark blackish green ripening to dark brown

DRIED: A warm black

SHAPE: Elongate, flattened, irregular, wrinkled, pointed apex; New Mexican chile/Anaheim type

SIZE: 6 to 12 inches long by ¾ to 1¾ inches wide

PUNGENCY: Medium to hot, 3 to 4

SUBSTITUTES:

FRESH: Poblano

DRIED: New Mexican chile, poblano-mulato

OTHER NAMES:

DRIED: Chile negro/black chilli, chile de Mexico, chile para deshebrar, quernillo, pasa, prieto

USES:

FRESH: In sauces; as a vegetable after charring and peeling

DRIED: In table sauces; as a garnish and condiment in soups; as an essential ingredient in *mole* and other cooked sauces

SOURCES:

FRESH: Probably not found outside Mexico; home gardens

DRIED: Many supermarkets in the Southwest, some ethnic food stores

PROCESSED: Not processed

SEEDS: Catalogs of specialty seed houses.

AVAILABLE CULTIVARS: 'Apaseo' and 'Pabellón 1'

This long, narrow, curved pepper with its dark chocolate color is very distinctive. In Spanish such a brownish-black color is termed *achocolatado*—appropriately, "chocolate colored." The brown color results from the mixing of green and red pigments when the plant retains the green chlorophyll into the mature stage, at which time red pigments are produced. This pepper dries into a very wrinkled fruit the color of a raisin, consequently it is called pasilla—the diminutive of *pasa* (raisin). The fresh form of this variety is known as *chile chilaca*, which derives from the Nahuatl *ácatl*, meaning "gray hair" or "old," a good description of the long, wrinkled, bent form.

There is too much confusion over the name of such a uniquely formed and colored chilli. In Baja California and the northwestern Mexican states, the name *pasilla* is given to the much wider and shorter ancho and mulato. Unfortunately, this practice has carried over into southern California, where I found them being sold in the fabulous Tianguis Latin American food markets as *chile negro*, while the mulato and ancho bore the name *pasilla*. It would be helpful if Californians would not perpetuate a misnomer begun in Mex-

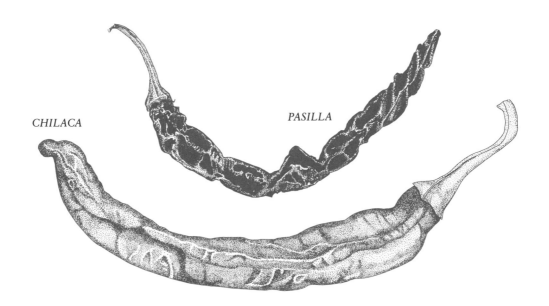

CHILACA

PASILLA

ico. At Tianguis I was told the labels bore the name by which the grower called the pepper whether it was correct or incorrect. To further complicate the issue, a Oaxacan chilli with the same color but an entirely different appearance and flavor is called pasilla. That Oaxacan pasilla is very likely the progenitor of the long green/red New Mexican chile that is said to have had the pasilla as an ancestor. In the Oaxaca area the true pasilla is known as *pasilla de Mexico,* while the local cultivar is the *pasilla de Oaxaca* or just *pasilla.*

The chilaca is used primarily in the central and northwestern regions in Mexico. The more popular dried pasilla, with its rich, mellow flavor, is desirable in cooked sauces, or toasted and crumbled, or ground into a table sauce.

Little is known of the origin of this sweet cultivar, from which only the green fruits are used to make the pickled pepper that is always found in Italian salads. The name comes from the Italian word for chilli, *peperone.* It was probably developed from a pepper of Italian origin, but we don't know for certain. It is grown in Louisiana and some of the other southern states. There is a very similar yellow form, 'Golden Greek', originally grown in Greece and used pickled in the same manner.

PIMENTO
Capsicum annuum var. *annuum* Linné

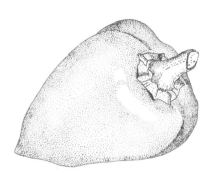

COLOR: Green to red; glossy
SHAPE: Conical, pointed apex, often heart-shaped; pimento type
SIZE: 4½ inches long by 3½ inches wide at shoulder
PUNGENCY: Sweet, 0
SUBSTITUTES: Red bell, tomato pepper
OTHER NAMES: Pimiento
USES: Fresh, in salads or in any recipe calling for bell; canned, in casseroles, cheese spreads, as a garnish, to stuff olives
SOURCES:
  FRESH: Home gardens, farmer's markets, occasionally in food markets
  DRIED: Not dried
  PROCESSED: Canned, common in supermarkets
  SEEDS: Catalogs of most large seed companies.

'PEPPERONCINI'
Capsicum annuum var. *annuum* Linné

COLOR: Green to red
SHAPE: Elongated cylinder, pointed apex, wrinkled; New Mexican chile/Anaheim type
SIZE: 3 to 5 inches long by ¾ inches wide at shoulder
PUNGENCY: Sweet to mild, 0 to 1
SUBSTITUTES: 'Golden Greek'
OTHER NAMES: None
USES: Green fruit pickled with salads
SOURCES:
  FRESH: Home gardens, farmer's markets
  DRIED: Not dried
  PROCESSED: Pickled, in most food stores
  SEEDS: Most large seed company catalogs, specialty seed suppliers.
  AVAILABLE CULTIVARS: 'Golden Greek', 'Pepperoncini'

AVAILABLE CULTIVARS: 'Bighart', 'Canada Cheese', 'Mississippi Nemaheart', 'Perfection', 'Perfection-D', 'Pimiento-L', 'Pimiento Select', 'Sunnybrook', 'Truhart', 'Truhart Perfection', 'Yellow Cheese'

Most of the commercially grown pimentos are found in the South and in California. The name comes from the Spanish word for pepper, *pimiento*. The second "i" was dropped when the Georgia Pimento Growers Association adopted that spelling for this sweet, heart-shaped fruit; however, many processors still use "pimiento." Its aromatic flavor and distinctive red color make it highly desirable. When red bell peppers or the tomato peppers are canned, their color is not the alluring, bright red of the pimento. It is peeled before canning, but fresh ones can just be sliced or chopped for salads or as a garnish.

POBLANO, FRESH; ANCHO AND MULATO, DRIED
Capsicum annuum var. *annuum* Linné

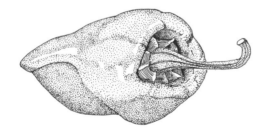

POBLANO
COLOR: Dark green; matures to red or brown
SHAPE: Tapered to a blunt point, wrinkled; ancho type
SIZE: 4 inches long by 2½ inches wide
PUNGENCY: Mild to hot, 3
SUBSTITUTES: 'Mexi-bell', New Mexican chile
OTHER NAMES: Ancho, chile para rellenar, joto, mulato, pasilla
USES: Stuffed (*relleno*); as strips (*rajas*); in soups and sauces; roast, seed, and peel before using

SOURCES:
FRESH: Food stores throughout the Southwest. More food stores in other parts of the country are carrying it in the imported produce section
DRIED: See ancho and mulato (page 83)
PROCESSED: Not processed
SEEDS: Specialty seed suppliers. Poblano does not always produce typical fruit in the United States, except in the area around Oxnard, California.
AVAILABLE CULTIVARS: 'Ancho', 'Ancho Esmeralda', 'Chorro', 'Miahuateco', 'Mulato Roque', 'Verdeño'

The poblano, or *chile poblano,* as it is known in Mexico, originated near the city of Pueblo, southeast of Mexico City; hence its name *poblano,* or "pepper from Pueblo." It is one of the most popular cultivars in that country. The fruit is undulating and more or less triangular in shape. The flesh is moderately thick but not as thick as the bell pepper; therefore it dries well. Several similar cultivars are known as poblanos when in the very dark, dusky green immature stage, but when they are fully ripe and dried they each have another name. These are the ancho, mulato, 'Miahuateco', and 'Chorro'. These cultivars vary from a mild to medium pungency. Growers have found that in the United States the poblanos seldom attain their typical form; consequently, those found in our markets are virtually all imported from Mexico and are not always readily available. When they are, select firm, unwrinkled, rich dark green fruits.

In Baja and southern California, both the dried forms and the fresh green fruit are incorrectly known as pasilla (see page 80); however, the flavors and shapes are different. In that area, if a stuffed pepper recipe calls for a pasilla, it probably means poblano because the true chilaca/pasilla is too long and "skinny" to be stuffed. This is very confusing, for a true fresh chilaca/pasilla cannot be substituted for a fresh poblano.

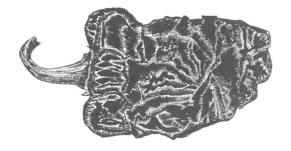

ANCHO

COLOR: Dark brown, brick red after soaking
SHAPE: Flattened, wrinkled; ancho type
SIZE: 4 inches long by 2½ inches wide
PUNGENCY: Mild to rather hot, 3 to 4
SUBSTITUTES: Mulato, New Mexican chile, pasilla
OTHER NAMES: Chile colorado (in Texas), mulato, pasilla
USES: In sauces for enchiladas, chili con carne, *adobados* (meat prepared with a sour seasoning paste in *adobado*), commercial chili powders
SOURCES:
  FRESH: See poblano (page 82)
  DRIED: Most food stores in the Southwest, ethnic specialty stores
  PROCESSED: Sold as chili powder in spice section
  SEEDS: Specialty seed suppliers.
  AVAILABLE CULTIVARS: 'Chorro', 'Esmeralda', 'Flor de Pabellon', 'Verdeño'

In Mexico the unripe green pepper is never referred to as *ancho* (which means "wide"), but in the United States many growers and seed suppliers call it ancho from the seed on, making no distinction between the fresh and dried state. The dried ancho is a type of poblano that is a deep red when fully mature and dries to a very wrinkled, blackish brown, flattened form. After it has been soaked, it becomes brick red. Soaking for more than an hour is usually unnecessary and will reduce the flavor and food value of the pepper, as the nutrients dissolve in the water. Reserve/save the soaking water for sauces and soups (see the remarks under mulato, next column).

The three robust dried Mexican *chiles*—ancho, mulato, and pasilla—are ground separately and made into a paste, which is sold in little blocks that look rather like baking chocolate. This paste is known as *chile pisado*—not *pasado* (see page 79).

MULATO

COLOR: Dark brown
SHAPE: Flattened, wrinkled; ancho type
SIZE: 4 inches long by 2½ inches wide
PUNGENCY: Mild to hot, 3 to 4
SUBSTITUTES: Ancho, pasilla
OTHER NAMES: Ancho, pasilla
USES: In sauces like *mole poblano*
SOURCES:
  FRESH: See poblano (page 82)
  DRIED: Imported from Mexico, sold in food stores throughout the Southwest, usually in mixed lots with ancho
  PROCESSED: Canned mole sauce now available where Mexican products are sold
  SEEDS: A few specialty seed suppliers carry it, but the poblano/mulato does not produce typical fruit when grown in the United States.
  AVAILABLE CULTIVARS: 'Mulato V-2', 'Mulato Roque'

The mulato (a person of mixed white and black ancestry; in Spanish, "tawny colored") ripens to a deep chocolate brown color, which is called *achocolatado*. Like the ancho, it also becomes blackish brown, very wrinkled, and flattened when it is dried. The two are difficult to distinguish until soaked; the mulato retains its brown color after soaking, while the ancho rehydrates to red. The chocolatelike flavor of the mulato is sweeter, richer, and a little more pungent than that of the ancho. The ancho, mulato, and true pasilla are ground into a paste and sold as *chile pisado,* and one square is equal to one tablespoon of powdered dried chillies.

Because the dried anchos and mulatos are so

difficult to distinguish before soaking, they are often used interchangeably. Not only are they difficult to identify in the marketplace, but the confusion is compounded in Baja and southern California, where both the dried forms and the fresh green fruit are mistakenly referred to as pasilla (page 80). In that area caution must be used in recipes calling for pasilla; they very likely mean ancho or mulato, and it will make a difference in the final taste of the dish.

Select clean, flexible, insect-free fruits. Store in an airtight container in a cool, dry place. Wash and soak in boiling water for no more than 1 hour before use. Longer soaking removes both flavor and nutrients. Reserve the soaking water for use in sauces and soups.

ROCOTO
Capsicum pubescens Ruiz & Pavon

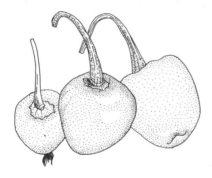

COLOR: Green to golden yellow or red

SHAPE: Globose to oblate

SIZE: 1½ to 2 inches long by 1½ to 2 inches wide

PUNGENCY: Undetermined, but very, very, very hot, 10 +

SUBSTITUTES: Nothing really, but try 1½ to 2 habaneros or 6 to 8 jalapeños for 1 rocoto

OTHER NAMES: Caballo in Guatemala and bordering Chiapas, Mexico; canario, locoto, manzana, and perón in Mexico; in Costa Rica it is also manzana, but more often jalapeño

USES: In table sauces, vegetable and meat dishes; as a seasoning; stuffed

SOURCES:

FRESH: Not available in the United States

DRIED: Not dried

PROCESSED: Not available

SEEDS: Perhaps in a specialty seed catalog

Although this species is not available commercially in the United States today, you need to know about it because it probably will be soon. This chilli is really different, unmistakably so. To begin with, the stems are very hairy (hence "pubescent," the Latin name meaning hairy), the flowers are always purple, the irregular seeds are coal black, and it requires a cool climate at altitudes of thirty-five hundred to six thousand feet. On top of all that, it must be the hottest chilli going. It takes a lot of getting used to. No Scoville rating is available. I used to buy it in the market in San Jose, Costa Rica, where it is called *jalapeño*—pungent/hot foods are not traditional there, so all hot peppers are called jalapeños. There are many varieties of *Capsicum pubescens* in the Andean region but, unlike the cultivars of *C. annuum* var. *annuum,* they do not have individual names. Down there, all are called rocoto or locoto, and Eshbaugh has measured the sprawling vinelike plant to be sixty feet long. The rocoto was a latecomer to the North American continent, perhaps as late as the twentieth century. The fruit spoils rather quickly. If you find some, wash and seed them (with gloves on), cut them into strips, blanch for 1 to 2 minutes, and freeze. Use as you would habaneros or datils but only half the amount.

'SANTA FE GRANDE'
Capsicum annuum var. *annuum* Linné

COLOR: Pale greenish yellow to orange to red; glossy

SHAPE: Conical, pointed apex; wax type

SIZE: 3½ inches long by 1½ inches wide at shoulder

PUNGENCY: Medium hot to very hot, 6

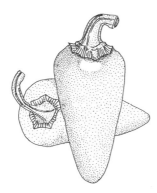

SUBSTITUTES: Any hot yellow pepper, such as caricillo, 'Cascabella', 'Floral Gem', 'Hungarian Wax'

OTHER NAMES: 'Caloro', 'Caribe', cera, güero

USES: In table sauces; pickled; as a seasoning

SOURCES:

FRESH: Many food markets, home gardens, farmers' markets

DRIED: Not dried

PROCESSED: Pickled, infrequently found in food stores

SEEDS: Catalogs of specialty seed houses, in some of the larger seed companies' catalogs.

AVAILABLE CULTIVARS: 'Caloro', 'Caloro PS', 'Caribe', 'Grande Gold' (sweet), 'Hybrid Gold Spike', 'Santa Fe Grande', 'TAM Rio'

This is a beautiful pepper plant when full of fruit in all stages—yellow, orange, and red. This prime example of a yellow wax pepper is the same pepper as the 'Caribe' in Mexico and the 'Caloro' in California. The ripe red fruit is difficult, if not impossible, to distinguish from the ripe red 'Fresno', but try to remember that the 'Fresno' never passes through yellow or orange stages, nor the 'Santa Fe Grande' through a green stage.

Like other peppers with fairly thick flesh, the 'Santa Fe Grande' will not air-dry satisfactorily. In Mexico any yellow pepper is called *güero*, or "blond," even though some of them may be red when mature. In the northern part of Mexico the 'Santa Fe Grande' is grown for export to American food markets, and is not used to any degree in Mexico. When Americans sent Mexican growers the bitingly hot 'Santa Fe Grande' seeds, the Mexicans called it 'Caribe' after the cannibalistic Indians who inhabited the Caribbean Islands at the time of Columbus. It can be used in any recipe calling for jalapeño, but will not have the typical jalapeño flavor.

SCOTCH BONNET
Capsicum chinense Jacquin

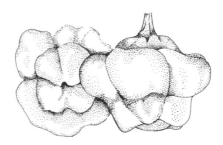

COLOR: Green to yellow-orange or orange

SHAPE: Stem end (base) is depressed. The deeply inverted, always rounded apex folding into a crimped periphery just below the base gives the rounded fruit the appearance of a Scottish tam-o-shanter, a cap with a tight headband and a full flat top with a large pompon, or a small unidentified flying object. Scotch bonnet type

SIZE: 2 to 2½ inches in diameter, 1¼ to 1½ inches deep

PUNGENCY: Very, very hot, 10 +

SUBSTITUTES: Habanero, dátil, West Indian hot, several serranos

OTHER NAMES: Scot's bonnet, bonnie

USES: In table sauces, cooked sauces; as a seasoning

SOURCES:

FRESH: Markets catering to West Indians, home gardens

DRIED: Does not dry well; retains pungency but loses flavor

PROCESSED: Bottled sauces in specialty shops

SEEDS: Catalogs of some specialty seed companies, not easily found

The Scotch bonnet was first mentioned in *The Gardener's Dictionary* by Philip Miller in 1768 when he listed a West Indian pepper with wrinkled leaves and a bonnet shape. There has been much confusion between this cultivar and other cultivars of *Capsicum chinense,* especially habanero. In the first three editions of *Peppers* I held it to be another name for habanero, as it was commonly thought to be at that time. Since then my visits to the West Indies with Brian Cooper, agronomist with the Caribbean Agricultural and Development Institute (CARDI), have convinced me that they are two distinct cultivars and that the habanero is a Mexican cultivar not widely grown in the West Indies, although many look-alikes of the same species grow there. "Look for the rounded apex and depressed base," Dr. Cooper stresses. There are many intergrades, but the purest strain is found in Jamaica. Even though they look like Scotch bonnet, the varicolored squash pepper (*C. annuum* var. *annuum*) and the rocotillo (*C. chinense*) both have a neck and a very pointed apex.

Both the Scotch bonnet and the habanero, along with the datil and West Indian hot (a habanero type), probably derive from the same Amazonian ancestor brought to the West Indies before the arrival of Columbus. Its primary use is in table sauce.

SERRANO
Capsicum annuum var. *annuum* Linné

COLOR: Green to red, glossy

SHAPE: Elongated cylinder, blunt apex; serrano type

SIZE: 2¼ inches long by ½ inch wide

PUNGENCY: Hot to very hot, 6 to 8

SUBSTITUTES: Chiltepín, 'Fresno', jalapeño, Thai

OTHER NAMES: Balín, chile verde, cora, serrannito, típico

USES: In table sauces, guacamole, relishes, vegetable dishes; as a seasoning or garnish

SOURCES:

FRESH: Most food markets, but less common than the jalapeño; in home gardens, farmers' markets

DRIED: Does not dry well. The dried japonés (page 90) are *not* dried serranos

PROCESSED: Mexican pickled (*escabeche*) serranos are occasionally found in specialty stores

SEEDS: Catalogs of most large seed houses and specialty seed companies.

AVAILABLE CULTIVARS: 'Altimira', 'Cotaxtla Cónico', 'Cotaxtla Gordo', 'Cotaxtla Típico', 'Cuauhtemoc', 'Huasteco 74', 'Panuco', 'Serrano Chili', 'Tampiqueño'

The slick little serrano is the favorite green chilli for table sauces and guacamole in Mexico and my kitchen. Its crisp, fresh flavor makes it quite distinctive. It is also wonderful in uncooked fruit chutney. The name comes from *serranias* (meaning "foothills") because it is believed that it originated in the foothills north of Puebla in Mexico. Although the serrano has very adaptable growth habits, it is not grown commercially to any extent in the United States. It is not necessary to peel or seed them, just slice thinly. Serranos freeze well, and if you blanch them before freezing, their pungency is not lost. After blanching 2 minutes, freeze them in a shallow, metal pan, then quickly separate and bag them in plastic. Frozen this way you can reach in the bag for one or as many as you need for up to a year. Like the jalapeño, the serrano does not dry well.

'TABASCO'
Capsicum frutescens Linné (page 4n)

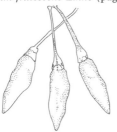

COLOR: Pale yellow-green to yellow to orange to red

SHAPE: Elongate cylinder, pointed apex; Tabasco type

SIZE: 1 to 1½ inches long by ¼ to ¾ inch wide

PUNGENCY: Very hot, 8 to 9

SUBSTITUTES: Chiltepín, 'Cascabella', 'Louisiana Sport', 'Mississippi Sport', Thai, Chilpequin

OTHER NAMES: None

USES: In sauces; as a seasoning

SOURCES:

FRESH: Home garden

DRIED: Not dried

PROCESSED: Pepper sauces made with 'Tabasco' peppers abound; occasionally pickled whole peppers are available in food stores

SEEDS: Specialty seed catalogs, a few major seed catalogs. The seed you get will probably be 'Greenleaf Tabasco'.

This little firebrand has been the subject of much litigation over the use of its name, and much dispute over its origin. Whatever went before, the chilli we now know as 'Tabasco' was developed by the McIlhenny family of Avery Island, Louisiana, who fiercely protect its name. The cultivar was named after their fermented pepper sauce. All the peppers used in their Tabasco Brand Pepper Sauce are grown from seed that the McIlhenny Company selects and furnishes to growers. Any seed you might find elsewhere is probably the 'Greenleaf Tabasco', which is a little hotter and deeper red and was the result of a cross with *Capsicum chinense* to resist infection by tobacco mosaic, a disease which was killing the 'Tabasco' plants. Other sauces may be made with the 'Tabasco' pepper, but you will have to read the fine print on the label because they cannot use Tabasco in their name. These sauces are used in soups, stews, bloody Marys, on oysters, in egg dishes, and anything needing a dash of fire. Use Tabasco Brand Pepper Sauce only if you desire your dish or drink to have its characteristic flavor, which is the result of the addition of vinegar and the fermentation process by which it is made.

A detailed, documented discussion of this cultivar can be found in *Peppers*. The new-found popularity of peppers has brought a plethora of sauces to the marketplace to compete with Tabasco Brand Pepper Sauce—so many, in fact, that for the first time in the long history of the Avery Island sauce, its makers have not only branched out into farm stores and many other products, even T-shirts flaunting their world-famous trademark, but also bought Trappey's, a competing pepper processor in New Iberia. 'Tabasco' peppers are not grown commercially to any extent in this country today because, as is the case with other very small chillies, no one will pick them. They make a beautiful potted plant. I had one espaliered in a sun room for five years.

The range of the wild and semiwild varieties of *Capsicum frutescens* is more limited than that of *C. annuum* var. *glabrisculum*; however, throughout their ranges both tiny chillies are called bird peppers by the local people. This long-standing interchange of vernacular names for the two has caused much confusion to everyone but the birds—they greedily harvest them no matter what the name is.

TOMATO
Capsicum annuum var. *annuum* Linné

COLOR: Green to red

SHAPE: Globular, tomatolike, or squash shaped; tomato type

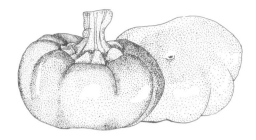

SIZE: 3 inches in diameter

PUNGENCY: Sweet, 0 to 1

SUBSTITUTES: Pimento, red bell pepper

OTHER NAMES: Paprika, Spanish paprika, sweet squash pepper

USES:

FRESH: Same as for bell pepper (page 66)

POWDERED: Sold as paprika

CANNED: As pimento (page 81). Also as a food and industrial coloring agent

SOURCES:

FRESH: Home gardens, farmers' markets

DRIED: Not used

PROCESSED: Canned sold as pimento; pickled; commercial coloring agent; powdered

SEEDS: Catalogs of most large seed companies.

AVAILABLE CULTIVARS: 'Canada Cheese', 'Early Sweet Pimento', 'Sunnybrook', 'Tomato Pimento', 'Yellow Cheese Pimento'

Few tomato peppers, if any, are grown today in Mesoamerica where they originated. This thick-fleshed, sweet capsicum is thought to be the precursor of the ubiquitous bell pepper. It is extolled in Spain and Morocco for the high-quality paprika produced from it, although it is not the only capsicum used for making paprika. For the most part, the tomato pepper is grown in the southern United States, where it is not only sold for paprika and as a coloring agent, but also as a substitute for the true pimento. When canned it is more yellowish red than the canned true pimento.

Miscellaneous Cultivars

These varieties of *Capsicum* are not commonly available in this country; however, you might read about them occasionally or see them in a farmers' market or ethnic food store or a seed catalog. I predict, though, that some will soon enter the market as "gourmet peppers." If there are large ethnic groups living in a community, you can be sure there is at least one food store to supply the ingredients their ethnic cuisines require.

CARIBBEAN ISLAND PEPPERS

As related earlier, Columbus first encountered the *Capsicum* pepper on Española in the Caribbean region, where only *Capsicum chinense, C. frutescens,* and possibly *C. annuum* were thought to be established at that time. Many of the varieties found there are of the first two species, which are known for their extreme pungency. They have taken many forms and carry many local names, which vary from island to island. The Scotch bonnet type and West Indian hot (a habanero type), along with a duke's mixture of *C. chinense* such as congo, bonnie, Peggy mouth, St. John's market, Jamaica red, and *ají gustos,* are grown in the West Indies for local use and export to Great Britain, Canada, and Holland, where large populations of West Indians can be found. They are also occasionally found in ethnic and farmers' markets in the United States. They are used primarily in table sauces; however, they may be used in the same manner as other, similar chillies. In the Caribbean area West Indian farmers have a different attitude about growing peppers than capsicum growers elsewhere. Keeping one *C. chinense* cultivar separate from the other is not important to them or their customers. Their fields of mixed *C. chinense* are allowed to cross at will. People who are familiar with peppers in the United States and Mexico recognize that the Caribbean chillies are similar to one another, yet different from those jalapeños, bell peppers, and other types of *C. annuum* var. *annuum* they are familiar with in the U.S.A. The only comparable pepper most Americans may have seen is a habanero—so, they call the Caribbean look-alikes habaneros. Indeed, many are habanero types, but not the actual habanero cultivar, which is a native of Yucatán, Mexico (page 75).

The only *Capsicum annuum* var. *annuum* I saw being cultivated were poor specimens of the bell type. The "bird pepper," a tiny, pointed, rod-like or elongated cone that has been called *C. frutescens,* grows spontaneously in gardens and under trees. This is probably very similar to the malegueta of Brazil. If you travel in the West Indies, please collect seed *with the local name,* make notes on how it is used and send it to me because I have only visited Antigua, Jamaica, and St. Croix.

ETHNIC PEPPERS

These are large, thick-fleshed, undulating, sweet fruits known in the trade as frying or ethnic peppers. The 'Cubanelle' and 'Romanian' are typical of this type. People from the Balkans, Greece, and Italy favor these served as a fried vegetable dish or with meats. Look for them in ethnic food markets where there are concentrations of people of those origins.

INDIAN PEPPERS (MIRCH)

Most *hari* (green) *mirch* are 2 to 4 inches long and used fresh. *Lal* (red) *mirch* are only used dried. Both are long, slim, curved *Capsicum annuum* var. *annuum* chillies of the cayenne type that mature from green to red. When used fresh, only the green ones are selected. Pepper vendors can be seen carefully removing from the pile any pepper that has begun to turn red. Cayenne, serrano, Thai, japonés, and other small cayenne types, or ground cayenne pepper may be substituted. Before mixing them with other ingredients, Indians toss the unseeded dried peppers into hot oil for a few seconds, along with other spices, in order to bring out the flavor. In India not many varieties are found, but those few are used in great quantity. Fields throughout the countryside are accented by huge, bright red squares of chillies spread to dry. A little round variety is also used dried, but to a lesser degree. In India the more recently introduced sweet bell-type peppers are called capsicums and are used as a vegetable, while the pungent varieties are called chillies (or "chillys"). Another rather recently introduced Hungarian wax type is used in the pale yellow-green stage as a vegetable.

INDONESIAN PEPPERS

These are used more as a condiment (*sambal*) than for seasoning the main dishes. Although some are used in cooking, the food is not as blistering as Thai and Indian victuals can be. The variety of capsicums available in Indonesia is more limited than in Thailand and India, and those few cayenne types found in the markets vary from island to island. Most are grown in home gardens instead of large commercial plantings. Kalimantan (Borneo), Java, Irian Jaya (western New Guinea), Sumatra, Sulawesi (Celebes), Bali, and the islands of the Lesser Sundas use a small (½ inch to ¾ inch), elongate-cylindrical *Capsicum frutescens* and a couple of larger (1½ inches to 4 inches) *C. annuum* var. *annuum* of the cayenne type. In addition to these, I found a bright red habanero-type *C. chinense* being used in Sulawesi, but did not find it elsewhere. As in Thailand and India, no common names are used. Until the Dutch came to Indonesia and applied the

Nahuatl-Mexican name *chilli* to the peppers introduced by the Portuguese, the most common name was *cabé* for *C. annuum* var. *annuum* and *cabé rawit* for *C. frutescens,* the tiny "bird pepper." *Cabé hijau* are green and *cabé merah* are red chillies. *Lombok* is the Javanese word for peppers. "Bird peppers" are known as *cabé burong* in Malaysia and *lombok rawit* in Indonesia. Only pungent peppers are used, and they are called chillies by those who speak English.

JAPONÉS, SANTAKA, AND HONTAKA

These are small (2 inches by ½ inch), very pungent chillies of the cayenne type. Green ones, like the hawk's bill (called *hontaka* in Japan), are used in sauces, and the dried red ones are made into a powder for seasoning. These cultivars may be of Japanese origin. No matter what you may read in books or on labels, the japonés is *not* a dried serrano. I know, because I grew plants using seeds from several different brands of japonés peppers and I can say that the resulting plants were *Capsicum annuum* var. *annuum* of the cayenne type. Let me know if you learn where this pepper got its name and where it comes from. Surely someone who buys it to sell will know where it is being grown.

MEXICAN PEPPERS

These are almost too numerous to list, each region having its own variety that is usually not grown or shipped elsewhere. These local types are called *criollos,* a Creole person being one born in the Americas of Spanish or French parents. When the term is applied to a *Capsicum* cultivar, it means a very local type, native to a particular land area and not widespread. They

are also called *chile corriente* (common chile) and *chile casero* (household chile). In Mexico, each of these varietal names would be prefaced with the word *chile,* i.e., *chile amarillo, chile carricillo,* etc. The locals claim no gringo can truly comprehend the *chile* mystique, and scoff at those of us gringos who profess to be *chile* authorities. All of the following are *C. annuum* var. *annuum* Linné. Some of the less familiar are:

AMARILLO. A beautiful, deep gold-colored, elongate chilli about 2 inches long and quite narrow and pointed. It dries to a translucent ocher color. These dried fruits are comparatively expensive in the markets of Oaxaca. Save the seed, as it will do well in your garden.

CARRICILLO. A pungent, pale yellow, narrow-shouldered, wrinkled, curved fruit of the cayenne type that ripens into vermilion. It is not used fresh or dried, but rather is pickled in its yellow stage and used in fish dishes. This *güero* (page 91) is also called *chile cristal, chile largo,* and *x-cat-ik.*

CATARINA. Shaped like the beak of the parakeet, or *catarinita,* this small (¾ to 1 inch), green to red, very pungent chilli is used dried. The dried translucent red fruits allow the seeds to rattle. It is favored for tamales and is used green in table sauces, as is the serrano. The fresh green form is sometimes called *mirasol* because it grows erect, or is "looking at the sun." It is also called *cascabelillo.*

CHILACATE. This is the Mexican name for the dried long red New Mexican chile (page 78). It is also called *chile del norte, chile colorado, chile largo colorado,* and *chile magdalena.*

CHILHUACQUI. A very variable chilli that looks like the guajillo in some areas; in others it produces a wider red fruit, called *chilhuacqui negro,* which dries black and is more like the ancho. Another, *chilhuacqui amarillo,* is yellow with narrow shoulders. These are grown on the Pacific coast of Chiapas and bordering Guatemala.

CHIPOTLE. Any chilli dried by smoking (*ahumado* or *pocchilli*) is a chipotle. Although *chiles moros* and *chiles bolitos* (two small jalapeño types), serranos, and others are smoke dried to a wrinkled, tough, fairly dark brown fruit, it is the jalapeño that is most commonly used for chipotles. Its varieties are known as *típico, meco,* and *morita*. They can be purchased dried or lightly pickled and canned (*adobado*). Picked ripe red, they are hotter than green jalapeños. Most chipotles are produced in the region of the Gulf of Mexico.

CHIPOTLE

COSTEÑO. A medium-sized (very variable, up to 6 inches), green to red, narrow-shouldered chilli that dries a translucent reddish brown, the costeño is grown in the state of Guerrero, Mexico. It may be a variation of the guajillo. The fruits are used dried.

DE AGUA. The large, thick-fleshed water (*agua*) *chile* comes from Oaxaca and Guatemala. Looking like a pale green, longer poblano, it matures to vermilion and is roasted and peeled before being made into sauces. It is too succulent to dry.

DE ONZA. This is a cayenne-type bright red chilli that is used dried like the *chile costeño*. In fact, it looks like a little fatter version of that cultivar.

GÜERO. This is not any cultivar in particular. The word means "blond" and is the name given to any yellow pepper or any pepper used in the yellow stage.

MORO/MORITO. A small variety of jalapeño, it is often smoked for chipotles. Some Mexicans call all pickled chipotle jalapeños by this name.

PULLA/PUYA. A 3- to 4-inch, elongate cylinder with narrow shoulders and pointed apex. This chilli becomes a translucent deep red when dried. It is probably a local variation of the guajillo and is used in the same way.

THAI PEPPERS

Peppers are indispensable to Thai cooking, which is my favorite of the Far Eastern cuisines. To me it is more subtle than Indian and more flavorful than Indonesian. The larger varieties are *Capsicum annuum* var. *annuum* and appear to be almost the same as the Indian varieties and used in the same quantity, if not more. There are at least ten kinds of varying size and pungency available in the markets. Even after attending a cooking school in Bangkok, I am not able to assign distinct flavors to the different varieties, but they do have different degrees of hotness. Some are pale green, others yellow or red, but all are hot. They are not seeded before being put in a dish. The various colors are used to enhance the dishes—presentation is important in Thailand. Both fresh and dried fruits are often used whole with the stems on. Substitute serranos, chiltepínes, or jalapeños for fresh Thai peppers, and for the dried ones, fill in with ground cayenne pepper or japonés. I did find a tiny cylindrical red pepper that was *C. frutescens*. It was semidomesticated and used as our chiltepínes (page 69). In rural and tribal villages, baskets of scarlet peppers drying on rooftops or porches made already colorful scenes even more vibrant. Most common names are only the word for pepper, *prik,* with some additional descriptors, such as *hang* (dried), *yuk* (fresh). The practice of giving each variety a name like "jalapeño" or "bell pepper" does not seem to be prevalent. English-speaking Thais use the word "chillies" for pungent peppers. 'Santa Fe Grande'/'Caribe' and some sweet bell types have been recently introduced, but their use is not widespread as yet.

UNITED STATES, MISCELLANEOUS

Several small varieties that have limited distribution need to be defined because they have been significant in the pepper industry from time to time. They are all *Capsicum annuum* var. *annuum*.

'CASCABELLA'. This small (1¼ inch by ¾ inch), wax-type fruit is similar and closely related to the larger 'Fresno' (page 74); both cultivars were developed in California by the same plant breeder. It grows on a very bushy plant and is yellow at first, turning orange and becoming red upon maturity. The conical fruit with a pointed apex is generally used in the yellow state for hot pickled peppers. The small size makes it highly desirable to pickle packers. The Spanish *cascabella* is formed from two words— *cascara* (skin, husk), referring to the waxy outer covering, and *bella* (beautiful). The name sounds and looks similar, but is not related, to another Spanish word, *cascabel* (jingle bell), which is used as the name of a round, red Mexican *chile* (page 67).

PAPRIKA. You may find a paprika pepper listed in seed catalogs; however, there is no single paprika pepper used for making paprika (page 102).

SPORTS. Two hot sauce and pickling varieties, 'Louisiana Sport' and 'Mississippi Sport' are small (1 to 1½ inches by ¼ to ¾ inch), erect-growing, elongate-cylindrical, green to red peppers. They were used as substitutes in vinegar-packed whole fruits when a disease threatened the 'Tabasco' pepper crop. Neither are used to any extent today.

SQUASH. This beautiful red or golden chilli pepper splashed with purple, about 2 inches in diameter, is shaped like a pattypan squash. Although it is a *Capsicum annuum* var. *annuum*, many call it rocotillo because the red form looks very much like that mild South American *C. chinense*, and the seeds are frequently sold as such. The squash pepper is pale green when young and very hot but with little flavor. It is great for garnishes or used as an ornamental in the garden or in pots. This small pepper is quite different from a larger, sweet, tomatolike pimento known as a squash pepper.

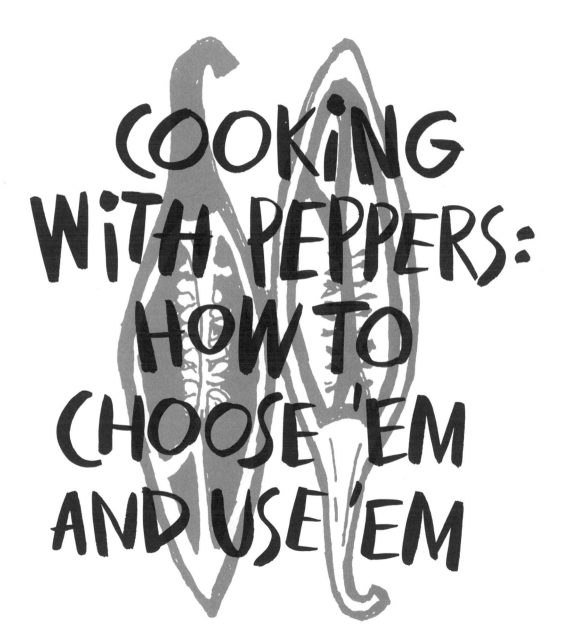

COOKING WITH PEPPERS: HOW TO CHOOSE 'EM AND USE 'EM

ow that we know where chillies came from, and where they went, and what they are or are not—let's eat them. As I said in my earlier book *Peppers*, before cooking with or eating capsicums you should familiarize yourself with the methods for selecting, preparing, and handling our precious pods in order to ensure an enjoyable experience. Please, in your rush to become a pod fellow, take the time to follow instructions. Peppers are expensive, so you don't want to waste them, but most of all, DON'T GET BURNED. Wear protective gloves if preparing more than one or two chillies. Work in a well-ventilated area—the fumes are tear jerkers. Do not put your hands in your eyes, or any body orifice for that matter. If you get too much on your hands, wash them in a mixture of one part household bleach to five parts water (see page 63). Do this at the start—don't wait until you are burned beyond relief. Repeat if necessary. It really works! An ammonia mix will also work, but it smells worse. When making relish or anything requiring quite a few chillies, I keep a small bowl of the chlorine solution by the sink to dip my hands in as needed, a practice born of sad experience.[1]

Keep peeled and cut peppers well covered. Vitamin C is destroyed by contact with oxygen. According to food scientist Harold McGee, the only plastic food wrap that does not let in too much oxygen is polyvinylidene chloride (Saran Wrap). Press and draw all the air out before sealing the package.

Selection

FRESH. Capsicums are a fruit that is used like a vegetable. The chilli aficionado will either grow his or her own peppers or buy them in a food market, supermarket, or farmers' market. By whatever means they are come by, you should be aware of a few points when selecting peppers. Capsicums of any type can be picked when they are green or when a fully mature red, though they can also mature to orange, yellow, or brown. Both the compounds that furnish the flavor (page 62) and the pungency (page 60) of peppers do not develop immediately, rather increasing gradually with maturity. Consequently, the green fruits are less pungent and flavorful than the fully mature ones. This accounts for the chipotle being so much hotter than the familiar green jalapeño, because only the fully mature red jalapeños are smoked to create them. It also justifies my opinion that green bell peppers are a poor excuse for a pepper. Now that the big, brightly colored flavorful bells are in the supermarkets on a regular basis, I don't ever have to buy the green ones except for garnish or decoration, and I burp less. That opinion is probably not acceptable to the bell pepper growers, but I feel better.

In your gardens choose fruits that have smooth, glossy skins and are firm to the touch. If you have to really tug to get it off the stem, it is not quite ready. These same qualities should be looked for by those who must buy peppers in the marketplace. Except for those insipid, obsequious, omnipresent green bell peppers, which grow in some places year round, peppers are a seasonal crop, and the best selection will be in the summer and fall. In the store you are often met with a bin of chillies that are wrinkled has-beens. In that

---

1. At our local farmer's market I was admiring one of the "farmer's" pepper displays when a basketful of habaneros reminded me of how I discovered my chlorine bleach cure for capsaicin burn. After telling the grower, a retired professor, about the process, she exclaimed, "That's it! My partner and I always thought we were immune to capsaicin burn when our employees' hands always got burned and ours never did, now I know why. We have always kept a bowl of water with chlorine bleach in it on the counter so that we could keep our cleaning rags sterile. Every time we do something we use a rag from the bowl to wipe up with. All this time it has been neutralizing the capsaicin while we thought we were immune."

case, all you can do is pick around for those with the least amount of wrinkles. Try buying them in season, when they are bright, shiny and crisp, to freeze for later use (page 97).

DRIED. Not all peppers will air-dry or sun-dry satisfactorily. Those that dry well have thinner skins than the succulent ones such as the bell pepper, jalapeño, serrano, 'Santa Fe Grande', 'Fresno', and many sweet ethnic varieties. If possible, select dried peppers that are unpackaged because you can pick the better ones. Look for clean, insect-free (tiny holes in the skin are made by bugs; also, powdery dust may be a sign that insects have been present) peppers that are still pliable, not brittle. There should be no light-colored blotches or transparent spots. Many packaged dry chillies are tagged with incorrect names. Pay no attention to those labels but do look at the size, shape, and color and determine the variety for yourself after studying pages 65–92.

Storage

FRESH. If you are not going to use the peppers immediately, they may be stored in the refrigerator for 4 or more weeks by drying fresh pods with a clean cloth, then placing them in an airtight container or a *tightly* sealed heavy ziplock plastic bag from which you have expelled all air.[2] Place the container in the refrigerator (optimum temperature 45° to 46° F). Each time you use peppers from the container, dry the unused pods before removing the air and resealing—a home vacuum-packer would be ideal. Every 6 days remove the container from the refrigerator

---

2. Kitchen stores sell Vacu Products in several sizes. These plastic containers have stoppers and a pump to remove air like those used to preserve opened champagne. In lieu of those, displace air with paper towels and/or suck air out with a straw or tube before completely sealing.

and allow the peppers to come to room temperature, dry them, return to the container, remove the air, and seal. This is a method of storage that I've recently discovered. If you cannot store them this way and are not going to use them within a week, it is best to freeze them and use them for cooking (page 97).

If peppers are to be shipped or kept out of the refrigerator, put them in a paper container. NEVER put them directly into a plastic bag before packaging them to transport or mail, as they will spoil immediately.

DRIED. Dried peppers will keep almost indefinitely if stored properly. Make certain they are dry, then put them in tightly closed, heavy plastic bags or glass or plastic jars in a cool, dry place, preferably the refrigerator or freezer. Check them from time to time to be certain they are not deteriorating or beginning to mold. Mildew will usually start on the inside where the seeds attach to the placenta (see the illustration on page 55). Peppers with traces of mildew should be disposed of right away.

HOW TO USE FRESH PEPPERS

The best way to use peppers is right off the bush; unfortunately, that is seldom possible. They will need to be washed, stemmed, deveined, and seeded before they are chopped or otherwise utilized in a favorite dish. All this business of roasting and peeling peppers before you cook with the precious pod is enough to scare most novice pepper cooks away. (The only fresh peppers that really need to be skinned are the poblano and the longer, tough-skinned New Mexican chile—

whichever of its cultivars you may be using—and even that ritual can be forsaken with certain cultivars if the recipe calls for chopped, minced, or pureed chillies; experiment with one pod first.) However, this blistering and peeling is all part of the pepper mystique. Pepper buffs just like to get right in there with their charismatic pods.

The big bell pepper, 'Cubanelle', poblano, and others of these types should be parboiled or blanched for 2 to 3 minutes before they are used whole for stuffing if the filling is not to be cooked in the pepper shell. If you have a microwave, put them in a plastic bag with a couple of tablespoons of water and microwave them for a minute or two on high, depending on the size and quantity. Either way, care must be taken not to cook them to a point that they cannot hold their shape. As soon as they are removed from the heat, plunge the peppers into cold or iced water to stop the cooking.

Small chillies can be washed, stemmed, seeded, and deveined without skinning. In Mexico, India, Indonesia, and the Orient, none of those steps are followed before the fiery fruit is plopped into the pot or wok, whole or chopped. It is recommended that, if you do decide to clean more than one or two pods, you wear plastic or rubber gloves and keep the tissue box handy. When seeding only a couple, handle them gingerly, taking care to not touch the cut surface, and use a small tool to remove the seeds. I have designated a metal cuticle pusher for the job. The principal reason for removing the "innards" of a chilli is to reduce the pungency. In Mexico peppers that have had the veins and seeds removed are called *capones,* which, like the caponized chicken, means they have been castrated. *Chipotles capones,* which require more preparation time, bring a much higher price than those left intact.

Usually, if a recipe calls for a pepper to be roasted, it is done not only to remove the peel but also because that charred flavor is desired. Like skinning a cat, there is more than one way to roast and skin a pepper.

Peeling

Before peeling a batch of New Mexican chiles or poblanos, test one to see if the skin is so tough that all that work is necessary. If you have very fresh, young peppers and plan to grind or chop them, they may not require peeling. However, I tried the lazy way one time (and only one time) with some supermarket New Mexican chiles, cultivar unknown. I did them in the food processor without peeling. I ended up having tiny pieces of ground up cellophanelike skin in my chiles. I had to cook and strain them before I dared use them in my sauce. New Mexican chiles offer the most "skin" problems, and some of the myriad cultivars are worse than others. Test one to see if you have tough or tender ones.

Peeling peppers can be done by "blistering" the pods, using one of several methods, and by using a hot paraffin dip. We won't go into the troublesome paraffin dip here (see my *Peppers* book on page 226). The actual blistering or roasting can be done in a number of ways. Your choice will probably be determined by your source of heat. Don't forget to keep a little bowl of chlorine solution handy!

BLISTER METHODS FOR PEELING

STEP 1: Before blistering the skin, always pierce or make a tiny slit in the pod to vent it so that it will not explode.

Burner roasting. If you have a gas stove, set the flame at medium and place your peppers on the burner trivet. If the openings in the burner are too large or if you have an electric stove, place a cake rack, hardware cloth, steel cooling rack, or one of the new stove burner racks designed for stove-top grilling over it. Never let the skin of the pepper touch the electric element. Set the burner on high. Use kitchen tongs to rotate the pods as they start to char. Continue turning until the entire pepper is blackened and blistered. Remove as soon as they are charred to prevent cooking.

Broiler. Arrange the peppers on an aluminum foil-covered broiler pan or cookie sheet and place it 3 to 5 inches under the broiler. As in the burner method, keep turning the pods until completely charred. This method cooks the peppers more because the oven holds the heat. If shape and firmness are required in your peeled pepper, do not use this method; however, it is a quick way to blister a number of pods at the same time for making stews and sauces. Constant attention is required.

Oven roasting. Preheat the oven to 550° F. Place the peppers on the oven rack and roast until blistered, 3 to 7 minutes. No turning is required.

Miscellaneous methods. The same principles of roasting as explained in the three previous methods can be used with a charcoal grill or barbecue grill, or in a heavy griddle or skillet on top of the stove. Roasting in hot oil in a saucepan is not recommended. Commercial chilli roasters using revolving cylindrical cages set over gas flames have become commonplace in New Mexico and parts of the Southwest where New Mexican chiles are sold in bulk.

STEP 2:

STEAMING. Remove the blistered pod from the heat and cool immediately in one of the following ways:

1. Place in a plastic or paper bag for 10 to 15 minutes.
2. Wrap in a cold, wet cloth and allow to steam 10 to 15 minutes.
3. Plunge into ice water. This method will result in a crisper pepper because it stops the cooking process immediately.

STEP 3: When the peppers are cool, begin peeling at the stem end while holding it under running water. A small knife will help. Wear rubber or disposable plastic gloves to protect sensitive hands from the fierce capsaicin. For freezing, do not peel in order to retain more flavor, color,

and vitamins. The charred skins will slip off easily when the peppers are thawed. Don't forget the chlorine water for your hands!

STEP 4: Slit the pod; remove the veins and seeds by cutting and washing. For stuffed chillies, leave the stems attached.

Freezing

Frozen peppers may be used in cooking for seasoning, or as stuffed peppers; they are too soft for salads. Most of the nutritive value is retained if care is taken not to expose the peeled or cut fruit to the air, as oxygen destroys vitamin C rapidly. Leave the blistered and steamed peel on the pods as long as possible to guard against this loss.

For New Mexican chiles and poblanos:
1. Blister and steam in a damp cloth but do not peel. When thawed, the skin comes off readily.
2. If space is a problem, remove the stem and seeds; otherwise, freeze the entire pod to prevent exposure to oxygen.
3. Flatten the whole pods to remove air and fold once for easy packing and handling.
4. Pack in a moisture-vapor-proof package, excluding as much air as possible. Double layers of waterproof paper between the pods will facilitate separation when peppers are needed.

For bell peppers and large sweet peppers:
1. Wash, core, seed, and dry the peppers. Cut in half; place the halves on a metal pan or baking sheet and freeze.
2. Stack the frozen halves one inside the other and pack in a moisture-vapor-proof package, excluding as much air as possible. Freeze. Use from the bag as needed.

For chillies (jalapeños, serranos, etc.):
1. Wash and dry the peppers. Place the whole pods on a metal pan or baking sheet and freeze.

2. Place the frozen pods in a moisture-vapor-proof package, excluding as much air as possible. Freeze. Use from the bag as needed.

Drying Peppers

SUN-DRYING. Sun-drying is an ancient method best adapted to arid climates and not feasible in humid areas.

For green New Mexican chiles:
1. Select full-grown but immature pods. Wash, peel, and slit the pod and remove the seeds, veins, and stem.
2. Spread the peppers in single layers on trays or racks. Cover with cheesecloth to exclude pests and dust. Tilt the rack to face the sun. Turn the pods occasionally. A clear plastic or glass covering will increase the heat. Dry for two to three days, bringing the trays in at night to prevent moisture from condensing on them. The product should be crisp, brittle, and medium green.

For the red pods of New Mexican chiles, guajillos, or any thin-fleshed variety:
1. Allow the pods to remain on the plant until fully mature. Select only ripe, red pods. Using heavy twine, run a string through the stem end and hang in the sun to dry. Or,
2. Let the pods ripen and remain on the plant until deep red; place on trays or heavy paper to dry in the sun. Bring in at night, Or,
3. Allow the fruit to mature on the plant; place the pods on a sunny windowsill to dry. Store the whole dried pods in tightly closed jars or zip-lock bags from which all the air has been removed.

OVEN-DRYING. This works for red bell peppers.
1. Core, seed, and remove the ribs/veins from the peppers. Quarter the peppers, or cut them into ¾-inch strips.
2. In a large steam basket, steam the peppers for 10 minutes, then dry on paper toweling.

3. Place the peppers, cut side down, on cheesecloth-covered racks. Set the racks on baking sheets. Dry the peppers in a preheated 140° F oven until just short of being crisp, or to crisp if desired, 8 to 10 hours or more. Turn the pepper pieces once about midway through the drying time, and keep the oven door propped open slightly to allow moisture to escape.
4. Let the peppers cool completely before packing.

SMOKING. Another method of drying peppers is to smoke them. Although this practice is not followed in the United States, it is the procedure by which chipotles are produced in Mexico. Fully ripened red jalapeños or other chillies are placed on a bamboo grate over a pit in the ground. A tunnel carries the smoke from the fire pit to the grate. This is very similar to the workings of a Chinese smoke oven. The chillies may be processed with or without the seeds. The smoky flavor imparted by this pre-Columbian method is a subtle addition to sauces and mayonnaise. Try a Mr. Smokey type cooker.

DEHYDRATION. Dehydration is drying with heat generated from a man-made source. Studies show that not only is the job done faster but the product is cleaner, retains more of the nutritive value, and has better color than chillies dried in the sun. To dehydrate:
1. Peel the fruit if necessary.
2. Place the pods in a colander and blanch in boiling water for 10 minutes to destroy the enzymes that cause changes in color and flavor. This step can be omitted with New Mexican chiles but not with jalapeños, bells, or poblanos because their flesh is thicker.
3. Cut the pods in half.
4. Spread the pods in a single layer between two pieces of cheesecloth on racks, nylon screen, or trays. Place in a dehydrator at 130° to 135° F for about 8 hours.

The dehydrated product can be placed in a blender or processor to be flaked or powdered.

The ground product will keep better refrigerated. Whole pods may be used in recipes that require a long cooking time and a large amount of water.

A whole fresh green New Mexican chile can be smoked or roasted before it is dehydrated. This imparts a unique flavor to the dehydrated pepper—called *chile pasado* in Mexico.

REHYDRATION

Anchos, pasillas, mulatos, guajillos, cascabels, chipotles, and other dried peppers are usually rehydrated (plumped with water) before being used in food preparation. To do this, either place the chillies in a pan, cover with water, bring to a boil, remove from the heat, and let stand for an hour, or place in a bowl and cover with boiling water and let stand for an hour. Drain the chillies and reserve the soaking water for use in sauces, soups, stews, etc. You can leave the chillies in the water for more than an hour if necessary, but you must realize that the longer they remain in the water, the more the flavor and nutrients are dissolved. After they have been drained, remove the stems, seeds, and veins. Now they are ready to be used as they are, shredded, chopped, or pureed.

MAKING A PASTE.   Rinse the chillies in cold water. Remove the stem and seeds and break the pods into pieces. Soak in enough warm water to cover for 30 to 40 minutes but never more than 1 hour. Place them in a blender with some of the soaking water and puree. Add water as needed to make the desired consistency. The paste can be cooked in hot oil with other ingredients to make a sauce. Store in a covered jar in the refrigerator until needed (see recipe page 158). For a variation, use toasted chillies.

TOASTING CHILLIES.   Rinse the chillies under cold running water and pat dry. Heat a heavy skillet over medium-high heat until a drop of water will sizzle. Place a few chillies in the skillet and toast until just fragrant, turning frequently to avoid scorching. Large types such as the ancho should be pliable; if not, soak them in

a bowl of boiling water for a few minutes. Remove the seeds and veins from the larger types, but this is not necessary for small chillies. Rehydrate the toasted chillies as directed in the paragraph above.

Another option is to rinse and dry the chillies, they fry them in ½ to 1 inch of hot oil in a skillet over high heat until aromatic and puffy. Drain on paper toweling and proceed as above.

MAKING A POWDER.   Dried peppers can also be made into a powder by removing the stems, seeds, and veins and grinding 4 to 6 pods at a time in a blender until pulverized. Sift and regrind the larger pieces. Store in a covered container in the refrigerator and use when the recipe calls for powdered red pepper or chilli powder. One tablespoon is equal to 1 dried ancho, mulato, or pasilla, or 2 New Mexican chiles. One-eighth teaspoon of ground dried chillies like cayenne can be substituted for 1 chiltepín, de árbol, or japonés.

LET'S COME TO TERMS: INGREDIENTS AND TERMS

A claim could be made that no other cultivated plant has such a multiplicity of fruit types with such diverse uses over such an expanse of the world as does *Capsicum*. The publication of *Peppers* in December of 1984 coincided with an increase in the acceptance of the pretty, pungent pod; that popularity has continued to grow, and I'm delighted—and so are the burgeoning number of producers of peppers and pepper products.

Peppers are not only colorful flavor enhancers but they also have many uses as comestibles—as vegetable, spice, and condiment—and the list is growing. Let's look at a few of the types of products found on the shelves of the supermarket. The important attributes valued in *Capsicum* products are the color, pungency level, and aroma. Within these types of pepper products there are so many variations and brands that it would not be possible to include them all.

Pepper Products

ACHAAR (ACĆAR). A pickled, oily Indian condiment often, but not necessarily, *very* hot. Limes, lemons, mangoes, ginger, eggplant, and other things might be used to make an achaar, but the decisive ingredient is chilli. It is served with curries. Contrary to the origin of the word *achaar/achar* given in my *Peppers* (page 5), *achaar* is Persian, not Portuguese, and it does not mean "chilli." The word, and probably the pickle, came to India early in the sixteenth century with the Moghuls from the northwest at the same time the Portuguese entered the southwest, bringing the chillies. The two met and melded on the subcontinent to become the favored hot pickle in India. Achaar can be bought in Indian food stores or gourmet food shops.

CAYENNE PEPPER. A ground product made from the small peppers that contain large amounts of capsaicin. It is not obligatory to make this seasoning from cayenne peppers, although it may contain some, along with African, Mexican, and Louisiana chillies. The name came from Cayenne, French Guiana, but it is not manufactured there. The powder ranges in color from orange-red to a deep red; as a result, it is sometimes labeled simply "red pepper," a term the American Spice Trade Association considers to be inappropriate.

CHILI POWDER. (Note the one "l" spelling.) Dried pods of milder cultivars such as the

long red New Mexican chile and/or the ancho are the principal ingredients of this blend of several peppers and other spices—oregano, cumin, cayenne, garlic powder, paprika. It was first produced commercially by Willie Gebhardt, a German Texan in New Braunfels, Texas, in 1892 to be used in making chili con carne. A popular brand still bears his name. Reams have been written about chili con carne, and those who want to know more can refer to them. Purists would never dream of using a commercially prepared chili powder in their chili pot. *Warning:* Chili powder *cannot* be substituted for ground ancho, mulato, or pasilla if they are called for in a recipe. Chilli/chile powder is pure ground dried chillies (see entry after next).

CHILLI OIL. A seasoning oil made with pulverized dried red chillies. Make your own by heating ½ cup vegetable oil in a small skillet over medium heat; add 4 teaspoons ground cayenne pepper (preceding columns), ground dried red New Mexican chiles, hot paprika, or ground dried small red chillies. Remove from the heat and carefully add ½ cup hot water while guarding against spattering. Simmer over medium heat for 10 minutes, then cool. After the oil rises to the top, skim it off and put it in a tightly sealed jar. Discard the chilli sediment. Use when a recipe calls for chilly oil, chilli/chili oil, Chinese chilli/chili oil, etc.

CHILLI/CHILE POWDER. This contains only one type of ground red chilli and is *not* a blend of ground peppers and other spices, as is chili powder. They can't be interchanged. Some chilli powders are finely ground, others may be coarse, while others have seeds ground with the flesh. The pungency is dependent on the types and combinations of peppers used. You can make your own (page 99) or order some (page 224).

CHILLI/CHILI SAUCE. The name is misleading; commercial chilli sauces have little or no peppers in them. Instead they are seasoned crushed tomato catsups with tomato seeds, onion, garlic, sugar, vinegar, some spices, and perhaps a little chilli. They are usually more textured than catsup. This sauce is one of a breed of sauces and catsups that were developed from chutneys and pickles when English cooks found the liquid in the pickle bottle was more interesting than the pickled vegetable.

CHINESE PEPPER MIX. A freshly ground mixture of whole black, white, and Szechuan peppercorns (see page 103) that have been roasted in a dry skillet over medium heat until fragrant.

CHUTNEY. The principal type of this delightful Indian accompaniment to curries and meats usually has as its base two fruits or two vegetables or a fruit and a vegetable, plus onions, tamarind, ginger, garlic, and chillies cooked with vinegar, sugar, and salt. Many of these are "put up" as you would preserves; however, today we enjoy many innovative uncooked chutneys. Create your own combination!

CRUSHED RED PEPPER. The acceptance of this product has grown in recent years along with the fame of pizza. The long red New Mexican chile is the primary, though not necessarily the only, pepper dried and crushed, including the seeds, to be used in this product. It is often called pizza pepper or *pepperone rosa*.

CURRY POWDER. This condiment originated in India from garam masala (freshly ground dry spices; page 106) and spread to other areas under Indian influence, where it is used to prepare a variety of sauces (curries) to be mixed with meat, seafood, and/or vegetables and served with rice and condiments. Since the eighteenth century, when English interest in and occupation of India began in earnest, curry powder has been used in Great Britain and Europe. A standard-ized, prepared curry powder does not exist in India, and what we buy here is a poor substitute for a freshly ground batch of spices. In the home of the curry, combinations of spices are ground with peppers specifically for the dish being prepared. It might consist of as few as five or as many as fifty ingredients. "Storebought" curry powder usually contains fifteen to twenty spices, herbs, and seeds, primarily chilli, thoroughly dried and ground.

The pungency of curry powder depends on the amount of chilli used. Commercially prepared curry powders are made by grinding slightly roasted chillies to a powder and mixing that with ground turmeric for color and adding coriander along with other spices, which may be one or more of the following: allspice, anise, bay leaves, caraway, cardamom, celery seed, cinnamon, cloves, cubeb berries, dill, fennel, fenugreek, garlic, ginger, juniper berries, mace, mint, mustard, nutmeg, pepper (white and black), poppy seeds, saffron, salt, sumac seeds, and zeodary root. After my extensive travels in the curry belt, I can only say that the product on our food market shelves pales by comparison to the freshly ground spices.

Get a spice mill, mortar, or electric blender and try the mixes on page 210. Store in the refrigerator with the air removed and tightly closed.

HARISSA. Tunisia in North Africa is the home of this fiery blend of dried red chillies, lemon juice, olive oil, garlic, salt, and spices. Harissa sauce both flavors and colors such traditional dishes as couscous. Look for it in specialty or Oriental food stores.

NAM PRIK (Thai hot sauce). A very hot mixture of ground shrimp, garlic, sugar, and dried red chillies mixed with lime juice, fish sauce, and chopped Thai or serrano peppers. Use on chicken or grilled meats. Look for it in Oriental food stores.

PAPRIKA. No single cultivar of pepper is used to make paprika. Paprika is a ground product prepared from the highly colored, mild red fruits of one or more cultivars of *Capsicum annuum* var. *annuum,* and it is used to season and color food. Sweet paprika is primarily the flesh with more than half of the seeds removed, while hot paprika contains seeds, veins, calyces, and stalks, depending on the grade. *Paprika* is also the name by which all peppers are known in the Balkans. Hungarian paprika is prepared from a long cayenne type pepper and is somewhat pungent, while Spanish and Moroccan paprikas are prepared from a milder, tomato-shaped pepper. Paprika is produced in Bulgaria, Czechoslovakia, Yugoslavia, Hungary, Spain, Portugal, Morocco, Chile, and Arizona and California in the United States.

PEPPER JELLY. Not long ago pepper jelly could only be found at the county fair or those other places where ladies brought in their jams and jellies to sell, but now it's in every large food market. Most of it is made from a combination of bell peppers and chillies, such as jalapeño or habanero. It is eaten as an accompaniment to meat and poultry, as mint jelly is with lamb, and it is nice over cream cheese on a cracker for the snack tray.

PEPPER SAUCE (BOTTLED). In 1992, on the shelf of a supermarket in a Texan city of 250,000, I counted at least forty different pepper sauces. Six or seven years before that there would have been six to ten. No matter how many you may find, there are two basic types of pepper sauce:
1. That which used whole fruits of very hot varieties preserved in vinegar or brine. It is used to douse cooked vegetables, especially greens. The liquid can be replenished with more vinegar or brine (this can be done several times).
2. Mashed or pureed chillies that either have or have not been allowed to ferment. These are then used as is or mixed with vinegar and spices.

These sauces are generally put up in small bottles designed to dispense the fiery liquid one drop at a time. "Shots" of hot pepper sauce are added with caution to stews, eggs, soups, oysters, and Bloody Marys, to mention a few. Although Tabasco Brand Pepper Sauce has almost become the generic for the second type of pepper sauce, its makers are justifiably vehement in their insistence that the others are not Tabasco sauce, and that there is but one original fermented sauce made of Tabasco peppers and it is to be known as Tabasco Brand Pepper Sauce, not simply Tabasco sauce (see page 87). I get announcements of new pepper sauces made from all kinds of chillies—dátils, jalapeños, habaneros—in many styles—Malaysian, Thai, Jamaican, Yucatecan–regularly. Try them until you find one you like, or design your own.

Tabasco Brand Pepper Sauce is made from a pepper mash that is packed into fifty-gallon Kentucky white oak barrels, covered, layered with salt, and allowed to ferment for three years. At that time the mash is filtered, homogenized, diluted one to three with vinegar, and bottled in the world-famous bottle with its cherished trademark.

Vinegar or sherry pepper sauce is a simple favorite. Fill a sterile bottle with whatever small chillies you might have—chiltepínes, Tabasco, sports, Thais, 'Floral Gems'—then fill the bottle with a good vinegar or sherry. Let it sit for several weeks before using and refill when necessary. Use on vegetables, eggs, soups, and what have you.

PICKLED AND PROCESSED PRODUCTS. Today you cannot keep up with the growing array of pepper products appearing in our food markets. Pepper processors are hard put to keep up with the increasing popularity of the captivating capsicum. We now have canned peppers, pickled peppers, sauces, dips, cheeses, vegetables with chillies, chilli-flavored potato chips, chilli con queso soup, hot corn chips, candy, jellies, stuffed olives—the list goes on and on. A commonly used Spanish term for "pickled" is *escabeche*. These products are used in place of fresh or dried chillies to add zip to any recipe or to prepared traditional dishes requiring them. Pickle processors like to use little bite-size chillies to eliminate the danger of "spurting" that may occur when biting into a large pickled pod. Many an unwary bystander has been temporarily blinded when a careless aficionado put the bite on a pickled jalapeño.

PIMENTO/PIMIENTO. "Pimento" is the name adopted by the Associated Pimento Canners of Georgia instead of the Spanish *pimiento* for the thick-fleshed, sweet, bright red capsicum that is usually cored, flame peeled, and canned whole or diced; however, *pimiento* is still used on many of the products on the grocers' shelves. The first pimento peppers grown in this country were from Spain. The large heart-shaped fruit is very aromatic. Pimento is used for garnishes, in cheese spreads and bricks, in casserole dishes, and wherever bits of color are desired in food.

RED PEPPER POWDER AND FLAKES. See entries for cayenne pepper and crushed red pepper.

SALSA PICANTE OR MEXICAN HOT SAUCE. The standard Mexican table sauce can now be purchased in bottles in any food market. This once humble preparation made fresh daily by every Mexican housewife is a mixture of chopped tomatoes, onions, and chillies with a few herbs, mainly cilantro, and garlic with some salt and sometimes a little vinegar and a pinch of sugar thrown in. Picante sauce, or *salsa picante,* is used as a dip for toasted tortilla chips (*tostadas*) and on Mexican dishes, as well as on eggs, tacos, and hamburgers. The market for this salsa is growing at a rate of 15 to 20 percent annually, and now outsells catsup.

There are literally hundreds of variations of *salsa picante. Pico de gallo* (rooster's beak) is a name occasionally given to this hot sauce; however, the original Mexican dish by that name is more of a salad made with jícama, oranges, onions, and a dash of serrano.

SAMBAL. Sambals are any kind of fiery hot or spicy relish or condiment served with food. Of Malaysian/Indonesian origin, the burning sambals are found wherever that influence is felt. The basis is always chillies plus a range of such ingredients as garlic, shallots, shrimp paste, tomatoes, tamarind, and even peanut butter. In East Africa mixtures of vegetables, such as cucumbers or carrots, with chillies accompany curried dishes. Southern India is known for a coconut sambal. Many are in the form of a paste or a thick sauce that varies in degree of pungency. Some are sour, while others are sweet. They can be likened to the *salsa picante* of Mexico and some are virtually the same as *salsa cruda* (uncooked salsa). All are made fresh daily in small amounts; however, for a sambal fan in a hurry, a reasonable facsimile can be bought in bottles like American catsup in Oriental food stores and some supermarkets.

On a long houseboat trip up a river in Kalimantan (Borneo), the native cooks let me prepare a fresh sambal for each meal. They are quite simple (see recipes page 151).

SATÉ SAUCE. An Indonesian sauce made of chillies and peanuts ground with lemon grass, shrimp paste, lemons, coconut milk, sugar, and salt to be used on grilled meat. Look for it at Oriental food stores or gourmet shops.

SZECHUAN PEPPERCORNS (*Zanthoxylum piperitum).* Not kin to either black pepper or capsicums, they are the small red-brown seeds from the prickly ash tree. Available in Oriental food stores.

WHOLE PEPPERS, DRIED. There are numerous types of chillies sold in bulk or in packages as dried whole pods. The varieties most commonly sold in this manner are the long red New Mexican chile, pasilla, mulato, ancho, cascabel, guajillo, de árbol, japonés, chiltepín/pequin, catarina, and others.

WHOLE PEPPERS, FRESH. In the United States and Canada the peppers most easily found commercially are the various bell pepper types, long green/red New Mexican chiles, and the yellow wax types. Some of the Mexican favorites found in our markets on a fairly regular basis are jalapeño, serrano, poblano. In ethnic food stores varieties favored by the ethnic group served there are often found. These are used fresh as vegetables, in sauces, and as a seasoning.

MISCELLANEOUS. In 1984 I wrote about jalapeño lollipops, jalapeño jelly beans, olives stuffed with jalapeños, "armadillo eggs" (deep-fried jalapeños stuffed with Italian sausage dressing), and the "Martinez" (a martini made with jalapeño-stuffed olives). Now the list could go on and on because chillies are put in almost anything you can think of. To the ranks of an old standby, the Jamaican Pickapeppa sauce, which is similar to Worcestershire sauce but hot, can be added sauces from all parts of the world, because as we travel more our earth gets smaller and our tastes broader. Now on the market are new imports like *mandram,* a West Indian stomachic made of ground chiltepínes, cucumber, shallots, chives or onions, and lime or lemon juice, and the Arabic *ras el hanout,* a mixture of spices—black pepper, chilli, turmeric, lavender, etc.—used in Moroccan dishes. If you go to various ethnic food shops and poke around for new things, you will find others too numerous to mention, but you can be certain they will have one thing in common—they are HOT!

Ingredients

Many of the recipes included in this book have had foreign inspiration or sources, and the ingredients called for are often exotic, with names that vary from country to country. I have included the scientific names because those are constant the world over and can be used if further information is desired.

ACHIOTE. *Bixa orellana,* the beautiful, small tropical annatto tree, a native of the West Indies, has fruit that look like bright red castor bean pods, which are made into a paste used to color foods more than to flavor them. Pre-Columbian Indians used powdered achiote to paint their bodies, hence the name "red Indians." Sometimes Eurasians substitute it for henna (*Lawsonia inermis*). Look for it in supermarket spice sections or Latin American and Indian food stores.

ADOBO. A dry marinade for meats made by pureeing together peppers—pungent and/or sweet—garlic, salt, pepper, spices, and vinegar or lime juice; the meat is rubbed with the mixture and allowed to sit for several hours or overnight, then it is *adobado* (pickled/preserved) and ready to cook.

BLUE CORNMEAL. This is cornmeal made from grinding the dry kernels of a blue-colored corn, *Zea mays,* favored by the Hopi Indians of Arizona. Available in southwestern supermarkets, or order from Native Seeds.SEARCH or hot food catalogs (see Sources).

CANOLA OIL (*Brassica rapus*). The name is an elision from Canada oil; also known as rapeseed oil. It comes from the rape plant, a relative of the mustard plant. *Lowest in saturated fat of all oils and second highest in monounsaturated fat after olive oil.* Substitute for any cooking oil or salad oil.

CARDAMOM. The very aromatic seed of a

member of the ginger family, *Elettaria cardamomum,* that is native to India. It has not gained the acceptance it deserves in America, but is an Asian, Arabic, and Scandinavian favorite. Do not buy it in powdered form. Get the small gray-green pods, remove the seeds, and grind them yourself. Or throw the pods in whole as is done in India, but be sure not to eat them. Cardamom is very expensive because of its specialized growing requirements, but a little goes a long way. Store tightly closed in the refrigerator or freeze.

CILANTRO (*Coriandrum sativum*). Although a native of the eastern Mediterranean, this herb is sometimes called Chinese parsley, culantro, or fresh coriander. The leaves (cilantro or fresh coriander) and the seeds (coriander), and, occasionally in Indonesia, the roots are used. It has gained in popularity because it is a component of many Mexican, North African, and Oriental dishes. It does not keep well. Put stems in water, cover, and keep in the refrigerator for 2 to 3 days. The only dependable source is a home garden.

COCONUT MILK. The liquid found in a fresh coconut, *Cocos nucifera,* called coconut water, is drunk as a refreshing beverage in the tropics. Coconut "milk" is a man-made milk. Make it by soaking grated coconut meat in hot water and squeezing out the liquid, as follows: Place 1 cup of grated coconut and 4 cups boiling water in a blender and process for a minute or two. Strain through a mesh cloth or piece of cheesecloth. Store in the refrigerator or freeze if not to be used in a day or two. It will keep 1 to 2 weeks. The same coconut meat can be used to make two batches, though the second will not be quite as rich as the first. Feed the remaining coconut to the birds.

CORIANDER. See entry for cilantro.

CRÈME FRAÎCHE. A thickened, nutty-flavored matured cream, not sour cream. To make it, stir 1 tablespoon of buttermilk into 1 cup whipping cream and heat until lukewarm. Remove from the heat, loosely cover, and allow to stand at room temperature until it thickens, 8 to 36 hours, depending on the temperature of the room. Refrigerate, covered, for up to 2 weeks.

CUMIN/COMINO (*Cuminum cyminum*). The flat, oval brown seeds of this eastern Mediterranean and Egyptian annual herb of the parsley family look like caraway or fennel seeds, but are very different in flavor. Essential to Thai, Indian, Middle Eastern, North African, Mexican, and southwestern U.S.A. cooking. No substitute.

EPAZOTE (*Chenopodium ambrosioides*). An annual herb with deeply serrated leaves and a strong, camphorlike odor. It is native to Mexico and Central America. A few chopped leaves of this almost weedlike plant give character to squash, black-eyed peas, and other vegetable dishes. Several sprigs added to a pot of beans are said to alleviate the problem of flatulence. Use fresh or dried. Store the easily dried leaves in a tightly closed jar. Grow your own, or purchase it in Latin American food markets where it may be labeled *pazote* or Jerusalem oak pazote. It grows very easily, but take care—it will take over your herb bed. There is no substitute.

FAGARA (*Zanthoxylum armatum* and/or *Z. planispinum*). In China these peppery seeds play the role black pepper does in our own cuisine. Look for them in an Oriental food store.

FISH SAUCE. A sauce made from layering fresh anchovies and brine that is used in southeast Asia as the Chinese use soy sauce. There is no substitute. Buy in an Oriental food store.

FIVE-SPICE POWDER. A blend of various spices including fennel, Szechuan pepper (see page 103), cloves, cinnamon, and anise used for chicken, fish, and marinades. No substitute. Buy in Oriental food stores.

GALANGA (*Allpinia galanga*). Also called Siamese ginger, hos, or galingale, this gingerlike root from Southeast Asia is used in Thai and Indonesian cooking. The rhizomes of the plant are dried, then powdered. Look for it in Oriental food stores or substitute fresh or ground ginger.

GINGER (*Zingiber officinale*). The root (actually a rhizome) of this tropical Southeast Asian native is indispensable in Oriental cookery. Select plump, smooth roots, scrape off the thin skin, place the roots in a jar, fill with sherry wine, cover, and store in the refrigerator, where it will keep for weeks. Do not freeze. It is also sold dried and powdered, and preserved in syrup or candied and coated in sugar to be used as is or chopped and sprinkled over desserts. Most supermarkets and all Oriental food stores sell both fresh and preserved ginger. There is no substitute.

GARAM MASALA. A blend of dried spices that have been roasted just before they are ground into a fine powder by a *masalchi* (the person who grinds) and are used sparingly toward the end of cooking or are sprinkled over the cooked food as a garnish. There are as many versions as there are chefs. Try making it yourself (page 210).

HOISIN SAUCE. A thick, spicy, sweet, dark brownish red Chinese condiment made of soy bean flour, garlic, chillies, ginger, and sugar used in stir-fried dishes, on mu shu pork, and in Chinese barbecue sauce. Sold in cans or bottles at Oriental food stores, it will keep for months tightly closed in the refrigerator. There is no substitute.

JÍCAMA (*Pachyrhizus erosus*). Jícama is the large, turniplike, brown-skinned root of a native Mexican legume that has a crunchy, slightly sweet white interior. Use fresh; crispness is lost when cooked. Store in the refrigerator for up to 2 weeks. More and more supermarkets carry this in their special vegetable section. Select firm roots.

KAFFIR LIME (*Citrus hystrix*). Substitute juice from regular fresh limes for the juice and any citrus leaf for the leaves of this Asian citrus fruit. Oriental food stores may have the leaves if you don't live where citrus trees grow.

LEMON GRASS (*Cymbopogone citratus*). A fairly tall, clumping grass. The bulbous white base and the leaves are essential to Thai, Vietnamese, and Indonesian cuisine and probably native to those areas. It is easy to grow, but a hard freeze will kill it. If you don't grow it, try an Oriental food store. You can substitute lemon peel.

MANGO (*Mangifera indica*). The fruit of a large tropical tree that is native to India. It is eaten both ripe or green, raw or cooked, dried or made into preserves and chutneys. There are many varieties of this aromatic fruit—some good, some stringy. The juice may cause skin problems for people hypersensitive to irritants in the sap. As a precaution, use one knife to peel the fruit, and a clean knife to slice the flesh to avoid contaminating it with the resin in the peel. Most supermarkets have mangoes, at least part of the year. Select rather firm partially ripe fruit with a taut skin that is blushed with red or yellow. Smell the stem end to make certain it has not begun to ferment.

MASA HARINA. A very finely ground yellow hominy (lime-treated dried corn) cornmeal used to make tortillas and tamales. Available in food stores in the Southwest and Latin American food stores elsewhere. It is also made by the Quaker Oats Company.

MENNONITE CHEESE. A white farm cheese made by Mennonites. Substitute a white farmer's cheese or Monterey jack.

MEXICAN CHEESES. Before the arrival of Columbus, people of the Americas had no dairy animals, hence, no cheese. There are now many,

many cheeses in Mexico but few of them are available in U.S. food markets. *Queso fresco* (fresh) and/or *queso blanco* (white) are mild, fresh cheeses used to crumble over the various tortilla dishes. Feta makes an adequate substitute. *Queso añejo* (aged) is a dry cheese similar to Parmesan. *Asadero* (roasting) is a cheese to be melted, like mozzarella.

MEXICAN CHOCOLATE. The name for chocolate derives from two Nahuatl words, *xoco* (bitter) and *atl* (water). In pre-Columbian Mexico a favored drink was made with chocolate in cold water sweetened with honey and spiced with vanilla, then beaten until foamy with a *molinillo* (a wooden beater that is twirled between the palms). Today, chocolate drinks are made in the same manner using small cakes of prepared chocolate sweetened with sugar. In the U.S., it can be purchased at most Latin American food stores.

MUSTARD OIL (*Brassica* spp.). A yellow oil made from mustard seed—pungent when raw but sweet when heated slightly. It is used in Indian cookery to prepare vegetables, fish, and for pickling. Peanut oil can be substituted. Look for it in Indian food stores.

NOPALES (*Opuntia engelmannii* or a similar species). New or very young green pads (these are flat stems, not leaves) of the prickly pear cactus, a New World native. The fruits, *tunas,* can be eaten when ripe. Many supermarkets now carry nopales in season (spring).

PALM SUGAR (*Coco nucifera* or *Borssaus flabellifer*). The sap of either the coconut palm or the sugar palm is formed into light brown cakes and used in cooking. If it cannot be found at an Oriental food store, soft brown cane sugar can be substituted.

PAPAYA (*Carica papaya*). Sometimes called papaw, this large herbaceous herb grows to twenty feet tall and bears large, melonlike, green to orange fruits with pinkish orange flesh that emerge from the trunklike stem. This native of tropical America was introduced to the Philippines by the Spaniards in the mid sixteenth century and from there became pantropic. The ripe fruit is commonly eaten fresh with lime or lemon, but unripe fruit is never eaten raw because of the latex content. It can be used in making pies, sauces, jams, and marmalades, alone or combined with pineapple. The fruit should be ripe and slightly soft. To ripen, put it in a paper bag in a dark place. Do not chill the fruit before it is ripe. Most supermarkets have papayas year round.

PEPITAS (*Cucurbita pepo*). Raw, hulled, unsalted pumpkin seeds, greenish in color with a nutty flavor, that are ground for sauces; used toasted or plain. Stored in the refrigerator in tightly closed containers, they will keep several months. Ground pepitas will not keep as long— try freezing them. Toasted pepitas can be bought in jars or cans in the nut section of supermarkets.

PILLÓNCILLO. A little loaf (*pilón*) of unrefined brown sugar from Mexico that can be in the shape of a cone, loaf, or cylinder. Substitute dark brown sugar.

RICE VINEGAR. A light amber-, red-, or black-colored condiment or flavoring agent made from rice. The light type is used in sweet-and-sour dishes, the black is used to darken the color of sauces, and the red is used mainly as a dip for meats and vegetables. Buy it at Oriental food stores; it will keep indefinitely. There is no substitute.

RICE WINE. There are two kinds of Shaosing, China's most popular wine—white and yellow. The sherrylike yellow is made from yellow rice and is warmed before drinking from tiny cups. In cooking, substitute Japanese sake, dry sherry, or gin, but never cooking or cream sherry. The clear, vodkalike white wine from north China is used in cooking not as flavoring but rather to neutralize strong odors. Purchase at Oriental food or liquor stores.

ROMA TOMATOES (*Lycopersicon esculentum*). A small, cylindrical, Italian-type tomato used for cooking and sauces. It has fewer seeds and less juice than regular tomatoes. Excellent for sauces and sun or oven drying.

SESAME OIL (*Sesamum indicum*). The flat, white seeds from this herbaceous annual have been ground for their oil in non-Hebrew cultures since a few thousand years before Christ. The nutty-flavored oil is consumed at or near the principal areas of production—Africa, India, China, and the Middle East. The whole seeds are used in cooking and baking. In a tightly closed bottle it will keep almost indefinitely in the refrigerator. The best is found in Oriental food stores.

SOFRITO. A traditional Spanish seasoning mixture of onions, garlic, capsicums—sweet and/or pungent—herbs, achiote seeds, and sometimes ham sautéed in olive oil or lard.

STAR ANISE (*Illicium verum*). The licorice-like flavor of the seeds of this small Chinese evergreen tree is rather new to American cooks. It is entirely different botanically from anise (*Pimpinella anisum*). Look for it in Oriental food stores.

SUGARS. Sugars are the rudimentary carbohydrates. Granulated sugar is sucrose taken from sugar cane or beets; glucose is the sugar found in fruits and vegetables; and fructose is the major component of honey and corn syrup. Crystalline fructose is more refined and less natural than sucrose. It must be used in its natural form to be a "healthy" substitute for sucrose.

TAMALES. Tamales are seasoned masa mixed with lard spread on corn husks or banana leaves (in the banana belt) and cooked; they may be unfilled or filled with any of a variety of seasoned fillings and rolled, ends folded, and steamed. The "shuck" is removed before eating. They are available canned (a very poor substitute wrapped in flavorless paper) and frozen in most supermarkets and fresh in southwestern supermarkets or Latin American food stores. In Texas almost everyone has a favorite local "tamale lady" to make them for special occasions—a Christmas Eve tradition in south Texas.

TAMARIND (*Tamarindus indica*). A tropical tree from India that produces a large brown bean pod. The seeds inside the brittle shell are enclosed in a sticky, brown pulp with a tart flavor. In India the pulp is an integral part of chutneys and sauces, and it gives Worcestershire sauce its characteristic flavor. Soak the dried pulp in enough lukewarm water to cover until soft—25 to 30 minutes. Squeeze until the pulp dissolves in the water, then strain to remove seeds and fibers. In the Southwest the dried pods are frequently available in supermarkets. A rather salty bottled tamarind paste is available in Indian food stores. Dilute the paste with water to prepare juice or reserve the soaking water to use when tamarind juice is called for.

TOMATILLOS (*Physalis ixocarpa*). The little Mexican green husk tomatoes are not really tomatoes but rather are kin to the Cape gooseberry. Their tartness adds distinction to many Mexican-style dishes and sauces. Select firm, unblemished fruit and remove the husks before using. Fresh ones can be found in southwestern supermarkets and canned ones are available in most places. Drain the canned ones before using. Green tomatoes can be substituted—but not fried ones.

TORTILLA. An unleavened, thin flat, round bread made of cornmeal or flour, it is the basis of Mexican, southwestern, and Tex-Mex cookery.

The ones made with wheat flour are handy substitutes for the typical breads of India and the Middle East. Available in the bread and/or refrigerator section of many supermarkets.

Cooking Notes

The cooking notes are few in number because most kitchens have a standard cookbook like *Joy of Cooking*, which can serve as a reference. The notes included here are for your convenience because they have been used frequently in the directions for preparation of the recipes.

BLANCH. To plunge food into boiling water and to cook until softened or partially or fully cooked. To do this in the microwave, place the vegetables in a recommended container, add a few tablespoons of water, cover, and microwave at high 2 to 5 minutes, depending on the quantity; stir. If needed, repeat. Plunge into iced water to stop the cooking.

CHOPPING HERBS. Wash and dry the herbs, as moisture causes sogginess. Remove any woodlike stems, then process in a food processor by pulsing on and off.

DEMI-GLACE. A demi-glace is made in a saucepan over high heat by bringing 1 quart of brown stock to a boil (see Stock, next column); reduce the heat and add 4 teaspoons of cornstarch mixed with 4 teaspoons cold water. Simmer until reduced by a half and the mixture is thick enough to coat a spoon. Stir until it is cool in order to prevent separation. Use in making sauces. This will keep up to a week in the refrigerator or several months if frozen. Note: canned beef bouillon can be substituted if homemade stock is not available.

GRINDING VEGETABLES. Ground vegetables have a distinct coarse texture as opposed to shredded or chopped vegetables and can be obtained with the coarse grind disk on an old-fashioned meat grinder (hand turned or electric) or a Braun type mixer/grinder (mine is 1970 vintage). It is almost impossible to get a comparable texture with a food processor—it will be either too coarse or too mushy. My late, noncooking physician husband loved Hayden's Relish (page 204) so much that he would volunteer to turn the crank on my grandmother's old grinder for hours during sweltering Texas summers before we had an air-conditioned kitchen (1944–1954) in order for the vegetables to have the desired texture for his favorite condiment.

NONREACTIVE CONTAINER. A glass, enamel- or agate-coated, stainless-steel, or any other type container that will not set up a chemical reaction with the food placed in it. Especially important when the foods are highly acidic.

REDUCE. To decrease the volume of a liquid by boiling, thereby concentrating its taste.

ROASTING VEGETABLES. Place the vegetable (tomatoes, garlic, shallots, eggplant) on an aluminum foil–lined pan 4 to 6 inches under the broiler flame. Broil until the skin is evenly charred, turning as needed. Remove only badly charred skin in order to maintain the desired flavor. Squeeze the garlic or shallots from their skins. Use as directed in the recipe.

SAUTÉ. To cook and brown food in a very small amount of really hot fat, usually in an uncovered skillet. The secret is to have the fat or oil very hot, the food dry, and to sear quickly to prevent loss of juices.

STOCK. The broth from boiled meat, chicken, or fish used in preparing soups and sauces. A flavorful stock is important. When boiling a chicken or other meat, add onion, celery, peppers, garlic, carrots, bay leaves, peppercorns, and herbs. Cook over low heat until the meat is tender. (For a richer stock, remove the meat, debone, then return the bones to the stock, and simmer for an hour or more.) Remove the meat (or bones), degrease, and strain. For a clear stock, never allow the broth to boil. Veal meat and bones produce stock with a neutral flavor. For a brown stock with a more robust flavor, cook the bones in a roasting pan in a 450° F oven, turning several times, until the bones are golden brown on all sides. Add the browned bones to the stock pot along with the vegetables.

SWEAT. See entry for wilt.

TOASTING SEEDS. Place seeds—sesame, cumin, pumpkin (pepitas), sunflower, or poppy —in a flat pan and toast for about 20 minutes in a 350° F oven and stir frequently, taking care not to scorch. This can also be done in a microwave by spreading the seeds in a shallow microwave container and cooking, stirring at ½- to 1-minute

intervals, until toasted. This brings out the nutty flavor. Prepare with or without a little vegetable oil. Yet another method is in a dry skillet over low heat on the top of the stove, using as little oil as possible, or none at all, and guarding against burning by watching carefully and stirring frequently.

USING A SPICE GRINDER. Whole spices and herbs may be ground in a small electric spice or coffee grinder, or by using a mortar and pestle. In order to maintain the volatile natural flavoring compounds of the spice, grind only the amount needed at the time. Do not overgrind.

WILT. Vegetables can be wilted (or sweated) in a covered skillet with a small amount of oil over medium heat, stirring frequently to prevent any browning. Cook them to a barely limp state. This can be done in a covered dish in the microwave without using oil, a plus for the calorie- and health-conscious cook.

PART II

THE RECIPES

Ordinary recipes using the captivating capsicum just wouldn't do! The recipes in this book are from prominent chefs who have been pioneers in the use of peppers. My book *Peppers: The Domesticated Capsicums* was published in December 1984, after eight years of research and preparation. During those years I never dreamed I was working with a plant that was about to become the darling of the food world. As a result, I have had the pleasure of meeting many of the creative food people interested in peppers, and when I decided to do this book my first thought was to turn to them for recipes. Invitations to submit a tested recipe of their own choosing in which peppers were an integral part, which took into consideration current health issues such as low sodium, low cholesterol, etc., which were designed for the American kitchen and for a busy cook, and which were uncomplicated went out across the land. The response was wonderful! They sent favorite recipes from one of their own books or ones created especially for this publication. The remainder are old favorites that I have concocted and served to family and friends for years or ones I compiled and tested in my kitchen from traditional recipes that I thought should be included.

Since 1984 the availability of peppers and pepper products has become so widespread that the reader will not have a problem finding the ingredients; however, a few mail-order sources are listed on page 224. In the recipes that follow don't be afraid to add or subtract chillies. It is best to use less and build up by tasting as you cook than to get the dish so strong that it is not comfortable to eat. Remember that the pungency of a particular variety of pepper is very variable, and I do mean variable!

Nothing tastes as good as butter, cream, eggs, and sugar but in this health-conscious age, many are trying to eat more nutritious foods. There are many alternatives, but here are a few of my favorite ways to make these already health-conscious recipes even more so without too much risk of spoiling them too badly:

• Use canola oil in place of any oil except olive, and in that case switch to "lite" olive. There is no substitute for the flavor of olive oil.

• Four tablespoons of egg product can be used instead of one egg, even in mayonnaise, with surprisingly good results. In mayonnaise or any similar sauce that forms an emulsion, add a few sprigs of parsley to ensure an emulsion.

• Use an equal amount of ground turkey in any recipe calling for a ground red meat.

• To reduce calories and fat, remove the skin from all poultry and fish, but only after cooking and not before in order to maintain flavor and prevent dryness.

• When a recipe calls for wilting or sautéing onions or other vegetables in any type of fat, omit the fat and wilt them in a covered container in the microwave.

• Use "lite" margarine when butter is called for. Most of the time you can get by with only a small part of the fat called for in a recipe.

• Use Morton's Lite Salt instead of salt and put it in only after all the cooking is complete to reduce the opportunity for the metallic flavor associated with salt substitutes to develop.

• Seasoning with chillies reduces the need for salt.

• Substitute no-fat or low-fat plain yogurt for sour cream and use dripped no-fat yogurt instead of cream cheese.

• Cook anything you can in a microwave oven in order to retain more nutrients and flavor. Almost any recipe can be prepared in a microwave now that special pans for browning in the pan before going in the microwave have been developed. If the recipe does not give a cooking time, just experiment by starting with a few seconds or minutes and repeating until the dish is cooked thoroughly. Stir the food from time to time to ensure all parts are cooked. Fish, fowl, and ham do well but other meats don't—especially roast beef.

Serrano Bloody Mary
MARK MILLER   *Coyote Cafe*

MAKES 12 SERVINGS

⅓ cup fresh lime juice
3 to 5 serranos (page 86), seeded
1 bunch cilantro (fresh coriander),
stemmed and chopped (reserve some
sprigs for garnish)
One 46-ounce can tomato juice
¾ cup tequila, chilled
Freshly cracked black pepper and salt
to taste

Place the first 3 ingredients in a blender and process until smooth. Mix with the tomato juice and tequila. Pour through a strainer into a pitcher (you may want to strain it twice). Serve over ice garnished with fresh cracked pepper, salt, and a sprig of cilantro.

Chile-Con-Queso with Rajas
PATRICIA QUINTANA

MAKES 6 TO 8 SERVINGS; MORE AS A DIP

¼ cup (½ stick) margarine
1 large red onion, finely chopped
12 green poblanos (page 82) or New
Mexican chiles (page 78), roasted,
peeled, veins and seeds removed; cut
in strips (rajas)
1 fresh or canned jalapeño (page 77),
minced
2 cups grated Monterey Jack cheese
2 cups grated Mozzarella cheese
1 cup milk
1 cup heavy cream or yogurt thinned
with milk to consistency of heavy
cream
Salt and freshly ground black pepper
to taste
1 large, ripe tomato, peeled, finely
chopped, and well drained

Melt the margarine in a frying pan over medium heat, then cook the onions, stirring, until transparent. Add poblano strips and jalapeño and cook, stirring, until softened. Add the cheeses and cook over low heat until the cheese begins to melt. Stir in the milk and heavy cream, and season with salt and pepper. Cook until a thick sauce is formed with the partially melted cheese, about 20 minutes. Add the tomatoes just before serving. Serve immediately in individual bowls or small plates with freshly made corn tortillas. In the Southwest, chile con queso is served from a chafing dish or fondue pot as a dip with tostadas (toasted tortilla chips).

Guacamole
JEAN ANDREWS

It's a long, long road to guacamole, and there are many variations of the dish along the way. Start with one and vary it to suit your taste.

MAKES 2 CUPS

4 ripe avocados, peeled, pitted, and
mashed with a fork (see notes below)
1 small, ripe tomato, chopped
1 tablespoon minced onion
Juice of 1 garlic clove (use a garlic
press)
1 to 2 serranos (page 86), seeded and
minced
2 teaspoons cilantro (fresh coriander),
finely chopped
Fresh lime or lemon juice to taste
Salt and freshly ground black pepper
to taste

Mix all the ingredients in a bowl. This mixture should have some texture. If a food processor is used, care must be taken to keep the mixture from becoming too smooth. The addition of 1 teaspoon of lemon juice or Fruit Fresh (ascorbic acid) and covering with plastic wrap touching the surface of the mixture will allow you to make this several hours ahead of serving time without fear of it turning black on top; otherwise, make it at the last minute. Serve with toasted tortilla chips.

NOTES: To peel an avocado, cut in half and remove the seed. Using a tablespoon, insert the spoon between the peel and meat and work it to the other side, scooping out the entire half. Dip the avocado quickly into a solution of water and ascorbic acid (a commercial preparation such as Fruit Fresh) or wipe it with lemon juice to prevent darkening.

If an avocado is not ripe, wrap it in newspaper or place it in a paper sack and set it in a microwave; at high power, using half-minute intervals, carefully heat the avocado until it is the desired consistency.

Grilled Quesadillas with Smoked Chicken
REED CLEMONS   *The Granite Cafe*

MAKES 8 SERVINGS

3 cups cooked black beans (recipe follows)
16 flour tortillas
1 pound smoked chicken, diced (or substitute grilled chicken)
1 pound Monterey Jack cheese, grated
3 poblanos (page 82), roasted (pages 96–97), peeled, and cut into strips
1 canned chipotle adobado (page 91), pureed (use more if desired)

Spread the pureed black beans on 8 of the tortillas and top with the smoked chicken, Jack cheese, and poblano strips. On the other 8 tortillas, spread the pureed chipotle. Place these tortillas on top of the others, chipotle side down.

Place the *quesadillas* on a preheated grill for a minute or so, and then, without turning the *quesadillas* over, turn them at a 45-degree angle for another minute or so, until there is a good crisscross pattern. Then repeat the same procedure for the other side. Be careful not to burn. Once they are done, take them off the grill and cut them into 6 to 8 wedges. Serve hot with the tomatillo sauce (page 147) and guacamole (page 114).

Black Beans

MAKES 8 SERVINGS

1 pound dried black beans, picked over
¼ cup vegetable oil
2 large onions, diced
1 garlic clove, minced
2 tablespoons ground cumin
Salt to taste
1 bunch fresh epazote (page 105), optional

Soak the beans in cold water to cover for several hours or overnight. Heat the oil in a large saucepan over low heat and cook the onions and garlic, stirring, for 5 minutes. Add the beans and enough water to cover, the cumin, salt, and epazote and bring to a boil. Reduce the heat to medium-low and simmer until tender, about 2 hours, stirring occasionally and making sure there is enough water to cover the beans. Puree the beans in a food processor (you may have to do this in batches).

Pickled Chiles Anchos

MIGUEL RAVAGO   *Fonda San Miguel*

MAKES 10 OR 20 SERVINGS

4 cups red wine vinegar
4 cups water
1½ cups piloncillo (Mexican cone
*   sugar) or 1 cup firmly packed*
*   brown sugar*
12 garlic cloves, peeled
10 bay leaves
2 tablespoons black peppercorns
2 tablespoons allspice berries
½ cup vegetable oil
½ cup olive oil
*   Sprigs of fresh herbs (such as thyme,*
*   sage, marjoram, oregano, mint, or*
*   tarragon)*
20 anchos (page 83), one side slit,
*   seeded, and deveined*

FOR THE FILLING
1 cup ricotta cheese
1 cup cottage cheese
*   Chopped green onions (scallions) to*
*   taste*
*   Minced cilantro (fresh coriander) to*
*   taste*
*   Salt and freshly ground black pepper*
*   to taste*

In a saucepan boil the vinegar, water, and piloncillo over high heat until the sugar dissolves; lower the heat. Add the garlic, bay leaves, and spices; allow to simmer for 10 minutes. Turn off the heat and add the oil, herbs and anchos; marinate overnight at room temperature.

To serve, drain the anchos and stuff with a mixture of equal parts of ricotta and cottage cheese to which has been added a little chopped green onion, minced cilantro, and salt and pepper to taste. Or use a filling of tuna salad, seafood salad, or guacamole salad.

Cheese-Stuffed Anaheims

FRIEDA AND KAREN CAPLAN   *Frieda's Inc.*

MAKES 36 APPETIZER SERVINGS

4 ounces sharp Cheddar cheese,
*   shredded*
3 green onions (scallions), chopped
2 fresh green chillies (serrano, 'Santa Fe
*   Grande,' 'Fresno,' or jalapeño; see*
*   index), seeded and minced*
⅓ cup black olives, pitted and chopped
2 tablespoons chopped cilantro (fresh
*   coriander)*
2 tablespoons milk
*   Salt and freshly ground black pepper*
*   to taste*
4 to 6 fresh green New Mexican (Anaheim)
*   chiles (page 78)*
*   Lettuce leaves*
*   Cilantro sprigs for garnish, optional*

In a food processor or using a mixer, combine the cheese, green onions, the 2 chillies, the olives, cilantro, and milk until well blended. Season with salt and pepper. Wash and trim with the stems from the New Mexican chiles. Slit them lengthwise; remove the ribs and seeds. Stuff the chiles with the cheese mixture, packing in the mixture with the back of a spoon. Chill several hours or overnight. To serve, arrange lettuce leaves on a platter. Slice the stuffed chiles crosswise into ½-inch-thick slices and arrange on the platter. Garnish with cilantro, if desired.

Caponata
JEAN ANDREWS

MAKES 8 CUPS

1 cup olive oil
2 large eggplants, peeled and cut into
   1-inch cubes, sprinkled with salt, and
   left to stand for 1 hour
3 medium-size onions, halved and sliced
   very thin
1½ cups minced celery (parboiled 2
   minutes, drained, and 1 cup
   measured)
1 red bell pepper, seeded and diced
¾ cup tomato sauce or puree
2 tablespoons Italian capers, rinsed and
   drained
1 dozen black olives, pitted and sliced
1 tablespoon pine nuts or sunflower
   seeds, or to taste
¼ cup red wine vinegar
2 tablespoons sugar
½ teaspoon salt
½ teaspoon ground cayenne pepper
¼ teaspoon freshly ground
   black pepper

Rinse and dry the eggplant. In a large saucepan heat the olive oil over medium-high heat. When hot, add the eggplant and cook, stirring, until browned. Remove with a slotted spoon and let drain on paper toweling. Cook the onions, stirring, in the oil until soft but not brown. Add ½ cup of celery, bell pepper, and tomato sauce and simmer over medium heat for 15 minutes. Add the capers, olives, pine nuts, vinegar, sugar, salt, cayenne pepper, black pepper, and the eggplant. Simmer until thick and condensed, about 20 minutes, stirring often. Add one cup of cooked celery and mix well. Add more tomato sauce if too dry. Adjust the seasonings to taste. Serve at room temperature with crusty Italian bread or crackers. This is a superb appetizer, and it freezes very well.

VARIATION: For a zippy caponata, sauté a minced fresh jalapeño or two (page 77) along with the celery and bell peppers.

Pita Pepper Confetti Hors D'Oeuvres
ROLLIE ANNE BLACKWELL   Gourmet Dallas

MAKES 40 HORS D'OEUVRES

¼ cup (½ stick) unsalted butter or
   margarine
1 large red bell pepper, seeded and cut
   into very small squares
1 large yellow bell pepper, seeded and
   cut into very small squares
1 large green bell pepper, seeded and
   cut into very small squares
6 small green onions (scallions), finely
   chopped
   Salt and freshly ground black pepper
   to taste
6 ounces Monterey Jack or ancho chilli
   cheese, grated
1 package pita bread, cut into triangles,
   brushed with melted butter or margarine, and toasted in a 400°F oven
   until crisp
   Fresh cilantro (fresh coriander) sprigs,
   optional

Melt the butter in a frying pan over medium heat, then cook the bell peppers and onions, stirring, until translucent, about 2 minutes. Season with salt and pepper and add the grated Monterey Jack Cheese, stirring until melted. Mound onto the toasted pita triangles and garnish with a sprig of cilantro, if desired.

Grilled Scallops with a Rocotillo Mango Relish
CHRIS SCHLESINGER   *East Coast Grill*

MAKES 8 APPETIZER SERVINGS

2 pounds sea scallops
1 cup seeded and diced rocotillo (page 9), fresh red pimento (page 81), or red bell peppers
1 small red onion, cut into small dice
1 green bell pepper, seeded and cut into small dice
1 jalapeño (page 77), seeded and cut into small dice
2 mangoes (page 106), cut into small dice
½ cup fresh orange juice
½ cup pineapple juice
½ cup fresh lime juice
¼ cup chopped cilantro (fresh coriander)
Salt and freshly ground black pepper to taste

Place the scallops on skewers and grill over a medium-hot fire until they are golden brown outside and opaque inside (about 2 to 3 minutes per side). In a mixing bowl, combine the remaining ingredients into an uncooked relish. Serve the scallops on a bed of relish seasoned with salt and pepper.

Seviche (Ceviche)
JEAN ANDREWS

MAKES 10 TO 12 SERVINGS

2 pounds redfish, snapper, trout, or a mixture (use any good fresh fish your favorite fisherman brings home), filleted and cut into very narrow strips
2 cups mixed chopped clams, oysters, shrimp, and/or snails (if none are available, use more fish)
3 cups fresh lime juice (Mexican limes preferred, but never bottled lime juice)
2 fresh green chillies (serranos, jalapeños, or 'Fresnos'; see index), seeded and chopped
1 large, ripe tomato, chopped
1 large onion, finely chopped
3 to 4 cilantro (fresh coriander) sprigs, chopped
1 to 2 tablespoons olive oil
Salt and freshly ground black pepper to taste

Place the fish and shellfish in a large nonreactive bowl. Cover with half the lime juice and marinate in the refrigerator at least 4 hours, preferably overnight. Drain and wash in cold water. Drain again. Return to the bowl. Pour in the remainder of the lime juice and add the remaining ingredients. (Some like to add sliced stuffed olives.) Serve in cocktail dishes before dinner, from a bowl sitting in ice as an appetizer, or on a bed of lettuce as a luncheon entrée. Accompany with soda crackers.

Hot Olives
JEAN ANDREWS

Prepare a jar of olives to have on hand for drinks, appetizers, or what have you.

1 jar giant whole or stuffed olives
Juice from the same-size jar or can of jalapeños (page 77)

Drain the juice from the olives and replace it with the juice from the jalapeños. Recap the jar and keep it in the refrigerator for 3 weeks before using. Replace the liquid in the jalapeño jar with equal amounts of vinegar and water. Recap and store in the refrigerator.

Creamy Chile Dip
JEAN ANDREWS

MAKES 1 CUP

> 6 *fresh green New Mexican chiles (page 78), peeled, seeded, and chopped, or one 4-ounce can, drained and chopped*
> One *8-ounce package cream cheese or dripped yogurt (see note below)*
> 2 *tablespoons milk*
> 3 *tablespoons finely chopped green onion (scallion)*
> 4 *garlic cloves, pressed*
> ½ *teaspoon ground cayenne pepper*

Combine all the ingredients in a medium-size bowl and beat until creamy. Add more milk if necessary. Allow to sit for at least 1 hour at room temperature before serving. Serve as a dip with chips or fresh vegetables or stuff into banana pepper halves (page 65) or celery.

NOTE: Drip yogurt by placing nonfat, plain yogurt in a drip bag or filter. Suspend it over a bowl and allow it to drip overnight in the refrigerator. This can be substituted for cream cheese in any recipe.

Macho Butter
JEAN ANDREWS

MAKES ABOUT 5 CUPS

> 3 *chipotles (page 91), rehydrated (page 99) and seeded*
> 4 *anchos (page 83), lightly toasted (page 99), rehydrated (page 99) and seeded*
> 1 *garlic clove, peeled*
> 3 *cups chunky peanut butter*
> 1½ *cups sesame seeds*
> *Ground cayenne pepper as needed*

Place the peppers and garlic in a blender and process until smooth, adding a little of the soaking water to make a paste. Gradually add the peanut butter, mixing well. Add the sesame seeds and mix until distributed throughout. Season with cayenne pepper. Serve as a spread with tortilla chips, bread rounds, or celery sticks.

Lillian's Tangy Cheese Ball
JEAN ANDREWS

MAKES 1 LARGE OR 2 SMALL CHEESE BALLS

> 6 *ounces Roquefort or blue cheese, at room temperature*
> 10 *ounces very sharp, crumbly Cheddar cheese, finely grated, at room temperature*
> 12 *ounces cream cheese, at room temperature*
> 1 *small onion, grated*
> 1 *tablespoon Worcestershire sauce*
> 1 *teaspoon ground cayenne pepper, or to taste*
> 1½ *cups pecans, finely chopped*
> 1½ *cups fresh parsley leaves, minced*

Place all the cheeses in a large bowl with the onion, Worcestershire, and cayenne pepper. Add ½ cup each of the nuts and fresh parsley, reserving the remainder. With your hands, process the mixture thoroughly. Do not use a mixer. Shape into 1 large or 2 small balls and place in a bowl lined with plastic wrap or aluminum foil. Refrigerate overnight. Before serving, roll the balls in a mixture of the remaining fresh parsley and pecans. Serve with unsalted or water crackers.

NOTE: Unused portions of the ball can be remolded and frozen.

Cheese Bites
JEAN ANDREWS

MAKES 24 OR MORE

1 pound sharp cheddar cheese, grated,
   at room temperature
½ pound (2 sticks) butter or margarine,
   at room temperature
2 cups all-purpose flour
½ teaspoon freshly ground black pepper
1 teaspoon salt
2 teaspoons ground cayenne pepper

In a processor or mixer, process the ingredients until they are creamed. Roll in a long roll in wax paper and chill thoroughly. Slice or use a cookie press. Arrange with space between each on an ungreased cookie sheet. Bake in a preheated 400°F oven for 7 minutes, or until slightly browned. Serve as appetizer with soups and salads. The dough can be made ahead and frozen. VARIATION: Half a cup of chopped pecans, walnuts, or Grape Nuts cereal can be mixed into the creamy dough before rolling.

Spicy Tortilla Soup
JEAN ANDREWS

MAKES 8 CUPS

1 small onion, finely chopped
2 to 4 cloves garlic, minced
1 tablespoon vegetable oil
6 cups chicken broth (homemade from
   chicken cooked with herbs, onions,
   celery, and carrots is best, but canned
   will do)
Two 10¾-ounce cans chopped tomatoes
   and green chiles
3 tablespoons chopped fresh coriander
   (cilantro)
1 teaspoon ground cumin

Salt and freshly ground black pepper
   to taste
1 teaspoon sugar
Juice of 2 limes
½ to 1 cup shredded cooked chicken
   (optional)
½ to 1 cup shredded Monterey Jack cheese
   Lightly salted tortilla chips, broken
   Sprigs cilantro (fresh coriander)

In a small skillet wilt the onion and garlic in the oil over low heat, or omit the oil and wilt them in a microwave. Place the onion mixture in a large stock pot and add all of the ingredients except the cheese, tortillas, and cilantro sprigs. Stir the mixture well, then cover and simmer the soup over low heat for about 1 hour. If it cooks down too much, add water to bring it back to 8 cups. When ready to serve, warm the bowls and bring the soup up to a boil, but don't boil. Put a heaping tablespoonful of the cheese and a handful of the tortilla chips in each bowl. Fill the bowls with very hot soup and top each with several sprigs of cilantro. Serve immediately. This soup, served with Jalapeño Dinner Muffins (page 190) or Jalapeño Cornbread (pages 191, 192), can make a meal. Serve smaller amounts if it is to be eaten before a meal.
NOTE: I have been served tortilla soup with a whole chipotle swimming on the surface, but I don't recommend it for the novice.

Grilled Corn Soup with Southwestern Creams
STEPHEN PYLES   *Baby Routh*

MAKES 6 TO 8 SERVINGS

4 ears fresh corn, partially husked
3 cups chicken stock
½ cup chopped carrots
¼ cup chopped celery

½ cup chopped onion
2 garlic cloves, roasted and squeezed
   from skins (page 109)
1 serrano (page 86), seeded and
   chopped
½ cup Cilantro Cream (recipe follows)
½ cup Ancho Chile Cream (next column)
   Salt to taste

Over a low charcoal fire, grill the corn 5 minutes on each side. Remove from the fire, and when cool remove the husks. Place the chicken stock, carrots, celery, onion, garlic, and serrano in a saucepan. Bring to a boil, then let simmer over medium-low heat for 5 minutes. Remove the kernels from the corn with a knife. Add the kernels to the stock and let simmer 10 minutes longer. Place all the ingredients from the saucepan into a blender and puree completely (you may have to do this in batches). Pass the mixture through a strainer and return to the saucepan. Add the creams and place the pan over low heat. Simmer for 5 minutes.

Cilantro Cream

MAKES ½ CUP

3 cups water
6 to 12 fresh spinach leaves, well washed
   and stemmed
1½ cups loosely packed cilantro (fresh
   coriander) leaves
4½ tablespoons milk
3 tablespoons sour cream or plain
   yogurt

Bring the water to a boil. Add the spinach leaves and cook for 1 minute. Drain off the liquid and place the leaves in ice water for 1 minute. (This first step is optional but ensures a deep green color.) Place the cilantro, milk, and spinach leaves in a blender and process until smooth. Pass the mixture through a fine strainer into a mixing bowl. Whisk in the sour cream.

Ancho Chile Cream

MAKES ½ CUP

1½ small anchos (page 83), cut in half
   and seeded
4½ tablespoons milk
3 tablespoons sour cream or plain
   yogurt

Place the ancho in a preheated 400°F oven for 45 seconds. Remove and place in a mixing bowl. Add warm water to cover and let stand for 10 minutes. When the ancho has softened, remove from the water and place in a blender with the milk. Process until smooth. Pass the mixture through a fine strainer. Whisk in the sour cream.

Chilled Tomato Cilantro Soup

JON JIVIDEN   Zagara's

MAKES 6 SERVINGS

2 tablespoons extra virgin olive oil
1 large Spanish onion, coarsely chopped
1 large carrot, chopped
3 to 4 large ripe tomatoes, chopped, or one
   28-ounce can whole tomatoes, drained
   and chopped
½ teaspoon crushed dried red chilli
   (japonés, de árbol, Thai; see index)
One 4-ounce can green chiles (page 78)
¼ cup cilantro (fresh coriander) leaves
   Cilantro sprigs for garnish

Heat the olive oil in a heavy 2-quart saucepan over medium heat. Add the onion and carrot, and cook about 4 minutes, stirring frequently. Add the tomatoes and dried chilli and cook 10 minutes more. Place the mixture in a food processor with the green chiles and cilantro and process until smooth. Serve the soup chilled, in chilled bowls garnished with cilantro sprigs.

Andalucian-style Gazpacho
JEAN ANDREWS

This recipe is the result of visiting kitchens and eating gazpacho every day for a month in Andalusia, Spain.

MAKES 6 TO 8 SERVINGS

> 6 cups peeled and chopped ripe tomatoes or canned plum tomatoes
> 1 small onion, coarsely chopped
> ½ cup seeded green bell pepper chunks
> 1 serrano (page 86), seeded
> ½ cup cucumber chunks
> 4 to 5 fresh basil leaves
> ½ cup stale French bread crumbs (or similar type bread)
> 2 cups tomato juice
> 1 garlic clove, minced
> Freshly ground black pepper to taste
> ¼ cup extra virgin olive oil
> ¼ cup white wine vinegar

FOR GARNISH
> ½ cup finely chopped onion
> ½ cup finely chopped cucumber
> ½ cup seeded and finely chopped green bell pepper
> ½ cup finely chopped ripe tomato
> Garlic croutons

In a blender, puree the tomatoes, onion, bell pepper, cucumber, basil, and bread crumbs. Add the tomato juice, garlic, and pepper. Stir in the oil and vinegar. Cover and chill. Serve this smooth, creamy soup in chilled bowls. Pass side dishes of chopped onion, bell pepper, cucumber, and tomato. Garnish with croutons.

Mexican Squash Soup
LINDA PARKER   *Native Seeds.SEARCH*

MAKES 4 TO 6 SERVINGS

> 2 tablespoons butter or margarine
> 1 small onion, chopped
> ¼ cup sliced celery
> 4 cups chicken or vegetable stock
> 1 dried red New Mexican chile (page 78)
> 1½ cups peeled and diced winter squash (Hubbard, acorn)
> 1 cup frozen whole-kernel corn
> Grated cheese for garnish
> Pepitas (toasted squash seeds; page 107)

Melt the butter in a saucepan over medium heat and cook the onion and celery, stirring, until soft. Add the stock and red chile and bring to a boil. Add the squash and cook until tender. Add the corn and cook 5 minutes. Remove the chile before serving. Serve sprinkled with grated cheese and/or pepitas. Great with Jalapeño Cornbread (pages 191, 192).

Sopa de Ajo (Garlic Soup)
DONALD COUNTS, M.D.,
AND KATHRYN O'CONNOR COUNTS

MAKES 6 SERVINGS

> 10 garlic cloves, peeled
> 3 fresh green New Mexican chiles (page 78) or canned green chiles (page 78), seeded and mashed
> 1 teaspoon tamari soy sauce
> ¼ cup water
> 8 cups chicken stock

⅓ cup chopped green onions (scallions)
1 cup cilantro (fresh coriander) leaves,
   chopped
3 large egg whites
3 tablespoons cornstarch or arrowroot
¼ cup dry sherry
   Cilantro sprigs for garnish

Crush 7 of the 10 cloves of garlic. Combine the green chiles, garlic, soy sauce, and water in a blender and blend until smooth. Mix with the chicken stock in a soup pot and bring to a simmer over medium heat. Slice the remaining garlic cloves and add to the stock. Add the green onions and cilantro to the stock and simmer, uncovered, for 30 minutes.

Slightly whip the egg whites and set aside. Mix the cornstarch with the sherry. Add it to the stock slowly, then stir constantly with a whisk until it reaches the desired consistency, 5 to 10 minutes. Pour the egg whites into the soup with a circular motion. Turn off the heat, cover, and let stand 5 minutes. Serve garnished with sprigs of cilantro.

Black Bean Soup
PATRICIA WINDISCH   *Beringer Vineyards*

MAKES 10 TO 12 SERVINGS

1 pound black turtle, pinto, black, or
   any dried dark beans
2 smoked ham hocks, blanched in boiling water for 8 minutes
2 to 3 quarts chicken stock
2 large onions, coarsely chopped
1 large carrot, coarsely chopped
5 to 9 garlic cloves, crushed
2 large red bell peppers, seeded and
   coarsely chopped

1 fresh green New Mexican chile (page
   78), seeded and coarsely chopped
1 fresh jalapeño (page 77), seeded and
   coarsely chopped
1 ancho (page 83), seeded and coarsely
   chopped
1 to 2 tablespoons ground cumin
1 tablespoon chili powder
2 to 3 whole cloves
10 sprigs fresh parsley
½ teaspoon dried thyme
1 bay leaf
   Salt and freshly ground black pepper
   to taste
   Sour cream for garnish
   Chopped fresh chives for garnish

Rinse and pick over the beans. Place in a large bowl, cover with cold water, and let soak for 8 hours. Drain, rinse, and place the beans in a stock pot (5 to 7 quart). Add the ham hocks, stock, onions, carrot, garlic, bell peppers, and New Mexican chile. Bring to a boil and skim the surface a few times to remove any residue. Reduce the heat to a simmer and add the rest of the ingredients. Cook until the beans are tender (black beans require longer cooking than other types), 3 to 5 hours. Remove the ham hocks, bay leaf, and cloves. Adjust the soup's consistency with boiling water. Serve with a dollop of sour cream and chopped chives.

Frijol Soup
JEAN ANDREWS

MAKES 8 SERVINGS

> 1 pound dried pinto, black, or red
> beans (frijoles), *rinsed and picked
> over (for the correct flavor, do not
> use kidney beans)*
> 2 quarts water
> 1 large onion, chopped
> 1 medium-size ripe tomato, chopped
> 3 serranos or fresh jalapeños, or 6 to
> 8 fresh or dried chiltepínes, or 3
> dried small red chillies (de árbol,
> japonés, Thai—don't use the large
> dried peppers; if habaneros are
> available, substitute 1 or 2 for a
> distinctive flavor. See index for chil-
> lies)
> Salt to taste
> 1 ham bone, optional
> 2 garlic cloves, chopped
> 10 to 12 sprigs cilantro (fresh coriander)
> Sour cream or plain yogurt, if de-
> sired, for garnish
> Additional 8 to 10 sprigs cilantro
> for garnish

Place the beans in a large, deep, heavy stockpot or Dutch oven, cover with water, and allow to sit overnight. Drain. Add the 2 quarts of water, on-ion, tomato, chillies, and salt. Cover and bring to a boil over high heat. Reduce the heat to medium and simmer, covered, until the beans are very soft, 4 to 5 hours. Be careful not to let the beans cook dry and burn. Add boiling water as needed, never cold water or the beans won't be tender. You can cook a ham bone with the beans if you like, but true Mexican beans seldom have added meat.

Once the beans are cooked, add the garlic and cilantro, then puree the soup in a blender in batches, adding water until the desired consis-tency is reached. This soup may be served thick and eaten as the main dish or thinner if served before the meal. Pour the soup into warmed bowls and add a dollop of sour cream and a sprig of fresh cilantro to each. Serve immediately, with toasted tortilla chips.

Caribbean-Style Bean Soup
JUNIE HOSTETLER   Native Seeds.SEARCH

MAKES 8 SERVINGS

> 2 cups dried pinto or black beans,
> rinsed and picked over, or three 15-
> ounce cans cooked beans, undrained
> (do not use kidney beans)
> ½ cup chopped onion
> 1 garlic clove, minced
> 2 teaspoons salt
> ¾ teaspoon dried oregano
> ½ teaspoon ground cumin
> ¼ teaspoon freshly ground black
> pepper
> 6 cups water (not necessary if using
> canned beans)
> One 4-ounce can chopped green New
> Mexican chiles (page 78)
> 3 cups peeled and chopped yellow
> winter squash (Hubbard, acorn)
> One 8-ounce can stewed tomatoes
> 2 cups or more steamed rice
> 1 to 2 cups small chunks Monterey Jack
> cheese

Soak the beans overnight or several hours in the water; drain. Pour into a stock pot (5 quart) and add the onion, garlic, salt, oregano, cumin, and pepper and enough water to cover and cook until the beans are tender (pintos require less time than black beans). Add the chiles, squash, and toma-toes and cook 25 to 30 minutes more over low heat. Serve with the hot rice and cheese.

Thai Chicken Coconut Milk Soup
JOYCE JUE

MAKES 6 TO 8 SERVINGS

4 cups thin coconut milk (page 105)
1½ cups chicken stock
3 pieces dried galanga (page 106) or 2 teaspoons powdered galanga or peeled and minced fresh ginger
3 stalks fresh lemon grass (page 106), cut in half lengthwise, then into 2-inch lengths and crushed
3 green serranos (page 86), halved and seeded
1 large, whole chicken breast, skinned, boned, and cut into ½-inch chunks
5 fresh or dried citrus or lime leaves (page 106), if available
½ cup canned straw mushrooms, optional
¼ cup fish sauce (page 105)
Juice of 2 limes
1 red serrano (page 86) or fresh red jalapeño (page 77), cut into rounds, for garnish
2 tablespoons cilantro (fresh coriander) leaves for garnish

Bring the coconut milk, stock, galanga, lemon grass, and green serranos to a boil in a large saucepan (2¾ quart). Reduce the heat to medium and simmer, uncovered, for 15 minutes. Strain and discard the galanga and lemon grass. Add the chicken chunks and citrus leaves and simmer until the chicken is tender, about 3 minutes. Stir in the straw mushrooms and fish sauce and simmer 1 minute longer. Pour into a soup tureen, stir in the lime juice, and taste for seasoning. Garnish with the red chillies and cilantro leaves. Serve hot.

Hot and Sour Soup with Poblanos and Tomatillos
JIMMY SCHMIDT   The Rattlesnake Club

MAKES 4 SERVINGS

3 cups chicken stock
3 cups duck stock
1¼ teaspoons roasted (page 96), peeled, seeded, and minced fresh jalapeños (page 78)
3 tablespoons balsamic vinegar
1 tablespoon champagne vinegar
Juice of ½ lime
1 teaspoon salt
¼ cup roasted (page 96), peeled, seeded, and diced poblanos (page 82)
¼ cup roasted (page 96), peeled, seeded, and diced red bell peppers
¼ cup roasted (page 96), peeled, seeded, and diced yellow bell peppers
½ cup husked and diced tomatillos (page 108)
½ cup diced raw duck breast
Twelve ½-inch-thick slices blue corn tamales (see note below)
2 tablespoons chopped cilantro (fresh coriander)

In a large saucepan (3¾ quart), combine the stocks and bring to a gentle simmer over medium heat. Add the jalapeño, vinegars, lime juice, and salt. Add the poblanos and bell peppers, tomatillos, and duck and cook until tender, about 5 minutes. Add the tamales, cooking until warm. Ladle into serving bowls. Sprinkle with the cilantro and serve.

NOTE: If blue corn tamales are not available, substitute regular tamales, fresh or frozen, but not canned. Also see page 108.

Red Anaheim Vichyssoise with Scallops
GREG HIGGINS   *Heathman Hotel*

MAKES 8 TO 10 SERVINGS

¼ cup olive oil
3 tablespoons minced garlic
1 large sweet yellow onion, diced
½ teaspoon ground cumin
1 tablespoon fresh thyme leaves
6 fresh red New Mexican chiles (page 78), roasted (pages 96–97), peeled, seeded, and diced
2 large red bell peppers, roasted (pages 96–97), peeled, seeded, and diced
2½ pounds russet potatoes, peeled and diced
6 cups chicken stock
Salt and freshly ground black pepper to taste
1 pound scallops, stirred in 1 tablespoon olive oil over medium heat until opaque all the way through
Cilantro (fresh coriander) leaves for garnish
Thin red bell pepper strips for garnish

Heat the olive oil in a large saucepan or Dutch oven (2¾ quart) over medium heat. Add the garlic, onion, cumin, thyme, and peppers and cook, stirring, until the onions become translucent, then add the potatoes. Continue cooking for 10 minutes, stirring often. Add the chicken stock and bring to a simmer. Cook until the potatoes are quite tender, 20 to 30 minutes, then remove from the heat and allow to cool.

Puree the soup in a food processor or blender until smooth (you will need to do this in several batches). Thin with more chicken stock if needed and adjust the seasoning with salt and pepper. Serve the soup chilled, in shallow bowls garnished with the scallops, cilantro, and bell peppers.

Red Pepper Chowder
MICHAEL FOLEY   *Printer's Row*

MAKES 4 SERVINGS

2 tablespoons olive oil
1 large onion, finely minced
6 large red bell peppers, roasted (pages 96–97), peeled, seeded, and chopped
3 cups chicken or vegetable stock
Salt and freshly ground black pepper to taste
½ cup heavy cream
1 cup ¼-inch diced potatoes, blanched
4 ounces bay scallops, dried in a towel
Chopped fresh marjoram to taste

Heat 1 tablespoon of the oil in a large saucepan (2¾ quart) over medium heat. Add the onion, cover, and let sweat for 5 minutes. Add the red peppers and continue to cook until all is worked together, about 5 minutes. Add the chicken stock and bring to a boil. Remove from the heat and taste for salt and pepper. In batches, process in a blender until smooth. Return to the saucepan, add the cream, then add the potatoes. At serving time, reheat over medium heat but do not let boil.

Heat another saucepan over high heat; add the remaining olive oil and bay scallops and toss until lightly brown. Season with chopped marjoram and divide among 4 soup bowls. Ladle in the hot soup and serve immediately.

Southwestern Raw Vegetable Salad
KURT KOESSEL   *Ginger Island*

MAKES 10 SERVINGS

1 medium-size jícama (page 106), peeled and julienned
2 red bell peppers, seeded and julienned
2 poblanos (page 82), seeded and julienned
2 fresh green New Mexican chiles (page 78), seeded and julienned
1 fresh jalapeño (page 77), seeded and chopped
1 medium-size red onion, thinly sliced
1 cup red seedless grapes

FOR THE DRESSING
1 tablespoon cumin seeds, toasted (page 110) and ground in a spice mill or coffee grinder
1 tablespoon chopped cilantro (fresh coriander)
1 tablespoon red New Mexican chile flakes
1 tablespoon fresh lime juice
1 teaspoon grated lime zest
2 garlic cloves, minced
½ teaspoon salt
¾ cup extra virgin olive oil
½ cup red wine vinegar

Combine all the salad ingredients in a serving bowl. Combine the dressing ingredients in a small bowl or glass jar. Pour the dressing over the salad, toss, and serve.

Romaine Salad with Crisp New Mexican Chile Rings
LINDA LAU ANUSASANANAN

MAKES 6 TO 8 SERVINGS

6 large dried New Mexican chiles (page 78)
¼ cup olive oil
⅔ cup cider vinegar
1 garlic clove, pressed or minced
1 tablespoon Worcestershire sauce
¾ pound romaine lettuce, washed, crisped, and torn into bite-size pieces
1 small red onion, thinly sliced
1 small cucumber, thinly sliced
2 small, ripe tomatoes, cored and cut into 1-inch wedges
½ pound tiny shelled cooked shrimp
1 cup cilantro (fresh coriander) sprigs
1 large, ripe avocado

Wipe the chiles. With scissors, cut the chiles crosswise into thin strips; discard the seeds and stems. In a 10- or 12-inch frying pan, stir the oil and chiles over low heat until the chiles are crisp, 2 to 3 minutes (watch closely to avoid burning). Lift the chiles from the oil; set aside. Whisk together the oil from the chiles, the vinegar, garlic, and Worcestershire.

In a large bowl place half of the romaine. Top with half of the onion, cucumber, tomatoes, shrimp, and cilantro. Repeat the layers. If made ahead, cover and chill up to 4 hours. To serve, pit, peel, and slice the avocados, then arrange the avocados and chiles over the salad. Spoon the dressing over the salad and mix.

Ensalada Favorita
LUCINDA HUTSON

MAKES 6 TO 8 SERVINGS

FOR THE MARINADE

    ¼ *cup mint vinegar or white wine*
      vinegar
    ¼ *cup fresh lime juice*
    3 *garlic cloves, minced*
    ½ *teaspoon brown sugar*
    Salt and freshly ground white pepper
    to taste
    ¼ *teaspoon red chilli pepper flakes*
    2 *tablespoons chopped fresh mint*
    6 *tablespoons olive oil*

FOR THE SALAD

    3 *medium-size zucchini, scored with a*
      fork and cut into ⅜-inch slices
4 to 6 *green Chile Gourmet Chiles (see note*
      below) or fresh green New Mexican
      chiles (page 78), roasted (pages 96–
      97), peeled, seeded, and cut into strips
    6 *green onions (scallions) with most of*
      the green tops, chopped
    4 *ounces cream cheese, cut into ½-inch*
      pieces
    2 *tablespoons chopped fresh mint*
    1 *tablespoon chopped cilantro (fresh*
      coriander) or parsley
    Salt and freshly ground black pepper
    to taste
    2 *ripe avocados, peeled, pitted, cubed,*
      and sprinkled with fresh lime juice
    1 *head red leaf lettuce*
    Fresh mint sprigs and cilantro sprigs
    for garnish
    Lime wedges for garnish

Make the marinade by combining the vinegar, lime juice, garlic, sugar, salt, pepper, chilli flakes, and mint; slowly whisk in the olive oil. Set aside. Bring a pot of water to boil. Place the zucchini in a steam basket and steam until crisp-tender, 2 to 3 minutes. Submerge in ice water immediately; drain. Pat the zucchini dry and place in a shallow glass dish. Add the chile strips, green onions, cream cheese pieces, mint, and coriander; sprinkle with salt and pepper. Drizzle the marinade over the squash mixture; gently mix together well. Marinate several hours or overnight, mixing occasionally. Before serving, add the avocados and mix well. Serve on chilled plates with crisp lettuce, mint and coriander sprigs, and lime wedges.

NOTE: Chile Gourmet Chiles are frozen New Mexican chiles that have been roasted and vacuum packed with the skins on to ensure year-round freshness and vitamin retention. When thawed, the skins slip off easily. They can be ordered from Chile Gourmet, P.O. Box 39, Mesilla, NM 88046.

VARIATION: Another way to serve this is to omit the green chile strips and serve each portion in a whole roasted and peeled green chile. Simply slit the chile down the middle, leaving the stem intact, and fill with the squash mixture. Serve on a bed of lettuce with a mint sprig, drizzling any remaining marinade over the chile.

Pepper, Endive, and Sprouts Salad
JEAN ANDREWS

MAKES 6 TO 8

    1 *head bibb lettuce, torn into bite-size*
      pieces
    1½ *cups sunflower sprouts*
    2 *Belgian endives*
    1 *large red or yellow pepper, seeded and*
      julienned
    1 *medium-size red onion, thinly sliced*
      and separated into rings
    Creamy Serrano Dressing (recipe
    follows)

Wash the lettuce, sprouts, and endive. Drain in a colander and shake off any excess moisture. Wrap in paper toweling, place in a plastic bag, and refrigerate for at least 1 hour. Cut the endives in half lengthwise, then cut each half into small strips. Place the endive, pepper, lettuce, sprouts, and onion in a salad bowl and toss with the dressing. Serve immediately.

Creamy Serrano Dressing
JEAN ANDREWS

MAKES ¾ CUP

> 1 teaspoon Dijon-style mustard
> ¼ teaspoon dried tarragon
> 1 garlic clove, peeled
> ¼ teaspoon sugar
> 1 to 2 serranos or 3 to 4 fresh green chiltepínes or fresh jalapeños (see index for chillies)
> Salt and freshly ground black pepper to taste
> 1 large egg yolk
> 2 to 3 fresh parsley sprigs
> 3 tablespoons fresh lime juice (never bottled)
> ½ cup olive oil

In a blender, combine the mustard, tarragon, garlic, sugar, chillies, salt, and pepper. Process. Blend in the egg yolk, fresh parsley, and lime juice. Pour the oil in very slowly.

This is a fairly thick dressing. Not only is it great for salads, but it is also delicious with boiled shrimp. Keep well covered in the refrigerator. Use within a week.

Jícama and Pepper Salad
JEAN ANDREWS

MAKES 8 TO 10

> 1 head bibb or leaf lettuce, washed and crisped
> 1 orange bell pepper, seeded and carefully cut into 8 thin rings
> 1 red bell pepper, seeded and carefully cut into 8 thin rings
> 1 yellow bell pepper, seeded and carefully cut into 8 thin rings
> 1 green bell pepper, seeded and carefully cut into 8 thin rings
> 1 purple bell pepper, seeded and carefully cut into 8 thin rings
> ¾ pound jícama (page 106), peeled, thinly sliced, and cut into ½- by 2- to 3-inch strips
> 1 medium-size red onion, thinly sliced and separated into rings
> Creamy Serrano Dressing (see previous recipe)

Tear the lettuce into bite-size pieces and prepare a bed of it on each salad plate. Overlap rings of each color pepper on the lettuce bed. Leave space for 4 to 5 jícama slices laced through several onion rings. In the center place a generous spoonful of the dressing. Serve very cold.

Garden Potato Salad

JEAN ANDREWS

MAKES 6 TO 8 SERVINGS

FOR THE SALAD

    2 pounds new potatoes
    1 tablespoon canola oil
    1 medium-size onion, thinly sliced
    5 garlic cloves, minced
    2 medium-size red bell peppers, seeded
        and julienned
1 to 5 fresh jalapeños (page 77), seeded and
        sliced (depends on desired
        pungency)

FOR THE DRESSING

    1 tablespoon dry mustard
    1 teaspoon freshly ground black pepper
    2 teaspoons salt
    ¼ cup olive oil
    2 tablespoons cider or herbed vinegar
        (page 209)

Boil the unpeeled potatoes in water to cover until tender (this can be done in the microwave). Drain and cool until easy to handle, then cut each potato into large chunks. Heat the oil in a heavy skillet over medium heat and cook the onion, garlic, and both peppers, stirring, until tender. Combine with the warm potatoes.

In a small bowl, blend the dressing ingredients with a wire whisk until smooth. Pour over the warm vegetables, tossing gently. Refrigerate several hours or overnight to let the flavors blend. Allow the salad to stand at room temperature 1 hour before serving.

Auntie's Perfection Salad

JEAN ANDREWS

MAKES 8 TO 10 SERVINGS

    3 cups tomato juice
    2 tablespoons unflavored gelatin soft-
        ened in ½ cup cold water
    ¼ cup sugar
    ½ cup herb vinegar (page 209)
    1 teaspoon salt
    ½ teaspoon freshly ground black pepper
    2 tablespoons Worcestershire sauce
    ½ teaspoon Tabasco Brand Pepper Sauce
    1 serrano (page 86), seeded and minced
One 2-ounce jar pimentos, chopped
    1 cup finely chopped cabbage
    1 medium red apple, cored and chopped
    2 cups finely chopped celery
    1 small red bell pepper, seeded and
        finely chopped
    1 tablespoon onion juice
    1 head bibb or leaf lettuce, washed and
        crisped
        Homemade mayonnaise, Chipotle
        Mayonnaise (page 155), or Creamy
        Serrano Dressing (page 129)

Heat 1 cup of the tomato juice to boiling and pour into a large mixing bowl. Dissolve the softened gelatin in the hot juice; add the sugar, vinegar, salt, pepper, Worcestershire, and Tabasco and stir until well mixed. Add the remaining juice and the serrano, pimentos, cabbage, apples, celery, pepper, and onion juice. Pour into a large rectangular Pyrex dish or mold. Chill until firm.

If you want, release from the mold, cut into squares, and serve on a bed of lettuce on individual salad plates, or serve directly from the pan. Top with a dollop of mayonnaise or dressing.

Ruby Red Grapefruit and Avocado Salad
JEAN ANDREWS

MAKES 3 SERVINGS

Leaf lettuce
1 grapefruit (ruby or pink preferred), peeled and sectioned
1 large, ripe avocado peeled (page 115), pitted, and sliced
1 small red bell pepper, seeded and sliced into thin rings
Zesty Poppy Seed Dressing (recipe follows) or Creamy Serrano Dressing (page 129)

On each salad plate prepare a bed of lettuce. Alternate overlapping slices of grapefruit, avocado, and bell pepper. Drizzle generously with the dressing and serve.

Zesty Poppy Seed Dressing
JEAN ANDREWS

This is delicious on fruit salads of any kind, but has a special affinity for grapefruit and in combinations where grapefruit is present.

MAKES 3½ CUPS

1½ cups sugar
2 teaspoons dry mustard
1 teaspoon salt
¼ cup white or cider vinegar
1 thick sliced onion
1 serrano (page 86), seeded, or 1 teaspoon ground cayenne pepper
2 cups vegetable oil (do not use olive oil)
3 tablespoons poppy seeds

Mix the sugar, mustard, salt, and vinegar in a blender. Add the onion and serrano and puree thoroughly. Add the oil slowly, processing constantly at medium speed, and continue to beat until thick. Add the poppy seeds and process for a few minutes. Store in the refrigerator. Stir before using.

Zesty Spinach-Chicken Salad
JEAN ANDREWS

MAKES 6 SERVINGS

FOR THE DRESSING

¾ cup extra virgin olive oil
¼ cup white wine vinegar
¼ cup Chilli Pepper Jelly (page 207)
2 tablespoons curry powder (page 101)
¼ teaspoon dry mustard
¼ teaspoon Tabasco Brand Pepper Sauce
Salt and freshly ground black pepper to taste

FOR THE SALAD

About 2 bunches fresh spinach, well washed and torn into bite-size pieces
2 cups thin red onion rings
2 red apples, cored and thinly sliced
1 yellow or red bell pepper, seeded and julienned, or ½ of each
½ cup sunflower seeds, toasted (page 110)
½ cup dried cranberries or golden raisins
1 cup bite-size pieces grilled chicken
Crumbled crisp bacon and sharp cheddar cheese cubes, optional

Mix all the dressing ingredients together well. Cover and refrigerate at least 24 hours. For the salad, toss all the ingredients in a large bowl. Add the dressing; toss to coat. Serve immediately.

Roasted Red Bell Pepper Mousse

JAMIE MORNINGSTAR   *Inglenook Napa Valley*

MAKES 4 TO 6 SERVINGS

> 2 tablespoons vegetable oil
> 2 shallots, diced
> 5 to 6 red bell peppers, roasted (pages 96–97), peeled, and seeded
> ½ cup good chicken stock
> 2 teaspoons unflavored gelatin
> ¼ cup very hot water
> ¾ cup whipped cream
> Salt and freshly ground black pepper to taste
> Fennel Salsa (recipe follows)

Heat the oil in a medium-size saucepan over medium heat. Add the shallots and cook, stirring, until limp. Add the peppers and cook, stirring, 5 minutes. Drain off any excess oil. Add the chicken stock and cook until soft. Pour the mixture into a blender and process until smooth. Dissolve the gelatin in the hot water and add to the puree. Strain through a fine sieve. Cool down over an ice bath (a bowl of ice water with the mousse in a separate bowl on top). When the mousse is cool to the touch, fold in the whipped cream and season with salt and pepper.

Fill individual molds with the mousse. For an added touch, place a cut-out star of roasted pepper on each mold bottom (which will be the top when unmolded). Tap the molds firmly on the counter to remove air bubbles and refrigerate 4 to 6 hours, overnight if possible. To unmold, place each in hot water for a few seconds and turn over onto a plate with the salsa underneath.

Fennel Salsa

MAKES ABOUT 2½ CUPS

> 1 cup finely diced fennel bulb
> 1 cup fresh, ripe tomato puree, no skins or seeds
> ½ cup finely diced red onion
> 2 tablespoons seeded and minced fresh jalapeño (page 77)
> Salt and freshly ground black pepper to taste

Combine all the ingredients and allow to stand at least an hour to let the flavors meld. Use fennel sprigs for additional garnish.

Grilled Stuffed Poblanos with Avocado Salsa

CINDY PAWLCYN   *Mustard's Grill*

MAKES 8 SERVINGS

> 8 poblanos (page 82)
> ½ cup grated fontina cheese (see note below)
> ½ cup grated Monterey Jack cheese
> ½ cup grated Jarlsberg cheese
> ½ cup grated white cheddar cheese
> ½ cup grated Asiago cheese (see note below)
> Cilantro (fresh coriander) sprigs for garnish
> Avocado Salsa (recipe follows)

Carefully slice off the shoulder of each poblano with the stem to form a lid. Remove the seeds and veins. Blanch lids and pods for 2 minutes in boiling, lightly salted water. Refresh in an ice bath and drain.

In a medium-size bowl, mix together all the cheeses. Stuff the chiles with the mixture and replace the top. Grill over a medium wood or charcoal fire until the cheeses are melted and you have nice grill marks on both sides of the poblanos. To serve, divide the Avocado Salsa among

8 plates and place a chilli on top. Garnish with cilantro sprigs

NOTE: You can substitute your choice of white cheeses for the fontina and Asiago.

Avocado Salsa

MAKES ABOUT 4 CUPS

 4 firm, ripe avocados, peeled (page 115), pitted, and diced
 1 fresh jalapeño (page 77), roasted, peeled, and minced
 ½ large red onion, peeled and minced
 1 cup cilantro (fresh coriander) leaves, minced
 1 cup minced green onions (scallions)
 ¼ cup rice vinegar (page 107)
 ¾ cup olive oil
   Salt and freshly ground black pepper to taste

In a large nonreactive bowl, mix all the ingredients together carefully so as to not mash the avocados.

Anaheim Stuffed with Apricots, Goat Cheese, and Almonds
STEPHEN PYLES *Baby Routh*

MAKES 6 SERVINGS

 12 fresh green New Mexican (Anaheim) chiles (page 78), roasted (pages 96–97) and peeled, but left whole
 3 garlic cloves, roasted (page 109), squeezed from skins, and pureed

 9 ounces goat cheese, crumbled
 4½ ounces caciotta or Monterey Jack cheese, grated
 1½ tablespoons chopped shallots
 1½ tablespoons chopped cilantro (fresh coriander)
 1½ tablespoons chopped fresh basil
 1½ tablespoons chopped fresh marjoram
 ¾ cup dried apricots, diced
 3 tablespoons toasted chopped almonds
   Salt and freshly ground black pepper to taste
 2 large eggs
 3 tablespoons heavy cream
   Oil for deep frying
   Yellow cornmeal for dredging
   Apricot Sauce (recipe follows)
   Pico de Gallo (page 136)

Carefully slice the chiles down one side and remove the seeds and ribs, leaving the stem attached. Set aside. In a bowl, combine the garlic, goat cheese, caciotta, shallots, cilantro, basil, marjoram, apricots, and almonds. Season with salt and pepper. Mix well and carefully stuff the chiles with the mixture. Do not overfill. Close the chiles and refrigerate until needed.

In a small bowl beat the egg into the cream. In a heavy, high-walled saucepan or deep fryer, heat enough oil to cover chiles to 325°F. Dip the stuffed peppers into the egg mixture, then dredge in the cornmeal. Slip the chiles, a few at a time, into the oil and fry until they are lightly browned. Remove and drain well on paper towels. Serve on top of the apricot sauce and garnish with the pico de gallo.

Apricot Sauce

MAKES 2 CUPS

> 2 cups chicken stock
> 1 cup dried apricots, diced
> 2 tablespoons sugar
> ½ cup dry white wine
> 1 shallot, minced
> ½ pound (2 sticks) butter or margarine,
>   softened and cut into pieces
> Salt to taste

In a small saucepan, bring chicken stock to a boil. Add the apricots and sugar, reduce the heat to medium and cook until soft, about 15 minutes. Place the apricots and stock in a blender and puree. Return to the saucepan and keep warm over low heat. Combine the wine and shallot in a medium-size saucepan over high heat and reduce the liquid to 2 tablespoons. Lower the heat to medium and begin whisking in the butter, piece by piece, until it is all incorporated. Remove from the heat. Stir in the apricot puree, season with salt, and strain. Keep warm over low heat.

Pico de Gallo

MAKES 3 CUPS

> 6 ripe tomatoes, seeded and cut into
>   ¼-inch dice
> 2 tablespoons chopped cilantro (fresh
>   coriander)
> 2 garlic cloves, minced
> 1 cup minced onion
> Juice of ½ lime
> 4 small serranos (page 86), seeded and
>   minced
> Salt to taste

Combine all the ingredients in a bowl and let stand for 30 minutes before serving.

Roasted Peppers in Olive Oil
JEAN ANDREWS

I was told how to make this dish by a native Italian, Enzo Domani, of St. Augustine, Florida, the largest eggplant processor in the world, who said every self-respecting Italian cook always kept these peppers on hand for the family to snack on.

MAKES ABOUT 1 QUART

> 6 pounds red, green, and yellow bell
>   peppers or 'Cubanelles' (page 71) or
>   any ethnic type, roasted (pages 96–
>   97) and peeled
> 2 sprigs fresh thyme, rosemary, and/or
>   basil
> 2 garlic cloves, halved
> 1 tablespoon red or white wine vinegar
> ¾ cup extra virgin olive oil, or to cover

Place the peeled peppers in a large bowl. Quarter them and remove the cores, seeds, and ribs over the bowl to catch the juices. Place the peppers in a wide-mouthed quart jar with the herbs and garlic. Strain the juices over the peppers. Add the vinegar and enough oil to cover the peppers. Stir to release any air bubbles; cover. In a tightly covered container these peppers will keep for 2 to 3 weeks in the refrigerator and even longer in a container designed so that the air can be removed with a pump (page 95).

Serve as an accompaniment to meat dishes, on crusty, warm French bread, or on sandwiches. Use the oil for seasoning.

ALTERNATE METHOD: Core, seed, and remove veins from the raw peppers. Cut into strips. Heat the olive oil in a heavy skillet and fry the peppers until limp. Place the peppers, garlic, and herbs in a wide-mouthed glass jar. Add the vinegar, the oil they were cooked in, plus enough more olive oil to cover. Stir to release any air bubbles; cover. Will keep in the refrigerator for a week or so.

Tucson Chile Festival Green-Corn Tamales

JEAN ANDREWS

In the field, when the milk in the corn sets it is called "green-corn." It is the first edible corn-on-the-cob stage of soft Indian corn, dent corn, or flint corn. It is never a sweet corn such as 'Golden Bantam'. Buy a few extra ears of corn in order to have enough good shucks. If you must use sweet corn, add 1 teaspoonful of cornstarch for each ear of corn because field corn has much more starch than sweet corn.

MAKES TWENTY-EIGHT 2½- TO 3-INCH TAMALES

> 12 ears of dent or flint corn, if possible
> ½ cup (1 stick) butter or margarine
> ¾ cup cubed Monterey Jack cheese
> ¾ cup cubed mild cheddar cheese
> 1¼ cups masa harina (page 106)
> 1½ teaspoons salt
> ¾ cup chicken stock, if needed
>   Green Chile Sauce (page 148), Salsa
>   Cruda (page 148), or Salsa Chipotle
>   (page 155)
> 6 large fresh green New Mexican chiles
>   (page 78), roasted (pages 96–97),
>   peeled, seeded, and chopped, or one
>   24-ounce can chopped green chiles
>   (page 78)

With a cleaver, chop off the stem ends of the corn and remove and discard the ugly outer shucks. Carefully remove the inner shucks to keep them whole. Using kitchen scissors, trim the pointed ends of each shuck. To make the shucks more pliable, some tamale makers bring a stockpot of water to a boil, drop the shucks in, and turn the heat off, leaving them in the hot water until they are ready to be filled. At that time, the shucks are removed and drained. The shucks should not be allowed to dry out before being filled. Leave the last several husks on the extra corn to keep them from drying out before you use them.

Hold each ear in a deep bowl and cut the kernels from 7 to 8 ears, enough to have 5 cups. Cream the butter in a food processor, taking care to scrape the sides of the bowl down several times. Add 4 cups of the corn, the cheeses, masa, salt, and a little of the stock if the mixture is too thick (it must be spreadable but not runny; the type of corn used will determine the consistency). Blend until smooth. Coarsely chop the reserved cup of cut corn; mix it and the chiles into the smooth mixture but do not process again.

To fill the shucks, spread a husk out so that it will curl over the filling. Place about 2½ tablespoons of the filling in the center of the shuck lengthwise. Fold the sides in over the filling and then fold the ends up. Stand the tamales in a steamer or colander, folded ends down. Place the steamer or colander in a large stockpot with enough water to come just below the bottom of the steamer. The tamales should not be standing in water. Cover and place over high heat. When the water comes to a boil, lower the heat to a simmer, and steam the tamales for about 1½ hours. Take care to not let the steamer run out of water. Using tongs, transfer the tamales from the steamer to a serving platter and serve hot, along with a table sauce.

NOTE: Tamales freeze well if wrapped properly. Put cool tamales in a plastic bag, close tightly, wrap in freezer paper, and seal. Label and date the package.

Cheese Grits with Green Chiles
JEAN ANDREWS

MAKES 12 SERVINGS

6 cups water or chicken stock
1½ cups instant grits
2 teaspoons salt
1 teaspoon sweet paprika
1 teaspoon ground cayenne pepper
3 large eggs
1 pound sharp cheddar cheese, grated,
or try a mixture of Monterey Jack
and chèvre
One 4-ounce can chopped green chiles
(page 78)

Bring the water to a boil in a large saucepan; stir in the grits gradually. Cover and cook over low heat until thickened. Stir occasionally to prevent sticking. Stir in the salt, paprika, and pepper.

In a large mixing bowl, beat the eggs lightly. Add a small amount of hot grits to the eggs, stirring constantly so the eggs do not cook. Gradually stir in the remaining grits. Add the grated cheese and green chiles. Pour into a buttered 2-quart casserole and bake for 45 minutes at 325° F. Serve immediately.

Corn and Green Chile "Pudding"
JEAN ANDREWS

My grandmother called it pudding when she made it, but it's not sweet—I added the chiles.

MAKES 8 TO 10 SERVINGS

4 cups fresh corn kernels (thaw if
frozen, but do not use canned)
3 tablespoons butter or margarine
4 large eggs
2 tablespoons cornstarch

2 cups milk
1 teaspoon salt
1 teaspoon freshly ground black pepper
½ cup chopped canned green chiles
(page 78) or fresh green New Mexi-
can chiles; if using fresh, peel them
first (page 96)

Put 3 cups of the corn in a blender with the butter, eggs, cornstarch, ½ cup of the milk, the salt, and pepper and process, being careful to not make too smooth a puree (the mixture should resemble scraped corn). Stir this mixture into the remaining corn, milk, and the chiles in a 2 quart-greased baking dish. Set the dish in a larger pan filled with hot water that comes 1 inch up the sides of the dish. Bake in a preheated 325°F oven until a knife blade comes out clean or the pudding is firm, about 1 hour.

VARIATION: If using a microwave, cook for 10 minutes on high, then give the dish a quarter turn and stir the mixture. Repeat, without stirring, until the pudding is set (times will vary). Brown the pudding in the oven if desired.

Vinita Parthasarathy's New Potatoes with Poppy Seed
JEAN ANDREWS

Vinita, who was a graduate student from Madras, India, is one of the people I have studied Indian cookery with.

MAKES 6 SERVINGS

1 to 2 tablespoons vegetable oil
6 medium-size new potatoes, cubed
2 to 3 dried red chillies (de árbol, japonés,
Thai; see index), crumbled
1½ tablespoons white poppy seeds
(available in Indian food markets)

½ *teaspoon turmeric*
½ *teaspoon ground cayenne pepper*
1 to 2 *serranos (page 86) or fresh
    jalapeño (page 77), minced*
1 *cup hot water*

Heat the oil in a large saucepan over medium-high heat. Add the potatoes and cook, stirring, until golden. Remove from the oil and set aside.

To the same oil, add the dried chillies and poppy seeds. When lightly browned, return the potatoes to the pan. Add the turmeric, cayenne, green chillies, and water. Simmer over medium heat until the potatoes are tender and most of the water is absorbed. This is hot, so use less chillies if desired.

Chef Grewal's Khatta Aloo (Potatoes)
JEAN ANDREWS

Chef Grewal was my cookery teacher in Aurangabad, India. Indians have a way with potatoes.

MAKES 4 SERVINGS

2 *tablespoons canola or vegetable oil*
⅛ *teaspoon ground cumin*
⅛ *teaspoon caraway seeds*
½ *teaspoon cumin seeds*
⅛ *teaspoon ground coriander*
1 *small red onion, finely chopped*
1 *garlic clove, minced*
1 *serrano (page 86) or fresh jalapeño
    (page 77), seeded and finely chopped*
1 *teaspoon peeled and minced fresh
    ginger*
1 *teaspoon turmeric*
½ to 1 *teaspoon ground cayenne pepper*
1½ *cups diced new potatoes, boiled until
    tender*

2 *tablespoons chopped cilantro (fresh
    coriander)*
2 *tablespoons chopped fresh mint leaves
    Juice of 1 lime
    Salt and freshly ground black pepper
    to taste*

Heat the oil in a heavy skillet over medium-high heat. Add the ground cumin, caraway, cumin seeds, and coriander and stir until fragrant. Add the onion, garlic, serrano, and ginger; cook, stirring until soft. Add the turmeric and cayenne. Mix well. Add the potatoes, cilantro, mint, and lime juice and stir to mix. Season with salt and black pepper. Heat thoroughly. Serve with grilled meats.

Pepperonata
JEAN ANDREWS

MAKES 4 SERVINGS

¼ *cup olive oil*
1 *large onion, coarsely chopped*
1 *garlic clove, minced*
2 *large potatoes, peeled and cubed*
2 *large, ripe tomatoes, peeled, seeded,
    and cut into large chunks*
3 *large bell peppers of several colors,
    seeded and julienned*
1 *fresh jalapeño (page 77), seeded and
    chopped*
¼ *teaspoon dried thyme, crumbled*
½ *teaspoon dried basil*

In a large skillet, heat the oil over medium heat. Add the onion and garlic and cook, stirring, until the onion is limp. Stir in the potatoes, cover, and cook 10 minutes, stirring occasionally. Stir in the remaining ingredients, cover, and cook 10 minutes longer, until the potatoes and peppers are crisp-tender.

My Garden Ratatouille
JEAN ANDREWS

MAKES 4 TO 6 SERVINGS

> 1 large eggplant, peeled and cut into
>   1-inch cubes
> One 6-inch-long zucchini, cut into 1-inch
>   cubes
> ¼ cup olive oil
> 2 onions, finely chopped
> 6 ripe tomatoes, peeled and cut up
> 1 bell pepper, seeded and chopped
> 1 fresh jalapeño (page 77) or serrano
>   (page 86), seeded and chopped
> 1 garlic clove, minced
> 1 tablespoon chopped fresh parsley
> 1 bay leaf
> 1 tablespoon Worcestershire sauce
>   Salt and freshly ground black pepper
>   to taste

Boil in water to cover or microwave the eggplant and zucchini until just tender. Drain. Heat the oil in a large saucepan over medium heat. Add the onions and cook, stirring, until browned. Stir in the rest of the ingredients and simmer until the juices are cooked down and the mixture is semi-dry. Allow to cool. Serve the next day either hot or at room temperature.

NOTE: This freezes well in freezer containers and is a good way to put up hard-to-freeze squash.

VARIATION: In some of my travels I had a delicious ratatouille that used those cucumbers that get yellow and too big—try it.

Stuffed Eggplant Jaipur
JEAN ANDREWS

MAKES 8 SERVINGS

> 1 cup uncooked rice
> 3 cups chicken stock
> 1 small red onion, finely chopped
> 2 serranos (page 86) or fresh
>   jalapeños (page 77), 1 red and 1
>   green, minced
> 1 large, ripe tomato, finely chopped
> 8 small Oriental eggplants or 4 small
>   eggplants, cut in half
>   Tomato Sauce (recipe follows)

Place all the ingredients, except the eggplants, in a 2-quart saucepan, cover, and cook over low heat until the rice is tender and fluffy. Meanwhile, bake the eggplant in a preheated 325°F oven until tender, but not mushy. Hollow one side of the eggplant and fill generously with the rice mixture, pressing it into the cavity. If halves of the larger type are used, hollow out a cavity for the rice mixture and fill. Place the stuffed eggplant in a baking dish and heat in the oven until thoroughly warmed before serving with the tomato sauce.

Tomato Sauce

MAKES 2 CUPS

> 2 cups chopped fresh, ripe or canned
>   tomatoes, with juice
> 1 small onion, finely chopped
> 1 garlic clove, minced
> 1 tablespoon chopped fresh basil
> 1 tablespoon Worcestershire sauce
> ½ to 1 teaspoon ground cayenne pepper
>   Salt and freshly ground black pepper
>   to taste
> 2 tablespoons olive oil

Place all the ingredients, except the oil, in a blender and puree. Heat the oil in a skillet, add the tomato mixture, and bring to a boil. Reduce the heat to medium and cook until slightly reduced. Serve hot on the stuffed eggplant. Extra sauce can be served in a small bowl.

Southwestern Pepper Tart

ROLLIE ANNE BLACKWELL   *Gourmet Dallas*

MAKES 12 TO 14 SERVINGS

> 3 tablespoons unsalted butter or
> margarine
> 1 small poblano (page 82), seeded and
> finely chopped
> 1 small red bell pepper, seeded and
> finely chopped
> 1 small purple bell pepper, seeded and
> finely chopped
> 5 green onions (scallions), finely
> chopped
> 3 large eggs, beaten
> 2 cups heavy cream or 1 cup each low-
> fat milk and plain yogurt
> Salt and freshly ground black pepper
> to taste
> 8 ounces ancho chile cheese (see note on
> page 185), grated, or substitute
> Monterey Jack, grated, with 2 tea-
> spoons of chopped anchos (page 83)
> 1 ear fresh corn, kernels cut off
> 2 fresh tomatillos (page 108), husked
> and thinly sliced
> 2 Roma tomatoes, thinly sliced
> 2 tablespoons chopped cilantro (fresh
> coriander) or fresh parsley
> Ground cayenne pepper, optional

Melt the butter in a medium-size saucepan over medium heat. Add the poblano, bell peppers, and green onions and cook, stirring, until softened. In a large bowl, combine the eggs, cream, salt, pepper, and grated cheese. Pour the egg mixture into a 13 × 9 × 2-inch baking dish, or into two glass pie plates. Top with the sautéed peppers, corn kernels, slices of tomatillo, tomatoes, and cilantro. Bake in a preheated 375°F oven until set, about 30 minutes. Cut into squares or triangles to serve. You can sprinkle cayenne pepper on if you so desire.

Pepper and Spaghetti Frittata

JEAN ANDREWS

MAKES 6 TO 8 SERVINGS

> 6 tablespoons olive oil
> 2 medium-size onions, chopped
> 5 medium-size garlic cloves, minced
> 6 to 8 red, orange, and green bell peppers,
> seeded and chopped (about 4 cups)
> ¼ cup sun-dried tomatoes (page 208),
> chopped
> 1 fresh jalapeño (page 77), seeded and
> minced
> ½ teaspoon dried oregano
> 1 teaspoon salt
> ¼ teaspoon freshly ground black pepper
> 6 ounces thin spaghetti, cooked
> according to package instructions
> and drained
> 8 large eggs
> ½ cup freshly grated Parmesan cheese
> ¼ cup minced fresh parsley
> 1 tablespoon minced fresh basil

In a large ovenproof skillet, heat the olive oil over medium-high heat. Add the onions, garlic, bell peppers, tomatoes, and jalapeño and cook, stirring frequently, until the vegetables begin to brown, taking care not to burn them. Season with the oregano and half of the salt and black pepper.

Add the cooked spaghetti to the skillet and toss well. Cook, stirring occasionally, until the pasta is lightly browned, about 10 minutes. In a medium-size bowl, beat the eggs with ¼ cup water and remaining salt and black pepper. Stir in ¼ cup of cheese, 2 tablespoons of the fresh parsley, and the basil. Pour the egg mixture over the pasta and stir with a fork to distribute evenly. Cook without stirring until the eggs are set around the edges. Place in a preheated 350°F oven and bake until the eggs are set, about 10 minutes. Slide onto a platter and cut into wedges. Toss together the remaining cheese and parsley and pass separately.

Green New Mexican Chile Quiche
JEAN ANDREWS

Real men will like this quiche!

MAKES 6 TO 8 SERVINGS

> 3 tablespoons butter or margarine
> 1 tablespoon vegetable oil
> ½ cup minced leeks, including the green top
> 1 tablespoon all-purpose flour
> 4 large mushrooms, sliced
> 1 canned jalapeño (page 77), seeded and minced, optional
> 4 large eggs, beaten
> 1 cup half-and-half
> 6 ounces Monterey Jack cheese, chilled and shredded
> ¼ teaspoon freshly ground pepper
> ½ teaspoon salt
> 1 teaspoon dry mustard
> One 10-inch prebaked deep-dish pastry shell
> 3 to 4 fresh green New Mexican chiles (page 78), peeled (page 96), seeded, and opened flat, or one 4-ounce can green chiles (page 78), drained and seeded
> 2 tablespoons minced fresh parsley
> 1 teaspoon dried oregano
> ½ red bell pepper, seeded and sliced into rings

Heat the butter and oil in a skillet and wilt the leek over medium-high heat. Stir in the flour and warm it, but do not let it cook. Remove the skillet from the heat. Stir the mushrooms and jalapeño into the leek mixture. Mix the eggs and half-and-half together in a large bowl and blend in the leek mixture, cheese, pepper, salt, and mustard.

Cover the bottom of the baked pastry shell with the opened and flattened chiles. Pour the egg mixture over the chiles only to ¼ inch from the top. Sprinkle the top with the parsley and oreg-ano. Place the red pepper rings decoratively on top. Bake in a preheated 375°F oven until the top is well colored, about 40 minutes. Transfer the quiche to a rack and let it stand 15 minutes before serving. Can also be served at room temperature.

VARIATION: Minced cook ham can be spread on the baked pastry shell before layering the chiles. The quiche filling can be baked without a crust in a well-greased shallow 4-cup baking dish. Sprinkle the bottom of the dish with ¼ cup of the shredded cheese. Ladle the filling over the cheese and bake as described above.

Enchiladas
JEAN ANDREWS

MAKES 18 ENCHILADAS; ALLOW 2 OR 3 PER SERVING

> Vegetable oil for heating tortillas
> 18 fresh corn tortillas
> Enchilada Sauce (page 154)
> 2 pounds longhorn cheese, shredded
> 1 large onion, finely chopped

Heat enough oil to cover a tortilla in a skillet over high heat. Dip each tortilla in the oil until pliable and heated, or 4 to 5 seconds. Drain the tortillas on paper toweling and stack them until all are dipped in the oil.

Place the sauce in a saucepan and warm it over low heat. Dip a tortilla in the sauce and place it on a large plate. Place 2 tablespoons of the cheese and ½ tablespoon of onion in the center of the tortilla and roll it up. Place it with the rolled edge down in a 13 × 9-inch baking dish. Repeat until two baking dishes are filled.

Pour the remaining sauce over the enchiladas and sprinkle with the cheese. Bake in a preheated 400°F oven until the enchiladas are bubbling. Sprinkle with onion and serve on a heated plate.

VARIATIONS: The enchiladas may be filled with shredded, cooked chicken or pork, small boiled shrimps, mashed *frijoles,* or whatever you care to try.

For chicken enchiladas with green sauce use one of the sauces on page 147 or one of the other green sauces and top each with a dollop of sour cream.

Red Chile Pasta

BRYAN BROADFOOT

MAKES 4 SERVINGS

1 teaspoon olive oil
1½ cups all-purpose flour, or more as needed
½ teaspoon salt
2 large eggs
1 tablespoon water, or more as needed
½ cup Gebhardt's Chili Powder or an available chili powder

Combine all the ingredients in a large mixing bowl and mix until the consistency of fine meal. Adjust the water or flour as necessary to make the mixture stick together when kneaded. Knead the dough by hand for 5 minutes; cover and let rest for 30 minutes.

Set the pasta machine to the thickest setting. Work a quarter of the dough through the pasta machine at one time, taking care to cover the remainder with a damp cloth. Repeat 8 times, then gradually reduce the thickness. Hang the processed pasta to let it rest and air dry for 20 minutes before cooking.

Place the pasta in a large pot of rapidly boiling water. Cover and boil until tender but still firm (this cooks very quickly). Use fresh; if refrigerated too long it breaks apart.

Serve with your favorite sauce in a contrasting shade of red. Experiment with colors and flavors for desired effect. See the sauce section beginning on page 145.

Green Chile Pasta

BRYAN BROADFOOT

MAKES 4 SERVINGS

One 7-ounce can Herdez Salsa Verde or Salsa Verde with Green Chiles and Tomatillos (page 147)
¼ cup tightly packed, finely chopped fresh spinach
2 large eggs
1½ teaspoons olive oil
2½ cups all-purpose flour
1 teaspoon salt

Strain the salsa through cheesecloth to remove all the seeds. Place it in a small saucepan over medium-high heat and reduce it to 2 tablespoons. Place the spinach and eggs in a blender and puree. Combine the salsa and puree with all the other ingredients in a large mixing bowl. Mix until it has the consistency of fine meal. Adjust the water or flour as necessary to make the mixture stick together when kneaded. Knead dough by hand for 5 minutes; cover and let it rest for 30 minutes.

Set the pasta machine to the thickest setting. Work a quarter of the dough through the pasta machine at one time, taking care to cover the remainder with a damp cloth. Repeat 8 times, then gradually reduce the thickness. Hang the processed pasta to let it rest and air-dry for 20 minutes.

Place the pasta in a large pot of rapidly boiling water. Cover and boil until tender but still firm (this cooks very quickly). Use fresh; if refrigerated too long, it breaks apart. Serve with your favorite sauce or a pesto in a contrasting shade of green. Experiment with colors and flavors for desired effect. See the sauce section beginning on page 145.

Roasted Pepper and Goat Cheese Pasta
PAULA LAMBERT   *Mozzarella Company*

MAKES 4 SERVINGS

3 to 5 bell peppers, preferably 2 green, 2 red,
*   and 1 yellow, roasted (pages 96–97),*
*   peeled, seeded, and cut into long*
*   strips*
1 garlic clove, minced
10 fresh basil leaves, cut into very thin
*   strips*
¼ cup extra virgin olive oil
1 pound spaghetti or bucatini
5 to 6 ounces goat cheese, crumbled

Toss the peppers with garlic, basil, and the olive oil. Cook the pasta in boiling water until tender but still firm, *al dente*. Drain and toss with the goat cheese. Add the pepper mixture and toss gently. May be served warm or at room temperature.

Penne with Sun-Dried Tomatoes and Chile
NANCY GERLACH AND DAVE DEWITT

MAKES 6 SERVINGS

¼ cup crushed red pepper (page 101)
½ cup oil-packed sun-dried tomatoes
*   (page 208), cut into slivers and 2*
*   tablespoons of the oil reserved*
1 cup black olives cured in oil, pitted
*   and halved*
½ cup fresh basil leaves, chopped
½ cup chopped fresh parsley
1 teaspoon dried marjoram
3 garlic cloves, minced
½ cup olive oil
2 teaspoons freshly ground black pepper
¾ pound Parmesan cheese, grated
1 pound penne pasta

Combine all the ingredients, except the cheese and pasta, and let sit at room temperature for a couple of hours or overnight to blend the flavors. Cook the pasta in salted water until tender but still firm, *al dente*. Drain. Toss with the sauce and cheese until well coated and serve.

Pasta from Hell
CHRIS SCHLESINGER   *East Coast Grill*

MAKES 4 SERVINGS

2 tablespoons olive oil
1 red bell pepper, seeded and cut into
*   small dice*
1 onion, cut into small dice
3 bananas, cut into small dice
1 cup pineapple juice
*   Juice of 3 oranges*
*   Juice of 2 limes*
¼ cup chopped cilantro (fresh coriander)
1 tablespoon finely chopped habanero
*   or Scotch bonnet or 2 to 3 table-*
*   spoons finely chopped fresh jalapeños*
*   (see index for chillies; see also note*
*   below)*
8 ounces fettuccine
*   Salt and freshly cracked black pepper*
*   to taste*
¼ cup grated Parmesan cheese

Heat the oil in a large nonreactive saucepan over medium heat. Add the bell pepper and onion and cook, stirring, for 4 minutes. Add the bananas and juices and cook until soft, 4 to 6 minutes. Remove from the heat and add the cilantro and chillies. Cook the fettuccine in boiling salted water until tender but still firm, *al dente,* and add to the mix. Season and garnish with the cheese and serve.
NOTE: It takes at least 2 jalapeños to equal 1 habanero; adjust to your taste. The amount of chillies given here quarters those called for in the original recipe.

auces are any kind of liquid or semiliquid seasoning for food. They may or may not use spices. The ancient Latin word for broths or soups (sauces) was "juices," or *ius* in singular form. The French *sauce* and the Spanish and Italian *salsa* succeeded *ius*. "Sauce" is derived from the Latin for "salted," *saltus*. Humans first seasoned their food with salt, then sauces. During the evolution of sauces, only the more-or-less liquid consistency has remained relatively constant, with taste being the unlimited element. Obviously there are many categories of sauces to accommodate myriads of concoctions and their variations that have been incorporated into virtually every cuisine. In medieval European households, sauces were mainly served with foods preserved by brining and pickling to make them more palatable in a period without refrigeration and slow transportation. In most of the rest of the world they were used as a vehicle for legumes, vegetables, and/or meat that were served with the local starch—rice, maize, manioc, potatoes, pasta.

When one thinks of French cuisine, sauces are probably the first thing to come to mind. However, the art of sauces came to France when Catherine de Médicis married the French king Henry II and brought her Italian cooks with her as part of her entourage. The French do not have a monopoly on sauces, only a greater variety of them. Some French sauces and techniques have migrated to Latin America, where you can be certain peppers have been added. Capsicums are no longer strangers to French-type sauces found in nouvelle, southwestern, and Cajun cuisines.

Gravies are sauces made just before serving to accompany meat. They utilize the fat and browned drippings of cooked meat along with a thickening agent and a liquid—stock, vegetable juices, milk, water. The English-type gravy uses flour for the thickener but cookery in other cultures may use vegetable purees, cornstarch, or root starches such as potato or arrowroot. Gravies serve as the basis for many Indian dishes that use different combinations of chillies and spices according to the desired outcome. Although no longer commonly used in France, in the fourteenth century French cooks served birds and other meats with a *grané* made with cooked juices or drippings. Today we call it gravy because a medieval English transcriber copied the "n" as a "v." The addition of chillies does wonders for your everyday gravy.

Sauces can be cooked or uncooked, hot or cold, sweet or sour, spicy or mild, thick or thin, smooth or lumpy, emulsified or thickened with a starch or gelatin—almost anything goes. Sauce is incorporated into many dishes in Latin America, China, India, Africa, and the Far East. Each has some form of chilli sauce served as a table sauce to be consumed at the discretion of the user. In Latin America these uncooked table sauces, or *salsas,* are traditionally added to food after it is cooked or served as a condiment instead of being incorporated in the dish, as are other sauces such as *adobo* (a chilli-vinegar marinade), *recado* (a simple to elaborate ground herb and spice mixture similar to garam masala), *mole* (an elaborate, rich sauce flavored and thickened with chillies), and *pipián* (sumptuous sauces thickened with ground seeds and/or nuts).

Elizabeth Lambert Ortiz is probably the leading authority on table sauces throughout the world—certainly on those using peppers. With her gracious consent, I have borrowed heavily from her in the sauce section in order to present a representative table sauce from as many countries as possible. She sent me pepper seeds and sauce recipes from her travels so I could grow the peppers to test the sauces.

The sponsor of a salsa-making contest called me for a list of the types of sauces to include in the competition so that in fairness to the sauces' creators the jury would not judge one type against another. It is not easy to codify pepper sauces. In her authoritative work on Latin American cookery, Ortiz surmises that if codification could be done, it would probably complicate rather than simplify matters. The sauce recipes that follow are divided into two major categories—table sauces and incorporated sauces. Within those two groups are cooked and uncooked sauces. By the way, I did not accept the sponsor's invitation to judge the contest because I remembered the tears and fits of coughing, gagging, and often pain that accompanied my testing of all the peppers I grew during the years I worked on *Peppers*. It did not promise to be a "fun" afternoon.

A word about uncooked sauces. Hand chopping of all uncooked, fresh ingredients is recommended. If a blender or food processor is used, it is very easy to overprocess the ingredients, thereby destroying the desired texture. Some of the vegetables, especially tomatoes, will become frothy and pale. Well-drained canned tomatoes can be chopped in the food processor because cooking took place during the canning process.

Sauces are extremely important to capsicum cookery. That old saying "Sauce for the goose is sauce for the gander" ain't necessarily so. These sauces are more specialized than that.

I wish I had said what Kathy Gunst did about pepper sauces in her book *Condiments*: "A really good hot sauce takes you by the shoulders, gives you a good shake, and slaps your face to say 'HELLO.' "

Pepita Salsa Verde
JEAN ANDREWS

MAKES ABOUT 4 CUPS

> 2 tablespoons pumpkin seeds or pepitas
> (page 107)
> 1 cup roasted (page 78), seeded and
> chopped fresh green New Mexican
> chiles (page 78)
> ¾ cup chopped fresh parsley
> All-purpose flour, if needed

¼ cup vegetable oil
3 cups chicken stock
Salt and freshly ground black pepper
to taste

Toast (page 110) pumpkin seeds until browned, or use toasted pumpkin seeds (pepitas). Puree the chiles and fresh parsley together in a blender. Add a little flour if a thicker sauce is desired. Heat the oil in a medium-size saucepan over medium heat. Add a little of the chicken stock and stir, then strain through a sieve. Add the strained mixture and remaining stock to the hot oil, heat thoroughly, season and serve. Use as a table sauce or on chicken enchiladas.

Salsa Verde with Green Chiles and Tomatillos
JEAN ANDREWS

MAKES 2 CUPS

> 8 large, fresh tomatillos (page 108),
> husked and washed, or one 13-ounce
> can, drained
> ½ cup fresh green New Mexican chiles,
> or one 4-ounce can
> 1 to 2 serranos (page 86), seeded if
> desired
> 1 to 2 garlic cloves, peeled and crushed
> 1 tablespoon cilantro (fresh coriander)
> leaves, chopped
> ½ teaspoon salt
> ¼ teaspoon sugar

If using fresh tomatillos, steam until just tender. Puree the tomatillos with the chiles, garlic, cilantro, salt, and sugar in a blender. This can be used as is or it may be simmered with a tablespoon of olive or vegetable oil for a few minutes and served hot. Use as a table sauce or on chicken enchiladas with a dollop of sour cream on each.

New Mexican Chile Salsa Verde
JEAN ANDREWS

MAKES 1 GENEROUS CUP

6 to 8 canned or fresh roasted (pages 96–97) green New Mexican chiles (page 78), seeded and chopped, to make 1 cup
1 teaspoon seeded and chopped jalapeños, fresh or canned (page 77)
1 garlic clove, peeled and crushed
½ teaspoon salt
1 tablespoon cilantro (fresh coriander), leaves, chopped
2 tablespoons chopped onion
½ to 1 teaspoon olive oil
¼ teaspoon sugar

Place the chiles and garlic in the bowl of a food processor and pulse for a few seconds until the mixture is pureed but still has texture. Add the other ingredients and pulse the processor several times. Adjust seasoning. Serve at room temperature. This salsa keeps well for several days, covered, in the refrigerator.

VARIATION: *Jalapeño Salsa Verde*

Substitute *jalapeños en escabeche* for green New Mexican chiles or use fresh jalapeños with 2 tablespoons vinegar or lime juice.

Salsa Cruda
JEAN ANDREWS

This is the most commonly used condiment/table sauce in Mexico and it goes by many names—*salsa picante, ranchero salsa, pico de gallo*—but it is good no matter what it is called.

MAKES 1 TO 1½ CUPS

1 medium-size ripe tomato, finely chopped
½ medium-size onion or 2 to 3 green onions (scallions), finely chopped
6 sprigs cilantro (fresh coriander), minced
1 garlic clove, minced
3 fresh green chillies (serranos, jalapeños, 'Fresnos'; see index), finely chopped
½ teaspoon salt
¼ teaspoon sugar
⅓ cup fresh lime juice or half vinegar and half water

Mix together in a bowl. Make fresh daily for the desired fresh crunchy taste. If any is left over, it can be simmered with a little oil for a few minutes and used over eggs. If you keep it in the refrigerator longer than the day that it's made it is no longer *salsa cruda*. You can eat it, but it is not the same. Please call it something else.

Roasted Serrano Salsa
MARK MILLER   *Coyote Cafe*

MAKES 3 CUPS

6 serranos (page 86)
1 pound ripe Roma tomatoes, finely diced
2 tablespoons minced sweet red onion
¼ cup fresh orange juice
2 tablespoons seeded and very finely diced yellow bell pepper
2 tablespoons finely chopped cilantro (fresh coriander)
1 tablespoon rice vinegar (page 107)
½ teaspoon salt
½ teaspoon sugar

Cook the serranos in a black iron skillet over medium-high heat until blackened. Remove about half of the blackened skin, and then chop fine. Mix together with the remaining ingredients. Let stand for 1 hour. Cover, and refrigerate until ready to serve.

Ixni-Pec (Yucatecan Habanero Sauce)
ELISABETH LAMBERT ORTIZ

This sauce from Yucatán in Mexico is not only extremely hot but is flavorful, as well, unlike piri-piri (see page 151), which is just concentrated fire. The sauce, pronounced *schnee-peck,* is served separately from the dishes it accompanies, appearing on tables in small bowls to be used at the diner's discretion. The pepper used is the golden habanero. The Jamaican Scotch bonnet and the dátil have a similar flavor, as well as a comparable degree of heat. Use freshly made.

MAKES ABOUT 1 CUP

> ¼ *cup chopped onion*
> ¼ *large, ripe tomato, peeled, seeded, and chopped*
> ¼ *cup habanero (page 75), seeded and chopped*
> ¼ *cup Seville (bitter) orange juice, or substitute a mixture of 1 part orange juice to 2 parts fresh lime juice*
> *Salt to taste*

In a bowl combine all the ingredients, seasoning with salt. Serve whenever a chilli sauce is called for.

Brazilian Chilli-Pepper Sauce
ELISABETH LAMBERT ORTIZ

The peppers used in Brazil are the small, very, very hot maleguetas (probably *Capsicum frutescens* or bird peppers), not usually available here. Any small chilli can be substituted. I have found pickled Caribbean peppers, usually from Jamaica or Trinidad, to be a good substitute, but you can use chiltepines.

MAKES ½ CUP

> *6 to 8 fresh chiltepines (page 69) or 3 to 4 hot red or green chillies, stemmed*
> *1 onion, chopped*
> *1 garlic clove, minced*
> *Salt to taste*
> ½ *cup fresh lime or lemon juice*

Crush the chillies, onion, and garlic with the salt using a mortar and pestle, adding the lime juice little by little, or puree in a blender or food processor. Serve in a bowl to accompany meat, poultry, and fish, and dried bean dishes. Use with caution.

Chilean Pebre
ELISABETH LAMBERT ORTIZ

MAKES ABOUT 1 CUP

> *1 medium-size onion, quartered*
> *1 garlic clove, peeled*
> *2 tablespoons chopped cilantro (fresh coriander)*
> *1 tablespoon chopped fresh parsley*
> *1 serrano (page 86) or fresh jalapeño (page 77), or to taste, seeded*
> *3 tablespoons olive oil*
> *1 tablespoon fresh lemon juice*
> *Salt to taste*

Combine all the ingredients in a food processor and mince but do not puree. Let stand for about 1 hour before serving for the flavors to develop. Serve with any meat.

Ecuadorian Chilli-Pepper Sauce
ELISABETH LAMBERT ORTIZ

This sauce is also used in Costa Rican homes.

*Red or green serranos (page 86) or
fresh jalapeños (page 77), seeded and
cut into thin strips
Finely chopped red onion
Fresh lemon or lime juice
Salt to taste*

Combine the chillies with an equal amount of onion in a glass container. Add lemon juice to cover. Season with salt and let the sauce stand 3 to 4 hours before using. Dilute with hot water if desired.

Banana Pepper Sauce
JEAN ANDREWS

This sauce is not hot and can be served cold with fish, tongue, or veal. When your garden is full of banana peppers, try this sauce.

MAKES ABOUT 2 CUPS

*1 medium-size onion, cut into chunks
1 cup cooked English peas
3 small, ripe tomatoes, cut into chunks
½ teaspoon dried oregano
¼ teaspoon dried thyme
3 fresh or pickled yellow banana
peppers ('Cubanelle' or any sweet
ethnic type)
1 tablespoon vegetable oil
3 tablespoons vinegar
1 tablespoon capers, rinsed and drained
12 green olives, pitted and sliced*

Combine all the ingredients except the capers and olives in a blender. Process until creamy.

Stir in the capers and olive slices. Store tightly covered in the refrigerator, but use within the week.

Moroccan Harissa Sauce
JEAN ANDREWS

MAKES 1 CUP

*1 cup chicken broth
1 teaspoon Harissa Paste (recipe
follows)
1 tablespoon fresh lemon juice
1 to 2 tablespoons olive oil
¼ teaspoon ground cumin
1 teaspoon minced cilantro (fresh
coriander)*

Place all the ingredients in a small saucepan over high heat and stir until warmed through. Remove from the fire and beat well; pour into a small sauce dish.
  Serve immediately.

Harissa Paste

MAKES ½ CUP

*2 ounce dried japonés (page 90), de
árbol (page 73), or any red chilli
2 garlic cloves, peeled
4 teaspoons caraway or coriander seeds
Salt to taste
Olive oil to cover*

Soak the chillies in hot water to cover for 1 hour; drain and chop. Place in a blender or spice mill with the garlic and caraway and puree. Season with salt. Place in a jar and cover with olive oil. Cover tightly and keep in the refrigerator for several weeks.

African Hot Sauce
JEAN ANDREWS

MAKES 2½ CUPS

One 12-ounce can tomato sauce
¼ cup chopped onion
1 garlic clove, minced
Juice of 1 lemon
2 to 8 small fresh red chillies (Thai,
  chiltepín, cayenne, or jalapeño; see
  index)
1½ teaspoons grated fresh horseradish

Put all the ingredients in a blender or food processor and puree. Store in a tightly covered jar in the refrigerator. Serve with meats, poultry, or fish. VARIATION: Add 1 tablespoon to 1 cup of mayonnaise and use as a dressing for seafood or poultry.

Iberian Piri-Piri Sauce
JEAN ANDREWS

The fiery piri-piri chilli, a migrant to the Iberian peninsula from Angola, Africa, when it was Portuguese, is used to make a sauce that bears its name. This very pungent table sauce can be made at home or bought in little bottles.

MAKES 1½ CUPS

1 cup piri-piris or chiltepines (page 69)
  or any small chilli, stemmed and
  chopped
1 cup olive oil
½ cup red wine vinegar
1 teaspoon salt

Put all of the ingredients in a glass jar, cover tightly, and shake well. Allow the mixture to sit for several weeks before using. Shake well before using the pungent liquid on anything that needs a little punch. Keeps, tightly closed, almost indefinitely in the refrigerator. Additional oil and vinegar can be added to the chillies as it is used.

Javanese Sambal
JEAN ANDREWS

MAKES ½ CUP OR MORE

¼ whole coconut, peeled and rough
  chopped
3 fresh green chillies (Thai, page 91,
  or serrano, page 86)
½ teaspoon shrimp paste, or substitute
  mashed anchovy
1 garlic clove, peeled
¼ teaspoon palm sugar (page 107)
  or granulated sugar
1 tablespoon tamarind (page 108)
  or fresh lime juice
Salt to taste

Pound all the ingredients together into a paste or puree in a blender. Serve as a table sauce with everything.

Bornea Sambal
JEAN ANDREWS

In Kalimantan (Borneo) this is made fresh daily —a table sauce to eat with everything.

MAKES ½ CUP

5 fresh green chillies (Thai, page 91,
  or serrano, page 86)
1 shallot or green onion (scallion)
1 garlic clove, peeled
¼ teaspoon shrimp paste, or substitute
  mashed anchovy
½ teaspoon brown sugar
Juice of 1 small lime
¼ teaspoon salt

Boil the whole chillies in water to cover for 6 minutes; drain. Pound all the ingredients together in a *molcajete* (mortar) to make a creamy paste or puree in a blender.

Spanish Romesco Sauce
JEAN ANDREWS

This is my version of a traditional sauce for seafood made with the cayenne-type romesco chilli. No need to limit this thick, red sauce to fish—try it on chicken, veal, pork, or as a spread for bread.

MAKES 2½ CUPS

> ¾ cup red wine vinegar
> 6 dried romescos, 3 dried red New Mexican chiles (page 78) or 4 guajillos (page 74), seeded
> 2 to 3 dried red chillies (japonés, de árbol, Thai, chiltepín; see index)
> 1½ cups extra virgin olive oil
> Three ½-inch slices French bread
> 1 cup peeled and chopped fresh tomatoes
> 5 garlic cloves, minced
> ½ cup blanched almonds, pecans, or skinned hazelnuts, toasted
> 2 tablespoons chopped fresh parsley
> Salt and freshly ground black pepper to taste

Heat the vinegar in a saucepan over medium heat or in a microwave. Tear all of the chillies into small pieces and allow to soak in the hot vinegar for 30 minutes.

Heat ½ cup of the oil in a small skillet over medium-high heat and fry the bread until both sides are golden. Cook the tomatoes and garlic in the same oil over medium heat for 3 to 4 minutes. Remove from heat and allow to cool, then place the tomatoes, vinegar, parsley, nuts, and chillies in a blender with the remaining oil and puree. Tear the bread into pieces and add to the blender with the nuts and puree into a smooth thick sauce. Add salt and pepper to taste. If a thinner sauce is desired, add water or tomato juice, as additional vinegar will make it too sour and additional oil separates out.

Make the sauce several hours or a day before using. Beat the sauce lightly and serve at room temperature. It will keep, covered tightly, for several weeks in the refrigerator.

Red New Mexican Chile Sauce
JEAN ANDREWS

To be used over enchiladas (page 142) or anything.

MAKES 4 CUPS OR MORE

> 2 tablespoons vegetable oil
> 1 tablespoon margarine
> 2 tablespoons all-purpose flour
> ¼ teaspoon ground cumin
> ½ cup freshly ground New Mexican chile powder (page 99)
> 1 cup cold water
> 2 to 3 cups chicken stock
> 1 garlic clove, minced
> Salt to taste

Heat the oil and margarine; stir in the flour until it reaches a golden color. Add the cumin. Mix the ground chile with the cold water until there are no lumps. Whisk it into the flour paste off the heat. Return to the heat and slowly add the stock. Simmer for 15 to 20 minutes, stirring frequently. Add the garlic and season with salt to taste. Simmer 5 minutes longer. If lumpy, run in the blender for a few seconds.

This sauce will keep well for a week in the refrigerator. Use over enchiladas, chiles rellenos, burritos, or anything.

Sauces

Southwestern Chile Sauce
JEAN ANDREWS

MAKES 4 CUPS

15 dried red New Mexican chiles (page
78) or equal parts anchos (page 83)
and New Mexican chiles, soaked
(page 99), deveined, and seeded,
soaking water reserved
1 garlic clove, peeled
3 tablespoons canola or vegetable oil
2 tablespoons all-purpose flour
1 teaspoon dried oregano
Pinch of salt
Pinch of ground cumin
Pinch of ground cloves
1 to 2 tablespoons cider vinegar
½ to 2 cups chicken, turkey, or beef stock

Puree a third of the chiles at a time in a blender
with ½ cup of the reserved water each time. Add
the clove of garlic and puree. If necessary, strain
this puree to remove bits of skin. Heat the oil in
a large skillet over medium heat. Stir in the flour
and cook until golden, not brown. Add the chile
puree, seasonings, vinegar, and enough stock to
make a sauce consistency. Simmer the chile sauce
for about 20 minutes to blend the flavors. Use
this sauce for enchiladas or stews.

Homemade 'Tabasco' Sauce
JEAN ANDREWS

Use the true 'Tabasco' pepper if possible; however, other small, fresh, ripe chillies may be substituted.

MAKES 1 CUP

1 dozen large 'Tabasco' chillies (page
87) or small, red chillies, stemmed
1 garlic clove, peeled
½ cup Herbed Chilli Vinegar (page 209)
½ teaspoon salt
½ teaspoon sugar

In a small nonreactive saucepan, boil the chillies
and garlic in the vinegar until tender. Place in a
blender with the salt and sugar and puree. Run
through a metal sieve if necessary. Dilute this
paste with more vinegar until it is the consistency
of rich cream. Pour into a nonreactive saucepan,
bring to a boil, then pour into a hot, sterilized
(page 197) bottle to within ½ inch of the rim and
run a sterilized knife around the inside of the
bottle to release air bubbles. Wipe the rim clean
and seal with a scalded top. Store in the refrigerator once opened.

Chipotle Sauce
JEAN ANDREWS

MAKES 4 CUPS

2 tablespoons vegetable oil
1 medium-size onion, chopped
2 garlic cloves, peeled and crushed or
pressed
One 16-ounce can solid-pack tomatoes,
drained chopped
One 12-ounce can tomato sauce
1 chipotle (page 91), or to taste,
chopped
Salt to taste

In a medium-size saucepan over medium heat,
heat the oil. Add the onion and cook, stirring,
until clear. Add the remaining ingredients and
cook over medium heat for 15 to 20 minutes.
Serve with grilled or barbecued meats.

Enchilada Sauce
JEAN ANDREWS

MAKES 3 TO 4 CUPS

> 8 dried red New Mexican chiles (page 78) or anchos (page 83) or some of each
> 2 tablespoons ground cumin
> 2 teaspoons dried oregano
> 1 medium-size onion, chopped
> 2 garlic cloves, minced
> 3 tablespoons vegetable oil
> 2 tablespoons all-purpose flour
> One 6-ounce can tomato paste
> 2 cups water or chicken stock
> Salt and freshly ground black pepper to taste

Wash the chiles. Cover with boiling water and let stand at least an hour. Drain and reserve the water. Remove stems, seeds, and veins. In a blender puree the chiles, spices, onion and garlic, with a cup (more if desired for consistency) of strained soaking water (see note below).

In a skillet, heat the oil, add the flour, and stir until smooth and golden brown. Add the pepper paste, tomato paste, and remaining water. Simmer about 30 minutes or until thickened. Season with salt and pepper. Serve on enchiladas (page 142).

NOTE: If you have on hand Basic Red Chilli Paste (page 158), use ½ cup or more if desired, instead of going through the steps to make the paste here.

Ancho Chile-Hazelnut Mole
GREG HIGGINS   *Heathman Hotel*

MAKES 3 TO 4 CUPS

> 8 anchos (page 83)
> 2 fresh red jalapeños (page 77), roasted (pages 96–97), peeled, and seeded
> 4 ripe Roma tomatoes, peeled and seeded
> 1 cup hazelnuts, toasted
> 4 garlic cloves, peeled and browned in a little hot oil
> 2 cups chicken stock
> ½ teaspoon ground cinnamon
> 1 teaspoon ground cumin
> 1 tablespoon unsweetened cocoa powder
> Salt and freshly ground black pepper to taste

Wash the anchos in cold water, then remove the stems and as many of the seeds as possible. Let soak in warm water till soft. Remove from the water and dry. Puree the anchos, jalapeños, tomatoes, hazelnuts, and garlic in a food processor. Add chicken stock as needed to facilitate the puree. Add the cinnamon, cumin, and cocoa powder and continue processing. Add more chicken stock to thin to a sauce consistency. Adjust the seasoning with salt and pepper if needed.

Serve the mole with enchiladas of chicken or pork, or as a condiment with grilled poultry or pork dishes. Thinned with oil, it makes an excellent marinade for grilled items.

Fourth Street Grill's Chipotle Mole Sauce
SUSAN H. NELSON   *Ginger Island*

MAKES 1 QUART

> 3 pasillas (page 79)
> 3 mulatos (page 82)
> 2 anchos (page 83)
> 2 dried New Mexican chiles (page 78)

One-half 4-ounce can chipotles adobado
  (page 91)
  2 tablespoons minced garlic
1½ tablespoons ground cinnamon
  1 teaspoon ground cloves
  4 ounces Mexican chocolate or
  sweetened chocolate
  1 cup golden raisins
  1 cup whole almonds
  3 cups fresh orange juice, or to cover
  Chicken stock as needed
  Salt to taste

Briefly rinse and remove the stems of the first four chillies. Put all the ingredients, except the orange juice, chicken stock, and salt, in a large nonreactive saucepan. Pour the orange juice over the other ingredients to cover and bring to a boil. Turn off the heat and let the mixture sit until all the dried chillies are about softened, 20 minutes.

Puree the contents of the pot in a blender (you may have to do this in batches) and strain through a sieve into a heavy-bottomed saucepan. If necessary, thin the sauce with a little chicken stock, until the consistency is similar to that of heavy cream. Place the sauce over low heat and let simmer for no less than 1 hour, thinning again if necessary. Season with salt.

This sauce can be easily kept in the refrigerator for weeks in a covered container. Serve with Fourth Street Grill's Chilli-stuffed Pork Loin (page 170) or grilled meats.

Chipotle Mayonnaise
DONALD COUNTS, M.D., AND
KATHRYN O'CONNOR COUNTS

MAKES 2½ CUPS

  2 cups homemade mayonnaise (recipe
  follows)
½ cup Salsa Chipotle (recipe follows)

Fold the salsa into the mayonnaise and serve as a dip for boiled shrimp or other seafood or as a spread for sandwiches.

Homemade Mayonnaise

MAKES 4½ CUPS

  1 large egg
  1 large egg yolk
  1 teaspoon dry mustard
  1 tablespoon fructose (honey or corn
  syrup), or to taste
  1 teaspoon freshly ground white pepper,
  or to taste
  4 teaspoons white wine vinegar
  4 cups vegetable oil, or as needed

Place all the ingredients except the oil in a blender and blend at high speed for 2 minutes. Slowly dribble in the oil until the desired consistency is reached (the machine will begin to slow down). Add extra pepper or fructose to taste.
NOTE: The key to success in making this in a blender is using fresh eggs and adding the oil in a slow, steady stream.

Salsa Chipotle

MAKES ABOUT 4 CUPS

  One 7-ounce can chipotles adobado (page
  91), seeded
  One 28-ounce can whole tomatoes
6 to 8 fresh basil leaves
  1 small white onion, quartered
  1 tablespoon vinegar, optional

Place all the ingredients in a blender, including the liquid from the chipotles, and puree well. Keeps well in the refrigerator if tightly closed.

Green New Mexican Chile Pesto
JEAN ANDREWS

A southwestern answer to Italian pesto. Use in any recipe calling for pesto.

MAKES 1 TO 1½ CUPS

> 6 fresh green New Mexican chiles (page 78), peeled, seeded, and chopped
> ½ cup olive oil
> 2 cups packed well-washed fresh spinach, chopped
> ½ cup chopped fresh parsley
> 2 garlic cloves, peeled
> 2 teaspoons chopped fresh or dried basil
> 2 tablespoons pine nuts or sunflower seeds
> Salt to taste

In a blender, puree all the ingredients to make a smooth sauce. Thin with water if necessary.

Racy Pesto Sauce
JEAN ANDREWS

MAKES 2 TO 2½ CUPS

> 2 cups packed fresh basil leaves
> 2 garlic cloves, peeled
> ½ cup olive oil
> ½ cup freshly grated Parmesan cheese
> ¼ cup sunflower or pumpkin seeds, toasted (page 110)
> 1 serrano (page 86), seeded
> ½ cup water
> Salt and freshly ground black pepper to taste
> ¼ cup heavy cream

Blanch the basil leaves and garlic in boiling water for a few seconds. Roll in a towel to remove the water. Place the basil, garlic, olive oil, Parmesan, sunflower seeds, serrano, and water in a blender. Puree until very smooth. Season with salt and pepper. Pour the sauce into a saucepan and stir in the cream. Over medium-low heat, warm the sauce without boiling. Serve over freshly cooked pasta with grated Parmesan.

Texas Peach Hot and Sweet Dipping Sauce
STEPHEN LOMBARDI

Makes a tasty dipping sauce for *flautas, wontons,* or egg rolls, but don't limit yourself to just those three. Experiment.

MAKES 8 CUPS

> 2 tablespoons olive oil
> 2½ tablespoons peeled and finely chopped fresh ginger
> 3 to 4 fresh jalapeños, seeded and minced (see note below)
> 3 pounds fresh peaches, peeled, pitted, and sliced
> 2 tablespoons fresh lemon juice
> ⅔ cup white vinegar
> 1½ cups sugar

Heat the oil in a 4-quart saucepan over medium heat. Add the ginger and jalapeños and cook, stirring, until soft. Add the remaining ingredients and allow to simmer until the peaches are soft. Remove from the heat, chill, then puree, pushing the mixture through a metal sieve with the back of a ladle.

NOTE: Remember, some jalapeños are hotter than others, so if you think you have your hands on some zingers, use the lesser amount.

James T's Flame Sauce
W. C. LONGACRE

MAKES 3 CUPS

¾ cup water
12 habaneros (page 75) or dátils (page 71), seeded and chopped
2 cups seeded, peeled, and medium-chopped fresh papaya (page 107)
1 teaspoon dry mustard
3 fresh jalapeños (page 77), seeded and minced
1 large Bermuda onion, finely chopped
2 large, ripe tomatoes, medium chopped
1 teaspoon freshly ground white pepper
1 teaspoon ground cayenne pepper
2 tablespoons minced fresh oregano
1 tablespoon minced fresh parsley
1 tablespoon minced cilantro (fresh coriander)
1 tablespoon minced fresh basil
2 tablespoons balsamic vinegar
1 tablespoon salt
2 tablespoons firmly packed dark brown sugar
2 tablespoons minced garlic

Place all the ingredients in a saucepan and bring to a boil. Reduce the heat to medium and simmer for 3 to 4 minutes. Allow to cool, covered, overnight in the refrigerator before using. This sauce should last several weeks if kept refrigerated. Use as a condiment on eggs, with grilled meats, or as a dip with chips.

Ponchartrain Sauce
TONY BECKWITH   Green Pastures

MAKES 8 CUPS

4 cups chicken stock
4 cups beef stock
½ cup (1 stick) butter or margarine
½ cup all-purpose flour
2 large green bell peppers, seeded and chopped
2 large red bell peppers, seeded and chopped
2 white onions, chopped
1 bunch green onions (scallions), chopped
4 garlic cloves, minced
1 pound shrimp, blanched until just pink, shelled, and chopped into bite-size pieces
Salt and freshly ground black pepper to taste
1 teaspoon dried thyme
1 teaspoon crushed red pepper (page 101)
1 pound uncooked crabmeat, picked over for crab shell
½ cup dry sherry
1 tablespoon minced fresh parsley

As Cajun cooks always say, first make a roux. Heat together the stocks in a medium-size saucepan. In a large saucepan melt the butter over medium heat. Add the flour to the butter and stir constantly. When the roux is an aromatic, nutty brown, gradually add the heated stocks. Stir until well blended and thickened to the consistency of a heavy gravy. Allow to simmer on low heat, stirring as needed, and strain through a fine sieve before use.

In a large heavy skillet or Dutch oven, cook the peppers, garlic, and onions, stirring, in a little butter or margarine over medium heat until soft and translucent. Add the shrimp and season with salt, pepper, thyme, and crushed red pepper. Add the strained roux. Simmer 10 minutes. Add the crab and sherry. Continue to simmer for 5 minutes. Garnish with the parsley and serve over grilled or sautéed fillets of red snapper or redfish.

Portuguese-Style Red Pepper Paste for Meats
JEAN ANDREWS

MAKES 1¼ CUPS

> 8 large red bell peppers, roasted (pages
>   96–97), seeded, and peeled
> 2 fresh jalapeños (page 77) or
>   serranos (page 86), roasted (pages
>   96–97) and seeded
> 1 teaspoon salt, or to taste
> 2 to 3 large garlic cloves, peeled
> 6 tablespoons olive oil

Place the peppers, salt, garlic, and half the oil in a blender jar and process until smooth. Slowly add the remaining oil and blend until the consistency of whipped cream. Place in a jar; seal tightly; store in the refrigerator.

When ready to use as a dry marinade for poultry, pork, or lamb, allow the paste to return to room temperature before rubbing on all sides of the meat. Allow to sit several hours or overnight. Scrape off excess before cooking in skillet or grill. There is a temptation to eat this before putting it on the meat.

VARIATION: After deglazing the skillet with a little boiling water, several tablespoonsful of the paste can be added to the deglaze to make a sauce for the meat. Cook down to the desired thickness.

Red New Mexican Chile Butter
JAMIE MORNINGSTAR *Inglenook Napa Valley*

MAKES ½ POUND

> 1 teaspoon crushed dried New Mexican
>   chile (page 78)
> 1 tablespoon chopped garlic

> ½ pound (2 sticks) unsalted butter or
>   margarine, butter at room tempera-
>   ture (see note below)
> Salt and freshly ground black pepper
>   to taste

Combine all the ingredients in a food processor and pulse a few times to get the mixture going. Then let the machine run until all the ingredients are well mixed.

NOTE: If using margarine, make sure it is well chilled.

Basic Red Chilli Paste
JEAN ANDREWS

MAKES 2 TO 3 CUPS

> 4 anchos (page 83)
> 2 guajillos (page 74)
> 2 chipotles (page 91)
> 1 large onion
> 4 garlic cloves, peeled
> 2 teaspoons ground cumin
> 2 teaspoons dried oregano
> 1 teaspoon salt

Soak the chillies in hot water to cover about 1 hour. Remove from the water and remove the seeds, stems, and veins. Reserve 2 cups of the soaking water. Place the chillies and remaining ingredients in a blender and process until a smooth, thick paste. Use the soaking water as needed. Store in a covered jar in refrigerator for several weeks or freeze. Use to flavor chilaquiles (page 165), enchiladas (page 142), and other sauces.

Pancetta Chile Butter

PATRICIA WINDISCH   *Beringer Vineyards*

This butter and the one that follows are wonderful on grilled steak, salmon, chicken, or anything else you may want to try.

MAKES ½ TO 1 CUP

> *½ cup (1 stick) unsalted butter or margarine, softened*
> *One ½-inch-thick slice pancetta, diced (see note below)*
> *2 shallots, minced*
> *3 garlic cloves, blanched for 3 minutes, peeled, and mashed*
> *1 fresh red New Mexican chile (page 78), peeled (page 96), seeded, and diced*
> *½ red bell pepper, seeded and diced*
> *2 teaspoons Tabasco Brand Pepper Sauce*
> *¼ teaspoon freshly ground black pepper*
> *1 tablespoon minced fresh chives*
> *1 tablespoon fresh lemon juice*
> *Salt to taste*

Sauté the pancetta in a small skillet until browned. Remove from the skillet to paper towels and cool. In the same skillet, sauté the shallots until translucent. Cool, then combine with the rest of the ingredients. Place on a sheet of plastic wrap and shape into a 1-inch cylinder. Refrigerate.

Remove from the refrigerator 30 minutes before serving and slice into ¼-inch rounds.
NOTE: Pancetta is a very peppery Italian bacon. Substitute any good bacon, but increase the black pepper to ½ teaspoon.

Green New Mexican Chile Butter

JAMIE MORNINGSTAR   *Inglenook Napa Valley*

MAKES ½ POUND

> *One 4-ounce can chopped green chiles (page 78), drained*
> *½ pound (2 sticks) unsalted butter or margarine, butter at room temperature (see note below)*
> *Salt and freshly ground black pepper to taste*

Combine all the ingredients in a food processor and pulse a few times to get the mixture going. Then let the machine run until all the ingredients are well mixed. Butter will be a light green color.
NOTE: If using margarine, make sure it is well chilled.

Roast Chicken with Wild Mushrooms and Pasilla Sauce
ROBERT DEL GRANDE   *Cafe Annie*

MAKES 6 SERVINGS

One 3- to 4-pound roasting chicken
Salt and freshly ground black pepper
to taste

FOR THE SAUCE
4 pasillas (page 79)
2 corn tortillas
½ cup shelled pumpkin seeds
2 tablespoons butter or margarine
½ yellow onion, chopped
4 garlic cloves, chopped
8 ounces fresh wild mushrooms (like
shiitake), stemmed and roughly
chopped
4 cups chicken stock
2 teaspoons pure maple syrup
1 teaspoon fresh lime juice
Salt and freshly ground black pepper
to taste

To roast the chicken, lightly salt and pepper it, then roast in a preheated 300°F oven until the juices at the joint run clear, 45 to 60 minutes.

Heat a dry skillet over medium heat. Heat the pasillas until lightly toasted on both sides, then stem and seed them. Set aside. In the same skillet, lightly toast the corn tortillas, break into pieces, and set aside. Then toast the pumpkin seeds in the skillet until puffed and crunchy. Set aside.

Melt the butter or margarine in the skillet over medium heat. Add the onion and garlic and cook, stirring, until lightly browned. Add the mushrooms and cook, stirring, until their liquid has evaporated. Transfer the mixture to a blender. Over medium-high heat, pour the stock into the skillet, scraping the bottom to loosen any browned deposits. Pour into the blender. Add the pasillas, tortillas, and pumpkin seeds. Puree for 10 to 15 seconds. Do not overpuree; the sauce should not be too smooth. Transfer the puree to a saucepan. Bring the sauce to a boil, then lower the heat to medium-low and simmer for 30 minutes. Add the maple syrup and lime juice and season with salt and pepper. Quarter the roasting chicken and serve with the sauce.

VARIATION: Instead of roasting the chicken, quarter it, then brown the pieces in a large deep pan in a little oil over medium-high heat. When the pieces are well browned, add 2 cups chicken stock and the sauce and bring to a simmer. Cook the chicken in the sauce until cooked through, 30 to 45 minutes. Remove the chicken pieces from the sauce and serve.

Lemon and Chilli Roasted Chicken
TIM COLTMAN-ROGERS

MAKES 6 OR MORE SERVINGS

1 large roasting chicken (figure ½
pound per serving)
½ pound (2 sticks) butter or margarine
2 large lemons
6 to 8 fresh or dried chiltepínes, or substitute
Thai, de árbol, or serrano (see index
for chillies)
2 to 6 garlic cloves, minced
Freshly ground black pepper to taste
2 tablespoons honey

Wash the chicken and dry thoroughly. Clarify the butter. Peel the lemons, being careful not to include any of the bitter white pith. Chop the rind finely and put in boiling water for 1 minute; drain. Squeeze the lemons; reserve the juice. Mash the chiltepínes together and add to the butter, lemon rind, garlic, and black pepper in a saucepan. Heat for 2 to 3 minutes over medium heat.

Gently lift the skin from the chicken's breast and fill the space between the skin and the breast meat with the lemon-pepper mixture. Use any surplus sauce to cover the chicken inside and out. Place the uncovered bird on a roasting rack in a pan. Bake in a preheated 400°F oven, basting from time to time. Allow 15 minutes per pound, plus another 15 minutes. The chicken is done when the juices run clear at a joint. Transfer the chicken to a serving platter. Place the roasting pan over medium-high heat and deglaze it with some boiling water, lemon juice, and honey (about 1½ to 2 cups total), scraping the bottom to loosen browned deposits. Serve the chicken and its gravy separately.

Breast of Chicken and Green Chiles in Phyllo with Chipotle Sauce
JEAN ANDREWS

MAKES 8 SERVINGS

2 tablespoons olive oil
¼ cup chopped shallots
½ pound mushrooms, chopped
1½ cups canned chopped green New Mexican chiles (page 78), drained
¼ teaspoon dried thyme
¼ teaspoon dried marjoram
½ cup dry sherry
½ cup low-fat plain yogurt
3 tablespoons freshly grated Parmesan cheese
Salt and freshly ground black pepper to taste
Dash of freshly grated nutmeg
3 large egg whites
16 sheets phyllo pastry
¾ cup (1½ sticks) butter or margarine, melted
8 boneless, skinless chicken breasts

FOR THE CHIPOTLE SAUCE
3 tablespoons butter or margarine
3 tablespoons all-purpose flour
1½ cups milk
½ cup sherry
1 chipotle adobado (page 91)
Salt and freshly ground black pepper to taste
Chopped fresh parsley for garnish

Heat the oil in a large skillet over medium-high heat, then add the shallots and cook, stirring, until they are soft. Add the mushrooms and cook, stirring, 4 to 5 minutes. Add the chiles, thyme, and marjoram and cook, stirring, 3 to 4 minutes. Add the sherry and cook until the moisture evaporates. Reduce the heat and stir in the yogurt and Parmesan; stir until well mixed. Season with salt, pepper, and nutmeg. Allow to cool.

Beat the egg whites in a large bowl until stiff and fairly dry peaks form. Gently fold the egg whites into the cooled mushroom mixture.

Use 2 sheets of phyllo for each breast. Put one on top of the other, brushing each with melted butter. Fold in half. Keep unused phyllo well covered with a dampened towel. Place 1 generous tablespoon of the mushroom mixture in the middle of the folded phyllo; then place a chicken breast on top. Put another tablespoon of the mushroom mixture on top of the chicken breast. Fold both sides of the phyllo over to the center. Fold each end toward the center and brush that side with butter. Place, folded side down, in a shallow baking pan; brush the top with butter. Repeat until all 8 breasts are wrapped. Bake in a preheated 350° F oven for 30 to 40 minutes.

Make a light white sauce by melting the butter in a saucepan, stirring in the flour until creamy, gradually adding the milk so as to prevent lumps, and cook over low heat or in the microwave; stir frequently. Add the sherry and mix. Mash the chipotle with a little of the white sauce, then press through a metal sieve into the pan of sauce; mix well. Season with salt and pepper.

Spoon the chipotle sauce on top of the phyllo envelope or spoon on the plate and place the baked phyllo envelope on top and garnish.

Kung Pao Chicken
PAT TEEPATIGANOND

MAKES 4 SERVINGS

FOR THE MARINADE

1 tablespoon dark soy sauce
1 tablespoon rice wine (page 107)
½ tablespoon sugar
1 tablespoon Chinese sesame oil (page 108)
1 teaspoon tapioca

FOR THE STIR-FRY

1 cup diced chicken breast
3 tablespoons peanut oil
3 ounces unsalted peanuts, raw or roasted
½ teaspoon peeled and minced fresh ginger
4 garlic cloves, minced
6 dried red chillies (Thai, de árbol, or japonés; see index)
½ cup diced celery
½ can bamboo shoots, drained and diced
½ can water chestnuts, drained and diced
½ cup diced carrots
2 tablespoons light soy sauce
½ tablespoon sugar
1 tablespoon chilli paste (page 99)

In a small bowl, mix together the marinade ingredients. Add the chicken, stir to coat, and set aside.

Over medium heat, heat 1 tablespoon of the peanut oil in a wok, then stir-fry the peanuts until golden brown. Remove to a paper towel to cool. Heat the remaining oil in the wok, stir-fry the ginger and garlic until fragrant, then add the dried chillies and stir. Add the chicken and stir well. If the mixture is too dry, add some hot water, a little at a time, then add the vegetables and stir. Again, if too dry, add some hot water and stir well. Add the soy sauce, sugar, and chilli paste, then turn off the heat, add the peanuts, and stir well. Serve with steamed rice.

Hot Pepper Chicken (A Szechuan Dish)
CECILIA CHIANG   *The Mandarin*

MAKES 4 TO 6 SERVINGS

1 to 1½ tablespoons vegetable oil
1½ pounds boneless, skinless chicken, diced
¼ cup dry sherry
½ teaspoon salt
¾ cup 1-inch seeded green bell pepper chunks
½ cup diced bamboo shoots
6 to 8 dried red chillies (japonés, de árbol, or Thai; see index)
5½ tablespoons chicken stock
1 tablespoon soy sauce
1 tablespoon cornstarch, optional

Heat the oil over high heat in a wok or wide frying pan. Toss and stir the diced chicken in it for about 2 minutes. Sprinkle with the sherry and salt. Add the bell pepper, bamboo shoots, and chillies, then the chicken stock, soy sauce, and cornstarch. Quick-stir for a minute or so and serve with rice.

Chicken Tikka
JEAN ANDREWS

MAKES 4 TO 6 SERVINGS

2 tablespoons white wine vinegar
¼ cup fresh lime juice
½ to 1 teaspoon ground cayenne pepper
½ teaspoon ground cumin
1 teaspoon turmeric
¼ cup cilantro (fresh coriander), chopped
1½ teaspoons fresh paprika
¼ cup chopped fresh parsley

1 tablespoon peeled and minced fresh
    ginger
1 cup low-fat plain yogurt
One 8- to 12-ounce boneless chicken breast
    per serving
    Indian Mint Chutney (page 201) or
    any chutney

Place all the ingredients, except the chicken, in a blender and puree. Put the chicken in a nonreactive bowl, pour the blended ingredients over it, and mix well. Cover and let marinate overnight in the refrigerator.

Scrape off excess marinade, then cook the chicken on a charcoal grill 4 to 6 inches above coals. Cover with the lid and cook until tender. Serve with Indian Mint Chutney or any chutney.

NOTE: *Tikka* is a Persian word used in Iraq, Pakistan, and India for meat threaded on a skewer.

If available at an Indian market, the spice mix *tikka masala* can be substituted for the dry spices.

Chilaquiles con Pollo (Chicken Chilaquiles)

JEAN ANDREWS

MAKES 6 TO 8 SERVINGS

FOR THE SAUCE
    6 guajillos (page 74)
    2 anchos (page 83)
    1 cup hot water
1 to 2 fresh jalapeños (page 77)
    ½ cup chicken stock
    ½ medium-size onion, chopped
    2 garlic cloves, minced
    ¼ teaspoon cumin seeds
    Salt to taste
    2 tablespoons olive oil

TO FINISH THE DISH
    About 2 dozen tortillas or 1 pound
        dried tortilla quarters or 1 pound
        packaged natural tostado triangles
2 to 3 cups shredded cooked chicken
    1½ cups grated Monterey Jack cheese
3 to 4 cups chicken stock
    1 cup sour cream or low-fat plain
        yogurt
    1 medium-size red onion, sliced into
        thin rings
    1 lime, cut into 6 to 8 wedges

Soak the dried chillies in the hot water for 1 hour. Remove, drain, devein, and seed. Place them, the jalapeño, and the stock in a blender with the onion, garlic, cumin seeds, and salt and puree. Heat the oil in a skillet and cook the puree, over low to medium heat, stirring until it is darkened.

Layer the bottom of a large flameproof dish or casserole with a third of the tortilla pieces. Cover with a third of the chicken, a third of the sauce, and a third of the cheese. Repeat the layers twice. Add the stock and bring to a boil. Simmer over medium heat until the stock is cooked down. Use your judgment; some like this dish soupier than others. This can also be done in a preheated 350°F oven, but it takes longer.

When the desired consistency is reached, cover the top with sour cream and garnish with the onion rings and lime wedges just before serving. Do not assemble this until you are ready to start cooking, as the tortillas will disintegrate.

Chicken Breasts in Pepper-Apricot-Lime Glaze with Dipping Sauce

W. C. LONGACRE

MAKES 4 SERVINGS

4 boneless, skinless chicken or turkey
  breasts (6 to 8 ounces each)
Juice of 2 lemons
3 tablespoons extra virgin olive oil
2 tablespoons pressed garlic
Juice of 2 limes
  Grated zest of 1 lime
2 tablespoons honey
¾ cup water
12 dried apricot halves, roughly chopped
1 teaspoon salt
2 tablespoons seeded and minced fresh
  jalapeño (page 77), more if desired
3 tablespoons pine nuts
1 teaspoon ground cinnamon
2 tablespoons firmly packed dark brown
  sugar
3 tablespoons cornstarch
  About ½ cup fresh orange juice

Coat the chicken breasts with the lime juice. Set aside in a nonreactive dish for 5 minutes. Mix together the olive oil, 1 tablespoon of the garlic, the lime juice, lime zest, honey, ½ cup of the water, the apricots, salt, jalapeño, pine nuts, cinnamon, and brown sugar in a small nonreactive saucepan, and bring to a rolling boil. Dissolve the cornstarch in the remaining water and pour into the mixture, stirring constantly until clear. Broil the chicken for 10 minutes; remove and add a generous portion of glaze to each breast; broil 2 minutes more.

Prepare a dipping sauce by mixing the remaining glaze with an equal amount of orange juice. Spanish rice and guacamole with cucumber slices accompany this well.

Zinfandeli's White Chili

DAVID JAMES *Zinfandeli's*

MAKES 6 TO 8 SERVINGS

4 garlic cloves, minced
1 pound dried Great Northern beans,
  picked over
6 cups chicken stock
3 medium-size onions, diced
1 tablespoon vegetable oil
4 serranos (page 86), seeded and finely
  chopped
2 teaspoons ground cumin
¼ teaspoon ground cloves
½ teaspoon ground cayenne pepper
1½ teaspoons chopped fresh epazote
  (page 105)
4 cups diced cooked chicken
  Salt to taste
3 cups shredded sharp white cheddar
  cheese
  Chopped fresh parsley for garnish,
  optional

Combine the first 3 ingredients and half the onion in a large pot. Bring to a boil. Reduce the heat to medium and simmer until the beans are soft, adding more stock if necessary.

Heat the oil in a medium-size saucepan over medium heat. Add the remaining onion and cook, stirring, until translucent. Add the serranos and cook another minute before adding to the beans. Add the cumin, cloves, cayenne pepper, chicken, and salt, and simmer for 5 more minutes. Sprinkle the chili, in bowls, with the cheddar cheese and finish under a broiler until golden. Garnish with chopped parsley if you like.

Ancho Roasted Turkey Breast with Corn and Tomato Salsa

ELMAR E. PRAMBS   *Four Seasons Hotel*

MAKES 6 SERVINGS

FOR THE CHILLI PASTE
> 3 anchos (page 83)
> ½ cup boiling water
> 1 garlic clove, peeled
> ½ medium-size onion, quartered
> 1½ teaspoons fresh lime juice
> 1½ teaspoons corn oil
> Salt to taste
> ½ turkey breast (skin on), about
>   3 pounds
>   Corn and Tomato Salsa (recipe
>   follows)

Preheat the oven to 350°F, then turn up to 500° F. Arrange the anchos on a baking sheet and heat in the oven until softened, about 2 minutes. Cut open the anchos, discard the stems, seeds, and veins, rinse the anchos and place in a small bowl. Cover with boiling water and let soak for 30 minutes. In a food processor, combine the anchos with some of the soaking liquid, the garlic, onion, lime juice, oil, and salt. Process until smooth, about 2 minutes. The ancho puree can be made up to 3 days ahead and refrigerated in a covered container.

Score the turkey skin at 1-inch intervals and rub the ancho puree over the turkey breast. Let marinate at room temperature for about 1 hour. Cook the turkey breast in a preheated 400°F oven for about 30 to 40 minutes. The internal temperature should register 180°F. Slice and serve with the salsa.

Corn and Tomato Salsa

MAKES 3 CUPS

> 1 medium-size ear fresh corn
> 1 large, ripe tomato, peeled, seeded, and
>   minced
> 1 small cucumber, peeled, seeded, and
>   minced
> 1 small celery stalk, minced
> 1 small onion, minced
> 1 large garlic clove, minced
> 1 fresh jalapeño (page 77), seeded and
>   diced
> 3 tablespoons fresh lime juice
> ½ teaspoon ground cumin
> ½ teaspoon salt
> ¼ cup chopped cilantro (fresh coriander)

Cook the corn in salted water to cover until tender, about 2 to 4 minutes. Drain and rinse under cold water, then scrape the kernels from the cob. In a medium-size bowl, stir together the corn and remaining ingredients until well blended. Cover and refrigerate until ready to serve.

South Texas Turkey with Tamale Dressing
JEAN ANDREWS

ALLOW ½ POUND PER PERSON

One 10- to 12-pound nonbasted or butter-basted turkey, with neck and giblets (allow ½ pound per person)
6 to 8 fresh red chiltepínes (page 69) or dried, if you must
2½ dozen tamales (page 108), allow at least 3 for each guest
3 to 4 tablespoons vegetable oil (more if necessary)

FOR THE GRAVY
Giblets and neck from turkey
1 large onion, quartered
8 to 10 fresh basil leaves or 1 tablespoon dried
1 serrano or jalapeño, seeded and chopped
2 celery stems with leaves, chopped
Salt and freshly ground black pepper to taste
½ cup all-purpose flour (add more for thicker gravy)

Thaw the turkey thoroughly if frozen, then remove the giblets and neck and put them aside. Wash the turkey well, making certain the cavity is clean, then dry it with a clean cloth or paper toweling. Place the turkey breast up on a cooking rack in a pan. Do not put any water in the pan. With a larding needle or ice pick, make 6 to 8 evenly distributed deep holes in the breast. Push 1 whole chiltepín into each hole as far as possible, as if you were larding the meat.

Remove the shucks from the tamales and break each into about 3 pieces, being careful not to crumble them (do not use canned tamales, only fresh or frozen ones wrapped in corn shucks). Lightly fill both the stomach and neck cavities with the tamale pieces. Close the cavity securely by sewing it together with cord and a large needle. Rub the entire bird with some of the oil. Cut four pieces of aluminum foil large enough to wrap around each wing and drumstick to prevent them from overcooking and drying out. Mold a sheet or two of paper toweling over the turkey breast, then saturate the paper with the remaining oil, using more if necessary. Next, mold a 12-inch square of foil over the towel. This keeps the skin from becoming hard and too brown.

Cook the turkey in a preheated 300°F oven for 20 minutes per-pound unstuffed or 25 minutes stuffed. Remove both the toweling and the foil during the last hour of cooking so the turkey can become a golden brown. If you want to speed up the cooking you can start with the microwave, putting the turkey on a large Pyrex dish with foil on the wings and drumsticks but not on the breast. Five minutes in the microwave at full power will equal 20 minutes in the oven at 300°F. Every 5 minutes give the turkey a quarter turn. After four 5-minute cooking periods, place the bird on the rack of your roasting pan, cover the breast with foil and cook it for the remaining time in the oven as directed above. A meat thermometer should register 180°F.

When the turkey is done, place it on a serving platter. Remove any stitching. Cover it with the turkey baker lid or clean dish towels. The bird will slice better if it's allowed to sit covered while you prepare the gravy.

FOR ADDITIONAL DRESSING

If the number of tamales required for the guests exceeds the space in the bird's cavity or if extra dressing is desired, layer those extra broken tamales in a square Pyrex dish and set the uncooked turkey on the tamales. Place this in the oven and proceed with the roasting. In this position some of the turkey drippings will go into the tamales, infusing them with the turkey flavor. Check the extra tamales from time to time—you may want to remove them before the bird is done so the dressing doesn't become dry.

Place all the gravy ingredients except flour in a 1-quart saucepan; cover with water. Bring to a boil. Reduce the heat to medium and allow to simmer until you have a rich stock, adding more water as necessary to maintain a quart of liquid. (This may take an hour.) Remove the meat when tender and set it aside.

Next, strain the stock, return it to the saucepan, and put 1 cup of it in a blender with the flour; process until smooth. Mix this with the stock in the saucepan.

When the turkey is done, remove as much of the melted fat in the pan as possible, saving all the browned juices and carmelized drippings. Then add a cup of hot water to the pan and use a spoon to loosen the browned juices; stir until they're dissolved. Add the brown juices to the flour-and-stock mixture in the saucepan; they'll give the gravy a rich color and delicious flavor. Place the mixture over high heat until it boils; reduce the heat to medium and stir constantly until the gravy reaches the desired thickness. Season with salt and pepper.

Grilled Pork Tenderloin with Apple and Red New Mexican Chile Chutney

MARK MILLER   *Coyote Cafe*

For this dish, prepare the brine, marinate the pork, and make the chutney the day before serving. On the day of serving, prepare the coals and grill the pork.

MAKES 6 SERVINGS

  ½ cup sugar
  2 tablespoons salt
  4 allspice berries
  4 whole cloves
One 4-inch stick cinnamon
  1 tablespoon crushed red pepper
   (page 101)

  2 cups water
  4 pork tenderloins (6 to 8 ounces each)
¼ cup ground red New Mexican chile
  (page 78)
  1 cup apple cider
  ½ cup firmly packed brown sugar
  ½ cup pine nuts, toasted (page 110),
  optional
Apple and Red Chile Chutney (recipe
follows)

In a large dish mix together the sugar, salt, allspice, cloves, cinnamon, crushed red pepper, and water. Add the pork tenderloins, coating them with the mixture, and let marinate overnight in the refrigerator.

Make a basting sauce with the ground chiles, cider, and brown sugar. Drain and pat dry the tenderloins, then grill them over hot charcoal for 7 to 10 minutes (to an internal temperature of 135° F), basting with the sauce. When done, serve garnished with pine nuts and chutney.

Apple and Red New Mexican Chile Chutney

MAKES ABOUT 3 CUPS

  4 Granny Smith apples, peeled, cored,
  and chopped
  4 fresh red New Mexican chiles (page
  78, if not available, rehydrate dried
  chiles or use frozen; do not use
  canned), diced
½ cup firmly packed brown sugar
⅓ cup cider vinegar
  8 garlic cloves, peeled and crushed
  1 cup water
  1 tablespoon chopped fresh marjoram

Place the apples and chiles in a heavy nonreactive saucepan with the brown sugar, vinegar, garlic, and water. Cook over medium heat until the apples are tender. Stir in the marjoram. Make the day before to allow the flavors to develop.

Fourth Street Grill's Chilli-Stuffed Pork Loin

SUSAN H. NELSON   *Ginger Island*

MAKES 6 SERVINGS

> Olive oil for sautéing
> 15 pasillas (page 79) or anchos
>   (page 83), seeded and minced
> 10 serranos (page 86), seeded and
>   minced
> 10 shallots, minced
> Salt to taste
> 1½ cups pistachios, toasted (page 110)
>   and ground
> 4 bunches cilantro (fresh coriander),
>   minced
> 1 pork loin, boned and trimmed of
>   excess fat
> Fourth Street Grill's Chipotle Mole
>   Sauce (page 154)

Heat a little oil in a small saucepan over low heat. Add the chillies and shallots and cook, stirring. They should remain slightly crunchy. Season with salt. Transfer the mixture to a bowl and let cool. Stir in the nuts and cilantro.

Cut the pork loin lengthwise around the loin to "unroll" it into a single flat piece and salt lightly. Spread the chilli-nut mixture over the entire surface. Beginning at the side closest to you, roll the coated meat up like a jelly roll. Tie with kitchen string several times along the roll so it won't unroll while roasting.

Place a large sauté pan over a high flame. When the pan is very hot, add the pork loin, turning the meat until it is seared on all sides. Then put the loin, uncovered, in a preheated 325°F oven. Roast until the meat thermometer reaches 135°F, approximately 50 minutes. Remove the meat and let it rest for 5 minutes before removing the string and slicing it into 1-inch slices. Serve with the mole sauce, rice, and warm tortillas.

Jerked Pork with Habanero

JON JIVIDEN

MAKES 6 TO 8 SERVINGS

> 5 pounds pork (lean shoulder, leg, or
>   roast), trimmed of excess fat
> 1 large, ripe tomato, finely diced
> 2 fresh green New Mexican chiles
>   (page 78), roasted (pages 96–97),
>   peeled, seeded, and finely chopped
> 1 habanero, seeded and finely chopped
>   (or substitute Scotch bonnet, dátil, or
>   3 serranos or 3 fresh jalapeños; see
>   index for chillies)
> 1 large onion, finely chopped
> 1 bunch fresh thyme, stemmed and
>   finely chopped
> 1 bunch green onions (scallions), finely
>   chopped
> 2 to 3 garlic cloves, minced
> ½ cup soy sauce
> ¼ teaspoon ground cayenne pepper
> ¼ cup fresh lime or lemon juice
> 1 cup water
> Salt and freshly ground black pepper
>   to taste

Place the pork on a cutting board and, with a sharp knife, punch holes, or "jerk," all over. In a medium-size bowl, mix together all the ingredients except the soy sauce, lemon juice, water, salt, and pepper. Using your fingers, stuff the mixture into the holes. Place the pork roast in a bowl and pour the remaining mixture and the soy sauce over it. Cover and let marinate overnight in the refrigerator.

Place the roast in a suitable roasting pan with the lime juice and water. Season with salt and pepper. Cook the roast in a preheated 450°F oven for 1½ to 2 hours. When fork tender, remove the cover and allow to brown. While browning, keep the pork moist by basting it with juices from the pan (see note below). Serve with rice or potatoes.

NOTE: If gravy is desired, remove the roast from the pan, pour off all but 1 to 2 tablespoons of the juices and place the pan on a burner over high heat. Brown the juices, then deglaze the pan with a little boiling water. Return the juice to the pan and add enough hot water to make about 1½ cups of gravy. If a thicker gravy is desired, a slurry of 1 tablespoon of cornstarch to ½ cup of water can be added gradually while stirring until desired thickness is reached.

Carnitas with Poblanos and Fruit
JERRY DI VECCHIO

The cut for this dish is from the shoulder of the pig; curiously, this part is also called butt in some parts of the country. It is usually an inexpensive cut, readily available boned, and because it is laced with fat and connective tissue, it cooks to melting succulence. Here it is roasted to render out excess fat, and the savory brown morsels are served with mildly hot roasted chillies, warm bananas, cool orange slices, and a piquant peanut sauce reminiscent of Indonesia. Dark, relatively mild green poblanos are the first choice, but slender light green New Mexican chiles also work well.

MAKES 6 TO 8 SERVINGS

3 to 4 poblanos (page 82), about 4 inches long, or green New Mexican chiles (page 78), about 6 inches long
3½ pounds boned pork butt or shoulder, trimmed of fat and cut into 1- to 2-inch cubes
3 large oranges
3 firm, ripe bananas
Piquante Peanut Sauce (recipe follows)
Salt to taste

Rinse the chillies and wipe dry. Cut in half lengthwise. Lay them, cut side down, in a 15- × 10-inch baking pan; broil 3 or 4 inches from the heat until the chillies are blistered and blackened, about 15 minutes. Transfer to a bowl, drape with a sheet of plastic wrap, and set aside to cool.

Rinse and dry the pan. Place the pork in the baking pan, spreading the pieces apart. Bake in a preheated 325°F oven, turning the pieces several times, until the pork is well browned and very tender when pierced, 1½ to 2 hours.

Meanwhile, pull the charred skin, seeds, veins, and stems from the chillies. With a knife, cut the peel and membrane from the oranges and slice crosswise. Lift the meat from the pan with a slotted spoon and put on a platter; keep warm. Peel the bananas and slice in half lengthwise. Coat them with the drippings in the pan and return to the oven until warm, 2 or 3 minutes. Arrange the hot bananas, chillies, and sliced oranges around the meat. Accompany with peanut sauce, seasoning with salt.

Piquant Peanut Sauce

MAKES 1 CUP

½ cup chunky peanut butter
½ cup plum jam
Seeded and minced fresh jalapeños (page 77) or serranos (page 86) to taste
Fish sauce (page 105) or salt to taste

Combine all the ingredients and serve. Can be made ahead; cover and chill up to 1 week.

Portuguese-Style Pork Chops or Chicken Breasts
JEAN ANDREWS

MAKES 6 SERVINGS

Six 1-inch-thick pork chops or boneless
    chicken breasts
6 tablespoons Portuguese-style red
    pepper paste (page 158)
2 cups dry white wine
½ teaspoon freshly ground black pepper
    Salt to taste
2 tablespoons olive oil
    Chopped fresh parsley for garnish

Rub the meat on both sides with the pepper paste; place in a shallow bowl, pour on the wine, cover, and refrigerate overnight, turning the meat once or twice.

Make a basting sauce by placing the marinade and olive oil in a saucepan; simmer over medium heat until it's the consistency of gravy. Season with pepper and salt and add boiling water if too thick.

Cook the meat on a charcoal grill (see note below), basting with the sauce. Sprinkle with chopped fresh parsley, and serve with rice or pasta.

NOTES: To cook in a skillet, heat a little olive oil over high heat until almost smoking; add the meat and brown both sides. Add the basting sauce, reduce the heat to low, cover, and cook until cooked thoroughly. Watch closely, as this sauce burns easily.

A gravy can be made by deglazing the pan with a little boiling water and adding the remaining basting sauce, stirring constantly.

Green Chili
PAUL PRUDHOMME *K-Paul's Kitchen*

MAKES 6 SERVINGS

3 tablespoons plus 2 teaspoons Chef
    Paul Prudhomme's Meat Magic (see
    note below)
1 tablespoon ground cumin
⅜ teaspoon ground nutmeg
1½ pounds boneless pork, ground
½ cup lard or chicken fat (preferred) or
    vegetable oil
1½ corn tortillas (6 inches in diameter)
1 teaspoon dried oregano
2½ cups chopped onions
2 cups seeded and chopped green bell
    peppers
1¼ cups diced canned green chiles (page
    78) and their juice
¼ cup minced jalapeños (see note below)
1½ teaspoons minced garlic
⅓ cup all-purpose flour
5 cups Basic Pork or Chicken Stock
    (recipe follows)

In a small bowl combine 1 tablespoon plus 1 teaspoon of the Meat Magic with ½ teaspoon of the cumin and ⅛ teaspoon of the nutmeg; mix well. Sprinkle the pork evenly with the seasoning mixture; mix by hand until thoroughly combined.

In a thick-bottomed, 4-quart saucepan melt the lard over high heat until hot (about 300°F). Brown the meat in the hot oil, then, with a slotted spoon, remove to a plate and set aside. (Remove as many of the tiny pieces of meat from the oil as possible.) In the same oil fry the tortillas over high heat until brown and very crisp; drain on paper towels. Remove the pan from the heat.

In a small bowl combine the remaining Meat Magic, cumin, nutmeg, and the oregano, mixing well. Add this seasoning mixture to the hot oil and cook over high heat until the seasonings roast, about 10 to 15 seconds, stirring constantly. Add 1½ cups of the onions; cook about 10 to 15 seconds, stirring constantly and scraping the pan bottom well. Stir in 1 cup of the bell peppers, ½ cup of the green chiles, and 2 tablespoons of the jalapeños; cook about 8 minutes, stirring fairly often (constantly toward the end of cooking time) and scraping the pan bottom well each time. Stir in the garlic and cook, stirring, a few seconds. Add the flour, stirring until well blended and scraping the pan bottom clean; cook 2 to 3 minutes, stirring and scraping almost constantly to make sure the mixture doesn't scorch. (Soups containing ground meat and flour stick more than other types of soup.) Add 1 cup of the stock, scraping the pan bottom until all the browned matter is dissolved. Then add the remaining 4 cups stock; stir until well blended, being sure to scrape the pan bottom clean again. Continue cooking over high heat, stirring occasionally.

Meanwhile, remove 1 cup of stock from this mixture and place in a food processor. Crumble the fried tortillas into the processor. Process until the tortillas are finely chopped, 30 to 45 seconds. Stir the tortilla mixture into the cooking stock mixture. Stir in the remaining onions and bell peppers. Add the meat, stirring well. Bring the mixture to a boil, stirring occasionally, then reduce the heat to medium-low and simmer 50 minutes, stirring and scraping fairly often (be careful not to let the mixture scorch).

Stir in the remaining green chiles and jalapeños and let simmer, stirring, 10 minutes. Adjust the seasoning, if desired, with additional Meat Magic; simmer and stir 5 minutes more. Skim any oil from the surface and serve immediately.

NOTE: Magic Seasoning Blends™ are available in most supermarket chains. If you cannot find them in your supermarket, call 1-800-457-2857 (outside Louisiana) or 1-504-731-7576 (in Louisiana) or 1-504-942-7576 (FAX) for ordering information.

Fresh jalapeños are preferable. If you have to use pickled ones, rinse as much vinegar from them as possible. See page 198.

Basic Pork or Chicken Stock

MAKES 5 CUPS

>   10 cups cold water (always start with
>   cold water, enough to cover the other
>   stock ingredients)
> 1½ to pounds pork neck bones (preferred)
>   2 or other pork bones and/or chicken
>   backs, necks, giblets (excluding the
>   liver), and/or bones
>   1 medium-size onion, quartered
>   1 celery stalk
>   1 large garlic clove, quartered

Place all the ingredients in a large stock pot; bring to a boil over high heat, then gently simmer at least 4 hours, preferably 8, replenishing the water as needed to keep about 5 cups of liquid in the pan. Strain, cool, and refrigerate until ready to use.

NOTE: If you are short on time, using a stock simmered 20 or 30 minutes is far better than using just water in any recipe.

Medallions of Beef with Ancho Chilli Sauce and Jícama–Black Bean Garnish

DEAN FEARING   *The Mansion on Turtle Creek*

MAKES 4 SERVINGS

>*Eight 3-ounce beef tenderloin fillets, trimmed of fat and any silver skin (the translucent skin that encloses groups of muscles)*
>*Salt to taste*
>*The Mansion on Turtle Creek Pepper Mixture (recipe follows) to taste*
>*3 tablespoons peanut oil*
>*Ancho Chilli Sauce (recipe follows)*
>*Jícama–Black Bean Garnish (page 175)*
>*¼ bunch cilantro (fresh coriander), stemmed*

Season the fillets with salt and the pepper mixture. Heat the oil in a large sauté pan over medium-high heat. Place several fillets in the hot pan. Do not crowd them (cook in batches if necessary). Brown one side, turn, and brown the other. Cook to the desired degree of doneness, about 3 minutes on each side for medium-rare. Remove from the heat and keep warm.

Ladle ancho chilli sauce over the bottom of each of four warm dinner plates. Place 2 beef medallions on each plate. Sprinkle the black-bean garnish evenly around the meat. Sprinkle with the cilantro leaves.

The Mansion on Turtle Creek Pepper Mixture

MAKES APPROXIMATELY 1½ CUPS

>*1 cup freshly ground black pepper*
>*⅓ cup freshly ground white pepper*
>*1½ tablespoons ground cayenne pepper*

Combine all the ingredients. Cover tightly and store in a cool place. Use to season red meats and game before cooking.

Ancho Chilli Sauce

MAKES 1 QUART

>*4 anchos (page 83), seeded (if peppers are small, use 5)*
>*1 tablespoon peanut oil*
>*1 yellow onion, cut into medium dice*
>*2 shallots, chopped*
>*2 garlic cloves, chopped*
>*1 fresh jalapeño (page 77), seeded and chopped*
>*3 sprigs cilantro (fresh coriander)*
>*1 cup chicken stock*
>*1 medium-size, ripe tomato, chopped*
>*½ cup brown veal demi-glace (page 109)*
>*½ cup heavy cream*
>*½ tablespoon honey, or to taste*
>*Salt to taste*
>*Juice of ½ lime, or to taste*

Place the anchos in a bowl and cover with hot water. Soak for 30 minutes, then drain. Place in a blender, adding some of the water in which they were soaked, and blend until smooth. Set the mixture aside.

Heat the oil in a medium-size saucepan over medium heat. Add the onion and cook, stirring, for 2 minutes. Add the shallots, garlic, and jalapeño and cook, stirring, for 2 minutes longer. Add the cilantro, chicken stock, ancho puree, and tomato; simmer for 12 minutes. Add the demi-glace, increase the heat slightly, and cook until the liquid is reduced by half, about 10 minutes. Add the cream and heat just to boiling. Pour the hot mixture into a blender or food processor and process until smooth. Add the honey, increasing the amount slightly if a sweeter sauce is desired. Season with salt and lime juice. Keep warm.

Jícama–Black Bean Garnish

MAKES 1½ CUPS

> 1 tablespoon peanut oil
> 1 cup jícama, cut into medium dice
> (page 106)
> 1 red bell pepper, seeded and cut into
> medium dice
> ½ cup cooked black beans (page 115,
> or use canned)
> Salt to taste

Heat the oil in a medium-size sauté pan over medium-high heat. Cook the jícama, pepper, and black beans, stirring, just until heated through, about 2 minutes. Season with salt. The sauce may be made several hours ahead and kept warm. Reheat gently, if necessary.

Fajitas with Tomatillo Sauce
KURT KOESSEL   *Ginger Island*

MAKES 4 SERVINGS

FOR THE MEAT

> 6 tablespoons pure New Mexican chile
> powder (page 99)
> ¼ cup pure ancho chilli powder (page
> 99)
> 1 tablespoon ground cumin
> 1 tablespoon kosher salt
> 2 teaspoons dried orange peel
> 2 teaspoons ground cayenne pepper
> 1½ teaspoons dried thyme
> 4 bay leaves, crumbled
> 2 garlic cloves, peeled and lightly
> crushed
> 1½ cups dark beer
> ⅔ cup fresh orange juice
> 1 pound flank steak, trimmed of fat

FOR THE TOMATILLO SAUCE

> 10 fresh tomatillos (page 108), husked,
> rinsed, and finely chopped
> 3 tablespoons finely chopped cilantro
> (fresh coriander)
> 2 tablespoons finely minced fresh
> jalapeños (page 77) or serranos
> (page 86)
> 2 tablespoons fresh lime juice
> Kosher salt to taste

> Corn tortillas

In a nonreactive container, mix together the chilli powders, cumin, kosher salt, orange peel, cayenne pepper, thyme, bay leaves, garlic, beer, and orange juice. Put in the meat, coating it entirely with the marinade. Cover the container with plastic wrap and marinate overnight in the refrigerator.

To assemble the tomatillo sauce, mix together the tomatillos, cilantro, jalapeños, and lime juice in a nonreactive bowl. Season with salt. Make at least an hour before serving to allow the flavors to blend.

To make the fajitas, let the meat come to room temperature. Meanwhile, build an intense charcoal fire. When the coals begin to turn gray, the fire is ready. Scrape off any excess marinade from the meat. On a well-oiled grill, sear the meat on both sides to desired doneness (about 4 minutes on each side for medium-rare). Slice thin and wrap in fresh corn tortillas. Garnish with tomatillo sauce and more fresh cilantro, if desired.

Tabasco Steak
GEORGE O. JACKSON

MAKES 10 TO 15 SERVINGS

5 pounds 3½-inch-thick sirloin butt beef-
steak
2 small bottles Tabasco Brand Pepper
Sauce, depending on amount of meat
2 to 4 garlic cloves, peeled and crushed
½ cup (1 stick) soft butter

Place the piece of beef in a plastic zip-lock bag with the contents of 2 bottles of Tabasco. Soak the beef in the sauce in the refrigerator for 3 days; turn often.

Remove the beef from the sauce and cook over mesquite wood coals. When the coals are at the hottest stage, put the steak on a grill 2 inches above the fire. Care must be taken to prevent flame-ups during the cooking. Cook for 10 minutes; turn and cook on the other side for 10 minutes; repeat for two more 10-minute periods. While the meat is cooking, blend the garlic with the softened butter and slightly melt.

After the meat has cooked for 40 minutes, remove from fire and place on a cutting board; allow to rest for 10 minutes before carving. After carving, brush the slices with the garlic butter. The meat will have a tangy crust but is not pungent in spite of the Tabasco.

NOTE: If the meat is room temperature at time of cooking, the final product will be medium rare; if it has just come from the refrigerator, it will be rare. If it is too rare for some tastes, return the meat slices to the grill for a bit more cooking.

Chipotle Ribs
JERRY DI VECCHIO

Buy the so-called English-cut beef short ribs for this dish, they are on the leaner end of the rib. Have the butcher saw through the bones at sev-eral intervals so you can bend the ribs to fit into the pan more readily. The ribs take several hours to bake, but you don't have to pay any attention to them. And the aromas that develop certainly give promise of good tastes to come. The chipotle flavor permeates and colors the drippings of the beef, and a few tablespoons of the resulting orange-red oil are used to season and tint the rice to serve with the ribs. The rice is lightly toasted in the drippings, so the grains remain separate and plump as they cook in the stock. The fat-skimmed juices from the ribs then become a lean and flavorful sauce to anoint both ribs and rice.

MAKES 4 TO 5 SERVINGS

4 to 5 English-cut beef short ribs (about 4
pounds total), bones cracked and
trimmed of fat
1 large onion, chopped
1 tablespoon mustard seeds
1 teaspoon cumin seeds
2 canned chipotles adobado or dried
chipotles (page 91)
2½ cups regular-strength beef or chicken
stock, homemade or low-sodium
canned
1 cup cilantro (fresh coriander) leaves,
coarsely chopped
Chipotle Rice (recipe follows)
1 to 2 limes, cut into wedges
Salt to taste

Arrange the ribs in a 3- or 4-inch-deep 4- to 5-quart metal pan. Sprinkle the ribs with the onion, mustard seed, and cumin seeds, then push the peppers down between the pieces of meat. Add 1 cup of the stock, then cover the pan tightly. Bake in a preheated 400°F oven until the ribs are tender enough to pull easily from the bones, about 3 hours. Check once or twice as the meat cooks to be sure there is moisture in the pan, adding a little of the remaining 1½ cups stock if the meat begins to brown.

Uncover the meat and skim off and reserve 2

tablespoons of the fat from the pan juices. Then bake the meat, uncovered, until it browns on top, 15 to 20 minutes. Lift the meat from the pan onto a platter and keep warm. Add the remaining stock to the pan; skim off the floating fat and discard. Bring to a boil over high heat, stirring to free browned bits and mash the chipotles. Pour the stock into a small pitcher. Spoon the chipotle rice around the ribs and sprinkle with the cilantro. Serve the meat and rice with the stock, limes, and salt.

Chipotle Rice

MAKES 4 TO 5 SERVINGS

> 2 tablespoons drippings reserved from
> Chipotle Ribs (previous recipe)
> 1 cup long-grain white rice
> 2 cups beef or chicken stock, homemade
> or low-sodium canned

In a 2- to 3-quart saucepan, combine the drippings and rice. Stir over medium-high heat until the grains look opaque, about 5 minutes. Add the stock and bring to a boil over high heat. Cover and simmer over very low heat, until the rice is tender to the bite and the liquid is absorbed, 15 to 20 minutes.

Pre-Columbian Carne Machaca con Chillies y Verduras, Reconstructed Sonoran Style

GARY NABHAN   *Native Seeds.SEARCH*

Native Americans of the desert Southwest undoubtedly used the wild chiltepín even before the domestication and distribution of cultivated chillies to the north of Mexico. Given the fact that meat was often scarce, but a variety of wild greens, cacti, and herbs were seasonally abun-

dant, I have tried to reconstruct what a pre-Columbian chilli dish might have been like for native peoples living in what is now southern Arizona or northern Sonora. *Carne machaca con verduras y chiltepíns* is still common fare in that desert region, but I have excluded post-Columbian ingredients to the extent that I could. In this recipe, wild chillies are but one of several native plants in the matrix, rather than being the primary ingredient of the sauce. Nevertheless, I guess that something akin to this dish served as the precursor to *carne con chile colorado*.

MAKES 6 TO 8 SERVINGS

> 1½ cups dried carne machaca (usually
> beef jerky today, but prehistorically it
> was dried venison, javalina, or
> antelope meat)
> 2 cups water
> 18 dried red chiltepínes (page 69),
> crushed
> 3 tablespoons dried or ½ handful fresh
> wild oregano leaves
> 2 cups hot water
> 2 to 3 cups freshly picked wild amaranth
> (careless weed) greens, coarsely
> chopped
> 1 cup dethorned, 1-inch-long tender,
> young prickly pear pad strips (page
> 107)
> 1 cup husked and chopped fresh
> tomatillos (page 108)
> 12 fresh green chiltepínes (page 69),
> seeded and finely chopped
> ¼ cup oil rendered from venison fat, or
> sunflower seed oil

Rehydrate the meat by soaking it in the water with the red chiltepínes and oregano for 1 hour; drain off the excess water. Heat a small amount of oil in a skillet over medium-high heat and cook, stirring, until browned. Add the remaining ingredients, mix well, and cook, stirring, for another 5 minutes. Serve with tortillas.

Mussamum (Muslim) Curry

CHARLIE AMATYAKUL   *Oriental Hotel Cooking School*

MAKES 6 TO 8 SERVINGS

FOR THE SAUCE

Vegetable oil
13 dried red chillies (de árbol, guajillo, Thai, New Mexican chiles; see index)
½ cup finely chopped shallots
½ cup finely chopped garlic
1 tablespoon sliced galanga (page 106) or fresh ginger
1 tablespoon finely chopped cilantro (fresh coriander) root
1 tablespoon finely chopped lemon grass (page 106)
1 teaspoon chopped kaffir (page 106) or regular lime peel
1 teaspoon black peppercorns
1 tablespoon salt
1 tablespoon coriander seeds
½ teaspoon ground mace
½ teaspoon ground nutmeg
½ teaspoon ground cinnamon
½ teaspoon ground cloves
1 tablespoon shrimp paste
4 cups medium-thickness coconut milk (page 105)
¼ cup thick tamarind water (combine 1 cup pulp, page 108, with ½ cup water)
2 to 3 tablespoons palm sugar (page 107) or white sugar
2 tablespoons fish sauce (page 105)
5 shallots, peeled
½ cup roasted peanuts
5 bay leaves
5 cardamom pods

TO FINISH THE DISH

1½ to 2 pounds lean, boneless beef (¼ pound per serving), cut into 1-inch cubes
3 to 4 cups coconut milk (½ cup per serving; page 105)

In a large sauce pan heat a small amount of oil over medium heat. Add the chillies, shallots, garlic, galanga, coriander root, lemon grass, kaffir, and spices and cook, stirring, until fragrant and the shallots are soft. Remove from the pan and pound together to make a paste. Add the shrimp paste. Pound until well blended. Heat 1 cup of the coconut milk and cook the paste in it over medium heat until fragrant. Season with the tamarind water, sugar, and fish sauce. Add the remaining coconut milk and simmer until reduced and thick. Add the whole shallots, peanuts, bay leaves, and cardamom, and cook 5 to 10 more minutes.

In a wok or skillet, simmer the beef in the coconut milk until tender. Add to the sauce and mix well.

Serve with rice on the side; accompanied by chutneys (pages 199–201).

Creamed Chipped Beef with Chiles (S.O.S.)

JEAN ANDREWS

MAKES 6 TO 8 SERVINGS

3 tablespoons butter or margarine
3 tablespoons all-purpose flour
2 cups milk
4 to 6 fresh green New Mexican chiles (page 78), peeled, seeded, and chopped
4 ounces canned mushrooms, sliced
1 tablespoon minced onion
4 ounces pimentos, chopped
⅛ teaspoon ground cumin
¼ teaspoon sweet paprika
¼ teaspoon ground cayenne pepper
⅛ teaspoon salt
One 2½-ounce jar dried beef, chopped
2 tablespoons dry sherry
1 tablespoon grated Parmesan cheese
6 to 8 slices hot buttered toast, English muffin, or Pepperidge Farm puff pastry shells
6 hard-boiled egg slices for garnish
Additional sweet paprika for garnish

In a skillet, melt the butter; sprinkle the flour into melted butter to make a paste and slowly add the milk, stirring constantly over medium-low heat to make a smooth, medium-thick white sauce. Add the chiles, mushrooms, onion, and pimentos; mix well. Add the cumin, paprika, cayenne, and salt; mix well. Stir in the chipped beef; simmer until thickened to desired consistency. Remove from the heat and stir in the sherry and cheese; taste and adjust the seasoning. Return the sauce to low heat. As soon as it begins to bubble, serve on hot buttered toast, English muffins, or puff pastry shells. Garnish with hard-boiled egg slices and sweet paprika.

Anatolian Eggplant Stew

JEAN ANDREWS

MAKES 8 SERVINGS

2 tablespoons olive oil
1 medium-size red onion, chopped
1 medium-size red bell pepper, seeded and chopped
1 to 2 fresh jalapeños (page 77) or serranos (page 86), seeded and chopped
1 pound ground beef or turkey
One 28-ounce can Italian-style tomatoes, chopped, with liquid
1 medium-size egglant, peeled and cut into large dice
½ cup diced carrots
½ cup chopped celery
3½ cups beef, chicken, or turkey broth
1 tablespoon chopped fresh basil
1 teaspoon salt
1 teaspoon sugar
½ teaspoon ground nutmeg
½ cup uncooked pasta (small shells)
2 tablespoons chopped fresh parsley
1 to 2 garlic cloves, minced
Grated Parmesan cheese for garnish

Heat the oil in a large stockpot over medium-high heat. Add the onion, bell pepper, and jalapeños and cook, stirring, until soft. Add the meat and brown; drain off any fat. Add the tomatoes, eggplant, carrots, celery, broth, basil, salt, sugar, and nutmeg. Bring to a boil and cover. Reduce the heat to medium-low and simmer 1 to 1½ hours. Add the pasta, parsley, and garlic, cover, and simmer until the pasta is tender.

This is a thick stew. Add hot water for desired consistency. Ladle into bowls and sprinkle with Parmesan. Serve hot, with hot garlic toast and a green salad.

NOTE: Standing improves flavor.

Stuffed Peppers Nogada
JEAN ANDREWS

MAKES 8 SERVINGS

    2 tablespoons vegetable oil
    1 medium-size onion, chopped
One 16-ounce can tomatoes, drained and
    chopped
    2 tablespoons chopped fresh parsley
    ½ teaspoon ground cinnamon
    ½ teaspoon ground cayenne pepper
    2 pounds ground beef, pork, or
    turkey
    ¼ cup raisins, plumped in hot water
    to cover and drained
    ½ cup pecans, roughly chopped
    2 large eggs, lightly beaten
    Salt and freshly ground black pepper
    to taste
    4 large red or green bell peppers,
    seeded, halved, parboiled 3 minutes,
    and patted dry
    Nogada Sauce (recipe follows)
    Fresh parsley sprigs for garnish

Heat the oil in a large saucepan over medium-high heat. Add the onion and cook, stirring, until soft. Add the tomatoes, parsley, cinnamon, and cayenne, then add the meat, raisins, and nuts. Cook, stirring, until browned, 20 minutes. Allow to cool, then stir in the eggs. Season with salt and pepper.

Stuff the bell pepper halves with the meat mixture. Bake in a preheated 325°F oven until thoroughly heated, 30 to 40 minutes. Pour the Nogada Sauce on top of the stuffed peppers and garnish with parsley. This may be served hot or at room temperature, as is done traditionally.

VARIATION: Instead of the rich Nogada Sauce, try the Tomato Sauce on page 185.

Nogada Sauce

MAKES ABOUT 4 CUPS

    3 slices whole-grain bread, no crust
    ½ cup cold milk
    2 cups milk
    1 cup pecans or almonds
    Salt to taste

Soak the bread in the cold milk. Puree in a blender with the 2 cups milk, the nuts, and salt. The sauce should be fairly thick; adjust with more milk. You may warm it slightly before serving on the hot stuffed peppers, but do not cook it.

Chipotle-marinated Lamb Chops
BRUCE J. AUDEN
Restaurant Biga & LocuStreet Bakery

MAKES 4 SERVINGS

One 7-ounce can chipotles adobado
    (page 91)
    ¾ cup balsamic vinegar, plus 1 table-
    spoon for the sauce
    6 garlic cloves, peeled
    6 sprigs fresh oregano
    2 bunches cilantro (fresh coriander)

16 lamb chops cut from the rack
2 tablespoons olive oil
4 carrots, cut into 2-inch-long julienne
4 leeks, well washed and cut into
   2-inch-long julienne
2 cups chicken stock
12 small, ripe tomatoes, seeded and
   chopped
   Mint Cream (recipe follows)
   Watercress Salad (recipe follows)

Combine the chipotles, the ¾ cup balsamic vinegar, the garlic, oregano, and half the cilantro in a blender. Process until smooth. Dip each lamb chop into this marinade while holding it by the bone. Try to keep the bone dry. Marinate overnight in the refrigerator or for 3 hours at room temperature.

In a large, heavy skillet, heat the oil over medium-high heat. Place the chops in the hot pan and cook 4 minutes per side, then transfer to a preheated 350°F oven in the same pan. Continue to cook for 5 minutes. Remove the pan from the oven and transfer the chops to a serving dish.

To make the sauce, pour the 1 tablespoon balsamic vinegar into the pan over medium heat and reduce while scraping the lamb juices and marinade from the bottom of the pan. At this time you may add more marinade, the amount depending on how hot you want the sauce (1 tablespoon should be enough). Add the carrots and leeks. Try to keep them on one side, as you will be removing them later. Next, add the remaining cilantro, reserving a few leaves for garnish, chicken stock, and tomatoes. Reduce the heat to low and cook until it starts to thicken.

Remove the carrots and leeks to the serving plate. Pour the sauce into a blender and process until smooth with some chunks. Place the lamb chops on the carrots and leeks and pour the sauce over. Garnish with the mint cream, cilantro leaves, and watercress salad.

Mint Cream

MAKES 1½ CUPS

1 cup sour cream
½ cup packed fresh mint leaves
1 teaspoon balsamic vinegar

Combine all the ingredients in a blender and process until smooth. Push through a sieve to remove excess leaves. Pour into a squirt bottle and garnish the chops and sauce by squeezing over the plate.

Watercress Salad

MAKES 4 SERVINGS

1 bunch watercress
1 jícama, (page 106) cut into 2-inch-
   long julienne
1 orange, cut into segments
2 tablespoons chilli oil (page 100)

Toss the ingredients together and arrange on a platter.

Chile con Queso with Sweetbreads

JOHN SEDLAR

Chile con queso in its most basic Southwestern form is a dip of melted cheese, usually Monterey Jack or a processed cheddar, spiced with chillies and served with corn chips. In this recipe, I've transformed the concept into a more delicate sauce to accompany veal sweetbreads. I like to use a good quality Parmesan-type cheese as the *queso,* and at St. Estephe we've been getting excellent results with an Argentine variety, Reggianito. To give the dish some spice without overpowering the other ingredients, I avoid the green jalapeños usually associated with *chile con queso,* and use fresh red jalapeños or New Mexican chiles instead.

MAKES 6 SERVINGS

> 2 quarts water
> ½ teaspoon salt
> 1½ pounds veal sweetbreads

FOR THE CHILE CON QUESO
> 5 ounces Parmesan or other mild
>   grating cheese, finely grated
> 3 cups heavy cream
> 2 medium-size garlic cloves, coarsely
>   chopped
> 1 teaspoon freshly ground white pepper
> 1 teaspoon salt
> 6 small fresh red jalapeños (page 77) or
>   3 green New Mexican chiles (page
>   78), roasted (pages 96–97), peeled,
>   seeded, and left whole
> ½ teaspoon freshly ground black pepper

Bring the water and salt to a boil in a large saucepan. Reduce the heat, carefully stir in the sweetbreads, and cook them for 30 minutes. When the sweetbreads are almost done, prepare a bowl of ice water. Drain the sweetbreads and plunge them quickly into the ice water to stop the cooking.

Carefully pull off any clear membrane from the sweetbreads and cut them into 1½-inch pieces. Set them aside.

While the sweetbreads are cooking, put the cheese, cream, garlic, pepper, and ½ teaspoon of the salt in a medium-size saucepan and bring to a boil over moderate to high heat. Boil briskly until the sauce has reduced to 1½ cups, 15 to 20 minutes. Sieve the sauce and keep it warm.

Season the sweetbreads and the chillies with the remaining ½ teaspoon of salt, and sprinkle the sweetbreads with the black pepper. Bring water to a boil in a steamer or a large pot with a steaming rack. Steam the sweetbreads and peppers until warmed through, about 4 minutes.

Spoon the sauce into the middle of each large warmed serving plate. Pat the sweetbread pieces dry with paper towels and place a cluster of them in the center of each plate. Drape the peppers over the sweetbreads.

Rabbit Cooked Two Ways with Hill Country Peach and Tequila Sauce

NORBERT BRANDT   *Louis B's American Cafe & Bar*

MAKES 2 SERVINGS

> One 1-pound rabbit

FOR THE MARINADE
> 1 medium-size onion, cubed
> 8 sprigs fresh parsley, crushed
> 4 garlic cloves, peeled and crushed
> 1 branch fresh rosemary
> 1 teaspoon crushed black peppercorns
> ½ teaspoon ground cayenne pepper
> 2 bay leaves
> 2 cups white Riesling

FOR THE STOCK

    1 tablespoon tomato paste
    5 cups unsalted chicken stock
    2 tablespoons oil

FOR THE SAUCE

    2 tablespoons butter or margarine
    1 cup cubed onions
    4 very ripe peaches, pitted and peeled
    1 teaspoon seeded and chopped fresh
      green jalapeños (page 77)
    3 cups rabbit stock
      Pinch of sugar
    1 tablespoon rice vinegar (page 107)
    1 cup Riesling
    3 ounces tequila
      Salt to taste
    1 teaspoon arrowroot

To prepare the rabbit (or have your butcher do this), remove the hind and front legs from the carcass and keep aside to marinate. Remove the back loin from the carcass and trim off all excess fat, skin, and silver skin (the translucent skin that encloses groups of muscles). Wrap well and set aside. Keep all bones and trimmings for use in the sauce.

Mix all the marinade ingredients and place the rabbit legs in the marinade. Let marinate for 24 hours in the refrigerator, moving the pieces every 6 to 8 hours. Remove the meat from the marinade and pat dry.

Make a rabbit stock by browning the bones and trimmings in a 400°F oven. Then add the vegetables from the marinade. Add the tomato paste, mix well, and continue to roast for 15 more minutes. Add the liquid from the marinade plus the chicken stock. Let simmer for 1 hour, then strain the stock.

In a heated braising skillet, heat the oil, then brown the rabbit legs. Remove the legs and fat from the skillet.

Melt the butter in the skillet. Over medium heat cook the onions, peaches, and jalapeños, stirring, 2 to 3 minutes. Add the rabbit legs, stock, sugar, vinegar, wine, tequila, and salt; cover and braise in a preheated 400°F oven for about 45 minutes. Then remove the front legs and cook the hind legs 15 minutes more. Remove all the meat from the sauce. Pour the liquid into a blender and mix well. Bring to a boil in a small saucepan and thicken with the arrowroot.

Place the legs on a serving plate and pour the sauce over the legs. Take the loins, season with salt and pepper, and grill over a medium-hot fire. Slice and garnish the legs with the loin pieces.

Hot Acapulco Shrimp
JEAN ANDREWS

MAKES 4 TO 6 SERVINGS

    2 pounds raw jumbo shrimp with tails,
      shells left on
    2 garlic cloves, peeled and crushed
    1 teaspoon ground cayenne pepper, or
      more to taste
    ¼ cup fresh lime juice, preferably from
      *Mexican **limones***
    ½ cup (1 stick) butter or margarine,
      melted

Split the unpeeled, raw shrimp down the belly, being careful not to cut through the back. Butterfly each shrimp by spreading it open; remove the vein. Mix the remaining ingredients in a small bowl; hold each shrimp by the tail and dip in the mixture until coated. Spread the opened shrimp on a cooking rack, shell side down. Cook until just pink on a charcoal grill or under the broiler.

Make a dip made of the same ingredients used on the shrimp before cooking and serve in individual ramekins. Jean's Own Chutney (page 200) or Romesco Sauce (page 152) is nice with these shrimp.

Shrimp Creole
JEAN ANDREWS

Most cooks tend to overcook this dish. You do not want it to be like a marinara sauce for pasta— Shrimp Creole is really just tenderly cooked shrimp in lightly stewed tomatoes.

MAKES 8 SERVINGS

FOR THE SHRIMP BOIL

1 small bunch celery with tops, chopped
1 large onion, quartered
12 bay leaves
4 garlic cloves, peeled and crushed
4 lemons, quartered
1 teaspoon ground cayenne pepper
2 tablespoons salt
1½ to 2 pounds medium-size shrimp, shells left on

FOR THE SAUCE

1 tablespoon olive oil
1 large onion, chopped
One 16-ounce can tomatoes or 12 large, ripe tomatoes, finely chopped
4 celery stalks, chopped
1 to 2 garlic cloves, crushed and minced
1 sprig fresh thyme or a pinch of dried
2 bay leaves
6 fresh basil leaves, chopped
½ to 1 teaspoon ground cayenne pepper

Place all the shrimp boil ingredients in a 6- to 7-quart stockpot and cover with water. Bring to a boil and let boil for 10 minutes. Add the shrimp and boil 10 minutes more, until the shrimp are pink no longer. Drain and peel the shrimp, leaving them whole; set aside.

Heat the oil in a deep skillet or Dutch oven over medium heat, add the onion, and cook, stirring, till clear. Add the rest of the ingredients.

Cook 20 minutes, stirring frequently. Add the peeled shrimp and cook 10 minutes more. (*Caution:* Never add water to stewed shrimp, as the tomato juice makes gravy enough.) Remove the bay leaves and serve over steamed rice.

Shrimp Amal
AMAL NAJ

MAKES 4 SERVINGS

¼ cup mustard oil or vegetable oil
6 dried red chillies (Thai, japonés, or de árbol; see index)
4 cinnamon sticks, broken
6 cardamom pods, crushed
6 whole cloves
1 teaspoon peeled and chopped fresh ginger
Bay leaves
1 pound large shrimp, shells left on
2 to 4 fresh green chillies (Thai, page 91, or serrano, page 86)
2 teaspoons ground cumin
1 teaspoon turmeric
1 teaspoon salt
½ cup white wine

Heat the oil in a large, heavy skillet over medium heat. When the oil starts to give off a pungent vapor, toss in the dried chillies, cinnamon, cardamom, and cloves. Stir until the chillies begin to darken, then add the ginger and bay leaves. Stir with a wooden spoon for 2 minutes. Raise the heat to high, add the shrimp, and stir for 2 minutes. Add the green chillies, cumin, turmeric, and salt and stir for 2 minutes. Add the wine, cover, and cook over medium heat 3 to 4 minutes. Serve the shrimp immediately with the shells on. These go well as an appetizer or as an accompaniment to another entrée served with steamed rice.

Ancho Chile Cheese and Shrimp Pizza

PAULA LAMBERT   *Mozzarella Company*

MAKES 2 SERVINGS

> Pizza dough for 10- to 12-inch pizza
> ½ cup Fresh Tomato Sauce (recipe follows)
> ½ pound Ancho Chile Caciotta cheese, grated (see note below)
> 8 to 10 grilled shrimp
> Cilantro (fresh coriander) leaves for garnish

Roll out the dough on a floured surface with a floured rolling pin, then cook the crust on a pizza stone or in a pizza pan in a preheated 450°F oven for approximately 5 minutes (or use a prebaked pizza crust). Remove the crust from the oven. Spread the tomato sauce on the crust, then top with the grated cheese. Arrange the shrimp on top of the cheese. Return to the oven and continue baking until the cheese has melted and the pizza is golden brown. Garnish with cilantro leaves.

NOTE: You can order Ancho Chile Caciotta cheese from the Mozzarella Company, 2944 Elm Street, Dallas, TX 75266; or substitute mild Monterey Jack cheese and chopped anchos.

Fresh Tomato Sauce

MAKES ABOUT 1 CUP

> 2 tablespoons olive oil
> 1 garlic clove, minced
> 1 cup drained and coarsely chopped canned tomatoes
> 10 fresh basil leaves, torn into pieces

Heat the oil in a small saucepan over medium heat. Add the garlic and cook, stirring, a few minutes. Add the tomatoes and heat to a simmer. Cook 2 minutes. Add the fresh basil leaves.

Over-Stuffed Peppers with Shrimp, Cajun Style

JUSTIN WILSON

MAKES 8 SERVINGS

> 8 large red or green bell peppers
> ¼ cup olive oil or bacon drippings
> 1 cup finely chopped onion
> ½ cup finely chopped green onions (scallions)
> ¼ cup drained and chopped canned pimento
> One 8-ounce can tomato sauce
> 4 garlic cloves, minced
> ½ cup dry white wine
> 1½ teaspoons salt
> 1 teaspoon ground cayenne pepper
> 1½ pounds shrimp, peeled, deveined, and coarsely chopped
> 2½ cups cooked rice
> 8 bacon strips, cut in half
> 1 to 2 cups chicken stock

Slice the tops from the bell peppers, remove the seeds, rinse out, and drain. Heat the oil in a large saucepan and cook the onions and green onions, stirring, over medium heat until the onions are clear. Stir in the pimento, tomato sauce, and garlic, then add the wine, salt, and pepper and stir. Stir in the shrimp, and remove from the heat. Stir in the rice and make sure everything is mixed together well. Fill each pepper with the rice mixture and place them side by side in a shallow pan, one large enough to hold all the peppers. Cross the bacon strips over the top. Fill the pan half full with stock, and bake in a preheated 350°F oven for 1 hour.

Fresh Mussels with Serranos and Fresh Mozzarella
JOHN ASH   *John Ash & Company*

MAKES 6 SERVINGS

36 *large mussels, poached on the half*
   shell, liquor reserved
¼ *pound bacon*
 3 *tablespoons extra virgin olive oil*
 3 *large garlic cloves, minced*
¼ *cup finely chopped green onions*
   (scallions) or shallots
 1 *teaspoon seeded and finely chopped*
   serrano (page 86)
 2 *tablespoons finely chopped fresh*
   parsley
¼ *cup plain dry bread crumbs*
 4 *ounces mozzarella cheese, thinly sliced*
 1 *large bunch spinach, well washed and*
   stems removed

Scrub mussels with a stiff brush, then wash in a colander in running water. Cook, covered, in a deep, heavy skillet over high heat about 6 to 8 minutes, agitating the pan to cook them evenly. Remove from the heat the moment the shells open. Leave the mussels in shell. Drain, reserving the liquid.

Cook the bacon until crisp. Drain well and chop fine. In a separate pan, heat 1 tablespoon of the oil over medium heat, then add the garlic, green onions, and serrano, and cook, stirring, until just soft. Do not brown. Combine the bacon, garlic mixture, and parsley in a bowl. In a separate bowl, add drops of the remaining olive oil to the bread crumbs to lightly coat.

Divide the bacon mixture and place some on top of each mussel. Moisten with a few drops of the reserved poaching liquor. Cover each mussel with a slice of mozzarella cheese. Sprinkle with the oiled bread crumbs. If not serving immediately, cover and refrigerate.

To serve, place the mussels on a bed of rock salt or crumpled aluminum foil to keep them level. Place them into a preheated 400°F oven or under a broiler until the cheese just begins to melt. While the mussels are cooking, quickly wilt the spinach leaves in the remaining olive oil in a saucepan over medium heat and place on six warm plates. Place 6 mussels on each and serve.

Grilled Salmon with Soy and Ginger
MICHAEL FOLEY   *Printer's Row*

MAKES 4 SERVINGS

FOR THE MARINADE
 6 *tablespoons soy sauce*
¼ *cup Chinese sesame oil (page 108)*
 3 *tablespoons sherry vinegar*
 1 *teaspoon ground cayenne pepper*
 1 *teaspoon chopped red banana pepper*
   (page 65) or red bell pepper
 3 *garlic cloves, peeled and crushed*
 5 *tablespoons peeled and minced fresh*
   ginger

TO FINISH THE DISH
 Four 7-ounce salmon fillets

Place all the marinade ingredients in a small bowl and stir. Add the fillets and turn over to coat. Marinate for 30 minutes.

Drain and squeeze the marinade from the fish. Wipe the grill with an oiled cloth, then grill the fish until cooked to the desired degree of doneness, 9 to 11 minutes.

Grilled Swordfish Ancho
LEWIS ALDRIDGE   *City Grill*

MAKES 4 SERVINGS

 6 *anchos (page 83), seeded*
 6 *garlic cloves, peeled*

1 cup vegetable oil
½ cup fresh lime juice
2 teaspoons dried oregano
  Salt and freshly ground black pepper
  to taste
1 cup sour cream
  Milk, if needed
12 green onions (scallions), trimmed to 6
  inches
4 swordfish (6 to 8 ounces each) mahi-
  mahi, tuna, marlin, or shark steaks, or
  boneless chicken breasts
1 dozen corn tortillas
  Lime wedges for garnish

Toss the anchos and whole garlic cloves in a little of the oil. Place them under a broiler until they soften and begin to brown. Be careful not to get them too brown or the basting sauce will be bitter. Remove from the broiler and process in a blender with the remaining oil and the lime juice. Add the oregano, salt, and pepper. Mix one third of the basting sauce with the sour cream. Thin with milk if too thick. Refrigerate.

Prepare the charcoal fire. When the fire is very hot, dip the whole green onions and swordfish steaks in the remaining basting sauce. Cook the onions until they are browned on the outside but still crisp in the center. The fish is usually done when both sides are lightly browned. If you have any doubts, just cut the center and check it. When done, place the fish in a warm oven.

Warm the tortillas, two at a time, in a lightly oiled Teflon or cast-iron skillet. Place an onion and a tablespoon of sour cream sauce on each tortilla, then roll. Arrange the rolls on the platter with the swordfish, and spoon the remainder of the sour cream sauce over the fish. For even more informality, let your guests roll the tortillas at the table. Garnish with large wedges of lime, and encourage everyone to use the lime, as it is the perfect finishing flavor for the spicy fish.

Grilled Red Snapper with Shrimp and Tomatillo Sauce
LEWIS ALDRIDGE   *City Grill*

MAKES 6 SERVINGS

1 pound fresh tomatillos (page 108),
  husked
3 serranos (page 86), seeded
6 garlic cloves, peeled
½ bunch cilantro (fresh coriander),
  stemmed and chopped
  Salt to taste, optional
  Olive oil for grilling
6 red snapper fillets (6 to 8 ounces
  each)
24 medium-size shrimp, peeled
  Lime wedges for garnish
  Cilantro leaves for garnish

Roast the tomatillos, serranos, and garlic cloves under a broiler until very browned, almost burned. Transfer to a food processor and process until smooth. Season with salt. This can be done ahead and reheated over very low heat. If the sauce thickens too much, thin with water.

Oil the red snapper and place on a grill over very hot wood or a charcoal fire. Brown lightly on one side, turn, and brown the other side. Ten minutes per 1 inch of thickness is a good rule of thumb for cooking time, but the best way to tell is to cut one fillet open and see if it is done in the middle. Just before the fish is ready, put the oiled shrimp on the grill. The shrimp take only a few minutes to cook.

To assemble, place the fish on a warm platter. Top each fillet with 4 shrimp and drizzle the sauce in a line down the center. Garnish with lime and cilantro leaves.

Salmon with Roasted Red Pepper Sauce and Cilantro Cream
RANDALL E. CRONWELL

MAKES 4 SERVINGS

2 pounds salmon fillets, cut into 8 equal pieces
Salt and freshly ground black pepper to taste
¼ cup olive oil

FOR THE RED PEPPER SAUCE
4 large red bell peppers
½ cup heavy cream
Ground cayenne pepper to taste
Fresh lemon juice to taste
Salt to taste

FOR THE CILANTRO CREAM
½ bunch cilantro (fresh coriander), stemmed and coarsely chopped
1½ cups sour cream
Fresh lemon juice to taste
Milk, if needed

Cilantro (fresh coriander) sprigs for garnish

Season the fillets with the salt and pepper and coat lightly with some of the olive oil. Set aside.

To prepare the red pepper sauce, roast the peppers over a grill or open flame until black and blistering. Put in a plastic bag and set aside to cool. Peel and seed the peppers. Puree in a blender and set aside. In a saucepan, blend the heavy cream with the puree and cayenne pepper. Add a little lemon juice and salt. Cook until smooth, about 5 minutes, over low heat.

For the cilantro cream, combine the cilantro, sour cream, and lemon juice. Pour into a blender and process until you have a smooth green sauce. Thin with milk if too thick—you want to be able to drizzle the sauce over the salmon. Set aside.

Heat the remaining oil in a large stainless steel skillet over high heat. Add the salmon fillets, brown one side, and flip over to finish cooking; place on paper towels. Put red pepper sauce on each warmed plate first, then the salmon. To finish, drizzle the cilantro cream over the fillets. Garnish with cilantro sprigs.

Spicy Beer Batter
JEAN ANDREWS

This batter is a delightful light, puffy coating for fish, chilli rellenos, shrimp, or anything that needs to be batter-fried. I like it better than tempura batter.

MAKES 8 TO 10 SERVINGS

1 cup all-purpose flour
1 teaspoon baking powder
½ to 1 teaspoon ground cayenne pepper
1 teaspoon paprika
½ teaspoon salt
One 8-ounce can light beer
Vegetable oil

Sift all the dry ingredients together in a large mixing bowl. Just before you are ready to fry the food, add the beer and mix well but do not beat. Dip the pieces of food to be fried into the batter one at a time. Heat enough vegetable oil to cover the food pieces in a deep skillet over high heat until a little sample of the batter sizzles. Lower the food into the oil a few pieces at a time—too many at one time will lower the temperature below the optimum for frying—and cook until golden on all sides turning as necessary. Remove the food from the fat with a slotted spoon or pancake turner and drain on paper toweling. Serve at once.

French Toast Caliente

INTERNATIONAL CONNOISSEURS OF
GREEN AND RED CHILE

MAKES 4 TO 6 SERVINGS

> 2 large eggs
> ½ teaspoon salt
> 1 cup milk
> ½ teaspoon pure vanilla extract
> 1 tablespoon mashed canned jalapeño
> (page 77)
> 6 to 8 slices bread
> Vegetable oil, optional

Beat the eggs lightly, then add the salt, milk, vanilla, and jalapeño; mix well. Dip the bread into the mixture and brown on both sides in heated vegetable oil in a skillet or on a grill over medium heat. Serve with your favorite syrup, honey, or try Chilli Pepper Jelly (page 207) or Capsicum Marmalade (page 206).

Cheese and Chilli Teacakes

KURT KOESSEL   *Ginger Island*

MAKES 12 TEACAKES

> 2½ cups all-purpose flour
> 1 cup whole-wheat flour
> 2 tablespoons firmly packed brown
> sugar
> 2 tablespoons baking powder
> 1 teaspoon baking soda
> 1 teaspoon salt
> ¼ cup bran
> ¾ cup (1½ sticks) cold butter or margarine, cut in small pieces
> 1 fresh green jalapeño (page 77), seeded and chopped (or substitute 'Sante Fe Grande', page 84, or red jalapeño)

> 1 red 'Fresno' chilli (page 74), seeded
> and chopped
> 1½ cups dried currants
> 6 ounces Asiago, Parmesan, or Romano
> cheese, cut into small cubes
> 2 large eggs
> 1 cup plain yogurt, or more as needed
> 1 large egg, beaten

Sift together the flours, sugar, baking powder, baking soda, and salt. Stir in the bran. Rub the butter in with your fingertips until the mixture resembles coarse crumbs. Add the chillies, currants, and cheese. Whisk the eggs and yogurt together and stir into the dry mixture. If necessary, add more yogurt to make a soft dough. Drop by large spoonfuls onto a greased baking sheet. Brush with the beaten egg. Bake in a preheated 350°F oven 10 to 12 minutes.

Jalapeño Dinner Muffins

JEAN ANDREWS

MAKES 12 LARGE OR 24 SMALL MUFFINS

> 2 cups all-purpose flour
> 1 teaspoon sugar
> ½ to 1 teaspoon ground cayenne pepper
> 1 tablespoon baking powder
> 1 teaspoon salt
> ½ cup (1 stick) margarine, cut into
> cubes
> ¾ cup cold milk
> 2 tablespoons drained and chopped
> canned jalapeños

In a large bowl stir together the flour, sugar, pepper, baking powder, and salt until well mixed. Add the margarine cubes to the flour mixture and work them together with your fingers until it looks like coarse cornmeal. Then add the milk and jalapeños and stir the mixture until it is just mixed. Do not beat or mix until smooth. Fill greased muffin pans about three-fourths full and bake in a preheated 350°F oven until just browned, 12 to 15 minutes. Serve them piping hot. These sconelike muffins get rather hard when leftover and do not warm up well, therefore, don't make more than you plan to serve.

Serrano and Blue Corn Muffins
STEPHEN PYLES   *Baby Routh*

MAKES 12 MUFFINS

> 1/2 cup (1 stick) butter or margarine
> 6 tablespoons vegetable shortening
>   Butter, margarine, or vegetable oil for sautéing
> 3 serranos (page 86), seeded and diced
> 1 large green bell pepper, seeded and diced
> 1/4 cup diced red onion
> 3 garlic cloves, minced
> 1 cup all-purpose flour
> 1 1/2 cups blue (page 104) or yellow cornmeal
> 2 tablespoons sugar
> 1 teaspoon salt
> 1 tablespoon baking powder
> 2 large eggs
> 1 cup buttermilk, at room temperature, mixed with a pinch of baking soda
> 1/2 cup heavy cream
> 3 tablespoons chopped cilantro (fresh coriander)

Lightly butter and flour 2 muffin tins. In a saucepan, melt the butter and shortening together, then set aside to cool. Heat a little butter in a small saucepan over medium heat. Add the peppers, onion, and garlic and cook, stirring, until the on-

ion is clear. Set aside. In a large mixing bowl, sift together the dry ingredients and set aside. In a separate bowl, beat the eggs lightly and add the melted butter and shortening. Stir in the buttermilk, cream, cilantro, peppers, and onion. Add the liquid mixture to the dry ingredients and beat just until smooth; do not overmix. Pour the batter into the muffin tin and bake in a preheated 375°F oven 12 to 15 minutes.

Easy Jalapeño Cornbread
JEAN ANDREWS

MAKES 4 TO 8 SERVINGS (DEPENDING ON APPETITE)

> 3 canned or pickled jalapeños (page 77), drained, seeded, and chopped
> 1 1/2 cups yellow stone-ground cornmeal
> 1/2 teaspoon baking soda
> 1 tablespoon sugar
> 1/2 cup all-purpose flour
> 1 teaspoon salt
> 2 teaspoons baking powder
> 2 large eggs, at room temperature
> 1 cup buttermilk (or add 1 tablespoon of vinegar to 1 cup of milk and allow to stand for an hour)
> 1 tablespoon vegetable oil

In a mixing bowl, combine the cornmeal, baking soda, sugar, flour, salt, and baking powder. Set aside. In a separate bowl, mix the eggs, buttermilk, and oil, and stir until smooth and creamy. Add the jalapeños and mix. Stir the liquid into the cornmeal-flour mixture. Blend with a spoon to form a smooth batter, but do not overstir. Grease a 9-inch skillet (preferably cast iron) with oil and preheat in a 400°F oven. Remove and pour the batter into the hot pan. Return to the oven and bake for 20 to 30 minutes, or until a wooden toothpick inserted in the corn bread comes out clean. Cut and serve immediately.

Mamie's Jalapeño Cornbread

MARY "PUD" LAUDERDALE KEARNS

Mary of Puddin Hill

MAKES 8 SERVINGS

> 1 cup grated American or cheddar cheese
> 2 tablespoons drained and chopped pickled jalapeños (page 77; see note below)
> 1½ cups yellow cornmeal
> 2 tablespoons baking powder
> ½ teaspoon salt
> 2 large eggs, beaten
> 1 cup buttermilk
> 3 tablespoons shortening, melted, or vegetable oil
> One 17-ounce can cream-style corn
> One 4-ounce can chopped hot or mild green New Mexican chiles (page 78)

Combine the cheese and jalapeños; set aside. In a large bowl, blend the cornmeal, baking powder, and salt. Combine the eggs, buttermilk, and shortening in a small bowl and mix thoroughly. Add to the dry ingredients, stirring until just blended. Stir in the corn and green chiles. Generously grease a 10-inch iron skillet with shortening and place in a preheated 500°F oven for 5 minutes. Pour the batter into the hot skillet. Sprinkle the reserved cheese-and-jalapeño mixture over the batter. Bake for 15 minutes. Remove and let stand 5 minutes before cutting. The cornbread should be very soft in the center and it does not have the texture of regular cornbread. NOTE: You may substitute more canned green chiles for the jalapeños if your system is not up to the heat!

Easy Confetti Cuban Bread

JEAN ANDREWS

MAKES 2 LOAVES

> 1 package dry yeast
> 2 cups lukewarm water
> 2 teaspoons salt
> 1 tablespoon sugar
> ½ teaspoon ground cayenne pepper
> 6 to 7 cups all-purpose flour
> 3 tablespoons dehydrated green New Mexican chile or green bell pepper flakes
> 2 tablespoons crushed red pepper
> 2 tablespoons white cornmeal

Dissolve the yeast in the water. Add the sugar and salt. Put the flour and cayenne in a food processor and pulse two to three times (can be mixed in a mixer with the dough hook). Pour the yeast liquid down the funnel gradually. Process until it forms a ball. After the dough is formed but no sooner (adding too soon will pulverize the flakes), add pepper flakes and crushed pepper, pulsing only until well distributed throughout the dough ball, taking care not to pulverize the pepper flakes. Put dough in a greased bowl and cover with a clean cloth. Turn on the oven to 110°F and place the dough in the oven. Let rise until doubled (temperatures above 120°F will kill the yeast), about 1 hour.

Remove the dough from the bowl, shutting off the oven. Cut the dough in half and shape into two long loaves. Slash the tops. Place on a shallow baking pan that has been dusted lightly with corn meal. Place a bowl of boiling water in the cold oven. Place the bread in the cold oven, then set at 400°F. Bake until done (about 40 to 45 minutes). Cool on a rack.

e can thank the Arabs for preserves, marmalades, jellies, jams, and those sweet condiments that grace our tables and rot our teeth. The Arabs took over the Greco-Roman practice of conserving fruits in honey, and extended or improved the process with the addition of sugar. Sugar had come to Arabia from India, where the technology of making "raw" sugar originated around 500 B.C., following the introduction of sugarcane (*Saccharum officinarum*), probably from New Guinea. As early as 325 B.C., the Greek geographer Strabo reported that sugarcane was present in India. Sugar was carried westward by the Persians in the sixth century A.D. The Arabs got it from them and introduced the cane to Syria, North Africa, and Spain. However, since the Far East was the only area in the Old World where the climatic conditions permitted the cultivation of sugar, only a small amount made its way to Europe via the Middle East and Venice before 1500. Throughout that period, honey was the primary sweetener, while the costly imported sugar was reserved for medicinal purposes. The English words "sugar" and "candy" are derived from the Arabic version of the Sanskrit *sharkar* and *khandh,* both of which mean "sugar."

In attempts to bring the price down, sugar cultivation was carried farther and farther west as settlers followed the early explorers to the New World. The sweltering New World sugar plantations were established in order to satisfy the European yearning for sweets, and millions of Africans were enslaved to appease that craving. With all of the new production, the price of that luxury item became somewhat lower, making it possible for people other than the wealthy to enjoy it. The amount and the range of sugar usage increased as worldwide sugar production increased. Now it was possible to afford it for other than medicinal purposes, and sugar-preserved fruits began appearing as a dessert course.

Not only did sugar effect a culinary change, but it also produced the fortunes that made the Industrial Revolution possible. A considerable addition to those fortunes came from rum, a by-product of the sugar industry, which became the official liquor of the English navy. For a single plant species that offers no special benefaction to the health or well-being of humankind, sugar has had an extraordinarily broad influence on Western history.

Sugar-preserved fruits and syrups had dual roles, first as healing (or therapeutic) potions and later as table delicacies. The knowledge of the making of these fruit confections migrated from the Middle East to medieval Europe, thence from Europe to America. The arrival of the art of making preserves and sweetmeats was the most outstanding addition to gastronomy in Renaissance Europe. Italians were the basic revolutionaries in the realm of preserves, and a significant book on preserving was *Bastiment de recettes,* an Italian publication that introduced the completely unknown art of making preserves, jams, and jellies into France. To me the desert seems an unlikely place, but during the same period, in sixteenth-century Egypt, there was a minor industry in preserves and sweetmeats. In my travels I have observed that speaking Arabic and eating sweets go hand in hand—obviously a very long-standing tradition.

During the sixteenth century the job of sweetmeat cooks, called *confituriers,* was to make not only jellies and preserves but also liqueurs and cordials. The Western world was in its formative stage of preserve-making when the French physician Michel de Nostradamus separated preserved fruit into two categories—dry and liquid—for his *Opuscule* in 1555. His liquid preserves included the fruit-based jellies, jams, and preserves in syrups similar to those we make today. Anything that could be eaten with the fingers—candied fruits, nuts, seeds, and vegetables—comprised dry preserves. His recipes used both sugar and honey as sweeteners for the liquid kind, but only sugar for the dry type.

During the period of European expansion, sugar was still a luxury. Europeans, who took their recipes for preserves and marmalades with them to their colonies in the New World, found that cane sugar was expensive in the North American colonies, so most early colonial cooks followed the Native American practice of using maple sugar, although white sugar was the ideal. At the end of the nineteenth century cane sugar became affordable and plentiful following the Spanish-American War, when the sugar-growing territories of Cuba and the Philippines came under American control. Sugar consumption in America soared right after that event, and Americans also started adding it to pickled vegetables and fruits such as cucumbers, radish pods, purslane, gherkins, peppers, and peaches. In the United States cooks began treating pickles as more than just a "salad" (served mixed with olive oil, as in the eighteenth century) or as a condiment eaten with meat. Pickles became something to be eaten alone or as a side dish.

Before you can have pickles you must have vinegar, and before you can have vinegar you must have alcohol, because vinegar is the product of a fungus-implemented (what's known as the "mother") fermentation of an alcoholic liquid. Consequently humans have had vinegar as long as they have had wine.[1] If the start-up liquid has been pasteurized, or if the percentage of alcohol is high enough, no "mother" will form, hence no vinegar. No one knows for certain when winemaking began, but it is estimated to have been between 8000 B.C. and 3000 B.C. As a condiment, vinegar has long been held in high regard, as testified by a reference to it in the Book of Ruth (2:14). "And Boaz said unto her, at mealtime come thou hither, and eat of the bread, and

---

1. When a cloudy, thick layer forms on the surface in an opened bottle of wine or unpasteurized vinegar, you are seeing the growing fungus, or "mother." When mother comes, vinegar is not far behind.

dip thy morsel in the vinegar [wine]." Pickles were known in Mesopotamia, ancient Egypt, Greek and Roman antiquity, and China, as well as in India. Pickles, in general, were made in European culture as early as vinegars were available to preserve them. The ancient Celts used cider vinegar, the Romans used wine vinegar—in short, pickles have been around for a very long time.

Chutney is a sweet-and-sour fruit condiment that originated in India and was introduced to Europe by early British or Dutch trading ships and later through the colonization of India by England. The word "chutney" may come from the Hindi *chatna,* meaning "taste." Making chutney was a means of preserving fruits in a tropical climate. Indian cooks are also big on very hot, spicy pickles called *achaar* (see page 100). Mixed vegetable pickles, also *achaar,* which we call chow chow, are another Indian specialty. I wondered whether the term "chow chow" could have come from India along with the relish, as a corruption of *achaar—chaar* or *char*—so I asked food historian William Woys Weaver, whose specialty is relishes and preserves, for an opinion. We decided that it was entirely possible that Dutch traders and colonists in southern India and Ceylon picked up the term with the relish because the early Pennsylvania Dutch used a corrupted form, *jar jar,* as their initial way of writing "chow chow." He went on to say that he believes the term can be traced to the U.S. Centennial in 1876, since a great many commercial foods were sold there, among them packaged pickles from India. Also, many Philadelphia hotels and food specialty shops offered Indian goods—they were quite chic in the 1870s. Today, chutney is having a well-deserved resurgence on our tables.

Not only in the art of making relishes, chutneys, and pickles are peppers a marvelous addition; I also find their acridity a perfect complement to the sometimes cloying sweetness of preserves, marmalades, and jellies. There is a physiological basis for this. When foods with different taste characteristics are mixed, these characteristics do not meld to produce a new taste, but rather suppress or enhance one another—salt added to sweet enhances the latter, while acid and acrid things mitigate sweetness. Don't be afraid to try chillies in your favorite plum or peach jam. Serranos or chiltepíns will add zest without changing your fruity flavor, while jalapeños impart a distinct flavor that may or may not be desirable.

It was through my hobby of pickling and preserving that I met and fell in love with peppers in the early 1970s. Peppers were indispensable to pickles and relishes, and now I find them equally vital to my preserves. The addition of capsicums to a sweet fruit enhances and complements the cloying sweetness of the sugar. The pickle and relish book I had begun, along with the recipes I had developed for it, went in the closet during my pursuit of peppers. Now, years later, I have rescued those tasty recipes from oblivion by including them in this book.

One hot Texas summer, while I was peeling and preserving a bumper crop, an old-timer dropped by and drawled to me, "Honey, you better put up enough for two or three years, cuz you might not make a crop next year." He was right. However, if your colorful, tasty products are to last more than a few weeks, care must be taken to make sure the homemade condiments and preserves are sterile before they are put in the pantry. There is so much hard work involved in preserving that it is a shame to risk losing all those ingredients and such effort through careless procedures. Unless you have ideal storage—30° to 50°F and dry and dark—giving the product of your labors a boiling water bath according to directions will ensure you and your friends enjoying the fruits of your garden.

The four things that cause spoilage in preserved food—bacteria, enzymes, molds, and yeast—can be controlled by heat, hence the boiling water bath. You will need a 6- to 7-quart nonreactive pot to cook in—too many boilovers will occur in anything smaller—a larger preserving kettle with a lid and a jar rack for the water bath, and a pair of tongs designed to lift jars from hot water. The directions for the water bath are on page 197.

PICKLING. Canning relishes and sauces that have been acidified with vinegar can be a very satisfying experience, and family and friends will be provided with taste treats throughout the year. For pickles the fruit and/or vegetables are left whole or cut to a specific size, while in relishes they are chopped. Only the very freshest, firmest fruits and vegetables, and whole spices (ground spices will cause darkening during storage), should be used and the recipe directions followed exactly. They are sealed and stored as are other canned foods, but they require a wait of at least 3 to 6 weeks before eating for the flavors to meld. A boiling water bath will guarantee a safe relish or pickle that will keep for several years at 50° to 70°F in a dark, dry place, although the contents may darken if kept too long. After opening they will keep in a tightly closed container in the refrigerator almost indefinitely.

PRESERVING. Preserving is an ancient procedure for safeguarding fruits and vegetables by increasing their sugar content to a concentration in which microbes are dehydrated by osmotic pressure, and are thereby destroyed. Sugar, fruit, pectin, and acid are the essential ingredients of four types of preserved fruit—jelly, which is made from the fruit juice; preserves, made of whole or large pieces of fruit in syrup; jam, made from ground or crushed fruit; marmalade, a soft jelly that has bits of citrus throughout.
Fruit. Select full-flavored, slightly underripe fruits to overcome the sweetness of the sugar.
Acid. Without acid no fruit will thicken or gel. Underripe fruit is higher in acid than fully ripe fruit. Lemon juice is frequently added to low-acid fruits.

Pectin. This is what makes jelly gel, not the sugar. Pectin occurs to some extent in all fruits and decreases with maturity. Commercial pectins—liquid or crystalline—take the guesswork out of jams and jellies. Capsicums require the addition of such supplemental pectin.

Sugar. This acts as a preservative and aids the formation of gels. Honey or corn syrup can be substituted for half the sugar in jams and marmalades but for only a quarter in jellies.

In the process of preserving, the fruit to be preserved—whole or cut up—is simmered for 10 to 20 minutes in a small amount of water to extract the pectin. If the fruit is deficient in either pectin or acid, then commercial pectin or pared lemon slices should be added. Follow the printed directions on the pectin package exactly. Additional or excessive cooking will break down the pectin molecules.

The correct amount of sugar is then added and the mixture is kept at a rolling boil until the desired consistency is reached. If a sample of the preserves fails to gel when cooled in a spoon, additional lemon juice or pectin can be added to stabilize the ingredients. Measure carefully and *never* double a recipe, because the additional cooking required not only darkens the fruit but also lessens the flavor. Experience or an experienced friend is a big help until you get the hang of preserving.

Properly sealed preserves stored in a dark, dry place at 50° to 70°F should keep indefinitely, however, they will darken. Opened jars of preserves should be tightly closed and stored at 32° to 50°F in the refrigerator, where they will keep for up to a year.

JARS, LIDS, AND STERILIZING THEM. Use modern self-sealing jars, unused flat lids, and reusable rings/bands, which can be purchased at the supermarket, hardware store, or feed store. If you have saved jars from previous years, be certain the rims are intact and use only new lids. The jars and lids must be washed thoroughly before each use. If a boiling water bath is to be used, they will not need to be sterilized prior to filling; however, the jars should be hot when they receive the boiling fruit. Before you start cooking, fill the clean jars one-quarter full of very hot water and place them in a flat pan in a 225°F oven so they will be the right temperature when the fruit is ready to be poured. Do not boil the self-sealing lids; instead, put them in a glass or metal container, scald them by covering them with boiling water, and let them rest until you are ready for them.

FILLING THE JARS. Fill the hot, clean jars to within ½ inch of the rim. If air bubbles appear, run a sterile knife down the inside of each jar to release the air. Wipe the rims clean and seal with scalded lids. Put the band on, then tighten it completely before the hot jars are placed in the boiling water bath. Do not tighten the lids after the bath or you will break the seal.

BOILING WATER BATH. After sealing the hot jars of goodies, place them on a rack in the canning kettle. Adding enough steaming hot water—never cold water—to cover the jars by an inch or two. Cover the kettle and turn the heat up. When the water reaches a rolling boil, start timing, 20 minutes for quart jars of whole dill or sour pickles, 5 minutes for jars of sweet pickles and relishes such as chutney, piccalilli, relish, peppers, chow chow, pickled jalapeños, and preserves. Be certain the water boils steadily throughout the processing period. If necessary, add boiling water to replace any that evaporates. When the processing time is up, remove the jars from the canner at once. Place on racks to cool out of the breeze. After the jars are cool, check the seal by pressing the lids. If the lid pops back, the jar is not sealed; store it in the refrigerator. If the lid stays down, store it in a cool (50° to 70°F), dry place.

NOTE: Jellies should not receive a boiling water bath but should be put up in sterilized jars (boiled for 15 minutes at 212°F) to within ½ inch of the rim and sealed immediately with a ¼-inch layer of melted paraffin in order to prevent surface mold. Cover with scalded lids. To melt paraffin, place it in a clean can that has been bent at the rim to form a pouring spout. Place the can in a saucepan of boiling water to melt. Never place it over the flame, as it catches fire easily. Be very careful when melting paraffin.

CANNING

The capsicum is a low-acid fruit/vegetable, which must be canned in a pressure canner for safety. The risk of botulism makes it unwise to can peppers at home.

Easy Pepper Sauce Pickles
JEAN ANDREWS

MAKES 8 PINTS

 1 gallon sliced "hamburger" dill pickles
 5 pounds sugar
One 2-ounce bottle chilli pepper sauce
  Pickling spice
  Mustard seeds

Drain the pickles well. Use the gallon glass pickle jar and return the sliced pickles to it in alternate layers with the sugar and pepper sauce. Screw the lid on tightly. Allow it to sit for 1 week in a cool place. Each day turn the jar of pickles upside down so that one day they sit with the top up and the next day the bottom is up.

After a week, remove the pickles and pack them into sterilized jars to which have been added 1 teaspoon pickling spice and ½ teaspoon mustard seed. Put the scalded lids on tightly. Refrigerate tightly closed once opened; they keep almost indefinitely. These easily prepared, very crisp pickles make great hostess gifts.

NOTE: A small, dried or fresh red chilli pepper added to the pickles so that it can be seen through the jar adds a bright touch.

Pickled Jalapeños or Hungarian Wax Peppers
JEAN ANDREWS

MAKES ABOUT 8 PINTS

 1 gallon Hungarian wax peppers, jalapeños, serranos or your own garden chilli mix (see index); or sweet peppers, if you must
 1 gallon plus 1 cup water
 2 cups salt
 5 cups 5 percent white vinegar
 2 tablespoons sugar
 1 tablespoon pickling spice
 2 small onions, quartered
 2 carrots, parboiled 3 minutes and sliced
 8 garlic cloves, unpeeled, parboiled 2 minutes
 ½ cup olive or vegetable oil

Thoroughly wash the peppers. Prick with a fork or make several small slits in each. Bring the gallon of water to a boil and dissolve the salt in it to make a brine solution. Let cool. Put the peppers in the cool brine in a crock (do not use a metal container). Place a quart jar full of water on a clean plate on top of the peppers to hold them down in the brine. Leave in the brine for 12 to 18 hours.

Rinse the peppers thoroughly to remove all salt. Drain. Combine the 1 cup water, the vinegar, sugar, and pickling spice in a stockpot and bring to a boil over medium heat. Simmer 10 minutes. In each hot, clean jar place an onion quarter, several carrot slices, 1 garlic clove, and 1 tablespoon of the oil, then pack the peppers into the jars. Pour in the hot liquid and process in a boiling water bath according to the directions on page 197. Store 3 weeks before using. Refrigerate tightly closed once opened. These pickled peppers will keep several months in the refrigerator.

Red Pepper and Tomato Chutney
JEAN ANDREWS

MAKES 10 CUPS

6 cups peeled and quartered ripe
*   tomatoes*
1 cup seeded red bell pepper slices (or
*   any sweet red pepper)*
2 fresh red chillies (jalapeños, serranos,
*   'Fresnos'; see index)*
2 Granny Smith apples, cored and sliced
*   into narrow wedges*
2 red onions, sliced and separated into
*   rings*
3 tablespoons mustard seeds
1 tablespoon salt
4 cups cider vinegar

IN A SPICE BAG

1 tablespoon whole cloves
1 tablespoon allspice berries
2 tablespoons peeled and sliced fresh
*   ginger*
2 tablespoons celery seeds
½ teaspoon cumin seeds
*   Pulp and seeds from 3 tamarind pods*
*   (page 108; see note below)*
3 cups firmly packed brown sugar
One 6-ounce pouch liquid pectin (Certo)

Place the tomatoes in a 6- to 7-quart nonreactive stockpot. Add the peppers, jalapeños, apples, onions, mustard seed, and salt. Simmer over medium-low heat gently for 30 minutes. Put all the spices and the pulp and seeds of the tamarinds in a spice bag or piece of muslin secured with a rubber band. Place the spice bag and the vinegar in a 2-quart nonreactive pan, bring to a boil, then reduce the heat to medium and simmer for 30 minutes. Remove the spice bag and strain the vinegar into the tomato mixture. Add the sugar and bring to a rolling boil. Reduce the heat to medium-low and simmer for 1 hour. Turn the heat off and cover. Let the chutney sit overnight.

Bring the chutney to a rolling boil and add the pectin (see note below). When it comes to a rolling boil again, boil for 1 minute. Remove from the heat and pour into hot, sterilized jars. Wait 3 weeks to allow the chutney to mellow before using. Refrigerate once opened.

NOTES: If tamarinds are not available, substitute 6 to 8 dried apricot halves and 3 tablespoons Worcestershire sauce.

Chutney can be made without the commercial pectin by boiling much longer, until it has thickened. This reduces the volume considerably and makes for a darker product.

Cranberry Chutney
JEAN ANDREWS

MAKES 3 TO 4 CUPS

2 cups fresh cranberries
½ cup water
½ cup golden raisins
1 small onion, sliced
1 to 2 serranos (page 86) or fresh
*   jalapeños (page 77), seeded*
*   and thinly sliced*
1 cup sugar
¼ teaspoon ground ginger
¼ teaspoon ground cinnamon
⅛ teaspoon ground allspice
⅛ teaspoon salt
1 cup diced fresh pineapple, or one
*   8-ounce can pineapple tidbits, drained*

Combine all the ingredients except the pineapple in a nonreactive Dutch oven or similar deep pan; stir well. Cook over medium heat, uncovered, until reduced and thickened, 10 to 15 minutes. Add the pineapple, bring to a boil, remove from the heat, and let sit, covered, until cool.

Serve at room temperature with turkey, lamb, or in baked acorn squash halves. Cover and keep refrigerated for 7 to 10 days—not for canning.

Jean's Own Chutney
JEAN ANDREWS

MAKES ABOUT 9 PINTS

> 4 cups firmly packed brown sugar
> 2 cups granulated sugar
> 1 teaspoon ground nutmeg
> 1 quart cider vinegar
> 1 pound golden raisins, pureed in
>   blender with 1 cup fresh lime juice
> 1 cup tamarind (page 108) juice
>   and puree or puree of ½ cup dried
>   apricots soaked in water to make
>   1 cup, plus 2 tablespoons Worcester-
>   shire sauce
> 1 cup chopped red onion
> 2 garlic cloves, minced
> 1 teaspoon salt
> 12 Kieffer or hard, green canning pears
>   (not Bartlett) and/or Granny Smith or
>   tart green apples, cored, peeled, and
>   diced (8 pounds before peeling)
> 3 tablespoons preserved ginger
>   (page 106)
> 4 tablespoons peeled and thinly sliced
>   fresh ginger
> 4 cups seeded and 1-inch diced red bell
>   peppers, or mixed sweet peppers, or
>   underripe mango (page 106); or 4
>   cups underripe peaches, peeled, pitted,
>   and sliced, or other fruits such as
>   citron melon, or green tomatoes
> 2 to 4 serranos (page 86) or fresh
>   jalapeños (page 77), seeded and
>   sliced

IN A SPICE BAG

> 2 cinnamon sticks
> 20 whole cloves
> 2 dried red chillies or ½ teaspoon
>   ground cayenne pepper
> 2 teaspoons ground allspice
> 1 teaspoon turmeric
> 1 teaspoon ground mace

Place the sugars, spice bag, and vinegar in a 6- to 7-quart nonreactive pan and cook until clear, stirring to dissolve sugar. Add the raisin and tamarind puree, onion, garlic, and salt and cook, uncovered, until thickened over a low-medium heat. Add sliced fresh fruits, gingers, and peppers; boil gently, uncovered, for 15 minutes, no more, stirring frequently. Cover immediately and let sit overnight.

Next day, adjust the seasonings and cook the chutney down over low-medium heat 15 to 20 minutes. This final cooking down may take more or less time but must be watched very carefully to prevent scorching. Remove the spice bag and pack the boiling chutney into hot, clean jars. Seal and process in a boiling water bath according to the directions on page 197. Allow flavors to meld for 3 weeks before serving.

This fairly dark colored chutney is great with meats, curries, over cream cheese as an hors d'oeuvre, or in sour cream on fruit salad. Cover tightly and refrigerate once opened. It will keep almost indefinitely in the refrigerator.

Fresh Chilli Papaya Chutney
STEPHEN LOMBARDI

MAKES 2 QUARTS

> 2 tablespoons butter or margarine
> ½ medium-size red onion, finely diced
> 2 medium-size poblanos (page 82),
>   seeded and finely diced
> 1 bunch green onions (scallions),
>   chopped
> 3 celery stalks, finely diced
> ½ large red bell pepper, seeded and
>   finely diced, optional
> 1 fresh jalapeño (page 77), seeded and
>   minced, optional; see note below

3 large papayas (page 107), cut into
   medium dice
½ cup raisins (preferably golden)
1⅓ cups sugar
⅓ cup red wine vinegar
2 tablespoons fresh lemon juice
   Pinch of salt

Melt the butter in a 4-quart saucepan, then add
the vegetables and sweat until soft (page 110).
Add the fruit and remaining ingredients, cover,
and simmer over low heat 12 to 15 minutes. Do
not allow to boil.

Can be served hot or cold, and works best
with fowl, pork, or seafood. Try adding some to
a quick hollandaise for a nice sauce. Can be safely
stored, covered, in the refrigerator for up to 2
weeks.

NOTE: The jalapeño may make the finished product too hot for some people. Taste the chutney
first and omit if necessary.

Indian-Style Mint Chutney

JEAN ANDREWS

MAKES 1 CUP

1 cup cilantro (fresh coriander) leaves
1 cup fresh mint leaves
1 large garlic clove, peeled
3 tablespoons onion
1 small green tomato, cored, or 2
   tomatillos (page 108)
4 to 6 fresh green chillies (serrano, Thai,
   'Fresno', 'Santa Fe Grande'; see
   index), seeded
2 tablespoons fresh lime juice
2 tablespoons olive oil
1 teaspoon salt

Put all the ingredients in a blender and process
until coarsely pureed. Serve with curry dishes or
any meats or as a dip with unsalted chips. *Warning:* This is addictive (but so good).

VARIATION: The timid may mix several spoonfuls
of this in plain yogurt or sour cream to taste. Use
as a dip with chips, cold chicken, lamb, or vegetables.

Indian Raita

JEAN ANDREWS

The cooling effect of this traditional Indian dish
is a delightful complement to the burning curries
or any other peppery foods.

MAKES 6 TO 8 SERVINGS

2 cucumbers, onions, or ripe tomatoes,
   or a combination, chopped
2 cups plain yogurt
   Salt to taste
½ teaspoon cumin seeds, sautéed in
   1 tablespoon vegetable oil till golden
   brown
½ teaspoon ground coriander
½ teaspoon ground cumin
½ to 1 teaspoon ground cayenne pepper
   Pinch of turmeric
   Pinch of garam masala (page 106)
¼ teaspoon freshly ground black pepper
   Cilantro (fresh coriander) sprigs for
   garnish

Mix together the vegetables and yogurt. Add the
salt, caraway seeds, and the oil it was sautéed in;
mix well. Sprinkle all the spices on top and toss
lightly. Garnish with cilantro sprigs.

Old-Fashioned Pepper Relish
JEAN ANDREWS

MAKES ABOUT 10 PINTS

8 cups seeded and coarse-ground (page 66) or medium-chopped bell peppers of all colors; or a garden mix of poblanos, banana peppers, 'Cubanelles', and New Mexican chiles (see index) (about 15 large)

4 fresh jalapeños (page 77) or serranos (page 86), or your garden chillies, seeded

8 cups coarse-ground (page 109) or medium-chopped red onions (about 8 to 10 large)

4 cups 5 percent white vinegar

1 cup water

3 cups sugar

2 tablespoons salt

3 tablespoons mustard seeds

2 tablespoons celery seeds

1 teaspoon peeled and minced fresh ginger

Place the ground peppers, chillies, and onion in a large container (a plastic dishpan will do), cover with boiling water, and let stand 10 to 15 minutes. Drain and return to the container. Mix 1 cup of the vinegar with the water; heat to boiling, then pour over the drained vegetables. Let stand 15 minutes. Drain again.

Place the vegetables in a large (6- to 7-quart) nonreactive pot, add the remaining ingredients, and place over high heat. Bring to a rolling boil. Pour the mixture into clean, hot jars, seal, and process in a boiling water bath according to the directions on page 197. Allow to mellow for a month before using. Store in the refrigerator in a tightly closed jar once opened. The opened relish will keep for several months in the refrigerator.

Serve with grilled or barbecued meats, in tuna or chicken salad, or on sandwiches and hamburgers.

Fresh Mango Chilli Relish
HEIDI INSALATA KRAHLING   *Smith Ranch*

MAKES ABOUT 1 QUART

2 cups diced mango (avoid the fibrous parts) or papaya (page 106 or 107)

¼ cup green onions (scallions), thinly sliced on the bias

¼ cup finely diced red onion

3 red jalapeños (page 77), seeded and finely diced

1 poblano (page 82), roasted (pages 96–97), peeled, seeded, and finely diced

1 bunch cilantro (fresh coriander), stemmed and chopped

3 tablespoons rice vinegar (page 107)

½ cup olive oil

2 teaspoons toasted (page 110) and ground cumin seeds
Zest and juice of 1 lime
Zest and juice of 1 orange
Salt to taste

Mix all the ingredients together in a nonreactive bowl. Adjust the flavor with citrus juices and salt. Serve with your favorite fish or fowl.

Pennsylvania Dutch Mango Relish
WILLIAM WOYS WEAVER

MAKES 8 TO 8½ PINTS

14 medium-size onions

12 large green bell peppers, seeded

12 large red bell peppers, seeded

4 small, fresh red chillies (cayenne, serrano, Thai; see index), seeded

3 cups vinegar

3 cups firmly packed brown sugar

3 tablespoons celery seeds

3 teaspoons pickling salt

Chop the onions, peppers and chillies to a fine, even texture. Put them in a nonreactive preserving kettle and add the vinegar, sugar, celery seed, and salt. Bring this to a gentle boil over medium-high heat and cook 15 minutes.

Put the relish in hot, clean jars, seal, and process in a 5-minute boiling water bath as described on page 197. Allow to mature for 1 to 2 weeks before using. Refrigerate once opened.

Chow Chow
JEAN ANDREWS

Chow chow is a mixed pickle in mustard. The name comes from *achaar* (*char char,* page 60), which is an Indian dish flavored with mustard seed. After studying numerous chow chow and mustard pickle recipes I have come to the conclusion that there is little, if any, difference between the two. We always had a jar labeled Crosse and Blackwell Mustard Pickle on our table, and my father called it chowchow in spite of its label. The main difference appears to be the size of the vegetable, smaller in chow chow. I prefer the smaller bits. The combination of vegetables is variable. A lot of folks call any vegetable relish chow chow.

MAKES 10 TO 12 PINTS

Use a mixture of the following vegetables to make 4 quarts:

Small (2-inch to 3-inch) cucumbers, sliced
1 red bell pepper, seeded and chopped
1 green bell pepper, seeded and chopped
Pearl onions, peeled (canned cocktail onions may be substituted)
1 head cauliflower, cut into florets
Tiny green tomatoes, cut in half if too large
Whole tiny snap beans
Lima beans, shelled
Tiny pickled gherkins (buy these bottled)

FOR THE BRINE
1 cup salt
4 cups boiling water

FOR THE SAUCE
1½ cups all-purpose flour
1 teaspoon ground cayenne pepper
6 tablespoons dry mustard
1½ tablespoons turmeric
2 quarts cider vinegar
2½ cups sugar
3 tablespoons celery seeds
1 tablespoon mustard seeds

Combine the vegetables in a crock. Stir the brine ingredients together until the salt is dissolved, then pour over the vegetables to cover. Let stand overnight.

In a large saucepan bring to a boil in the brine. Let stand 10 minutes. Rinse thoroughly in cold water. Drain. Combine the vegetables in a 6- to 7-quart nonreactive stockpot.

Make a paste of the flour and ground spices with a small amount of the vinegar. In a nonreactive saucepan, bring the remaining vinegar, sugar, and seeds to a boil. Slowly stir in the flour mixture and cook until smooth and thickened. Combine with the vegetables in the larger pot. Simmer over medium heat until the vegetables are just barely tender. Pour into hot, clean jars, seal, and process in a boiling water bath according to the directions on page 197. Refrigerate once opened.

VARIATION: For a snappier chow chow, add 1 tablespoon canned nacho-sliced jalapeños, or more, to the vegetables.

Creole Chow Chow or Mustard Pickle
JEAN ANDREWS

MAKES 10 TO 12 PINTS

    3 quarts cider vinegar
    2 tablespoons mustard seeds
½ cup celery seeds
    1 tablespoon grated fresh horseradish
    1 garlic clove, minced
2 to 3 fresh red and green chillies, (serrano,
        jalapeño, 'Fresno'; see index), seeded
        and chopped
    1 cup firmly packed brown sugar
    1 teaspoon turmeric
¾ cup dry mustard
½ cup salad oil

Put the vinegar in a nonreactive saucepan and bring to a boil. Add the mustard seed, celery seed, horseradish, garlic, and chillies. Boil 5 minutes, stirring constantly, then add the sugar and stir until dissolved. Make a paste of the turmeric, dry mustard, and oil with a little cold vinegar. Slowly pour into the hot vinegar mixture. Stir well and pour over the vegetables. Pour into hot, clean jars, seal, and process in a boiling water bath according to the directions on page 197. A small, bright red chilli pushed down the inside of the filled jars so that it can be seen against the glass is an attractive addition. Refrigerate once opened.

Hayden's Relish
JEAN ANDREWS

I have never known who Hayden was, but when I was a child a neighbor gave this recipe to my mother, and it has always been our very favorite relish. Thank you, Hayden, wherever you are!

MAKES 12 TO 18 PINTS

    1 gallon cored and coarse-ground (page
        109) or medium-chopped firm, ripe
        tomatoes (about 4 pounds)
    1 gallon seeded and coarse-ground
        (page 109) or medium-chopped green
        and red bell peppers (about 5 pounds)
    1 gallon coarse-ground (page 109)
        or medium-chopped cabbage (about 6
        pounds)
    1 quart coarse-ground or medium-
        chopped red onions (about 4 pounds)
    1 cup noniodized salt
    6 fresh jalapeños (page 77), seeded and
        chopped
    8 cups cider vinegar
    6 cups sugar
    2 tablespoons mustard seeds
    2 tablespoons celery seeds
    2 teaspoons turmeric
    2 teaspoons finely broken cinnamon
        sticks
    1 teaspoon whole cloves
    1 teaspoon peeled and minced fresh
        ginger

Place the ground ingredients in a large container such as a plastic dishpan and mix with the salt. Let stand for 2 hours. Lift from the juice and drain. Put in a large nonreactive pan (6 to 7 quarts or larger) and add the remaining ingredients. Boil the vegetables and spices for 30 minutes, stirring frquently.

Pack into hot, clean jars, seal, and process in a boiling water bath according to the directions on page 197. Refrigerate in a tightly closed jar once opened. The relish will keep for several months.

Delicious with meats, ham, mixed in mayonnaise for salad dressing, in deviled eggs, tuna salad, and on hamburgers.

Mediterranean Relish
JEAN ANDREWS

This is an uncooked eggplant and green New Mexican chile relish.

MAKES 2 CUPS

> One 1-pound eggplant
> 4 fresh mild, green New Mexican chiles (page 78) or sweet banana peppers (page 65), peeled, seeded, and chopped
> 1 fresh jalapeño (page 77)
> 1 garlic clove, peeled and crushed
> 2 tablespoons grated onion
> 3 tablespoons fresh lemon juice or white wine vinegar
> 1 tablespoon chopped fresh basil
> 6 tablespoons olive oil
> Salt and freshly ground black pepper to taste

Pierce the unpeeled eggplant with a fork in two or three places. For good flavor, bake in a preheated 375°F oven for 20 minutes, turning once. Place the baked eggplant over a gas flame, hot charcoal, or under a broiler and roast until softened and blackened. Remove the blackened skin under cold running water, then press gently to remove any bitter juices. Chop the pulp fine and mix with the peppers. Add the garlic, onion, lemon juice, and basil, then gradually stir in the oil. Season with salt and pepper. Chill before serving. Will keep in the refrigerator, covered, for a week.

Home-Canned Salsa
JEAN ANDREWS

MAKES 4 CUPS

> 2 cups fresh green chillies (New Mexican chiles, 'Fresnos', jalapeños, or 'Santa Fe Grandes'; see index), seeded
> 4 pounds ripe tomatoes (about 8 large), cored and quartered
> 1 large onion, quartered
> 4 garlic cloves, peeled and crushed
> 1 cup sugar, or to taste
> 1 tablespoon salt
> ½ teaspoon coriander seeds
> 1 teaspoon chopped fresh oregano leaves
> 4 cups cider vinegar

In a food processor in batches, puree the chiles, tomatoes, onion, and garlic together until smooth. For a chunkier salsa, pulse the processor until you reach the desired level of "chunkiness." Put into a large (6- to 7-quart) nonreactive stockpot and mix in the sugar, salt, spices, and 2 cups of the vinegar. Simmer over medium heat, uncovered, until the salsa is reduced by half, about 1½ hours, stirring frequently.

Add the remaining vinegar and continue simmering and stirring until the salsa is reduced to 1 quart, about 30 to 40 minutes. Remove from the heat.

To can, follow the instructions on pages 196–197. Store in the refrigerator once opened; the salsa will keep for several weeks if tightly closed.

If you have a garden or farmer's market, this recipe can be doubled and made several times to take advantage of the seasonal produce.

VARIATION: This basic *salsa picante* can be varied with the addition of any or all of the following: 2 red bell peppers; 1 cup banana peppers (page 65), seeded and chopped; ½ cup cilantro (fresh coriander) leaves, chopped; 1 teaspoon ground cumin; 1 teaspoon freshly ground black pepper.

Jean's Capsicum Marmalade
JEAN ANDREWS

MAKES 10 CUPS

> 2 lemons, peeled and juiced
> 2 grapefruit, peeled and juiced
> ½ teaspoon baking soda
> 6 large red bell peppers, roasted (pages 96–97), seeded, peeled, and chopped
> 4 to 6 chiltepínes (page 69) or other small fresh red chillies, minced
> 10 cups sugar
> 2 cups water
> One 6-ounce can frozen orange juice concentrate
> ¼ teaspoon salt
> Two 6-ounce pouches liquid pectin (Certo)
> Paraffin

Score the citrus skin in quarters and remove; cut the skinned fruit in half and juice. Set the juice aside. Cut the excess white from the peel and thinly slice the peel in the food processor. Place the citrus peel and soda, with enough water to cover, in a covered saucepan; bring to a boil and simmer until the rinds are tender (20 to 30 minutes). Remove from the heat, drain, and rinse. Place in a food processor and puree.

Place the fruit, peel, and peppers in a large bowl and mix—there should be 6 cups. Divide the mixture into two 3-cup portions to be cooked separately. Better results are obtained when making preserves by keeping your "batches" small. Never cook a doubled recipe of preserves.

Place 3 cups of the mixture in a 6- to 7-quart nonreactive pot and add 5 cups of sugar. Add 1 cup water, ½ can orange juice concentrate, salt, and the grapefruit and lemon juice to the citrus peel and pepper mixture. Bring to a boil over high heat, then reduce the heat and simmer, uncovered, for 5 to 10 minutes. Raise the heat to high and bring to a rolling boil that won't stir down and continue boiling and stirring for 2 to 3 minutes. Add one pouch of the pectin. Let the marmalade return to a boil and boil for exactly 1 minute. Remove from the heat. Skim the foam, if necessary.

Pour hot marmalade in hot, sterilized jelly jars. Wipe the rims with damp paper toweling. While still very hot, pour on a layer of melted paraffin (see page 198). Put scalded lids on the jars and tighten and place on a rack to cool. Repeat the process using the other half of the fruit, sugar, and pectin.

Keep tightly closed in the refrigerator once opened. Use it up so that it won't turn to sugar, but if it does, melt the marmalade in a saucepan over low heat or in the microwave and use it for a sauce with meats. Additional chillies can be used for a more pungent marmalade.

NOTE: During the winter when citrus fruits are at their peak, prepare the rind and freeze it until summer when the peppers are at their peak. This is a good way to utilize those grapefruit rinds.

Capsicum Marmalade
PHIL COLMAN

MAKES 5 TO 6 CUPS

> 4 oranges, thinly sliced
> 2 lemons, thinly sliced
> 6 red bell peppers, seeded and sliced
> Sugar

Combine the citrus fruits in a nonreactive saucepan with enough water to cover. Bring to a boil and cook until the rinds are tender. Drain and add the peppers. Measure the contents. For three parts of fruit, add one part sugar. Place the saucepan over low heat and cook until the sugar is dissolved. Increase the heat to medium and cook until thick.

Pour into hot, clean jars and seal with scalded lids (see page 197). Refrigerate once opened.

Chilli Pepper Jelly
JEAN ANDREWS

MAKES 7 CUPS

¼ *cup seeded and chopped fresh chillies (such as chiltepínes, jalapeños, habaneros; see index)*
¾ *cup seeded and chopped bell peppers (use same color as the chillies)*
6½ *cups sugar*
1½ *cups white vinegar*
One *6-ounce pouch liquid pectin (Certo)*
Food coloring (optional)
Paraffin

Mix the peppers, sugar, and vinegar together in a 6- to 7-quart nonreactive pan; boil 2 minutes. Let cool for 5 minutes. Add the pectin and 1 or 2 drops of food coloring, then bring to a rolling boil and boil for 1 minute (do not exceed pectin manufacturer's recommended time).

Pour into hot, sterilized jelly jars. Wipe the rims with a clean, damp cloth and seal immediatley with melted paraffin (see page 198). Place scalded lids on the jars and tighten. Place on a rack to cool. Store in the refrigerator once opened. If the jelly turns to sugar, melt it and use it as a sauce on meats.

NOTE: Any chilli—jalapeño, habanero, dátil, serrano, chiltepín; see index—can be used, but don't mix them if you want a distinct flavor typical of that variety.

Cayenne Pepper Catsup
JEAN ANDREWS

MAKES 4 TO 5 CUPS

4 *dozen fresh ripe cayenne chillies (page 68)*
4 *cups best-quality white or cider vinegar*
3 *tablespoons grated fresh horseradish*
5 *onions, sliced*
1 *teaspoon sugar*
1 *garlic clove, minced*
1 *cup hot water*

Place all the ingredients in a nonreactive stockpot and boil together, uncovered, until the onions become soft. Remove from the heat and mash and strain or puree in a blender. Return the puree to the saucepan and bring to a boil.

Pour into hot, clean jars, seal, and process in a 5-minute boiling water bath as described on page 197. However, this is not necessary if it is to be used in a couple of months. Refrigerate once opened.

This famous Creole preparation is very hot and excellent with oysters. Ripe red New Mexican chiles, 'Santa Fe Grandes', jalapeños, Hungarian wax, or serranos (see index) can be used, but the flavor will be a little different with each. Makes a great gift.

''Sun-Dried'' Tomatoes
JEAN ANDREWS

MAKES 2 TO 3 CUPS

*4 to 5 pounds ripe Roma tomatoes (use no
other kind)*
*Ground cayenne pepper and/or salt to
taste*

Go to a farmer's market or wait for a special on
Roma tomatoes. Select tomatoes approximately
all the same size, otherwise some will dry quicker
than others, causing you to have to watch them
closer. Buy enough to do several broiler pans full
at a time or whatever your oven will hold.

Oil broiler racks and place the racks in broiler
pans. Cut the tomatoes in half and place them cut
side down on the racks. Fill the pans and place
them in a preheated 190°F oven. The length of
cooking time will depend on the tomatoes. Turn
them once about mid-drying time. It will take
from 16 to 24 hours or a little more, depending
on the size of the tomatoes. If some "dry" before
the others, remove them and return the pan to
the oven. Don't let them get crisp.

When the tomatoes are as "dry" as you desire, remove the pans and cool. They can be
seasoned with cayenne pepper, salt, or whatever. I put them in a closed container unsea-
soned, but they keep longer packed with olive oil
and marjoram. Having them on hand plain, you
are free to use them in many ways. They will keep
several weeks in the refrigerator or longer if you
freeze them.

Try serving them as appetizers with a good
blue cheese or mozzarella chunks, a side dish of
olive oil with crushed fresh parsley and basil, and
pieces of fresh, crusty French bread to dip in the
oil.

Candied Chillies
JEAN ANDREWS

Try these in a drink instead of a cherry.

YIELD IS VARIABLE

*½ pound whole small fresh red chillies
(serranos, jalapeños, 'Cascabellas'; see
index) with stems (see note below)*
1 quart water
4 cups sugar
Red food coloring, optional

Place the whole chillies and the water in a saucepan and bring to a boil over medium heat. Reduce the heat immediately and simmer,
uncovered, over low heat for 15 minutes. Add 1
cup of the sugar and continue cooking, uncovered, over low-medium heat for 15 minutes. Add
1 more cup of granulated sugar and continue
cooking for 30 minutes. Add the third cup of
granulated sugar and cook for 30 minutes. Add
the food coloring and the final cup of granulated
sugar a little at a time while stirring. Put the lid
back on and cook for 30 minutes more. Care
must be taken to not caramelize the sugar.

Place an oiled rack on a sheet of waxed paper.
Remove the chillies with a slotted spoon and
place on the rack, allowing the excess syrup to
drip onto the paper. If any stems come off, re-
attach them. Allow the chillies to sit at room
temperature overnight. Store in an airtight container lined with waxed paper.
NOTE: If these are too hot, try to find some ripe,
red mild jalapeños or cherry peppers.

Herbed Chilli Vinegar
JEAN ANDREWS

MAKES 3 GALLONS

> 1½ gallons fresh herbs: salad burnet,
> lemon balm, and marjoram; lemon
> thyme, chives, and tarragon; or rose-
> mary, thyme, basil, and oregano
> 6 to 8 garlic cloves, peeled and crushed
> 2 to 3 fresh jalapeños (page 77) or
> serranos (page 86), slashed
> 1 small onion, sliced
> 3 gallons cider vinegar
> Dried red chillies
> Sprigs of rosemary or other herbs

Place the herbs and vegetables in a 3-gallon pickling crock or nonreactive container; press with a
wooden spoon to bruise. Pour the container full
of vinegar. Cover the container with plastic wrap.
Mark with the date.

Three weeks later, remove the wrap and strain
the vinegar through muslin, coffee filters, or two
layers of paper toweling. Sterilize enough bottles
(pretty wine bottles) to hold 3 gallons. Place a
dried red chilli and a sprig of rosemary (other
herbs will serve) in each bottle. Using a funnel,
fill each bottle to within 1 inch of top. Cork,
using a wooden mallet to insert the cork firmly.
Store as you would pickles, etc. (page 196).

Use this vinegar in salads, on vegetables, in
salad dressings, or to marinate meats.

Zesty Jalapeño Vinegar
JEAN ANDREWS

MAKES 3 CUPS

> 6 fresh jalapeños (page 77), or to taste
> 1 cup water
> 2 cups cider or white vinegar
> 2 tablespoons olive oil
> 3 garlic cloves, peeled and crushed
> ½ teaspoon fresh or dried oregano
> 1 slice onion
> 1 teaspoon black peppercorns,
> crushed

Cut the jalapeños in several places with a knife.
Place all the ingredients in a nonreactive saucepan and bring to a boil. Reduce the heat to medium and simmer for 5 minutes. Cool and place
in a sterilized glass jar or bottle with a tight lid or
cork. Store in the refrigerator.

Use on vegetables, cooked greens, in salad
dressings, or substitute for vinegar or lime juice
in sauce recipes.

Curry Powders or Masalas
JEAN ANDREWS

A visit to the huge Indian market in Durban, South Africa, and markets of all sizes throughout India made me realize that the spices used to make curries are very variable. Almost anything goes, except the commercially prepared, standardized stuff called curry powder in American supermarkets. Those colorful, aromatic piles of ground spices might vary in composition but not in freshness. They were all recently ground. If you want to grind your own, try one of the following combinatons; however, you can also use them as a base to compose your own. Use whole spices and crush them in a mortar, process in a blender, or grind them in an electric spice mill until fine, then sift and return any large particles for further powdering. Experiment! Tightly covered and stored in the refrigerator, it will keep a year. Better yet are the plastic containers with the type of rubber stoppers that allow the air to be pumped out like those used on wine bottles (see footnote, page 95).

CURRY POWDER NO. 1

MAKES ABOUT ¾ CUP

4½ teaspoons freshly ground black pepper
1½ teaspoons cardamom seeds
2 teaspoons ground cayenne pepper
1½ teaspoons ground cinnamon
1½ teaspoons cumin seeds
2 tablespoons plus 1½ teaspoons ground ginger
4½ teaspoons mustard seed
1 teaspoon sweet paprika
¼ cup turmeric
½ teaspoon crushed dried red chillies (de árbol, Thai, japonés, chiltepínes; see index)

CURRY POWDER NO. 2

MAKES ABOUT 6 TABLESPOONS

2 teaspoons freshly ground black pepper
½ teaspoon cardamom seeds
6 to 8 whole cloves
4 teaspoons ground coriander
4 teaspoons ground cumin
2 teaspoons ground ginger
½ teaspoon ground mace
½ teaspoon mustard seeds
4 teaspoons turmeric
½ teaspoon crushed dried red chillies (de árbol, japonés, chiltepínes; see index)

CURRY POWDER NO. 3

MAKES ABOUT ¼ CUP

1 teaspoon freshly ground black pepper
½ teaspoon cardamom seeds
¼ teaspoon ground cinnamon
3 teaspoons coriander seeds
½ teaspoon ground cumin
½ teaspoon fenugreek seeds
1 teaspoon ginger
1 teaspoon mustard seeds
3 teaspoons turmeric
¼ teaspoon crushed dried red chillies, (de árbol, Thai, japonés; see index)

DESSERTS

JEAN ANDREWS

Honeydew Compote with Lime, Ginger, and a Hint of Serrano
JOHN ASH   *John Ash & Company*

MAKES 6 SERVINGS

½ cup fresh lime juice
2 teaspoons grated lime peel
½ cup water
⅓ cup sugar
1 tablespoon peeled and minced fresh ginger
½ teaspoon seeded and finely slivered serrano (page 86)
1 teaspoon finely slivered fresh mint
1 large honeydew melon (3 pounds or so), seeded and cut from the rind in uniform pieces
Fresh figs and mint sprigs for garnish

Combine the first 7 ingredients in a small saucepan. Bring to a boil, reduce the heat to medium, and simmer until the sugar is dissolved, 5 minutes. Cool, then strain.

To serve, pour the syrup over the melon and, if possible, allow to marinate refrigerated for at least 1 hour. Garnish with slices of fresh fig and the fresh mint. Also very nice garnished with a slice or two of good prosciutto or Bayonne ham.

Toasted Chilli Custard
KURT KOESSEL   *Ginger Island*

MAKES 4 SERVINGS

2 large eggs
2 large egg yolks
⅓ cup plus 2 tablespoons firmly packed brown sugar
2 teaspoons toasted (page 99) de árbol or japonés chilli powder (page 99) or ground cayenne pepper
¼ teaspoon salt

2 cups heavy cream
¼ teaspoon pure vanilla extract

In a bowl, whisk together the eggs and egg yolks with the ⅓ cup brown sugar and the salt until just mixed. In a saucepan, scald the cream with the vanilla. Add half the scalded cream to the egg mixture, stirring constantly. Add 1¾ teaspoons of the chilli flakes and combine with the rest of the cream in the pan; cook over low heat, stirring constantly, until the custard coats the spoon. Pour the custard into four 4-ounce ramekins, place in a larger pan filled with water that comes halfway up the sides of the ramekins, and bake in a preheated 300°F oven for 35 minutes. Cool 3 hours in the refrigerator.

When ready to serve, sprinkle approximately ¼ teaspoon of the powdered chilli flakes over the top of each custard. Top with a thin layer of sifted brown sugar. Place under the broiler, watching constantly, until the sugar is melted but not burned. Serve immediately.

Fourth Street Grill's Chile Festival Brownie
KURT KOESSEL   *Ginger Island*

MAKES 10 TO 12 SERVINGS

¾ cup (1½ sticks) butter or margarine
6 ounces semisweet chocolate, broken into small pieces
3 ounces unsweetened chocolate, broken into small pieces
3 large eggs
¾ cup sugar
½ cup firmly packed dark brown sugar or ground piloncillo (Mexican cone sugar)
2 teaspoons pure vanilla extract
1 tablespoon chili powder or a combination of ancho (page 83) and dried New Mexican chile flakes (page 78), ground

½ *teaspoon ground cayenne pepper, or to taste*
½ *teaspoon ground coriander, optional*
⅛ *teaspoon ground cloves*
 1 *cup all-purpose flour*
½ *cup raisins, soaked overnight in 1 cup dark Mexican beer and drained*
½ *cup pecans, toasted (page 110) and chopped*
  Confectioners' sugar for garnish, optional

Combine the chocolate and butter in a heavy-bottomed pan and cook over low heat just until the chocolate melts. Cool. Beat the eggs in a mixing bowl until they start to thicken. Add the sugars and continue beating until the mixture is light and fluffy. Stir in the vanilla and chocolate mixture.

Lightly toast the spices in a skillet over low heat, stirring often to be careful they don't burn. Combine the spices and flour in a bowl with a whisk. Gently stir the dry ingredients into the wet ingredients. Gently add the raisins and nuts, stirring just until combined. Don't overmix.

Pour the mixture into a greased and floured 9-inch round cake pan. Bake in a 350°F oven just until set, 25 to 30 minutes. Cool in the pan. Turn out and cut into wedges. If desired, dust with confectioners' sugar and serve with vanilla ice cream.

Moctezuma's Brownies
CAROL ISENSEE KILGORE

This recipe was created just for this book.

MAKES 12 TO 16 SERVINGS

 2 *anchos (page 83)*
 6 *ounces (squares) unsweetened baking chocolate*
½ *cup (1 stick) butter*

½ *cup (1 stick) unsalted margarine*
 5 *large eggs*
2¾ *cups sugar*
1½ *teaspoons pure vanilla extract*
1½ *cups all-purpose flour*
1½ *cups pecans, toasted and coarsely chopped*

Select pliable anchos; do not wash them. With scissors, stem, seed, and cut them in half lengthwise. Microwave the anchos for 2 minutes on high; stir. Continue cooking and stirring at 1-minute intervals until the peppers are crisp, about 5 minutes, or place in a 350° F oven and stir occasionally until crisp. Crumble them gradually into an electric spice grinder or blender and reduce to a fine powder. Set aside.

In a large bowl, microwave the chocolate, butter, and margarine together at 1-minute intervals until just melted; stir occasionally. Remove and continue stirring until the chocolate mixture is well blended. (The chocolate, butter, and margarine can be melted in a small, heavy saucepan over low heat, stirring constantly.) Stir in the 2 tablespoons of the powdered anchos.

In a large mixing bowl, beat the eggs until light. Add the sugar gradually, then stir in the vanilla. Stir in the chocolate mixture. Add the flour, beating just until blended. Stir in the pecans. Pour the batter into a 13 × 9-inch pan sprayed with nonstick cooking spray. Bake in a preheated 375°F oven until a toothpick inserted into the cake center comes out with moist crumbs, 35 to 40 minutes. Take care not to overbake. Cool in the pan, then cut into rectangles. Serve warm.

New World Pie
JEAN ANDREWS

MAKES ONE 9-INCH PIE

> 1 cup semi-sweet chocolate chips
> 6 tablespoons (¾ stick) butter or
>   margarine, cut into pieces
> 2 large eggs, slightly beaten
> ¼ cup plus 1½ teaspoons sugar
> ¼ cup all-purpose flour
> 1 tablespoon freshly ground ancho,
>   mulato, or pasilla (see note on
>   page 215)
> ¼ teaspoon salt
> 1 teaspoon instant coffee granules
> ½ cup milk chocolate chips
> 1 cup pecans, coarsely chopped
> One 9-inch pie crust, lightly baked and
>   cooled
> ½ cup sour cream
> Paprika

Melt the semi-sweet chips and butter in a heavy medium-size saucepan over boiling water or in a microwave oven, stirring until smooth, then cool to room temperature. In a mixing bowl, whisk the eggs and sugar until well blended. Whisk in the melted chocolate-butter mixture, then gently fold in the flour, ground chilli, salt, and coffee until well mixed. Add the milk chocolate chips along with the pecans and stir until evenly distributed. Spread the batter over the cooled crust and bake in a preheated 325°F oven until a toothpick inserted in the center comes out clean, about 25 minutes, taking care to not overcook the pie. If the pie is to be served while still warm, cover the pie tightly with aluminum foil and allow to stand on a rack until ready to serve. Remove the foil and cut into wedges. Serve the slightly warm pie with a dollop of sour cream and sprinkle with paprika. If the pie is baked ahead of time and is completely cool, it can be warmed in a 200°F oven.

Apple Pie with New Mexican Chile
INTERNATIONAL CONNOISSEURS OF GREEN AND RED CHILE

MAKES ONE 9-INCH PIE

> 5 cups peeled and sliced apples (not
>   'Delicious')
> ¾ cup sugar
> 2 tablespoons butter or margarine
> 1 teaspoon ground cinnamon
> ½ teaspoon ground nutmeg
> 2 teaspoons pure red New Mexican
>   chile powder (page 99)
> 1 cup water
> Salt to taste
> One 9-inch double pie crust

Combine all the ingredients except the crust in a large saucepan and cook over medium heat until the apples are slightly tender and the juice is thick, 20 to 25 minutes. Pour into the unbaked pie shell, dot with additional butter or margarine, cover with the top crust and cut vents into it (or cover the top with lattice strips of crust) and sprinkle with additional sugar. Bake 30 to 40 minutes in a preheated 375°F oven.

New World Truffles
JEAN ANDREWS

MAKES 24

1½ *cups milk chocolate chips*
¼ *cup (½ stick) butter or margarine*
1 *tablespoon finely ground ancho (see note below)*
½ *teaspoon finely ground jalapeño or cayenne pepper*
½ *cup no-cholesterol egg product*
2 *tablespoons Kahlua liqueur or brandy*
 Ground pecans or other nuts

Place the chocolate and butter in the top of a double boiler over barely simmering water. Cover, and let stand until it is partially melted; remove the cover and stir until completely melted. Remove the top pan of the double boiler, keeping the water in the bottom heated. Add the ground chillies and mix well. Stir the egg product into the chocolate mixture and return it to above the pan of fully simmering water. Stir the mixture continuously until it is quite hot but not boiling. Continue cooking and stirring for 3 minutes. Remove the boiler top from the heat and add the liqueur gradually while stirring. Set the pan in a large bowl of iced water. Add ice as necessary to keep the water very cold. Stir constantly until the entire mixture forms a fairly firm, nonsticky ball. Place slightly rounded teaspoonfuls of the candy on a sheet of waxed paper and let them dry until firm enough to handle, 1 to 2 hours. Put the ground nuts on a sheet of wax paper and roll each truffle in the nuts. Allow the truffles to dry for 30 minutes to 1 hour, then shake off the excess nuts. These truffles will keep for 2 to 3 days at room temperature, but they are best fresh. They may be refrigerated in a tightly closed container for up to a week but should be allowed to return to room temperature before serving.

NOTE: To grind the ancho remove the stem, seeds, and veins from the dry pod. Break the pod into pieces and place it in a spice mill, blender, or mortar. Grind the ancho to a very fine powder. Store in a tightly closed jar or zip-lock plastic bag. It is best to do several at a time because the properly sealed powder will keep almost indefinitely in the refrigerator.

Sunset Jalapeño Truffles
JERRY DI VECCHIO

MAKES 25 TRUFFLES

6 *fresh jalapeños (page 77), seeded and minced*
¼ *cup white vinegar*
½ *to 1 teaspoon ground cayenne pepper*
½ *cup granulated sugar*
¼ *cup (½ stick) butter or margarine, softened*
1 *tablespoon grated orange peel*
3 *cups confectioners' sugar*
¼ *cup unsweetened cocoa powder*

In a 1- to 2-quart saucepan, combine the jalapeños, vinegar, cayenne, and granulated sugar. Stir until dissolved. Boil without stirring until the mixture reaches 220°F on a candy thermometer, 6 to 7 minutes. Remove from the heat and let cool for 15 minutes.

In a bowl, beat the butter with an electric mixer until fluffy. While still beating, add the jalapeño syrup and orange zest. Stir in the confectioners' sugar and beat until the mixture holds its shape when patted into a ball. Add more confectioners' sugar if necessary. Divide into 1-tablespoon portions. Shape into truffles and roll in the cocoa. Place on a plate and chill until firm.

Arizona Chiltepín Ice Cream

GARY NABHAN AND MARTHA AMES "MUFFIN" BURGESS *Native Seeds.SEARCH*

This was first custom-made for two Arizona events, the Fiesta de los Chiles at Tucson Botanical Gardens and a conference on wild chiltepín conservation and development at Desert Botanical Garden in Phoenix. The creators warn that "it's so hot that you immediately have to eat more ice cream to cool down your mouth!"

MAKES A BUNCH

> 1 gallon vanilla ice cream
> ¼ to ½ cup green chiltepínes (page 69) pickled in brine, thoroughly rinsed and pureed

Blend the ice cream and chiltepínes together in an electric blender until green flecks are thoroughly mixed into the ice cream. Firm in the freezer if necessary. Serve small portions.

Citrus-Güero Sorbet

JEAN ANDREWS

MAKES 8 SERVINGS

> 4 Hungarian wax-type or any güero (yellow) chilli, seeded and chopped (for flavor with less heat, use banana peppers or yellow bell peppers)
> 5½ cups water
> 2½ cups sugar
> 8 large oranges, peeled and chopped
> ¼ cup tequila, cointreau, or mixed
> ½ cup fresh lemon or fresh lime juice, or to taste
> 6 tablespoons light corn syrup

Combine 4 cups of water with the sugar in a saucepan and heat until the sugar dissolves, then bring to a boil. Cool to room temperature, then refrigerate for 2 hours.

Puree the remaining ingredients with 1½ cups water and refrigerate until well chilled, at least 2 hours. Stir the sugar mixture into the fruit. Pour the mixture into an ice cream maker and follow the directions for making ice cream.

Serve the sorbet as a dessert or as a refresher between courses of a large meal.

VARIATION: Use 4 white grapefruit and a drop or two of green food coloring instead of the oranges, and jalapeños (page 77) instead of güeros. Jalapeños have a flavor very different from the yellow chillies.

THE CONTRIBUTORS

ALDRIDGE, LEWIS. *Chef/Owner, City Grill, Austin, Texas* Lewis Aldridge was born in south Texas, where he developed his taste for chillies and spicy Mexican food. In 1984, after a stint with his first restaurant, The Yellow Rose in San Francisco, he and two partners opened the City Grill. This tree-shaded restaurant has a menu that is heavy in the chilli department.

AMATYAKUL, CHARLIE. *Executive chef, Oriental Hotel Cooking School, Bangkok, Thailand* Charlie Amatyakul, a native Thai, is director of the Thai Cooking School operated by the Oriental Hotel. He is a most cosmopolitan fellow, having studied interior design in Vienna and literature in France. He returned to Thailand to earn a degree in political science. Before heading up the cooking school he was food and beverage director for the Oriental and helped develop its catering and banquet business. His events caught the eye of Queen Sirikit, and he continues to cater state functions.

ANUSASANANAN, LINDA LAU
Linda Anusasananan, a native Californian of Chinese descent, graduated from Oregon State University with a degree in home economics and journalism. Since 1971 she has written, researched, and developed recipes for *Sunset* magazine, emphasizing the use of the food bounty of the West. She has written major articles about home cooking in China and Italy. She also takes an active part in the annual Berkeley Chile Festival.

ASH, JOHN. *Chef/Owner, John Ash & Company, Santa Rosa, California* John Ash graduated from college with a degree in fine arts and a major in painting. After pursuing food at the corporate level with Del Monte Foods in San Francisco (developing new food products), he began to cook professionally in the early 1970s following study in Europe. Ash opened his first restaurant in 1978, focusing on the foods and wines of Sonoma County, California.

AUDEN, BRUCE. *Chef/Owner, Restaurant Biga & LocuStreet Bakery, San Antonio, Texas* For a number of years Bruce Auden, a native of England, was the innovative executive chef at Polo's in San Antonio, Texas, where his food gained a reputation for its elegant simplicity. He developed recipes that require more time marinating and seasoning with fresh herbs than actual cooking.

BECKWITH, TONY. *Chef/Manager, Green Pastures, Austin, Texas* Tony Beckwith, a native of Argentina, has been with Green Pastures for more than ten of its forty-five years as a widely acclaimed restaurant founded by Mary Faulk Koock in the historic 1894 Faulk house. The restaurant is still owned and operated by a member of the Koock clan.

BLACKWELL, ROLLIE ANNE. *Chef/Owner, Gourmet Dallas, Dallas, Texas* Rollie Blackwell is a native Texan, self-taught chef, and innovative Dallas caterer. She uses exciting regional ingredients and flavors to create zesty and delicious gourmet cuisine.

BORG, JOHN. *Executive Chef, Papagayo, San Diego, California* John Borg, a Californian since 1979, is a native of Illinois with a degree in hotel and restaurant management from the University of Denver, and has a wide range of experience as both restaurant manager and chef. He was invited by chefs of the Republic of Georgia, Russia, to demonstrate the foods and wines of California.

BRANDT, NORBERT. *Chef, Louie B's American Cafe & Bar, Austin, Texas* Brandt is a native German who worked in Germany, France, Switzerland, Singapore, and Canada before coming to the United States. In 1983 he created and prepared a state dinner in honor of Queen Elizabeth, which President Reagan hosted in San Francisco. At present he owns and operates seven restaurants in Houston, Austin, and San Antonio, Texas.

BROADFOOT, BRYAN Bryan Broadfoot, a native Texan, is a retired Sperry Rand executive who resides in Austin, Texas. Bryan spends time between homes in Austin and San Miguel de Allende, Mexico, taking classes in gourmet cooking and delighting his guests with his skills. Pasta making is his specialty.

BURGESS, MARTHA AMES "MUFFIN" Muffin Burgess, a native of the Southwest, who holds an M.S. in geochronology/tree-ring dating, is the former education director of Native Seeds. SEARCH, an organization that preserves and studies the food plants and foodways of Native Americans.

CAPLAN, FRIEDA AND KAREN Frieda and Karen Caplan head up a Los Angeles-based wholesale produce business called Frieda's that pioneered much of the specialty produce market in this country. One of their introductions, the Chinese gooseberry, took off after they renamed it the kiwifruit.

CHIANG, CECILIA. *Chef/Owner, The Mandarin, San Francisco, California* Cecilia Chiang, a native of Beijing, started her first restaurant in Tokyo because she was unable to find the grand cuisine of North China to which she was accustomed. When she came to America in the early 1960s, Mandarin food was not available. Her award-winning restaurant, The Mandarin, is renowned for presenting the cuisines of northern China.

CLEMONS, REED. *Chef/Owner, The Granite Cafe, Austin, Texas* Reed Clemons, who has served at a number of Austin restaurants, received his professional culinary training at the New York Cooking School. He features creative dishes in a combination of ethnic styles but with southwestern overtones.

COLMAN, PHIL Phil Colman has been curator of invertebrates at the Australian Museum of Natural History in Sydney since the early 1960s. His interest in natural history has carried over to plants and cooking, especially peppers. My interest in mollusks led me to Phil, and his interest in peppers led him to me, and a friendship and sharing of shells and recipes followed.

COLTMAN-ROGERS, TIM Tim Coltman-Rogers is one of England's "landed gentry" who has greenhouses full of exotic peppers at his estate on the Scottish border. He is a world traveler who collects peppers from far-off places, grows them, and entertains friends with dishes he creates to use his fiery finds. Part of the year he calls Houston, Texas home.

COUNTS, DONALD, M.D., AND KATHRYN O'CONNOR COUNTS Don and Kathryn O'Connor Counts are private investors who are not only deeply interested in foods both from a gastronomical point of view but from a medicinal and nutritional one. Kathryn is a member of one of the oldest of the legendary south Texas ranching families and incorporates their culinary traditions into her interest in food, while Donald brings his medical expertise to bear on the health aspects of the recipes they present. They are the authors of *A Texas Family's Cookbook*.

CRONWELL, RANDALL E. Randall Cronwell is a 1978 graduate of the Culinary Institute of America in Hyde Park, New York, and is currently a resident of Portland, Oregon. Before going independent, he worked with Jeremiah Tower at the Santa Fe Bar and Grill in Berkeley, California, from 1981 to 1985.

DEL GRANDE, ROBERT. *Chef/Manager, Cafe Annie, Houston, Texas* Robert Del Grande, who holds a Ph.D. in biochemistry from the University of California, is an award-winning chef whose knowledge of chemistry has turned to the subject of food. His writings about food have been published in major food magazines.

DI VECCHIO, JERRY Jerry Di Vecchio, a Kansas native transplanted to California, received her degree in home economics and journalism at San Jose State College. Thirty years ago, after living in Europe for several years, she joined *Sunset* Magazine, where she is now the food and entertaining editor. Through the magazine and numerous books, she has been a significant force in shaping the fresh, innovative, and multicultural cuisine of the West that has captured the attention of the nation.

FEARING, DEAN. *Executive Chef, the Mansion on Turtle Creek, Dallas, Texas* The multi-award winning Dean Fearing, Corporate Chef of Rosewood Hotels, has achieved national acclaim for his development of American Southwest cuisine. This native of Ashland, Kentucky, the son of an innkeeper, is a graduate of the Culinary Institute of America and the author of *Mansion on Turtle Creek Cookbook* and *Dean Fearing's Southwest Cuisine*.

FOLEY, MICHAEL. *Chef/Co-owner, Printer's Row, Chicago, Illinois* When Michael Foley isn't cooking at either of his two Chicago restau-

rants, he's making road trips to search out new unique midwestern ingredients. He is well known for his dedication to quality, innovation, and regional foods.

GERLACH, NANCY, AND DAVE DEWITT Dave DeWitt and Nancy Gerlach are editors of *Chile Pepper Magazine*. They are the authors of several cookbooks on hot and spicy cooking and numerous magazine articles.

HIGGINS, GREG. *Executive Chef Heathman Hotel, Portland, Oregon* A pragmatic "working chef," Higgins strongly believes in utilizing classical cooking methods to enhance the phenomenal range of food products found in the Pacific Northwest. Under Chef Higgins' leadership, The Heathman Hotel and Restaurant have garnered numerous national and international awards and honors for its food program.

HOSTETLER, JANIE Janie Hostetler was born in Indiana, but has lived in the Southwest for twenty years. She is the distribution manager of Native Seed.SEARCH in Tucson, Arizona. Her hobby is experimental cooking and recipe development using foods common to that region.

HUTSON, LUCINDA Lucinda Hutson was born and raised in El Paso, Texas, and is bilingual. Her degree from the University of Texas is in anthropology, and her interest in other cultures has led to extensive travel throughout Mexico, Central America, the American Southwest, and Europe. She has become an expert in the field of herb gardening and cooking with herbs and is the author of *The Herb Garden Cookbook*.

INTERNATIONAL CONNOISSEURS OF GREEN AND RED CHILE, *Las Cruces, New Mexico* This is an international organization whose primary purpose is to develop, promote, and strengthen educational and research programs leading to the appreciation and enjoyment of the chile.

JACKSON, GEORGE O. Jackson, better known as George-O, was born in Houston of a Texan father and Mexican mother. As a result of his maternal family background, with their vast interests in Mexico, he has spent much of his life there. He was the originator of several restaurants in Houston and Austin, Texas, but is best known for his photography, hospitality, and love of peppers.

JAMES, DAVID. *Chef, Zuni Grill, San Antonio, Texas* David James, along with his wife, Jane Dunnewold, owned and operated Zinfandeli's. The eclectic menu ranged from Rack of Lamb to Eggplant Southwestern Style to Triple Decker Quesadilla—all with peppers.

JIVIDEN, JON. *Executive Chef, Zagara's Specialty and Natural Foods and Catering, Marlton, New Jersey* Jon Jividen, a California native, is a graduate of Mesa College with a degree in food service and restaurant management. After graduating from the Culinary Institute of America, he held various positions from sous-chef to executive chef in the San Diego area before moving to Philadelphia. For five years he was the executive chef of the prestigious Ridgewell's Caterers before transferring to their Washington operation to carry on his innovative work as executive chef and head of research and development.

JUE, JOYCE Joyce Jue is a native of San Francisco who has studied cooking and done research in Bangkok, Paris, Spain, and Singapore. She has been teaching cookery around the world since 1976, is the author of *Wok and Stir-Fry Cooking,* and conducts culinary tours to the Orient. She was one of the founders of the Thai cooking school at the Oriental Hotel in Bangkok.

KEARNS, MARY "PUD" LAUDERDALE Pud Kearns claims to be the only living person named after a fruitcake. She grew up in her parents' multimillion-dollar mail-order food business, Mary of Puddin Hill, which is based on that fruit cake. A fashion design graduate of Stephens Col-

lege, she worked and taught in that field before returning to Greenville, Texas, to join the family business, where she is now vice-president of marketing and director of new product development.

KILGORE, CAROL ISENSEE Carol Kilgore, who has a master's degree in bacteriology from the University of Texas at Austin, has managed a large farming operation since her graduation. She is a longtime friend, who had done the preliminary editing for several of my books. It was on her farm that I grew the peppers I painted for *Peppers: The Domesticated Capsicums.* She is a recognized herbalist and expert cook, besides being a most erudite lady.

KOESSEL, KURT. *Chef, Ginger Island, Berkeley, California* Susan Nelson, the owner of Ginger Island, says Kurt, whose gastronomic career spans more than eighteen years, "is one of the most creative and capable all-around talents I've ever encountered in this business, and I've worked with the best."

KRAHLING, HEIDI INSALATA. *Executive Chef, Smith Ranch, San Rafael, California* With a maiden name of Insalata and a gourmet chef for a father, Heidi Krahling's flavorful future with food seemed inevitable. After obtaining a degree in business administration from Cal Poly University, she utilized her business knowledge to rise from waitress to owner. She attended Tante Marie's Cooking School in San Francisco and now teaches there. In 1988 she was chosen as one of *USA Today*'s Best Women Chefs for that year.

LAMBERT, PAULA Paula Lambert is co-owner and president of the Mozzarella Company, which she founded in Dallas, Texas, in 1982. She lived in Italy for a number of years while she studied cheesemaking. Unable to find cheeses of equal quality when she returned to Texas, she began producing her own, incorporating southwestern and Texas ingredients.

LOMBARDI, STEPHEN Lombardi combines two major talents, artistic and culinary, to literally paint pictures with food. His style shows American cuisine with southwestern coloring, combining indigenous foods such as venison, cactus pears, and juniper berries.

LONGACRE, W. C. W. C. Longacre opened his first restaurant in Albuquerque so he could raise enough money to put himself through chiropractic school, and in so doing, fell in love with peppers. Now he is only taking the kinks out of cayennes. His experimenting nature has combined three culinary styles—Hong Kong, New Mexico, and Florida—to create his own cuisine. He is best known for his peppery curries, which are mild, medium, hot, and native.

MILLER, MARK. *Chef/Owner, Coyote Cafe, Santa Fe, New Mexico* Miller is a Bostonian transplanted to the Southwest. Trained in anthropology and Chinese art at the University of California at Berkeley, he continued postgraduate study and teaching there. When he broke from academia he began cooking at Chez Panisse with Alice Waters, the "mother" of the New American Cuisine. He was a founding partner of Fourth Street Grill in Berkeley, California. It was there that he developed his interest in southwestern ingredients, which led to his pioneering of modern southwestern cuisine. Mark and his innovative Coyote Cafe, and the creative Red Sage in Washington, D.C., have made a difference in what America eats. He is the author of *Coyote Cafe: Foods From the Southwest* and *The Great Chile Book.*

MORNINGSTAR, JAMIE. *Chef, Inglenook Napa Valley, Rutherford, California* Becoming resident chef at Inglenook Napa was like coming home to this Seattle native, for Morningstar is a descendent of the winery's founder. After graduating from San Francisco's California Culinary Academy, she entered the world of food, which led her to the winery, with its wine program and creative menus.

NABHAN, GARY Gary Nabhan, Ph.D., is an award-winning author, ethnobotanist, and founding director of Native Seeds.SEARCH, a research and conservation center in Tucson, Arizona. Nabhan is an authority on arid land food plants and their uses by Native Americans which he relates in his books *Gathering the Desert* and *Enduring Seeds.*

NAJ, AMAL Amal Naj is a native of Calcutta, India, transplanted to New York, where he is a writer for the *Wall Street Journal,* a job that led him to the *Capsicum.* In America he has had to learn to cook in order to satisfy his longing for the spicy Indian cuisine of his mother's kitchen. In his book, *Peppers: A Story of Hot Pursuits,* he has made a fascinating study of the diverse people involved with peppers—writers, botanists, growers, processors.

NELSON, SUSAN H. *Chef/Owner, Ginger Island, Berkeley, California* Susan Nelson, educated as an artist and art historian, is a trendsetting restaurateur and founder of the Berkeley Chile Festival, held in August each year. After her beginnings at Alice Waters' Chez Panisse, she and Mark Miller opened the innovative Fourth Street Grill, now Ginger Island, which reflected her love of California, Mexico, and good food.

ORTIZ, ELIZABETH LAMBERT Elizabeth Lambert Ortiz is a widely traveled Englishwoman whose husband was an official of the United Nations. Extended stays in each country allowed her to make in-depth studies of each cuisine. Their first duty station in Mexico resulted in *The Complete Book of Mexican Cooking.* That was followed by books of the cooking of Japan, Latin America, the Caribbean, and the Iberian peninsula. Her intense and continuing interest is in the effects of New World foods on Old World kitchens. One of the principal unifying ingredients of the cuisines examined in those works is peppers—she is probably the paramount authority on their usage in foods of the world.

PARKER, LINDA Linda Parker is a native of Pennsylvania who has lived in the southwestern United States for fifteen years and is the curator of collections at Native Seed.SEARCH in Tucson, Arizona. She has a B.S. degree in horticulture, is an avid gardener, and likes to cook the things she grows.

PAWLCYN, CINDY. *Chef/Co-Owner, Mustard's Grill, Napa, California* Cindy Pawlcyn, executive chef and co-owner of five popular California restaurants, has been working in professional kitchens since she was thirteen years old. Of Russian, German, and Norwegian extraction, her family meals were steeped in European traditions. Cindy earned a degree from Hennepin Technical Institute and from the University of Wisconsin in hotel and restaurant administration. She has also studied at the Cordon Bleu, La Varenne, and Ken Hom School, and was a member of the Shanghai/San Francisco Culinary Exchange program.

PRAMBS, ELMAR E. *Executive Chef, Four Seasons Hotel, Austin, Texas* Elmar Prambs, a native of Bavaria, Germany, has been with the Four Seasons chain for more than ten years. He trained in Germany, then worked with the Hilton Corporation in England, where he developed an international reputation. He was an award-winning member of a regional team competing in the Frankfurt Culinary Olympics and has been delighting diners in Austin since 1986.

PRUDHOMME, PAUL. *Chef/Owner, K-Paul's Kitchen, New Orleans, Louisiana* Paul Prudhomme was born and raised in the Louisiana Acadian country, and it was to that style of cooking he returned after twelve years traveling and apprenticing with chefs throughout the United States. He and his wife (she was the K in K-Paul's) opened their famous restaurant in 1979 and he now has a second in New York. His cookbooks, television appearances, and magazine articles have made Prudhomme a true homegrown American celebrity.

PYLES, STEPHEN. *Chef/Owner, Baby Routh, Dallas, Texas; Goodfellow's and Tejas, Minneapolis, Minnesota* Stephen Pyles, a native West Texan, has gone a long way from Big Springs, and we don't mean Dallas. After earning a degree in music education, he pursued postgraduate work in music in France, where he fell in love with French food and cooking. Back home, he taught himself cooking by studying cookbooks. As evidence of his teaching abilities, *Bon Appetit* has credited Pyles with "almost single-handedly changing Texas's cooking scene." He was named to *Food and Wine*'s Honor Roll of American Chefs, and he was the first Texan named to *Cook*'s magazine's Who's Who of Cooking in America. He is the author of *The New Texas Cuisine.*

QUINTANA, PATRICIA Patricia Quintana lives and teaches in Mexico but visits the United States, where she is a sought-after cooking teacher and restaurant consultant. She is one of the foremost authorities on her native cuisine, and has studied cooking in France. She writes a column in several Mexican publications and is employed by the Mexican Ministry of Tourism to promote the cooking of Mexico throughout the world. Her cookbooks, with photographs by Ignacio Urquiza, are outstanding.

RAVAGO, MIGUEL. *Chef/Owner, Fonda San Miguel, Austin, Texas* Mike Ravago was born and reared in Arizona by parents who were natives of Mexico. He met Tom Gilliland, an attorney, who lived at the Arizona home of Mike's grandmother while he studied foreign trade. Both men continued their studies at The University of Texas at Austin before becoming partners in a restaurant in Houston because Tom felt food like he had eaten while living with Grandmother Ravago should be available in Texas. After five years they returned to Austin where they have delighted their clientele with cuisine from the interior of Mexico for eighteen years. Annual visits to different states in Mexico add new dishes, art, and artifacts to their Fonda, a beautiful Mexican inn in the heart of Texas.

SCHLESINGER, CHRIS. *Chef/Owner, East Coast Grill, Cambridge, Massachusetts* Chris Schlesinger grew up in Virginia and at age eighteen dropped out of school to wash dishes. He soon graduated to fry cook, went on to receive his formal training at the Culinary Institute of America, and subsequently cooked in restaurants ranging from Hawaiian burger joints to New England's finest dining rooms. In 1985 he and partner Cary Wheaton opened the East Coast Grill, and in 1987 they opened Jake and Earl's Dixie Barbecue next door. In the early 1980s he discovered chillies in Barbados and has been challenged by them ever since. He is coauthor of *The Thrill of the Grill.*

SEDLAR, JOHN. *Chef/Owner, St. Estephe Restaurant, Manhattan Beach, California* John Sedlar, a native of New Mexico whose culinary development was greatly influenced by his Hispanic mother and grandmother, has created a cooking style founded on the tantalizing flavors and forms of that colorful region. Since he and his partner, Steve Garcia, opened the trend-setting St. Estephe restaurant in 1980, he has melded his European training in the French cooking tradition and his background in the Southwest into a unique cuisine which can be found in his book, *Modern Southwest Cuisine.*

SCHMIDT, JIMMY. *Chef/Owner, The Rattlesnake Club, Detroit, Michigan* A native Midwesterner, Jimmy Schmidt studied food and cooking extensively in France before receiving his professional Chef's Diploma from Modern Gourmet, Inc., Newton Centre, Massachusetts. After working as executive chef for several years, he and a partner opened The Rattlesnake Club in Denver, Colorado, and two other restaurants before dissolving the partnership. Jimmy has owned and operated the Detroit club since that time. A

frequent contributor to *Bon Appetit,* he's also the author of *Cooking for All Seasons.*

TEEPATIGANOND, PATATAMATIP Pat, a certified public accountant in Thailand, followed her husband to Texas in 1974, where they opened an Oriental food store. With that as a base and her inherent knowledge of Thai cuisine, she began teaching various types of Oriental cooking through the University of Texas. She grows the Thai peppers used in her cooking classes.

WEAVER, WILLIAM WOYS Bill Weaver is a native of Philadelphia who lives in the historic, twenty-eight-room Land Tavern (1805) in Devon, now almost encompassed by the city. It is in the restored kitchen of this notable old house that he indulges his passions—preserving and pickling and collecting culinary artifacts. Weaver is one of the foremost experts on the history of American cooking, a sought-after lecturer, and the author of five books dealing with the history of American cookery, including *America Eats.* This pioneering figure in his field is a specialist in edible folk art.

WILSON, JUSTIN This native Louisianian is better known as the "Old Cajun." Wilson, a humorist, raconteur, and author of four cookbooks, including *Justin Wilson's Homegrown Louisiana Cookin',* began his career in crime and accident prevention and still teaches in the training school of the Texas Highway Patrol. He has been starring in his own PBS and cable cooking shows since 1972. His food is fun, "I garontee."

WINDISCH, PATRICIA. *Chef, Beringer Vineyards, St. Helena, California* Patricia Windisch learned to cook from her Hungarian grandmother, going on for professional training in New Hampshire and France. She went to Beringer as the 1986 culinary scholarship winner, and as executive chef oversees the kitchens of Beringer's Culinary Arts Center. She has been a cooking instructor in Tokyo, Japan, and in California.

MAIL·ORDER SOURCES

INGREDIENTS

In the years since I wrote my first book about peppers, their usage has grown in leaps and bounds. A local ethnic food store or supermarket should be the first place to look; you probably won't need to order.

Chile Gourmet
P.O. Box 39
Mesilla, NM 88046

Chile Shop
109 East Water Street
Santa Fe, NM 87501
(505)983-6080

Don Alfonso
P.O. Box 20198
Austin, TX 78720-1988
(512) 335-2370

Frieda's by Mail
P.O. Box 58488
Los Angeles, CA 90058
(800) 241-1771

Great Southwest Cuisine
Catalog
206 Frontage Road
Rio Rancho, NM 87124
(800) 869-9218

Mo-Hotta-Mo-Betta
P.O. Box 4136
San Luis Obispo, CA 93403
(800) 462-3220

Mozzarella Company
2944 Elm Street
Dallas, TX 75226
(800) 798-2954

Native Seeds.SEARCH
2509 North Campbell
Avenue #325
Tucson, AZ 85719
(602) 327-9123

Pecos Valley Spice
Company
500 East 77th Street,
Suite 1224
New York, NY 10162

Pendery's
304 East Belknap Street
Fort Worth, TX 76102
(817) 332-9896

Santa Fe Chili Company
218 Old Santa Fe Trail
Santa Fe, NM 87501
(505) 988-1289

Tianguis Supermarkets
3610 North Peck Road
El Monte, CA 91731
(818) 459-4716

SOURCES OF SEEDS

Virtually all of the major seed catalogs in the United States will list several peppers; the following have more unusual cultivars.

Horticultural Enterprises
P.O. Box 340082
Dallas, TX 75234

The Pepper Gal
10536 119 Avenue North
Largo, FL 34643

Petoseed Company, Inc.
P.O. Box 4206
Saticoy, CA 93994-0206
(805) 647-1188

Plants of the Southwest
930 Baca Street
Santa Fe, NM 87501
(505) 983-1548

Seed Savers Exchange
Kent Whealy
Rural Route 3, Box 239
Decora, IA 52101

RECIPE CREDITS

Medallions of Beef with Ancho Chilli Sauce and Jicama-Black Bean Garnish reprinted by permission of Grove Press, Inc., from *The Mansion on Turtle Creek Cookbook* by Dean Fearing. Copyright © 1987 by Rosewood Hotels, Inc.

Pennsylvania Dutch Mango Relish reprinted by permission of HarperCollins Publishers, from *America Eats* by William Woys Weaver.

Jalapeño Truffles reprinted courtesy of *Sunset Magazine*.

Mamie's Jalapeño Cornbread reprinted with permission from *The Puddin' Hill Cookbook* by Mary "Pud" Lauderdale Kearns. Copyright © 1988.

Sopa de Ajo and Chipotle Mayonnaise reprinted with permission from *A Texas Family's Cookbook* by Joseph Lowery with Donald R. Counts, M.D., and Kathryn O'C. Counts. Copyright © 1985 by Donald R. Counts, Houston, Texas. All rights reserved.

Ensalada Favorita reprinted with permission from *The Herb Garden Cookbook* by Lucinda Hutson. Copyright © 1992 by Lucinda Hutson, Houston, Texas. All rights reserved.

Chile Con Queso with Sweetbreads from *Modern Southwest Cuisine* by John Sedlar. Copyright © 1986 by John Sedlar. Reprinted by permission of Simon & Schuster, Inc.

Salsa Cruda, Chilaquiles Con Pollo, Guacamole, Shrimp Creole, and Chiltecpin Jelly from *Peppers: The Domesticated Capsicum* by Jean Andrews. Copyright © 1984 by Jean Andrews. Reprinted by permission of the publisher, the University of Texas Press.

Serrano Bloody Mary, Pork Tenderloin with Apple Red Chile Chutney, and Roasted Serrano Salsa from *Coyote Cafe*. Copyright © 1989 by Mark Miller. Reprinted by permission of Ten Speed Press, Berkeley, Calif.

Overstuffed Peppers with Shrimp, Cajun Style reprinted with the permission of Justin Wilson and Macmillan Publishing Company from *Justin Wilson's Homegrown Louisiana Cookin'*. Copyright © 1990 Justin Wilson Company.

Green Chili copyright © 1987 Paul Prudhomme. Pork or Chicken Stock copyright © 1984 Paul Prudhomme.

Grilled Scallops with a Rocotillo Mango Relish from *The Thrill of the Grill* by John Willoughby and Chris Schlesinger. Copyright © 1990 by John Willoughby and Chris Schlesinger. Reprinted by permission of William Morrow & Co.

Ixni Pec and Brazilian Chilli Pepper Sauce from *The Book of Latin American Cookery* by Elisabeth Lambert Ortiz. Copyright © 1979 by Elisabeth Lambert Ortiz. Reprinted by permission of Alfred A. Knopf, Inc.

Chile con Queso with Rajas from the book *The Taste of Mexico*, copyright © 1986 Patricia Quintana. Reprinted by permission of Stewart, Tabori & Chang, Publishers, New York.

BIBLIOGRAPHY

AMERICAN DIETETIC ASSOCIATION
1985. Pepper research "heats up." *Journal of the American Dietetic Association,* 85 (July): 798.

ANDERSON, E.
1958. Anatolian mystery. *Landscape.* Pp. 14–16 Berkeley, Calif.:
1967. The bearings of botanical evidence on African cultural history. In *Reconstructing African cultural history.* Ed. by C. Gabel and N. R. Bennett. Pp. 167–80. Boston: Boston University Press.

ANDERSON, E. N., JR., and M. L. ANDERSON
1977. Modern China: South. In *Food in Chinese culture.* Ed. by K. C. Chang. Pp. 317–82. New Haven, Conn.: Yale University Press.

ANGHIERA, P. M. D'.
1904. *De Orbo Novo: The decades of the New World, or West India.* Vol. 5. Trans. from Latin by Rycharde Eden. London: Hakluyt Society.

ANDREWS, J.
1984. *Peppers: The domesticated Capsicums.* Austin: University of Texas Press.
1988. Around the world with chili pepper: The postcolumbian distribution of domesticated *Capsicum. The Journal of Gastronomy.* 4(3):21–35.
1991. A newly recognized variety of chili-pepper. (Capsicum Solanaceae) developed in the United States. *Phytologia.* 69(6):413–15.
1993 Diffusion of mesoAmerican food complex to southeastern Europe. *Georgia Review.* 83(2): 145–68.

ANDREWS, R.
1991. American's ancient mariners. *Natural History.* October, pp. 72–75.

ARBER, AGNES
1953. *Herbals: Their origin and evolution, a chapter in the history of botany.* Cambridge: Cambridge University Press.

ARBERRY, A. J.
1939. A Baghdad cookery book. In *Islamic culture.* Hyderabad, India. 13–47, 189–214.

ARNOTT, MARGARET L.
1975. *Gastronomy: The anthropology of food and food habits.* The Hague: Mouton Publishers.

BAILEY, L. H.
1923. *Capsicum. Gentes herbarum.* 1:128–29.

BAKER, H. G.
1970. *Plants and civilization.* Belmont Calif.: Wadsworth.

BARBOSA, D.
1918. *The book of Duarte Barbosa: An account of countries bordering on the Indian Ocean and their inhabitants.* Translated by M. L. Dames, Vol. 1, London: Hakluyt Society.

BARRACLOUGH, G.
1982. *The Times concise atlas of world history.* Maplewood, N.J.: Hammond.

BENNETT, D. J. and G. W. KIRBY
1968. Constitution and biosynthesis of capsaicin. *J. Chem Soc.,* no. 442.

BOXER, C. R.
1952. Maize names. *Uganda Journal.* 16(2):178–179.
1953. *South China in the sixteenth century.* London: Hakluyt Society. 2d. ser., vol. 106.
1963. *The great ship from Amacon: Annals of Macao and the old Japan trade 1555–1640.* Lisboa: Centro de Estudios Historicos Ultramarinos.
1967. Spaniards and Portugese in the Iberian colonial world: Aspects of an ambivalent relationship 1580–1640. In *Salvadore de Madariaga.* Bruges: Liber Amicorum.
1969a. *Four centuries of Portuguese expansion:* 14154825. Berkeley: University of California Press.
1969b. *The Portuguese seaborne empire, 1415–1825,* London: Hutchinson.
1975. *Mary and Misogny: Women in Iberian expansion overseas; some facts and personalities.* London: Duckworth.
1980. *Portuguese India in mid-seventeenth century.* Delhi: Oxford University Press.
1984. *From Lisbon to Goa 1500–1750. Studies in Portuguese maritime enterprise.* London: Variorum Reprints.
1985. *Portuguese conquest and commerce in southern Asia 1500–1750.* London: Variorum Reprints.

BRADFORD, E.
1971. *The Mediterranean: Portrait of a sea.* New York: Harcourt Brace Jovanovich.

BRAND, D. D.
1967. Geographical exploration by the Spaniards. Pp. 109–44.
Geographical exploration by the Portugese. Pp. 145–50, in *The Pacific Basin*. Ed. by D. R. Friis. New York: American Geographical Society.

BRAUDEL, F.
1976. *The Mediterranean and the world in the age of Phillip II*. Vols. I and II. New York: Harper and Row.
1979. *The wheels of commerce*. Vol. II. New York: Harper and Row.
1982. *The structures of everyday life: The limits of the possible*. New York: Harper and Row.

BROWNE, L.
1935. *Stranger than fiction*. New York: Macmillan.

BULLARD, R.
1961. *The Middle East, a political and economic survey*. London: Oxford University Press.

CANDOLLE, A. P. DE
1852. *Prodromous*. 13:411–29. Paris: Masson.

CASAS, B. DE LAS
1699. *An account of the first voyages and discoveries made by Spaniards in America*. London.
1967. *Apolgética historia sumaria, 1520–1561*. Ed. by E. O'Gorman. Mexico: Universidad Nacional Autónoma de. México. Vol. I.

CHANG, K. C. (ED.)
1977. *Food in Chinese culture: Anthropological and historical perspectives*. New Haven, Conn.: Yale University Press.

CIKOVSKY, N.
1988. *Raphaele Peale still-lifes*. New York: Harry N. Abrams.

COETZEE, RENATA
1892. *Funa food from Africa: Roots of traditional African food culture*. Durban/Pretoria: Butterworth.

COHEN, J. M. (Ed.)
1969. *The four voyages of Christopher Columbus*. Baltimore: Penguin Books.

COLES, P.
1968. *The Ottoman impact on Europe*. London: Thames and Hudson.

COLUMBUS, C.
1971. *Journal of first voyage to America by Christopher Columbus*. Freeport, N.Y.: Books for Libraries Press.

COLUMBUS, F.
1947. *Vida del Almirante don Cristobal Colon*. México: Fondo de Cultura Economica. [1571].

COVINGTON, J. W.
1959. Trade relations between southwest Florida and Cuba 1600–1840. *Florida Historical Quarterly*. 38:114–28.

CROSBY, A. W., JR.
1972. *The Columbian exchange: Biological and cultural consequences of 1492*. Westport, Conn.: Greenwood Press.
1986. *Ecological imperialism: The biological expansion of Europe 900–1900*. Cambridge: Cambridge University Press.

DAMES, M. L.
1918. *The book of Duarte Barbosa: An account of countries bordering on the Indian Ocean and their inhabitants*. Vol. 1. London: Hakluyt Society.

DAVIDSON, B.
1961. *The African Slave Trade*. New York: Little, Brown.

DOBBY, E. H. G.
1961. *Monsoon Asia*. London: University of London Press.

DRUMMOND, J. C., and A. Wilbraham
1969. *The Englishman's food: A history of five centuries of English diet*. London: Jonathan Cape.

DUNKLE, J. R.
1955. St. Augustine, Florida: A study in historical geography. Unpubl. Ph.D. diss. Worcester, Mass.: Clark University.

DUNLOP, D. M.
1971. *Arab civilization to A.D. 1500*. London: Longman Group.

DUYVENDAK, J. J. L.
1949. *China's discovery of Africa*. London: Arthur Probsthain.

ELTON, G. E. (Ed.)
1962. *The new Cambridge modern history*. Vol. II. Cambridge: Cambridge University Press.

ESHBAUGH, W. H.
1964. A numerical, taxonomic and cytogentic study of the genus *Capsicum*. Ph.D. diss., Indiana University.
1980. The taxonomy of the genus capsicum (Solanaceae). *Phytologia*. 47(3):153–66.
1983. The genus capsicum (Solanaceae) in Africa. *Bothalia*. 14(3 & 4):845–48.
1993. Peppers: history and exploitation of a seredipitous new crop discovery. In *Advances in New crops*. Proceedings of the Second National Symposium New Crops: Resources, Development, and Economics.

ESHBAUGH, W. H., S. I. GUTTMAN, and M. J. MCLEOD
1983. The origin and evolution of domesticated capsicum species. *J. Ethnobiology*. 3(1):49–54.

FAIRBANKS, G. B.
1975. *The history and antiquities of the city of St. Augustine, Florida* [1858]. Gainesville: University Presses of Florida.

FARB, P., and G. ARMELAGOS
1980. *Consuming passions: The anthropology of eating.* Boston: Houghton Mifflin.

FERET, B. L.
1979 *Gastronomical and culinary literature: A survey and analysis of historically-oriented collections in the USA.* Metuchen, N.J.: Scarecrow Press.

FERNÁNDEZ, M. G.
1971 The life of Las Casas. In *Bartolomé de las Casas in history.* Ed. by J. Friede and B. Keen. Pp. 67–125. DeKalb: Northern Illinois University Press.

FINAN, J. J.
1950 *Maize in the great herbals.* Waltham, Mass.: Chronica Botanica Co.

FISHER, W. B.
1978. *The Middle East.* London: Methuen & Co.

FORBES, J. G.
1821. *Sketches historical and topographical of the Floridas.* New York: C. S. Van Winkle.

FREYRE, G.
1966. *The masters and the slaves: A study in the development of Brazilian civilization.* New York: Alfred A. Knopf.

FRIIS, H. R.
1967. *The pacific basin: A history of its geographical exploration.* New York: American Geographical Society.

FUCHS, L.
1543. *New Kreuterbuch (De historia stirpium in 1542).* Basel: Isingrin.

GEERTZ, H.
1967. Indonesian cultures and communities. In *Indonesia.* Ed. by R. T. McVey. Pp. 24–96. New Haven: HRAF Press.

GERARD (GERARDE), J.
1597. *The herball or generall historie of plantes.* London: John Norton.

GIBAULT, M. G.
1912. *Histoire des légumes.* Paris: Librairie Horticole.

GODE, P. K.
1960. The history of maize (maká) in India between A.D. 1500–1900. In *Studies in Indian cultural history.* 2(32):283–294.

GOVINDARAJAN, V. S.
1985. Capsicum: Production, technology, chemistry and quality. Botany, cultivation and primary processing. *Crit. Rev. Food Sci. Nutr.* 22(2):108–75.
1986a. Capsicum: Production, technology, chemistry and quality. Processed products, standards, world production and trade. *Crit. Rev. Food Sci. Nutr.* 23(3):206–288.
1986b. Capsicum: Production, technology, chemistry and quality. Chemistry of the color, aroma, and pungency stimuli. *Crit. Rev. Food Sci. Nutr.* 24(3):244–355.

GOVINDARAJAN, V. S., V. S. RAJALAKSHMIA, and N. CHAND
1987. Capsicum: Production, technology, chemistry and quality. Evaluation of quality. *Crit. Rev. Food Sci. Nutr.* 25(4):185–282.

GREENHILL, B.
1956. The Karachi fishing boats. *Mariner's Mirror.* 42(1):54–66.

GREWE, R.
1987. The arrival of the tomato in Spain and Italy: Early recipes. *The Journal of Gastronomy,* 3(2):67–82.

GRIGSON, J. (Ed.)
1974. *The world atlas of food.* New York: Simon and Schuster.

GUNST, K.
1984. *Condiments.* New York: G. P. Putnam's Sons.

HABIB, I.
1982. *An atlas of the Mughal Empire.* Delhi: Oxford University Press.

HALASZ, Z.
1963. *Hungarian paprika through the ages.* Budapest: Corvina Press.

HANCE, H. F., and W. F. MAYERS.
1870. Introduction of maize into China. *Pharmaceutical Jour. Trans.* Dec. 31. pp. 522–25.

HARDING, C.
1964. *Trade and navigation between Spain and the Indies in the time of the Hapsburgs.* Glouester, Mass: Peter Smith.

HARLAN, J. R.
1975. *Crops and man.* Maidson, Wis.: Amer. Soc. of Agronomy, Crop Soc. of Amer.

HARMAN, J. E.
1969. *Trade and privateering in Spanish Florida 1732–1763.* Jacksonville, Fla: St. Augustine Historical Society.

HARRIS, M.
1974. *Cows, pigs, wars, and witches: The riddles of culture.* New York: Vintage Books.

Bibliography

HEISER, C. B., JR.
1965. Cultivated plants and cultural diffusion in nuclear America. *Amer. Anthropology.* 67:937–49.
1969. *Nightshades: The paradoxical plants.* San Francisco: W. H. Freeman and Co.
1973. *Seeds to civilization: The story of man's food.* San Franciso: W. H. Freeman and Co.
1976. Peppers: Capsicum (Solanaceae). In *Evolution of crop plants.* Ed. by N. W. Simmonds. Pp. 265–268. London: Longman.
1985. *Of plants and man.* Norman: University of Oklahoma Press.

HEISER, C. B., JR. and B. PICKERSGILL
1975. Names for the bird peppers [Capsicum-Solanaceae]. *Baileya.* 19:151–156.

HELPS, A.
1896. *The life of Las Casas the Apostle of the Indies.* London: George Ball & Sons.

HENDERSON, S. G., B. E. NICHOLSON, G. B. MASEFIELD, and M. WALLIS
1960. *The Oxford book of food plants.* Oxford: Oxford University Press.

HENKIN, R.
1991. Cooling the burn from hot peppers. *JAMA.* 226(19):2766.

HERNANDEZ, F.
1651. *Nova plantarum, animalium et mineralium Mexicanorum Historia, rerum medicarum novae.* Trans. into Latin from 1628 ed. by A. Reccho. Rome.
1943. *Historia de las plantas de Nueva Espana.* Vol. I. Mexico City: Inst. Biol. Univ. Autonomo.

HILLMAN, H., and D. SHILLING
1979. *The book of world cuisines.* New York: Penguin Books.

HO, P. T.
1955. The introduction of American food plants into China. *American Anthropologist.* 55:191-201.

HOOKER, S.H.
1985 *Herbals and closely related medico-botanical works, 1472–1753.* Lawrence, Kans: University of Kansas.

HOURANI, G. F.
1951. *Arab seafaring in the Indian Ocean in ancient and early medieval times.* Princeton, N.J.: Princeton University Press.

HOUSTON, J. M.
1959. Land use and society in the plain of Valencia. In *Geographical Essays in Memory of A. G. Ogilie.* Ed. by R. Miller and J. W. Watson. Pp. 166–194. Edinburgh: Nelson.
1949. The social Geography of the Huerta of Valencia. Unpubl. Ph.D. diss., University of Oxford.

HULTMAN, T. (Ed.)
1985. *The African news cookbook.* New York: Penguin Books.

HUNZIKER, A. T.
1958. *Synopsis of the genus Capsicum.* VIII Congress International de Botanique, Paris, 1954. Proceedings Sec. 4(2):73–74.

HSW, V. Y. N., and F. L. K. HSU
1979. Modern China: North. In *Food in Chinese culture.* Ed. by K. C. Chang. Pp. 295–316. New Haven, Conn.: Yale University Press.

IZZEDDIN, N.
1953. *The Arab world: Past, present, and future.* Chicago: Henry Regnery.

JEFFREYS, M. D. W.
1953. *Pre-columbian maize in Africa.* London: Macmillan Journals. 172(4386):965–66.
1954. Maize names. *Uganda Journal.* 18(2):192–94.
1975. Pre-Columbian maize in the Old World: An examination of Portuguese sources. In *Gastronomy: The anthropology of food and food habits.* Ed. by M. L. Arnott. Pp. 23–66. The Hague: Mouton Publishers.

JOHNSON, M.
1981. North Balkan food, past and present. In *National and regional styles of cookery, Proceedings,* Pp. 122–33, Oxford Symposium, 1981. London: Prospect Books.

KALRA, J. I. S., and P. D. GUPTA
1990. *Prashad: Cooking with Indian masters.* New Delhi: Allie Publishers.

KRAMARZ, I.
1972. *The Balkan cookbook.* New York: Crown Publishers.

LABORDE CANCINO, J. A., and O. POZO COMPODONICO
1982. *Present y pasado del chile en Mexico.* Pub. Especial Num. 85. Mexico City: Nac. de Invest. Agri.

LANE, F. C.
1940. Notes and suggestions: The Mediterranean spice trade. *American History Review.* 45:581–91.

LATOURETTE, K. S.
1964. *A short history of the Far East.* New York: Macmillan.

LAUFER, B.
1919. Sino-Iranica: Chinese contributions to the history of civilization in ancient Iran, with special reference to the history of cultivated plants and products. *Field Museum of Nat. His.* No. 201, 15(3):185–621.
1929. The American plant migration. *The Scientific Monthly.* 28:235–51.

LEE, T. S.
1954. Physiological gustatory sweating in a warm climate. *Jour. Physiol.* 124:528–42.

LE MAGNEN, J.
1981. Neurophysiological basis for sensory mediated food selection. In *Criteria of food acceptance.* Edited by J. Solms and and R. L. Hall. Zurich: Forster Verlag AG, p. 268.

L'ESCLUSE, C.
1611. *Curae posteriores post mortem.* Antwerp.

LEWIS, R.
1981. Turkish cuisine. *National and regional styles of cookery. Proceedings,* pp. 117–21, Oxford Symposium, 1981. London: Prospect Books.

LOAIZA-FIGUEROA, F., K. RITLAND, J. A. LABORDE CANCINO, and S. D. TANKSLEY.
1989. Patterns of genetic variation of the genus *Capsicum* (Solanaceae) in Mexico. *Plants Systematics and Evolution.* 165:159–88.

LOBELIUS, M.
1576. *Plantarum sev stirpium historia.* Antwerp.

LONG-SOLIS, J.
1986. *Capsicum cultura: La historia del chili.* Mexico: Fondo de cultura economica.

MACARTHUR, D.
1964. *Reminiscences.* New York: McGraw-Hill.

MAGA, J. A.
1975. Capsicum. In *Critical revisions in food science and nutrition.* Pp. 177–99. Cleveland: CRC Press.

MAJUPURIA, I.
1980. *Joys of Nepalese cooking.* Gwalior-1, India: Smt. S. Devi Madhoganj.

MANNIX, D. P.
1978. *Black cargoes: A history of the Atlantic slave trade, 1518–1865.* New York: Penguin Books.

MARCHANT, A.
1941. Colonial Brazil as a way station for the Portuguese India fleets. *Geographical Review.* American Geographic Society: New York. 31(July):454–65.

MARTINEZ, M.
1979. *Catalogo de nombres vulgares y cientificos de plantas Mexicanas.* Mex. DF: Fondo de Cultura Economica, Mex. DF, Amer. de. Univ. 975.

MARTYR, P. (see Anghiera, P. M. d')

MASADA, Y., K. HASHIMOTO, T. IMOUE, and M. SUZUI.
1971. Analysis of the pungent principles of *Capsicum annuum* by combined gas chromatography. *Journal of Food Science,* 36: 858.

MATHEW, A. G., Y. S. LEWIS, N. KIRISHNAMURTHY, and E. S. NAMBUDIRI.
1971. Capsaicin. *The Flavor Industry.* 2(12): 691–95.

MATTHI OLI, P. A.
1544. *Commentarii in sex libros Pedacii Dioscoridis.* Lyon: Anazarbeen de la matit.

MCCLURE, S. A.
1982. Parallel usage of medicinal plants by Africans and their Caribbean descendents. *Economic Botany.* 36(3):291–301.

MCCUE, G. A.
1932. The history and use of the tomato: An annotated bibliography. *Annals of the Mo. Bot. Gard.* 39:289–348.

MCGEE, H.
1984. *On food and cooking: The science and lore of the kitchen.* New York: Collier Books.
1990. *The curious cook: More kitchen science and lore.* San Francisco: North Point Press.

MCLEOD, M.J.S., S. I. GUTTMAN, and W. H. ESHBAUGH
1982. Early evolution of chili peppers (Capsicum). *Econ. Bot.* 36(4):361–68.

MCVEY, R.
1963. *Indonesia.* New Haven: Southeast Asia Studies, Yale University.

MEANS, P. A.
1935. *The Spanish Main: Focus on envy 1492–1700.* New York: Scribners.

MEILINK-RAELOFSZ, M. A. P., and GODINHO, V. M.
1962. *Asian trade and European influence in the Indonesian Archipelago, 1500–1630.* The Hague: Martinus Nishoff.

MINTZ, S. W.
1988. Food origins and syntheses in Carribean history. *Journal of Gastronomy.* 2(4):35–43.

MIRACLE, M. P.
1967. *Agriculture in the Congo basin. Tradition and change in African rural economics.* Madison: University of Wisconsin Press.

MONARDES, N.
1574. *Joyfull news out of the newe founde worlde.* Trans. by J. Frampton, New York: Alfred A. Knopf. Repr. 1925.

MONTAGNÉ, P.
1968. *Larousse gastronomique.* New York: Crown Publishers.

MOORE, F. W.
1970. Food habits in non-industrial societies. In *Dimensions of nutrition.* Ed. by J. DuPont. Pp. 181–221. Boulder: Colorado Associated Universities Press.

Bibliography

MORAN, E. F.
1975. Food, development, and man in the tropics. In *Gastronomy*. Ed. by M. L. Arnott. Pp. 169–186. The Hague: Mouton Publishers.

MORELAND, W. H.
1920. *India at the death of Akbar: An economic study*. London: Macmillan & Co. Ltd.
1939. The ships of the Arabian Sea about A.D. 1500. *Journal of the Royal Asiatic Society*.

MORISON, S. E.
1942. *Admiral of the ocean sea*. Boston: Little, Brown.

MOTE, F. W.
1979. Yüan and Ming. In *Food in Chinese culture*. Ed. by K. C. Chang. Pp. 193–258. New Haven, Conn.: Yale University Press.

MULHERIN, J.
1988. *Spices and natural flavorings*. New York: Macmillan.

MURAKAMI, N.
1917. Japan's early attempts to establish commercial relations with Mexico. In *The Pacific ocean in history*. Ed. by H. M. Stephens and H. E. Bolton. Pp. 467–480. New York: Macmillan.

MURATORI, C.
1952. Maize names and history: A further discussion. *Uganda Journal*. 16(1):76–81.

MURDOCK, G. P.
1959. *Africa, its peoples and their cultural history*. New York: McGraw-Hill.

MUROGA, N.
1967. Geographical exploration by the Japanese. In *The Pacific basin*. Ed. by D. R. Friis, pp. 96–108. New York: Amer. Geog. Soc.

NELSON, E. K.
1910. Capsaicin, the pungent principle of *Capsicum*, and the detection of Capsaisin. *J. Ind. Engl. Chem.* 2:419–21.

NEWMAN, B.
1945. *Balkan background*. New York: Macmillan.

NEWMAN, J.
1981. Regional and other differences of Chinese cookery. In *National and regional styles of cookery. Proceedings*, pp. 33–41, Oxford Symposium, 1981. London: Prospect Books.

NUTTALL, Z.
1906. The earliest historical realtions between Mexico and Japan. From original documents preserved in Spain and Japan. In *Univ. of Calif. Publications, American Archaeology and Ethnology*. 4(1):1–47.

O'GORMAN, E. (Ed.)
1967. *Apologética historia sumaria*. Vol. 1. Mexico: Universidad Nacional Autónoma de Mexico.

ORTA, GARCIA DA.
1563. *Colloquies on the simples and drugs of India*. London: Henry Southern. Repr. 1913.

ORTIZ, E. L.
1979. *The book of Latin American cooking*. New York: Alfred A. Knopf.
1986. *Complete book of Caribbean cooking*. New York: Ballantine.
1988. *The book of Japanese cooking*. New York: M. Evans.
1989. *The food of Spain and Portugal*. New York: Macmillan.

PANAGOPOULOS, E. P.
1966. *New Smyrna: An eighteenth century Greek odyssey*. Gainesville: University of Florida Press.

PARRY, J. W.
1945. *The history of spices*. New York: Chemical Pub. Co.
1953. *Europe and a wider world: 1415–1715*. London: Hutchinson's University Library.

PARRY, V. J., H. INALCIK, A. N. KURAT, and J. S. BROMLEY
1976. A history of the Ottoman empire to 1730. Chapters from the *Camb. Hist. of Islam and The New Cambridge Modern History*. Ed. by M. A. Cook. Vol. II. Cambridge: Cambridge University Press.

PERRY, C.
1983. Grain foods of the early Turks. In *Food in motion: Migration of foodstuffs and cookery techniques*. Ed. by Alan Davidson. Pp. 11–22. London: Prospect Books.

PICKERING, C.
1879. *Chronological history of plants*. Pp. 560, 976. Boston: Little, Brown and Co.

PICKERSGILL, B.
1969. The domestication of chili peppers. In *The domestication and exploitation of plants and animals*. Ed. by P. J. Ucko and G. W. Dimbleby. Pp. 443–450. London: Gerald Duckworth.
1984. Migrations of chili peppers, *Capsicum* spp. in the Americas. In *Pre-Columbian plant migration*. Ed. by Doris Stone. Pp. 106–123. 14th International Congress of Americanists. Cambridge: Peabody Mus. of Arch. and Ethnology, Harvard University.

PICKERSGILL, B., and C. HEISER, JR.
1976. Cytogenetics and evolutionary change under domestication. *Phil. Trans. Royal Soc. London*. 275:55–69.

PORZIO, F. (Ed.)
1989. *La natura morta in Italia*. Vol. 2. Milan: Electa.

POUNDS, N. J. G.
1979. *A historical geography of Europe 1500–1840.* Cambridge: Cambridge University Press.

PRAKASH, O.
1961. *Food and drinks in ancient India.* Delhi: Munshi Ram Manohar Lal.

PROCTOR, V. W.
1968. Long-distance dispersal of seeds by retention in digestive tract of birds. *Science.* 160(3825):321–22.

PURSEGLOVE, J. W.
1963. Some problems of the origin and distribution of tropical crops. *Genetics Agraria.* 17:105–22.
1968. *Tropical crops: Dicotyledons.* New York: Halsted Press.

QUINN, J.
1975. *Minorcans in Florida their history and heritage.* St. Augustine: Mission Press.

RAYCHUDHURI, H. and T. RAYCHANDHURI
1981. Not by curry alone: An introductory essay on Indian cuisines for a western audience. *National and regional styles of cookery. Proceedings,* pp. 45–56, Oxford Symposium, 1981. London: Prospect Books.

REVEL, J. H.
1982. *Culture and cuisine.* New York: Doubleday.

RICK, C. M.
1978. The tomato. *Scientific American.* 238:78–87.

RIDLEY, H. N.
1930. *The dispersal of plants through the world.* Ashford, Kent, England: L. Reeve & Co.

ROBELO, C. A.
1904. *Dictionario de Aztequismos.* Mexico: Ediciones Fuente Cutural.

RODEN, C.
1980. Early Arab cooking and cookery manuscripts. *Petis Propos Culinaries.* 6:16–27.
1983. The spread of kabobs and coffee. In *Food in motion: Migration of foodstuffs and cookery techniques.* Ed. by Alan Davidson. Pp. 74–79. London: Prospect Books.
1985. *A book of Middle Eastern food.* New York: Alfred A. Knopf.

ROMANS, B.
1961. *A concise natural history of east and west Florida.* Gainesville: University of Florida Press.

ROOSEVELT, A.
1984. Problems interpreting the diffusion of cultivated plants. In *Pre-Columbian Plant Migration.* Ed. by Doris Stone. Pp. 2–18. Cambridge: Peabody Mus. of Arch. and Ethnology, Harvard University.

ROOT, W.
1971. *The food of Italy.* New York: Atheneum.

ROOT, W. and R. ROCHEMONT
1976. *Eating in America: A history.* New York: Morrow.

ROSELLI, B.
1940. *The Italians in colonial Florida.* Florida: Drew Press.

ROSENGARTEN, F., JR.
1973. *The book of spices.* New York: Pyramid Books.

ROZIN, E.
1982. The structure of cuisine. In *The psychobiology of human food selection.* Ed. by L. M. Barker. Pp. 189–203. Westport, CN: AVI Publishing Co.
1983. *Ethnic cuisine: The flavor principle cookbook.* Brattleboro, Vt.: Stephen Green Press.

ROZIN, E. and P. ROZIN
1981. Culinary themes and variations: Traditional seasoning practices provide both a sense of familiarity and source of variety. *Natural History.* 90(2):6–14.

ROZIN, P.
1990. Getting to like the burn of chili pepper. In *Chemical Senses.* Ed. by B. G. Green, J. R. Mason and M. R. Morley. Pp. 231–69. New York: Marcel Dekker.
1982. Human food selection: The interaction of biology, culture, and individual experience. In *The psychobiology of human food selection.* Ed. by L. M. Barker. Pp. 225–252. Westport, Conn.: AVI Publishing Co.

ROZIN, P., L. EBERT, and J. SCHULL
1982. Some like it hot: A temporal analysis of hedonic responses to chili pepper. *Appetite: Journal for Intake Research.* 3:13–22.

ROZIN, P. and FALLON, A. F.
1981. The acquisition of likes and dislikes for food. In *Criteria of food acceptance.* Ed. by J. Solms and R. L. Hall. P. 35. Zurich: Forster Verlag AG.

RUMPHIUS, G. E.
1741–50. *Herbarium Amboinense.* Ed. by J. Burman.Vol. 5. Amsterdam: F. Chansuion, J. Catuffe, and H. Vywerf.

RUSSEL, R. J., and F. B. KNIFFEN, and E. L. PRUITT
1961. *Culture worlds.* New York: Macmillan.

SANNA, L., and R. J. SWIENTEK
1984. HPLC quantifies heat levels in chili pepper products. *Food Processing.* 10:70.

SASS, L. J.
1981. Religion, medicine, politics and spices. *Appetite: Jour. for Intake Research.* 2:7–13.

SAUER, C. O.
1952. *Agricultural origins and dispersals.* Cambridge: MIT Press.

1966. *The early Spanish Main.* Berkely: University of California Press.

1969. *Seeds, spades, hearth, herds: The domestication of animals and foodstuffs.* Cambridge: MIT Press.

SCHAFER, E. H.
1977. T'ang. In *Food in Chinese culture.* Ed. by K. C. Chang. Pp. 85–140. New Haven: Yale University Press.

SCHEVILL, F.
1972. *The Balkan Peninsula and the Near East: A History from the earliest times to the present day.* London: C. Bell and Sons.

SCHOPF, J. D.
1911. *Travels in the confederation 1783–1784.* Philadelphia: Wm. J. Campbell.

SCHORGER, A. W.
1966. *The wild turkey: Its history and domestication.* Norman: University of Oklahoma Press.

SCHURZ, W. L.
1939. *The Manila galleon.* New York: E. P. Dutton.

SIMON, ANDRÉ
1951. *A concise encyclopedia of gastronomy.* New York: Harcourt, Brace.

SIMOONS, F. J.
1961. *Eat not this flesh: Food avoidances in the Old World.* Madison: University of Wisconsin Press.

SIMPSON, B. B. and M. CONNER-OGORZALY
1986. *Economic botany.* New York: McGraw-Hill.

SINGER, I. (Ed.)
1905. *The Jewish encyclopedia.* Vol. XI. P. 485. New York: Funk and Wagnalls.

SMITH, C. D.
1979. *Western Mediterranean Europe: A historical geography of Italy, Spain and Southern France since the neolithic.* London: Academic Press of Harcourt Brace Jovanovich.

SMITH, P. G. and C. B. HEISER JR.
1951. Taxonomic and genetic studies on the cultivated peppers *C. annuum* L. and *C. frutescens. Amer. J. Bot.* 38:367–68.

1957. Taxonomy of *Capsicum sinense* Jacq. and the geographic distribution of the cultivated *Capsicum* species. *Bull. Torrey Bot. Club.* 84(6):413–20.

SOKOLOV, R.
1991. *Why we eat what we eat: How the encounter between the New World and the Old changed the way everyone on the planet eats.* New York: Summit Books.

SOLANKE, T. F.
1973. The effect of red pepper (*Capsicum frutescens*) on gastric acid secretion. *Journal Surgical Research.* 15:385–90.

SORRE, M.
1962. The geography of diet. In *Readings in cultural geography.* Ed. by P. L. Wagner and M. W. Mikesell. Chicago: University of Chicago Press.

SPIKE, J. T.
1983. *Italian still life paintings from 3 centuries.* New York: National Academy of Design

SPINDEN, H.
1928. Thank the American Indian. *Scientific American.* 138(Apr.):330–32.

STAVRIANOS, L. S.
1958. *The Balkans since 1453.* New York: Holt, Rinehart and Winston.

STOIANOVICH, TRAIAN
1966. *Le maïs dans les Balkans.* In *Annales: Économies sociétés civilizations.* 21(2):1026–40.

STONER, A. K., and B. VILLALON
1977. The popular cultivated tomato, peppers and eggplant. In *Gardening for food and fun.* Washington, D.C.: Yearbook of Agri.

STURTEVANT, E. L.
1885. Kitchen garden esculents of American origin. *The American Naturalist.* 19(6):542–53.

1961. Taino agriculture. In *The evolution of horticulture systems in native South America: Causes and consequences.* Ed. by J. Wilbert. Pp. 69–82. Caracas: Sociedad de Ciencias Naturales La Salle.

TANNAHILL, R.
1981. *Food in History.* New York: Stein and Day.

TEJERA, E.
1951. *Palabras indijenas de la isla de Santa Domingo.* Ciudad Trujillo, R. D.: Editora del Caribe, C. por A.

TODD, P. H., JR., M. C. BENSINGER, and T. BIFTU
1977. Determination of pungency due to *Capsicum* by gas-liquid chromatography. *Jour. of Food Sci.* 42(3): 660–65.

TREASE, G. E. and P. W. C. EVANS
1983. Drugs of biological origin. *1983 Pharmacognosy.* 12th Ed. Bailliere Tindall.

TURNBULL, A.
1788. The refutation of a late account of New Smyrna. *The Columbian Magazine.* pp. 684–88.

TURNER, W.
1538. *Libellus de re herbaria.* London: Ray Society. Repr. 1965.

UCKO, P. J., and G. W. DIMBLEBY
1969. The domestication and exploitation of plants and animals. London. Papers given at a symposium.

VARNER, J. G., and J. J. VARNER
1983. *Dogs of the conquest*. Norman: University of Oklahoma Press.

VERRILL, A. H.
1937. *Foods America gave the world*. Boston: L. C. Page.

WALDO, M.
1967. *Dictionary of international food and cooking terms*. New York: Macmillan.

WALSH, W. T.
1939. *Isabella of Spain*. London: Sheed and Ward.

WATT, G.
1889. *A dictionary of the economic products of India*. Vol. II. Delhi, India: Cosmo Pub. Repr. 1972.

WATTS, D.
1987. *The West Indies: Patterns of development, culture and environmental change since 1492 (1987)*. American Historical Assc. Recently Published Articles. Cambridge: Cambridge University Press.

WEAVER, W. W.
1989. *America Eats*. New York: Harper and Row.

WEST, R. C., and J. P. AUGELLI
1976. *Middle America: Its lands and peoples*. Englewood Cliffs, N.J.: Prentice-Hall.

WESTRIP, J. P.
1981. Some Persian influences on the cooking of India. In *National and regional styles of cookery. Proceedings*, pp. 67–95, Oxford Syposium, 1981. London: Prospect Books.

WHEATON, B.
1983. *Savoring the past: The French kitchen and table from 1300 to 1789*. Philadelphia: University of Pennsylvania Press.

WHEATON, B. K., and P. KELLY
1988. *Bibliography and culinary history*. Boston: G. K. Hall.

WITTHOFT, J.
1966. A history of gunflints. *Penn. Archaelogist*. 36:1–49.

WILSON, A. C.
1983. Sugar: The migrations of a plant product during 2000 years. *Proceedings*, pp. 1–10, Oxford Symposium, 1983. In *Food in motion: The migration of foodstuffs and cookery techniques*. Ed. by Alan Davidson. London: Prospect Books.

WINCHESTER, S.
1988. *Korea: A walk through the land of miracles*. London: Grafton Books.

WRIGHT, A. C. A.
1949. Maize names as indicators of economic contacts. *Uganda Journal*. 13(1):61–81.

YULE, H., and A. C. BURRELL
1886. *Hobson-Jobson: A glossary of colloquial Anglo-indian words and phrases and of kindred terms, etymological, historical, geographical, and discursive*. Ed. by W. Cooke. New Delhi: Munshiram Manoharlal Pub., 1979.

ZOHARY, D., and M. HOPF.
1973. Domestication of pulses in the Old World, *Science*. 182:887–94.

INDEX